T0306126

"Plural forms of leadership where two or more individuals share roles at the top have recently attracted a good deal of interest. The phenomenon seems to run counter to preconceived notions of leadership. Yet, co-leadership is common in the arts and culture sector. Fjellvær and Reid have independently conducted intensive qualitative studies of how and why this might work. This volume integrates their insights. It is beautifully researched and offers a sophisticated understanding of executive co-leadership, its challenges, and its potential. It is a must-read for academics, practitioners and policy makers interested in the governance and leadership of arts and cultural organizations".

Ann Langley, *Co-editor, Strategic Organization, Associate Editor, Academy of Management Journal and Emerita Professor, HEC Montréal*

"Reid and Fjellvær's book on co-leadership in arts and culture is a timely and welcome contribution to the literature on non-profit leadership. Their volume is among the first and most integrative on the topic, making an important contribution exploring the dynamics, dilemmas, and paradoxes of this oft-confusing management configuration. While this book focuses on arts and culture organizations, its content and insights offer important value and options for effective executive leadership to all third sector governance and management scholars and practitioners in an increasingly complex and dynamic environment".

David Renz, *Bloch School of Management, University of Missouri – Kansas City*

"A book focusing on the challenges and idiosyncrasies of co-leadership in the arts and cultural setting is much overdue. I am delighted that Wendy Reid and Hilde Fjellvær have undertaken this deep analysis around the distinct attributes of this phenomena. It will make an important contribution to our field, theoretically and practically, and be an essential teaching aide in arts leadership".

Jo Caust, *University of Melbourne*

"Co-leadership in arts and culture is a common but very delicate alchemy. Under-researched and under-documented, the tension in these relationships is central to success in these organizations. Understanding its dynamics and limitations will undoubtedly provide important answers to guide public policy in support of the arts, as well as offering practical insights for those who work within it daily".

Nathalie Maillé, *General Director, Conseil des arts de Montréal – Montreal Arts Council*

"What a joy to read a book that explores creating art within a dynamic, communal, and social context. For in the performing arts, we work together, in the spirit of creating values, culture, aspirations and ultimately art. It is anything but lonely. If, as some say, music really occurs between the notes, a similar alchemy happens between people who strive toward a shared purpose".

Antoni Cimolino, *Artistic Director, The Stratford Festival of Canada*

"Having extensive arts board experience, I can say this book will be very useful. It will help everyone interested in co-leadership understand the complexity of this form of management. I have seen every leadership problem over my 48 years of practice. Every manager should stop and think about how they do things. Reid and Fjellvær will guide their reflections".

François Colbert, *Carmelle and Rémi-Marcoux Chair in Arts Management and Codirector, Master of Management in International Arts Management, HEC Montréal*

"Understanding the dilemma of logics between artists and managers in the complex governance of arts and culture is indispensable. This book addresses the ambiguities of this interesting polarity. Hierarchy problems are inherent in governance, subject to context, but Reid and Fjellvær demonstrate their universality in the arts. This book is indispensable to foundational knowledge of arts and cultural management".

Jaime Ruiz-Gutierrez, *Universidad de los Andes, Colombia*

"This brilliant book rests on the simple but profound observation that leadership in arts organizations is different. Drawing from their extensive engagement in arts and culture, Reid and Fjellvær elaborate the concept of co-leadership, a model of distributed power that challenges our assumption of leadership as an individual phenomenon. This book will be an inspiration to arts managers and organizational scholars alike".

Roy Suddaby, *Winspear Chair of Management, Peter B. Gustavson School of Business, University of Victoria, Canada, and Professor of Entrepreneurship, Carson College of Business, Washington State University, USA*

"Scholars have paid frustrating little attention to the peculiar complexity of co-leadership, preferring to focus on individual leadership. Yet co-leadership is common in organizations of skilled professionals including the arts, where they embody and reconcile competing interests of stakeholder groups. Reid and Fjellvær's book is an important addition to the literature as an incisive and comprehensive overview of a fascinating and important topic".

Laura Empson, *Professor in the Management of Professional Service Firms, Bayes Business School (formerly Cass), University of London.*

"This MUST-read book will prepare readers to cope with post-pandemic changes in many settings. Although set in the arts, insights on co-leadership address the accelerating need for collaboration, co-operation, and co-construction to manage change with openness. Both authors have solid experience in observing, analyzing, and theorizing key success factors of co-leadership. Readers will be inspired and stimulated by this book".

Johanne Turbide, *Secretary-General, Director of Sustainability, Responsible for Equity, Diversity and Inclusion, HEC Montréal*

Co-Leadership in the Arts and Culture

This book is about co-leadership: A leadership practice and structure often found in arts organizations that consist of two or three executives who bridge the art and business divide at the top.

Many practitioners recognize this phenomenon but the research on this topic is limited and dispersed. This book assembles a coherent overview and presents new insights of the field. While co-leadership is well institutionalized in the West, it is also criticized for management's constraint of artistic autonomy and for its pluralism that dilutes leadership clarity. However, co-leadership also personifies the strategic objectives of art, audiences, organization, and community, by addressing plural logics – navigating the demands of artistic vision and organizational stability. It is an integrating solution. The authors investigate its specifics in the arts, including global practice and its interdisciplinary nature. The theoretical frame of plural leadership supports their empirical explorations of the dynamics within the co-leadership relationship and with organizational stakeholders. Data includes the voices of co-leaders, artists, staff, and board members from arts organizations in Canada and Norway. Their abductive reflection generates a stimulating research experience.

By viewing co-leadership in action, not as a study of static theories, the book will appeal not only to students and researchers but also resonate with practitioners in arts and cultural management and assist them to work with co-leadership and to manage its tensions.

Wendy Reid is an Honourary Professor with the Management Department of HEC Montréal (retired summer 2021 – formerly Associate Professor) after an executive career in arts management in Canada.

Hilde Fjellvær is Associate Professor with the NTNU Business School and a member of the Faculty Board. She is Chair of the Board at Rosendal Teater in Trondheim, Norway.

Routledge Research in the Creative and Cultural Industries
Series Editor: Ruth Rentschler

This series brings together book-length original research in cultural and creative industries from a range of perspectives. Charting developments in contemporary cultural and creative industries thinking around the world, the series aims to shape the research agenda to reflect the expanding significance of the creative sector in a globalized world.

Risk in the Film Business
Known Unknowns
Michael Franklin

Orchestra Management
Models and Repertoires for the Symphony Orchestra
Arne Herman

The Venice Arsenal
Between History, Heritage, and Re-use
Edited by Luca Zan

Managing Cultural Joint Ventures
An Identity-Image View
Tanja Johansson, Annukka Jyrämä and Kaari Kiitsak-Prikk

Public Relations as a Creative Industry
Elisenda Estanyol

Co-Leadership in the Arts and Culture
Sharing Values and Vision
Wendy Reid and Hilde Fjellvær

For more information about this series, please visit: www.routledge.com/Routledge-Research-in-the-Creative-and-Cultural-Industries/book-series/RRCCI

Co-Leadership in the Arts and Culture

Sharing Values and Vision

Wendy Reid and Hilde Fjellvær

First published 2023
by Routledge
4 Park Square, Milton Park, Abingdon, Oxon OX14 4RN

and by Routledge
605 Third Avenue, New York, NY 10158

Routledge is an imprint of the Taylor & Francis Group, an informa business

British Library Cataloguing-in-Publication Data
A catalogue record for this book is available from the British Library

ISBN: 978-1-138-58702-1 (hbk)
ISBN: 978-1-032-39649-1 (pbk)
ISBN: 978-0-429-50425-9 (ebk)

DOI: 10.4324/9780429504259

The Open Access version of chapter 1 was funded by Hilde Fjellvær.
The Open Access version of chapter 4 was funded by Wendy Reid.

From Wendy – Peter and Houdini, as well as my parents – James and Nancy Reid.

From Hilde – Erik, Siri, and Ida.

Contents

Tables

Figures

Foreword

Introduction

Co-leadership configurations vary around the world. The practice is not necessarily universal. For performing arts organizations, sharing executive responsibilities typically involves one or more artistic directors as well as a managerial partner who each report to a board of directors or to a government authority. Our data is centred in this configuration.

The mandate for this Routledge series involves original research, and accordingly we present new ideas and perspectives derived from our newly analyzed data. We expect that our findings will interest scholars of plural and co-leadership as well as those of arts management. This practice is found in many other professional sectors: Education, health, religion, journalism, and fashion organizations as well as legal, accounting and consulting firms, high-tech and investment banking (Alvarez & Svejenova, 2005) as well as many family businesses and entrepreneurships (Deschamps & Cisneros, 2012). We hope that our specifically situated work will inform research on the arts as well as this larger conversation (Huff, 2009).

We originally engaged in this research because of our personal and professional interest in the phenomenon. For Hilde, it was a newly mandated type of leadership. Her spouse was confronted with a change to co-leadership in a digital news-organization. This piqued her interest. Wendy had observed and participated in co-leadership practice during a career spanning 25 years in professional arts organizations in Canada.

Terminology

While we each initially used the term "dual executive leadership" in our individual research, we now follow the practice of other scholars, using "co-leadership" to describe our phenomenon (Denis et al., 2012). We regret leaving behind our previous label (Fjellvær, 2010; Reid & Karambayya, 2009, 2016) but the term co-leadership can include trios and other small groups in the configuration at the top (Alvarez & Svejenova, 2005). This is especially relevant as two or three artistic leaders are increasingly being engaged in the same organization.

Near the end of our work on this book, a new label for co-leadership appeared in the leadership literature: "Managerial shared leadership" (Döös & Wilhelmson, 2021). We chose to continue to use co-leadership for several reasons. First, we had already connected our theory development with the plural leadership literature (Denis et al., 2012) which provides a clear typology, naming four distinct forms of plural leadership, including co-leadership. Second, while claiming to fall within the field of plural leadership, the definition of managerial shared leadership confusingly conflates co-leadership with shared leadership. "Shared" as defined in plural leadership refers to emergent and multiple leaders in groups, whereas we study a discrete and separate empirical phenomenon (Pearce & Conger, 2003). Finally, we wished to remain within the leadership literature; the combination of management and leadership in the same term creates tension and blurs the definition by linking to two very different research traditions.

While outlining their new category of leadership, Döös and Wilhelmson (2021) also insist that the term "constellation" should be consistently deployed. While we agree that this terminology is useful to signal the link with one of the founding works of co-leadership (Hodgson et al., 1965), we also found that there is a structuring aspect to co-leadership in the arts. As a result, we also make use of the term configuration. This provides variety for our readers and different perspectives on the phenomenon.

Reflecting on our research approach

As a base to our research in this book, we independently published large research studies on co-leadership (Fjellvær, 2010; Reid, 2007). In these studies, our respective methods involved qualitative research using some inductive but also abductive approaches for comparative case analysis (Coffey & Atkinson, 1996; Eisenhardt, 1989; Eisenhardt & Graebner, 2007). However, given that we were seeking reflections on relationships, values, and logics, our data analysis studied our texts for personal reflections and feelings. We do not provide propositions. Subsequently, we decided to join forces for the purposes of this book: Review current theoretical literature, merge our data, and add new data. Given our previous familiarity with the data, our approach became exclusively abductive, recoding the data with new eyes to assist us and new literature to inform our vision.

With new theoretical insights from the updated literature, we revisited this data and distanced ourselves from our initial understandings, thus engaging in a form of "casing" the data with new and sometimes surprising frames of understanding (Timmermans & Tavory, 2012).

Researcher perspectives

As well, our collaboration has provoked mutual reflections, comparisons, and contrasts. Besides perspectives based in Europe and North America respectively, we are each inspired by a different school of management theory – organizational behaviour (OB) and organization theory (OT). Wendy's OB-related theorizing on leadership focused on individual and duo-level dynamics with observations on organizational impact (Reid & Karambayya, 2009, 2016). On the other hand, Hilde's research mobilizing OT principles focused on competing logics and hence broader social influences on the practices of the co-leaders (Fjellvær, 2010).

Our different professional experiences provide another counterpoint. While initially trained as a musician and in musicology, Wendy has been immersed in management in the performing arts in Canada, moving to a PhD and academic research later in her career. Hilde's early career in non-governmental organizations (NGOs) concerned with international development and exchange brings a crucial outside perspective. Her research on co-leadership covered a wide range of contexts, including institutional organizations (universities, theatres, and museums) and commercial enterprises (newspapers). She currently leads a volunteer board of directors for a professional theatre in Trondheim, Norway, having recently participated in the engagement of a new Artistic Director and an Executive Director for the company.

Both Wendy and Hilde have careers on faculty at university business schools. Wendy has taught at York University in Toronto and at HEC Montréal; she has just ended her career teaching mature artists and managers from the Québec arts community in a large postgraduate arts management programme there. Both schools host pioneering programmes in arts management in Canada. Wendy uses case method, which provides on-going sources of real-world data and reflection in interaction with the students. These programmes nourish a critical audience seeking insights to help explain how their world functions. At the business school of the Norwegian University of Science and Technology in Trondheim, Hilde also embraces experiential learning in her classrooms. She uses a mix of case methods, simulations, and roleplay as a basis for reflection and analysis in negotiation and management.

We engaged in regular bi-weekly conversations for four years. These conversations challenged and developed our mutual understanding of our data and our theorizing. This back-and-forth abductive approach between the data and theory has been at the core of our work (Coffey & Atkinson, 1996; Huff, 2009; Kelle, 1995; Timmermans & Tavory, 2012). Abductive theorizing is particularly appropriate for the performing arts where interpretation and reinterpretation enable artists to challenge an audience's understanding of the creative material being presented.

Choosing topics

Several factors led to our choice of topics in these chapters. First, our previous research suggested topics for future research (Fjellvær, 2010; Reid & Karambayya, 2009, 2016). Survey articles about plural leadership and other forms of co-leadership pointed out several gaps in the larger field of co-leadership (Bolden, 2011; Cullen-Lester & Yammarino, 2016; Denis et al., 2012; Sergi et al., 2012; Yammarino et al., 2012). As well, we were stimulated by articles published on co-leadership particularly in the arts and by arts case studies which diverged from our original insights (see Chapters 3 and 4).

Collecting data

The original primary data comes from several previous research projects and included over 150 interviews in 20 organizations. In the initial project in Canada, Wendy studied eight cases: Two dance, two opera and three theatre companies, and one symphony orchestra. In Norway, Hilde drew on five cases from her study of a larger pool of cases. This study also included many organizations outside the arts. But in the arts, she focused on two theatre companies and two symphony orchestras as well as one art museum. Subsequently, Wendy continued to explore other research sites for related topics like newly arrived artistic directors in the executive leadership, often interviewing over time. This research includes three theatre and two dance organizations, and two orchestras. The data allowed a comparison between North American and European practice enabling triangulated conclusions (Coffey & Atkinson, 1996; Timmermans & Tavory, 2012). But it also reflects the regional practice focused in Anglo-Saxon and Scandinavian arts organizations (Chapter 4). Other scholars have published cultural leadership cases from around the world (Caust, 2013, 2015; Rånlund et al., 2016; Ruiz-Gutiérrez et al., 2016). We make use of these cases to expand the readers' international perspectives on this topic.

The breadth of our organizational and interview data, including participants outside of the co-leadership, is apparently distinctive in co-leadership research, particularly in the arts (Döös & Wilhelmson, 2021). Its richness sustained our search for new insights through the structure of the abductive process articulated by Timmerman & Tavory (2012).

In the original set of eight cases in Canada, eight or nine interviews per organization were undertaken including the executive leaders, and staff employees who were familiar with production, financial, and marketing perspectives. An artist was often consulted as well as three board members: The president of the board, and other board members who could provide perspectives on financial, marketing, and funding functions of the co-leadership. For each case, a pertinent arts council agent, usually at the federal level, was interviewed. Our focus in the interviews was on relationships, decision-making, and practice.

Wendy also included seven additional Canadian cases from other research projects that were longitudinal. Fewer roles were considered in the data collection, but they were located across the organization in a similar manner to the original cases. Role incumbents were interviewed on several occasions, separated by a minimum of six months and sometimes a year. Three or four interviews were undertaken per person. While there were some changes in personnel along the way, the same roles were consulted.

Each interview in the Canadian research was undertaken to gain insight into the relationship(s) dynamics and how those dynamics had an impact on the functionality of the relationship and on the organization. Respondents who were not in a co-leadership role were questioned about how they perceived the nature of the relationship, leadership impact of the configuration, and how the individual leaders and the dynamic in the co-leadership affected the respondent's work. Respondents who had a closer relationship to one co-leader or the other revealed different influences and impact.

Strategic plans, organizational documents, and websites were consulted for an understanding of organizational context. We also attended performances and observed dynamics in offices and backstage to enrich our reflections. Subsequent organizational history in both Canada and Norway was available through websites and media reports as well as our general knowledge of the arts sector.

Analyzing and writing

In each interview, data were coded related to each topic developed for the book. The citations were then compiled according to chapter topic. This collection of citations was further coded and analyzed in relation to the range of theorizing on the topic. From this process, we drew out ideas that extended our interpretation of each topic (Timmermans & Tavory, 2012). We led the recoding, but we were assisted by a retired cultural worker with an extensive career in both theatre and film presentation – Peter Roberts. His insights were refreshing and extremely helpful.

Frequent conversations among the three of us generated new emergent reflections. This evokes the notion that Peirce suggests of "cultivated perceptual insight" (Timmermans & Tavory, 2012, p. 172) which enables novel judgement that may provide surprises and new theorizing about the data. Our respective cultural roots, professional experiences, and theoretical orientations shaped our individual perceptions. As a result, our conversations provoked insights that evolved our earlier individual views of the data.

Each of us wrote independently, leading the data analysis and theorizing for each topic. With early and subsequent drafts, new insights occurred that generated conversations between us about our respective texts. These conversations questioned our respective theorizing, generating further clarity and depth of insight. Some questions required further data analysis of the original interviews and more reading in the literature.

Occasionally, our process required us to abandon the work on the book to prioritize our other academic and pedagogical work. So, each chapter matured over time, allowing us to revisit the ideas within the chapters over four years. The refining of ideas is essential to the cohesion of the abductive process (Timmermans & Tavory, 2012).

Conclusion

The variety of topics chosen for this book provoked new collective insights, responding to a desire for surprising revelations through an abductive approach to research (Timmermans & Tavory, 2012). However, by linking our results to the principles and insights articulated by the founding researchers in co-leadership, we feel that the field has been moved forward. The interviews for our original research were conducted with questions focused on the originating concerns of the field, but also reflected our own practical understanding. The range of respondents for each case also provided many layers of data which we re-mined with new eyes. Cumulative learning was stimulating.

References

Alvarez, J. L., & Svejenova, S. (2005). Sharing executive power: Roles and relationships at the top. Cambridge University Press.

Bolden, R. (2011). Distributed leadership in organizations: A review of theory and research. *International Journal of Management Reviews*, *13*(3), 251–269. https://doi.org/10.1111/j.1468-2370.2011.00306.x

Caust, J. (Ed.). (2013). *Arts Leadership - International Case Studies* (1st ed.). Tilde University Press.

Caust, J. (Ed.) (2015). *Arts and Cultural Leadership in Asia*. Routledge.

Coffey, A., & Atkinson, P. (1996). *Making Sense of Qualitative Data*. Sage Publications, Inc.

Cullen-Lester, K., & Yammarino, F. (2016). Collective and network approaches to leadership: Special issue introduction. *The Leadership Quarterly*, *27*(2), 173–180. https://doi.org/10.1016/j.leaqua.2016.02.001

Denis, J.-L., Langley, A., & Sergi, V. (2012). Leadership in the plural. *The Academy of Management Annals*, *5*(1), 211–283. https://doi.org/10.1080/19416520.2012.667612

Deschamps, B., & Cisneros, L. (2012). Co-leadership en succession familiale: Un partage à définir. *Entreprendre & Innover*, *14*(2), 49–57. https://doi.org/10.3917/entin.014.0049

Döös, M., & Wilhelmson, L. (2021). Fifty-five years of managerial shared leadership research: A review of an empirical field. *Leadership*, *17*(6), 715–746. https://doi.org/10.1177/17427150211037809

Eisenhardt, K. (1989). Building theories from case study research. *Academy of Management Review*, *14*(4), 532–550.

Eisenhardt, K., & Graebner, M. E. (2007). Theory building from cases: Opportunities and challenges. *Academy of Management Journal*, *50*(1), 25–32. https://doi.org/doi.org/10.5465/AMJ.2007.24160888

Fjellvær, H. (2010). *Dual and unitary leadership: managing ambiguity in pluralistic organizations* (Publication Number 2010/10). Doctoral dissertation, Norwegian School of Economics and Business Administration, Bergen. https://openaccess.nhh.no/nhh-xmlui/bitstream/handle/11250/164362/fjellver%20avh%202010.PDF?sequence=1

Hodgson, R. C., Levinson, D. J., & Zaleznik, A. (1965). *The Executive Role Constellation: An Analysis of Personality and Role Relations in Management*. Harvard University, Division of Research, Graduate School of Business Administration.

Huff, A. S. (2009). *Designing Research for Publication*. Sage Publications, Inc.

Kelle, U. (1995). Theories as Heuristic Tools in Qualitative Research. In I. Maso, P. Atkinson, S. Delamont, & J. C. Verhoeven (Eds.), *Openness in Research: The Tension between Self and Other* (pp. 33–50). Assen.

Pearce, C., & Conger, J. A. (2003). All Those Years Ago: The Historical Underpinnings of Shared Leadership. In C. Pearce, & J. A. Conger (Eds.), *Shared Leadership: Reframing the Hows and Whys of Leadership* (pp. 1–18). Wiley.

Rånlund, S., Dalborg, K., & Löfgren, M. (Eds.). (2016). *The FIKA Project: Narratives by Cultural Change Makers*. Nätverkstan Culture.

Reid, W. (2007). *Conflict and Trust in Dual Executive Leadership*. Doctoral dissertation, York University.

Reid, W., & Karambayya, R. (2009). Impact of dual executive leadership dynamics in creative organizations. *Human Relations*, *62*(7), 1073–1112. https://doi.org/10.1177/0018726709335539

Reid, W., & Karambayya, R. (2016). The shadow of history: Situated dynamics of trust in dual executive leadership. *Leadership*, *12*(5), 609–631. https://doi.org/10.1177/1742715015579931

Ruiz-Gutiérrez, J., Grant, P., & Colbert, F. (2016). Arts management in developing countries: A Latin American perspective. *International Journal of Arts Management*, *18*(Special Edition Latin America), 6–31.

Sergi, V., Denis, J. L., & Langley, A. (2012). Opening up perspectives on plural leadership. *Industrial and Organizational Psychology*, *5*(4), 403–407. https://doi.org/10.1111/j.1754-9434.2012.01468.x

Timmermans, S., & Tavory, I. (2012). Theory construction in qualitative research: From grounded theory to abductive analysis. *Sociological Theory*, *30*(3), 167–186.

Yammarino, F., Salas, E., Serban, A., Shirreffs, K., & Shuffler, M. (2012). Collectivist leadership processes: Putting the 'we' in leadership science and practice. *Industrial and Organizational Psychology*, *5*(4), 382–402.

Acknowledgements

This book – and all of our work – would not be possible without the artists, administrators, and organizational members of small and large cultural organizations in Canada, Norway, and across the world who have contributed to over 20 years of research. They remain anonymous, but we are deeply grateful for their willingness to share their experiences, and we remain indebted to them for the trust they had in us, expecting that we would treat their information thoughtfully and with respect. They have opened our eyes, provoked ideas, and been a continuous source of inspiration.

No one works in isolation, and we would like to thank many of our colleagues with whom we discussed ideas and received constructive and interesting feedback and advice, both on the content and the process of writing a book. In particular, we would like to thank key early guides in our careers: Ann Langley, Arent Greve, Inger Stensaker, Rekha Karambayya, and Eileen Fischer.

We benefited greatly from the significant support of excellent and very committed librarians, computer support, and help with figures and references. Research funding from both our schools allowed us to meet in Canada and Norway to advance the project.

We would like to express our deepfelt thanks to the staff at Routledge for their professionalism and positive support throughout.

This isn't merely a book about co-leaders in the arts. It is a book about cooperation, potential for conflict, and how to manage original vision and ideas. In other words, it is also about writing a book together. We thank each other for keeping the communication going, for engaging in each other's lives, and for always keeping the objective in sight.

There was a willingness and ability to discuss and challenge ideas, always keeping our eyes on the next task and for learning so much from each other. We could not possibly have known that we embarked upon such a challenging and stimulating journey of exploration.

We thank all those friends and colleagues who listened patiently to our story – for the journey turned out to be longer than we perhaps naively anticipated.

Finally, we would like to thank the people in our lives:

For Hilde – Siri, Ida, mamma Kari, and Erik – you kept my mind on creating new lifetime experiences, provided perspective, and so much emotional and practical support.

For Wendy, Peter sustained my interest and ability to maintain the discipline to continue this important sense-making project. He is patient, constructive, and creative – so many intriguing and engaging conversations. The material provoked many memories in our respective careers in the arts.

In fact, Peter's support for the book provided both of us with invaluable editing expertise. We owe him our deepest gratitude. Everything is much more accessible, as a result. Thank you.

1 Introducing and summarizing the book

Overview

In this book, we investigate the dynamics of executive co-leadership as a strategic practice in arts organizations. Arts leaders are chosen for their specialized expertise in separate roles to lead either artistic achievement or organizational development. However, they also lead the whole organization together as joint executives in a "shared role space" (Gronn & Hamilton, 2004, p. 6). Arts organizations are pluralistic, driven by multiple objectives, values, and logics (Kraatz & Block, 2008, 2017; Thornton et al., 2012). Arts co-leaders import these guiding and diverse logics into their co-leadership role space where they attempt to integrate them (Fjellvær, 2010; Gibeau et al., 2020) and hence negotiate strategic direction of the organization (Gronn & Hamilton, 2004). Co-leadership has become an executive leadership solution to this pluralism.

> If we're an arts organization, how do we make sure that we balance our different stakeholders and that fiscal and financially credible responsibility that we have with our role as a community organization? On the other hand, how do we create excellence in an organization so that it can truly be a distinguishing characteristic of it? Always the challenge.
>
> Board president

As this board president from our research explains, co-leaders are influenced by multiple close and distant stakeholders: Artists, audiences, and funders (Denis et al., 2001). The values that these stakeholders hold are inherent in the arts' pluralistic logics. The artistic imperative is the distinctive driving logic, but market and business logics are essential for achieving organizational balance (Lampel et al., 2000). Figure 1.1 (below) illustrates the arts co-leadership practice situated at the centre of a triangle where powerful logics produce role and goal ambiguity.

With artists at the apex of the triangle and as the essence of the mission, their passion, and a sense of calling motivates their achievement of

DOI: 10.4324/9780429504259-1

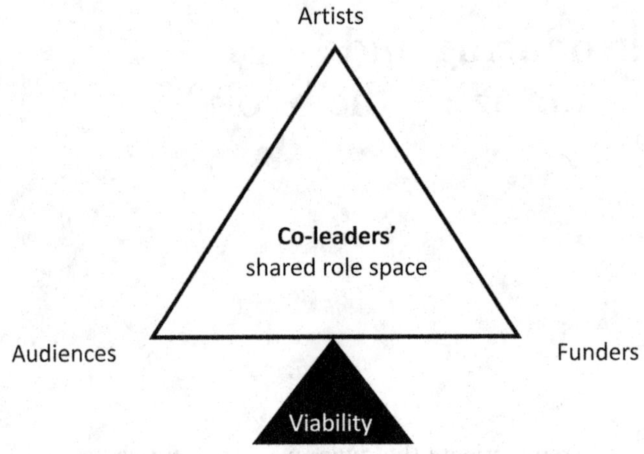

Figure 1.1 Stakeholder perspectives defining shared role space.

performance quality and new creation (Chiapello, 1998, 2004; Shiner, 2001). Audiences are the market focus of the art and are drawn to engaging experiences in the theatre or concert hall (Colbert & Dantas, 2019; Lampel et al., 2000). Funders and boards of directors prioritize both artistic quality and organizational viability (Baumol & Bowen, 1966; Rentschler, 2015). The distinct combination of mission, markets, and funders in the arts generates co-existing and sometimes strongly competing objectives. This competition can produce tension as well as an organizational culture of ambiguity (Cohen & March, 1974; Denis et al., 1996). The tension, ambiguity, and pluralistic competition among logics, values, and objectives is played out in the "shared role space" among the co-leaders (Gronn & Hamilton, 2004, p. 6).

The ongoing "balancing act" (Lampel et al., 2000, p. 265) that co-leaders perform influences how creation, programming, and organizational risks are managed. For instance, artistic ambitions can push production beyond predicted budget and time resources. Audience response to new work and programming is capricious, but ticket sales have the potential to generate significant revenue. Private and public funders, following different objectives and logics, can compensate for market-related revenue risks (Baumol & Bowen, 1966). Further, many arts organizations have recently extended their missions to reflect the social value of art, adding to their mix of objectives – and logics (Dragićević Šešić, 2020; Kawashima, 2006; Löfgren, 2016; Røyseng, 2019). The dynamic is complex.

Valuing pluralistic goals (Kraatz & Block, 2008, 2017) but making clear strategic and organizational decisions is a responsibility that co-leaders must manage together. To do so, they define differentiated but complementary roles that bridge across the multiple logics, shaping the shared role space (Chiapello, 1998; Fjellvær, 2010; Peterson, 1986;

Radaelli, 2012). This contrasts with the singular focus typical of unitary leadership (Locke, 2003).

Holding a separate artistic or managerial role and a joint organizational leadership role at the same time is distinctive of arts co-leadership and contrasts with other sectors like education and health where co-leaders often share the same role (Döös & Wilhelmson, 2021; Gibeau et al., 2020). The combination of the individual and joint roles presents a dilemma of ambiguity for these leaders since they must choose their perspective with each decision. The role space where the co-leadership is realized is rarely conceptualized in detail, particularly in relation to its specific institutional context (Denis et al., 2010). We explore this relationship in the arts through the rest of this book.

> Well, I call it the two-headed Hydra or Cerberus. How shall I put this? On the surface, this is a very good model, like democracy. Even if it isn't perfect, it is the best we have.
>
> Artistic director (AD)

In this chapter, we position co-leadership in the plural leadership literature and distinguish the presence of co-leadership within small companies and large institutions. Criticisms of co-leadership are considered, leading to an exploration of issues related to celebrity versus post-heroic leadership within the dynamics of arts co-leadership. To conclude this chapter, the structure of the book and its individual chapters are outlined briefly.

Understanding co-leadership as plural leadership

Scholars have identified co-leadership as one of several forms of plural leadership – called "pooling at the top to direct others" (Denis et al., 2012, p. 231). It is useful to understand co-leadership compared with the other forms of plural leadership that are theorized as emergent (Chapter 3). Leaders may delegate or "distribute" leadership responsibilities into the ranks (Bolden, 2011; Devereaux, 2019; Döös & Wilhelmson, 2021; Gronn, 2002). They may also encourage "shared" leadership to evolve from within organizational groups (Offerman & Scuderi, 2017; Pearce, 2004).

Several arts management scholars and policy makers highlight the use of distributed or shared practices for greater organizational effectiveness and as a counterbalance to artistic celebrity and power which can shape the dynamics of the triangle in Figure 1.1 (Caust, 2018; Hewison et al., 2013; Schrauwen et al., 2016). Individually or jointly, co-leaders may choose to encourage the development of distributed or shared leadership within their organizations (Denis et al., 2012; Pearce, 2004). Nevertheless, co-leadership is distinct from distributed and shared leadership because it leads others from the top of different types and sizes of organizations.

Applying the practice of co-leadership in the arts

Co-leadership practice is institutionalized in the arts, primarily in the West (Peterson, 1986; Radaelli, 2012). It may emerge as a practice among a small group of entrepreneurial artists (Järvinen et al., 2015) or as a conscious decision made by a governance body for an institution (Chapters 4 and 8). Executive leadership practices in the arts vary by art discipline, size and age of organization, legal jurisdiction, and governance orientation (Caust, 2015; King & Schramme, 2019). In Chapter 4, we explore the geography and traditions of arts leadership practice and develop a typology of co-leadership configurations in the arts. This variation across small and large organizations is fairly unique in the arts compared to other sectors, except the high technology sector where co-CEOs are found in both start-ups and major corporations.

Recent research on smaller or younger organizations reports less conflict arising from the tensions typical of pluralistic cultures, especially in the arts (Carneiro, 2019; Järvinen et al., 2015; Leung & Tung, 2015). While titles exist in these smaller organizations, the definition of certain roles can be ambiguous (Tremblay, 2014), making little distinction among the formal professional roles found in larger organizations. Artist collectives or artist entrepreneurs alone may share the artistic as well as administrative responsibilities, responding to the organizational, logistical, and funding needs of producing art with their personal expertise and preferences.

In larger organizations, arts co-leadership formally mandates artistic and management leadership as separate roles (Peterson, 1986), but also assigns joint responsibility to lead the organization as one. The mandated choice for co-leadership may be defined either through public regulation and funding agreements in Europe and some parts of Asia (Fjellvær, 2010; Tschmuck, 2006; Zan et al., 2012) or by boards of directors in the Anglo non-profit tradition (MacNeill & Tonks, 2013; Reid & Karambayya, 2009, 2016). In these cases, the co-leaders are rarely hired simultaneously and so have no prior relationship. In very large institutions, a celebrity artist is traditionally appointed as AD (Ostrower, 2002). Despite how well-established co-leadership has become in the arts, the practice is criticized by scholars in both arts management and leadership studies.

Criticizing co-leadership

One critical view proposes that co-leadership constrains the artistic mission (Macdonnell & Bereson, 2019). The romantic ideal about art suggests that creative artists need artistic autonomy to fully express their ideas (Chiapello, 2004; DeNora, 1991; Røyseng, 2008). In the shared role space, the managerial partner's concern about organizational stability contrasts with artistic autonomy and creates tension in the space that can impact organizational well-being and influence strategizing (Beirne & Knight,

2002; Cray et al., 2007). However, in many cases, the ongoing debates within the organization resulting from these tensions underscore the positive value of maintaining the differentiation (Røyseng, 2008). For example, managerial partners in certain film production companies in Europe protect the idiosyncratic vision of their film-makers from conforming pressures (Alvarez et al., 2005). Our research in this book provides macro and micro insights about how this tension occurs and how co-leaders respond to the balancing demands of this criticism.

The second criticism of co-leadership is expressed by scholarly advocates of single leadership (Fayol, 1949; Locke, 2003). They argue that a solo executive provides a unified and coordinated organizational direction in contrast to the potential dysfunctionality of co-leadership. Asking two or more leaders who value different logics to make joint assessments and decisions is certainly a more significant demand than a single leader would face. However, the pluralistic context of the arts would be difficult for one leader to confront, as well. Despite the challenges of co-leadership, by debating the opposing perspectives that they embody, arts co-leaders can bring a collective perspective to the shared role space responding to the demand of pluralistic dilemmas. Clearly, each criticism implies that a co-leader relationship needs to span and integrate competing logics to be effective and so lead as one.

As a further counter to the second criticism, plural leadership scholars argue that collective leadership approaches generate less directive leadership and so more coherent organizational process, especially in ambiguous and complex environments (Denis et al., 2012). In the arts, however, celebrity artists may be chosen not only as charismatic champions of artistic autonomy in the co-leadership but also for their capacity to lead and attract artists and audiences, enhancing organizational reputation (Nisbett & Walmsley, 2016). But artistic leadership can be quite directive (Abfalter, 2013), and recently, this strategy has been questioned due to revelations of artistic leaders' abuse of power (Alick, 2021; Schmidt, 2016). How this behaviour can be managed within the co-leadership relationship presents new frontiers for boards and co-leaders (Chapter 8 and 10).

Researching post-heroic and heroic plural leadership

Scholars have termed solo leadership as "heroic" (Crevani et al., 2007; Etzioni, 1965) because of its emphasis on inspiration and charisma (Burns, 1978; House, 1977). Plural leadership scholars frequently evoke "post-heroic" leadership when describing their approach (Crevani et al., 2007; Fletcher, 2004). While celebrity ADs appear heroic, scholars have argued that co-leadership mitigates the risks of charisma by promoting collaboration (Alvarez & Svejenova, 2005; Heenan & Bennis, 1999). Nonetheless, the presence of celebrity can unbalance the power parity in co-leadership leading to status conflict and dysfunction in the shared role space

(Bendersky & Hays, 2012) (Chapter 6). On the other hand, psychoanalysts argue that there is a human need to transfer emotions and allegiances to a strong individual in charge (Maccoby, 2004) suggesting a functional value for these heroic leaders in the larger organization (Shamir et al., 2007). However, particularly in the arts, the dark side of this transfer is revealed when the artistic imperative is used to justify destabilizing leadership and organizational dynamics that damage the artistic process (Abfalter, 2013; Kleppe & Røyseng, 2016; Lindgren, 2009; Quigg, 2007; Schmidt, 2016). Dependence on celebrity in the arts places strenuous demands on institutions and organizations, and their leadership.

But change is occurring. Just before and during the 2020 pandemic, social justice movements like #MeToo!, Black Lives Matter, and advocates of diversity, equity, and inclusion have forced arts boards to confront organizational and ethical issues in North America (Lederman, 2018). A recent report from the Sundance Institute on theatres in the US suggests that AD plurality is an antidote to the concentration of AD power and enables racial diversity (Alick, 2021), extending the practice of co-leadership. Increasingly, important US institutions have hired more than one AD (Cooper, 2019; Jones, 2021). As well, in Europe and Britain, trends in arts leadership training encourage collaborative leadership (Abfalter, 2013; Hewison & Holden, 2002; Järvinen et al., 2015).

In summary, co-leadership in the arts is a strategic mechanism that promotes leadership differentiation in response to the pluralism and diffuse power inherent in the arts. The balancing act between the logics of artistic autonomy and of market or managerialism is delicate and multi-faceted. Co-leaders work jointly through these multiple perspectives in the shared role space visualized by the triangle in Figure 1.1. Both large institutions and small entrepreneurships or collectives engage in co-leadership. Despite interest in a post-heroic view of leadership, artistic celebrity is a particular characteristic of leadership in the arts, and it works both for and against the organization's success and co-leadership effectiveness.

Justifying this topic ... in a book

Despite the call for contextual study of plural leadership (Denis et al., 2010), co-leadership scholarship has often been theorized outside of specific contexts (Alvarez & Svejenova, 2005; Arnone & Stumpf, 2010; Gibeau et al., 2016; Heenan & Bennis, 1999). Nonetheless, some scholars have contributed to generalized research by analyzing co-leadership in specific sectors like hospitals (Denis et al., 2001; Gibeau et al., 2020; Hodgson et al., 1965), schools (Court, 2002; Döös & Wilhelmson, 2021; Gronn, 1999), and professional service firms (Empson, 2017). In this book, we hope to contribute to theory about co-leadership, plural leadership, and, as a result, provide cohesion and insight regarding the specific co-leadership practice in the arts.

An impressive 19 articles on cultural co-leadership have appeared in journals that specialize in the arts or in general management (Chapter 3). We also considered three theses focused on co-leadership in the arts. There is clearly interest in the arts field about the phenomenon of co-leadership but, like the arts management field in general, theorizing is dispersed and not well-connected (DeVereaux, 2020). We observed two major theoretical themes: Strategic decision-making (Bhansing et al., 2016; Cray et al., 2007) and dynamics in the shared role space (Reid & Karambayya, 2009, 2016; Reynolds et al., 2017). These themes reflect the criticisms of co-leadership identified earlier. They address the different perspectives that emerge during decision-making. They also focus on the relationship of co-leadership in the role space as they attempt to lead as one. However, there is limited referencing across the literature or recognition of the criticism. In this book, we consolidate threads from both the cultural field and the management literature about co-leadership. Arts management research will benefit from the theorizing and precision that has emerged from management scholars concerned with plural leadership (Denis et al., 2012). Management scholars will appreciate the special dynamics of the arts where the specific logics integral to the triangle (Figure 1.1) meet with some intensity, raising questions about "post-heroic" leadership and governance (Chapters 2 and 5–8).

Our context is complex and pluralistic, volatile, and politically demanding with multiple objectives (Lampel et al., 2000; Schrauwen et al., 2016). Researchers can find analyzing such extreme situations informative, where factors with potentially broader relevance for theory building can be uncovered (Eisenhardt, 1989; Eisenhardt & Graebner, 2007). Plural leadership scholars may be attracted to opportunities to expand insights on bridging between potent logics like the artistic imperative, embedded in freedom of speech, and the audience and funders' role in organizational stability. These pluralistic risks can be organizationally life-threatening, and their tensions are unique among professional organizations with co-leadership. The power of celebrity and artistic imperative may be relevant to a general understanding of the balance needed between professional and managerial logics (Fjellvær, 2010; Gibeau et al., 2020). Arts management and leadership scholars rarely study co-leadership, but they may wish to further explore how co-leadership is a strategic response to dynamics in the arts context. We open doors to future research possibilities in Chapter 10.

Structuring the book

The book is organized in four sections:

Section I frames co-leadership within the research on organizational pluralism and plural leadership as well as its historical and international context. The arts management literature that explores influential stakeholders and logics like the artistic imperative is analysed. Our research consolidates an understanding of global and historical practices of arts leadership.

It deepens our understanding of co-leadership as embedded in its institutional context. (Chapters 2, 3, and 4)

Sections II and III present the empirical heart of the book focusing on co-leadership dynamics and practices, responding to the platform of theory provided in the first half of the book.

Section II analyses co-leaders' relationships and interdependence as they address their joint responsibilities in the shared role space. We look at how co-leaders perceive competing logics to make decisions and how the relationship evolves in the shared role space using conflict and trust as lenses for this investigation. This study enables an understanding of how a differentiated co-leadership can potentially lead with coherence and complementarity (Chapters 5, 6, and 7).

Section III investigates how organizational members work with co-leaders including implications for the shared role space. This perspective adds governance bodies like boards of directors and followers to gain and expand insight into the dynamics around co-leadership (Chapters 8 and 9).

Section IV builds on the investigation of arts co-leadership in this book, suggesting future research questions to support the creation of more strategic understanding of co-leadership in the arts (Chapter 10).

Summarizing the book

Chapter 1

We present a summary of the learning in the book highlighting key notions about arts co-leadership and anticipating the theoretical frames of upcoming chapters.

Section I – Framing the research

Chapter 2 – Interpreting organizational context for arts co-leadership

In this chapter, we set co-leadership within the theoretical platform of pluralism, and describe the impact of various logics on co-leadership found in Figure 1.1. Pluralism generates a culture of ambiguous roles and goals (Cohen & March, 1974; Denis et al., 1996; Kraatz & Block, 2008, 2017) suggesting challenges for trust-building, coherent collaboration and strategizing, and conflict management. While scholars of single leadership may view co-leadership's potential lack of coherence as its Achilles heel, the complementary expertise is its advantage.

The key to pluralism in this context lies in appreciating the tension of interdependence among the needs of the artistic imperative and the needs of the organization connecting art with its audience, suggesting hybrid dynamics (Battilana & Lee, 2014). This analysis provides a backdrop of institutionalized practices that clarify the tensions of pluralism in the arts.

Chapter 3 – Parsing co-leadership theory for the arts

We position arts co-leadership in the research tradition of plural leadership (Denis et al., 2012). Given its typically mandated and executive position in professional organizations, co-leadership is distinguished from other more emergent forms of plural leadership. These other forms are called shared, distributed, and collective or relational leadership (Denis et al., 2012; Döös & Wilhelmson, 2021).

In this chapter, we outline the foundational concepts in co-leadership research. These concepts are inspired by role theory which considers the dynamics involved in an array of associated roles that appear in social structures around a focal role like a leader or co-leaders (Gronn & Hamilton, 2004; Katz & Kahn, 1966; Merton, 1957; Stewart, 1991). The two concepts of executive role constellations and shared role space (Gronn & Hamilton, 2004) address how co-leadership manages pluralism. Inter-relational issues are traced through differentiation, specialization, and complementarity (Hodgson et al., 1965) and through other interpersonal and organizational theories in social psychology and strategy. These concerns are assembled as a theoretical baseline from which to launch an exploration of further dilemmas of arts co-leadership in this book. Several arts management scholars have delved into these issues, and we chart their work in our discussion.

Chapter 4 – Situating co-leadership in the arts globally

In this chapter, a contingency approach structures an understanding of the varied global practice of executive leadership in the arts (Alvarez & Svejenova, 2005). This approach confronts the normatively tinted debate around single versus plural leadership in the academic literature with examples of real-life practice drawn from interviews with globally situated experts in the field as well as published cases.

Co-leadership is prevalent in Anglo-Saxon and some European regions like Scandinavia and German-speaking countries. On the other hand, single or hierarchically configured leadership dominates in large parts of the Global South (e.g., India, Latin America, and Asia) often reflecting less anchored values or negative views about the role of artistic creation in society.

External influences generate a variety of practices in cultural leadership involving both societal and field-level values like the role of art in society, traditions rooted in specific art disciplines, funding policies, and the presence of arts management training. Internally, the organization's needs for leadership evolve as the operation grows from entrepreneurial to a more formal mode of functioning. This understanding provides an opportunity to create a typology of co-leadership in context.

Section II – Theorizing relational dynamics in arts co-leadership

Chapter 5 – Working with interdependence: Logics, values, and the shared role space

The triangle of perspectives in Figure 1.1 defines the role space shared by arts co-leadership. Different logics and values compete in this space, related to the variety of stakeholders present in this same figure. Each co-leader consciously chooses either a single dominant logic or a balance of logics (Fjellvær, 2010; Gibeau et al., 2020). Different combinations of logic dominance or balance across sets of co-leaders occurred in our data. Complementarity occurs when logics and values are integrated and balanced after solid debate (Hodgson et al., 1965). The ultimate combination type achieves an over-arching logic that can produce organizational innovation, but given the needs for other forms of innovation, this may not be the main goal for arts co-leadership. Suboptimal logic integration may evoke a state similar to negative peace, a concept developed by Johan Galtung. This idea suggests a state that is usually good enough for productive complementarity (Galtung & Fisher, 2013). However, the fluidity of circumstances as environmental influences change over time may induce co-leadership fragility (Denis et al., 2001; Denis et al., 2012).

Chapter 6 – Challenging equality: Pluralism, competitive conflict, and social hierarchy

Conflict can unbalance the power and status parity intended within the co-leadership role space (Alvarez & Svejenova, 2005; Reid & Karambayya, 2009; Schrauwen et al., 2016). In this chapter, status conflict provides a new micro view of competitive power and social hierarchy dynamics applied to co-leadership (Bendersky & Hays, 2012; Magee & Galinsky, 2008). Arts management scholars debate the presence of conflict in arts co-leadership (Järvinen et al., 2015; Reynolds et al., 2017), but it appears embedded in pluralistic contexts (Kraatz & Block, 2008, 2017) and complex organizations (Greenwood et al., 2011) with positive or negative consequences (Reid & Karambayya, 2009). Status asymmetry within co-leadership may influence decisional dynamics, shared role space logics integration, and leadership effectiveness.

Chapter 7 – Contending with ambiguity and vulnerability: Leaps of faith and mechanisms of trust

Trust is important in co-leadership relationships (Alvarez & Svejenova, 2005; Gronn & Hamilton, 2004). It supports bridge-building across competing values (Fjellvær, 2010), enables the negotiation of differences (Alvarez & Svejenova, 2005), and counters co-leadership fragility (Denis et al., 2001).

In the arts, pluralism presents ambiguous options to leaders for decision-making, rendering organizational life uncertain and vulnerable (Lampel et al., 2000). Artists are familiar with vulnerability, when live performance can be unpredictable and requires the audience to suspend disbelief (Goffman, 1959; Möllering, 2012). Trust also involves a suspension of doubt in order to positively regard others and thus contend with ambiguity and vulnerability. As a result, a leap of faith forms the threshold to initiate trust in the co-leadership role space.

However, to sustain a long-term relationship, the mobilization of trust-building mechanisms rooted in routines, rationality, and reflection are called for (Möllering, 2006). In this chapter, the leap of faith decision to hire a new member of the co-leadership is the empirical conceit deployed to explore trust processes in arts co-leadership. Focusing on the organizational mission is found to be a particularly powerful routine mechanism for subsequently supporting trust development and binding the co-leadership relationship.

Section III – Theorizing organizational dynamics with arts co-leadership

Chapter 8 – Managing risk: Board-staff relations, co-leadership, and information asymmetry

Formalizing executive co-leadership is frequently a governance decision (Alvarez & Svejenova, 2005), especially in medium and large organizations (Chapter 4). Non-profit board members face governance dilemmas and pluralism (Cornforth, 2003a, 2003b) arising from different governance and organizational logics. Hiring co-leaders can both complicate and solve organizational dilemmas in the arts but how the presence of co-leaders responds to governance logics has not been explored. The ADs charisma, public profile, and carefully guarded professional terrain are passionately motivating for arts boards (Ostrower, 2002; Rentschler, 2015), but challenging as well (Bieber, 2003; Rentschler, 2015). Creating and presenting art is a subjective and unpredictable risk (Lampel et al., 2000).

Overseeing the balance between financial and artistic risks and rewards is difficult for board members who rarely have a professional understanding of art at a level comparable to the AD. Agency theory explains this lack of understanding as information asymmetry (Fama & Jensen, 1983). As a result, the board is uncomfortable evaluating an ADs programming and artistic production (Ostrower, 2002). To solve their information asymmetry with an AD, boards delegate to the executive director (ED) a governance "watch-dog" responsibility. The pressure from this delegation may intensify the potential for co-leadership conflict. On the other hand, if strong trust occurs within the co-leadership, the leadership may work well, but the board may misperceive relational coherence as collusion. Extreme conflict or collusion invites board intervention at the operational level, including artistic decisions, challenging the initial purpose of appointing co-leadership. This dynamic has a major impact on the shared role space. This study of board-staff relations demonstrates the influence by boards on arts co-leaders and how co-leadership plays a role in governance effectiveness.

Chapter 9 – Following and influencing co-leaders

Our research is quite unique in the field of plural leadership because of its extensive organizational dataset (Döös & Wilhelmson, 2021; Ebbers & Wijnberg, 2017). Few research studies have ventured outside the role space and dynamics within co-leadership relationships. We examine a number of cases from our research using role theory to understand how key followers interact with co-leaders' relationship and decision dynamics. The possibility for followers' role crafting is explored through two types of situations: one is by understanding the well-being of the co-leaders' relationship and the other is by providing opportunities to participate in the shared executive role space (Ebbers & Wijnberg, 2017; Schrauwen et al., 2016). These strategies distribute leadership influence beyond the executive appointed co-leadership and into the organization.

Section IV – Structuring co-leadership research and practice

Chapter 10 – Charting insights and a future research course: What and who, how, where, and why?

Much remains to be explored about co-leadership. This chapter builds on the learning in the book by structuring the future possibilities for research in both theory and practice. This structure proposes a view of arts co-leadership through basic perspectives of what and who, where, and how to define topics that could be further considered. As well, we reflect on how the current environment, the pandemic, social justice, and environmental issues may influence arts organizations, their missions and viability. This raises strategic questions about how executive leadership configurations play an effective role in enabling the multi-level relationships among organizations, artists, and art in society.

References

Abfalter, D. (2013). Authenticity and respect: Leading creative teams in the performing arts. *Creativity and Innovation Management*, *12*(3), 295–306.

Alick, J. C. (2021). *Emerging from the cave: Reimagining our future in theater and live performance.* Sundance Institute.

Alvarez, J. L., Mazza, C., Pederson, J. S., & Svejenova, S. (2005). Shielding idiosyncrasy from isomorphic pressures: Towards optimal distinctiveness in European filmmaking. *Organization*, *12*(6), 863–888. https://doi.org/10.1177/1350508405057474

Alvarez, J. L., & Svejenova, S. (2005). *Sharing Executive Power: Roles and Relationships at the Top*. Cambridge University Press.

Arnone, M., & Stumpf, S. A. (2010). Shared leadership: From rivals to co-CEOs. *Strategy & Leadership*, *38*(2), 15–21. https://doi.org/10.1108/10878571011029019

Battilana, J., & Lee, M. (2014). Advancing research on hybrid organizing – Insights from the study of social enterprises. *The Academy of Management Annals*, *8*(1), 397–441. https://doi.org/10.1080/19416520.2014.893615

Baumol, W., & Bowen, W. (1966). *Performing Arts The Economic Dilemma: A Study of Problems Common to Theater, Opera, Music and Dance*. The MIT Press.

Beirne, M., & Knight, S. (2002). Principles and consistent management in the arts: Lessons from British theatre. *International Journal of Cultural Policy*, *8*(1), 75–89. https://doi.org/10.1080/10286630290032459

Bendersky, C., & Hays, N. (2012). Status conflict in groups. *Organization Science*, *23*(2), 323–340. https://doi.org/10.1287/orsc.1110.0734

Bhansing, P., Leenders, M., & Wijnberg, N. (2016). Selection system orientations as an explanation for the differences between dual leaders of the same organization in their perception of organizational performance. *Journal of Management & Governance*, *20*(4), 907–933. https://doi.org/10.1007/s10997-015-9330-4

Bieber, M. (2003). Governing Independent Museums: How Trustees and Directors Exercise Their Powers. In C. Cornforth (Ed.), *The Governance of Public and Non-profit Organizations: What Do Boards Do?* (pp. 164–184). Routledge.

Bolden, R. (2011). Distributed leadership in organizations: A review of theory and research. *International Journal of Management Reviews*, *13*(3), 251–269. https://doi.org/10.1111/j.1468-2370.2011.00306.x

Burns, J. M. (1978). *Leadership*. Harper & Row.

Carneiro, M. (2019). How *do dual executive leadership practices of theatre production companies around the world make decisions for their artistic and organizational wellbeing*? Master's thesis, HEC Montréal, Montréal.

Caust, J. (Ed.). (2015). *Arts and Cultural Leadership in Asia*. Routledge.

Caust, J. (2018). *Arts Leadership in Contemporary Contexts* (1st ed.). Routledge.

Chiapello, È. (1998). *Artistes versus Managers: Le Management Culturel face à la Critique Artiste*. Éditions Métaillés.

Chiapello, È. (2004). Evolution and co-optation: The 'artist critique' of management and capitalism. *Third Text*, *18*(6), 585–594. https://doi.org/10.1080/0952882042000284998

Cohen, M. D., & March, J. G. (1974). *Leadership and Ambiguity: The American College President* (2nd ed.). Harvard Business School Press.

Colbert, F., & Dantas, D. (2019). Customer relationships in arts marketing: A review of key dimensions in delivery by artistic and cultural organizations. *International Journal of Arts Management*, *21*(2), 4–14.

Cooper, M. (2019). City Ballet, Shaken by Turmoil, Chooses New Leaders. *New York Times*.

Cornforth, C. (Ed.). (2003a). Conclusion: Contextualising and Managing the Paradoxes of Governance. In *The Governance of Public and Non-profit Organisations: What Do Boards Do?* (pp. 237–253). Routledge.

Cornforth, C. (Ed.). (2003b). Introduction to the Changing Context of Governance - Emerging Issues and Paradoxes. In *The Governance of Public and Non-profit Organisations: What Do Boards Do?* (pp. 1–19). Routledge.

Court, M. (2002). Co-principalship and shared teacher leadership. Re-viewing international studies and introducing New Zealand initiatives. *NZEAS Conference*. Auckland.

Cray, D., Inglis, L., & Freeman, S. (2007). Managing the arts: Leadership and decision making under dual rationalities. *Journal of Arts Management, Law and Society*, *36*(4), 295–313. https://doi.org/10.3200/JAML.36.4.295-314

Crevani, L., Lindgren, M., & Packendorff, J. (2007). Shared leadership: A post-heroic perspective on leadership as a collective construction. *International Journal of Leadership Studies*, *3*(1), 40–67.

Denis, J.-L., Lamothe, L., & Langley, A. (2001). The dynamics of collective leadership and strategic change in pluralistic organizations. *The Academy of Management Journal*, *44*(4), 809–837. https://doi.org/10.2307/3069417

Denis, J.-L., Langley, A., & Cazale, L. (1996). Leadership and strategic change under ambiguity. *Organization Studies*, *17*(4), 673–699.

Denis, J.-L., Langley, A., & Rouleau, L. (2010). The practice of leadership in the messy world of organizations. *Leadership*, *6*(1), 67–88. https://doi.org/10.1177/1742715009354233

Denis, J.-L., Langley, A., & Sergi, V. (2012). Leadership in the plural. *The Academy of Management Annals*, *5*(1), 211–283. https://doi.org/10.1080/19416520.2012.667612

DeNora, T. (1991). Musical patronage and social change in Beethoven's Vienna. *American Journal of Sociology*, *97*(2), 310–346. https://doi.org/10.1086/229781

Devereaux, C. (2019). Practice versus a discourse of practice in cultural management. *The Journal of Arts Management, Law, and Society*, *39*(1), 65–72. https://doi.org/10.3200/JAML.39.1.65-72

DeVereaux, C. (2020). Arts Management: Reflections on Role, Purpose, and the Complications of Existence. In W. J. Byrnes & A. Brkić (Eds.), *The Routledge Companion to Arts Management* (1st ed., pp. 12–22). Routledge.

Döös, M., & Wilhelmson, L. (2021). Fifty-five years of managerial shared leadership research: A review of an empirical field. *Leadership*, *17*(6), 715–746. https://doi.org/10.1177/17427150211037809

Dragićević Šešić, M. (2020). Contemporary Arts in Adaptable Quality Management: Questioning Entrepreneurialism as a Panacea in Europe. In W. J. Byrnes & A. Brkić (Eds.), *The Routledge Companion to Arts Management* (pp. 39–54). Routledge.

Ebbers, J., & Wijnberg, N. (2017). Betwixt and between: Role conflict, role ambiguity and role definition in project-based dual-leadership structures. *Human Relations*, *70*(11), 1342–1365. https://doi.org/10.1177/0018726717692852

Eisenhardt, K. (1989). Building theories from case study research. *Academy of Management Review*, *14*(4), 532–550.

Eisenhardt, K., & Graebner, M. E. (2007). Theory building from cases: Opportunities and challenges. *Academy of Management Journal*, *50*(1), 25–32. https://doi.org/10.5465/AMJ.2007.24160888

Empson, L. (2017). *Leading Professionals: Power, Politics, and Prima Donnas.* Oxford University Press.

Etzioni, A. (1965). Dual leadership in complex organizations. *American Sociological Review*, *30*(5), 688–698. https://doi.org/10.2307/2091137

Fama, E. R., & Jensen, M. C. (1983). Separation of ownership and control. *Journal of Law and Economics*, *26*(June), 301–325.

Fayol, H. (1949). *General and Industrial Management*. Isaac Pitman.

Fjellvær, H. (2010). *Dual and unitary leadership: managing ambiguity in pluralistic organizations* (Publication Number 2010/10). Doctoral dissertation, Norwegian School of Economics and Business Administration, Bergen. https://openaccess.nhh.no/nhh-xmlui/bitstream/handle/11250/164362/fjellver%20avh%202010.PDF?sequence=1

Fletcher, J. K. (2004). The paradox of postheroic leadership: An essay on gender, power, and transformational change. *The Leadership Quarterly*, *15*(5), 647–661. https://doi.org/10.1016/j.leaqua.2004.07.004

Galtung, J., & Fischer, D. (2013). *Johan Galtung: Pioneer of Peace Research*. Springer.

Gibeau, É, Langley, A., Denis, J.-L.& van Schendel, N. (2020). Bridging competing demands through co-leadership? Potential and limitations. *Human Relations*, *73*(4), 464–489. https://doi.org/10.1177/0018726719888145

Gibeau, É, Reid, W., & Langley, A. (2016). Co-leadership: Contexts, Configurations and Conditions. In J. Storey, J. Hartley, J.-L. Denis, P. 't Hart, & D. Ulrich (Eds.), *Routledge Companion to Leadership* (pp. 225–240). Routledge.

Goffman, E. (1959). *The Presentation of Self in Everyday Life*. Doubleday.

Greenwood, R., Raynard, M., Kodeih, F., Micelotta, E. R., & Lounsbury, M. (2011). Institutional complexity and organizational responses. *The Academy of Management Annals*, *5*(1), 317–371. https://doi.org/10.1080/19416520.2011.590299

Gronn, P. (1999). Substituting for leadership: The neglected role of the leadership couple. *The Leadership Quarterly*, *10*(1), 41–62. https://doi.org/10.1016/S1048-9843(99)80008-3

Gronn, P. (2002). Distributed leadership as a unit of analysis. *The Leadership Quarterly*, *13*(4), 423–451. https://doi.org/10.1016/S1048-9843(02)00120-0

Gronn, P., & Hamilton, A. (2004). 'A bit more life in the leadership': Co-principalship as distributed leadership practice. *Leadership and Policy in Schools*, *3*(1), 3–35. https://doi.org/10.1076/lpos.3.1.3.27842

Heenan, D. A., & Bennis, W. (1999). *Co-leaders: The Power of Great Partnerships*. John Wiley & Sons.

Hewison, R., & Holden, J. (2002). *Task Force Final Report: An Investment in the Rising Generation of Cultural Leaders is Necessary, and Timely*. Clore Duffield Foundation.

Hewison, R., Holden, J., & Jones, S. (2013). Leadership and Transformation at the Royal Shakespeare Company. In J. Caust (Ed.), *Arts Leadership: International Case Studies* (1st ed., pp. 145–160). Tilde University Press.

Hodgson, R. C., Levinson, D. J., & Zaleznik, A. (1965). *The Executive Role Constellation: An Analysis of Personality and Role Relations in Management*. Harvard University, Division of Research, Graduate School of Business Administration.

House, R. J. (1977). A 1976 Theory of Charismatic Leadership. In J. G. Hunt, & L. L. Larson (Eds.), *Leadership: The Cutting Edge: A Symposium Held at Southern Illinois University, Carbondale, 1976* (p. 286). Southern Illinois University Press.

Järvinen, M., Ansio, H., & Houni, P. (2015). New variations of dual leadership: Insights from Finnish theatre. *International Journal of Arts Management*, *17*(3), 16–27.

Jones, C. (2021). Steppenwolf Theatre names two new artistic directors. *Chicago Tribune.*

Katz, D., & Kahn, R. L. (1966). *The Social Psychology of Organizations.* Wiley.

Kawashima, N. (2006). Audience development and social inclusion in Britain: Tensions, contradictions and paradoxes in policy and their implications for cultural management. *International Journal of Cultural Policy, 12*(1), 55–72. https://doi.org/10.1080/10286630600613309

King, I., & Schramme, A. (Eds.). (2019). *Cultural Governance in a Global Context: An International Perspective on Arts Organizations.* Palgrave MacMillan.

Kleppe, B., & Røyseng, S. (2016). Sexual harassment in the Norwegian theatre world. *Journal of Arts Management, Law and Society, 46*(5), 282–296. https://doi.org/10.1080/10632921.2016.1231645

Kraatz, M. S., & Block, E. (2008). Organizational Implications of Institutional Pluralism. In R. Greenwood, C. Oliver, K. Sahlin-Andersson, & R. Suddaby (Eds.), *The SAGE Handbook of Organizational Institutionalism* (pp. 243–296). SAGE Publications Limited.

Kraatz, M. S., & Block, E. (2017). Institutional Pluralism Revisited. In R. Greenwood, C. Oliver, T. Lawrence, & R. E. Meyer (Eds.), *The SAGE Handbook of Organizational Institutionalism (*2nd ed., pp. 532–557). SAGE Publications.

Lampel, J., Lant, T., & Shamsie, J. (2000). Balancing act: Learning from organizing practices in cultural industries. *Organization Science, 11*(3), 263–269. https://doi.org/10.1287/orsc.11.3.263.12503

Lederman, M. (2018). When the #MeToo reckoning came for Canadian arts. *The Globe and Mail.*

Leung, C. C., & Tung, K. Y. (2015). Dual Roles: Collaborative Leadership in a Newly Developed Music Ensemble: A Case Study from Hong Kong. In J. Caust (Ed.), *Arts and Cultural Leadership in Asia* (pp. 105–120). Routledge.

Lindgren, A. C. (2009). The National Ballet of Canada and the Kimberly Glasco legal arbitration case. *The Journal of Arts Management, Law, and Society, 39*(2), 101–116. https://doi.org/10.3200/JAML.39.2.101-116

Locke, E. A. (2003). Leadership: Starting at the Top. In C. L. Pearce, & J. A. Conger (Eds.), *Shared Leadership: Reframing the Hows and Whys of Leadership* (pp. 271–284). Sage.

Löfgren, M. (2016). On the Public Value of Arts and Culture. In K. Dalborg, & M. Löfgren (Eds.), *The FIKA Project: Perspectives on Cultural Leadership* (pp. 75–99). Nätwerkstan Kultur.

Maccoby, M. (2004). The power of transference: Why people follow the leader. *Harvard Business Review, September 2004*, 76–85.

Macdonnell, J., & Bereson, R. (2019). Arts Management and Its Contradictions. In W. J. Byrnes, & A. Brkić (Eds.), *The Routledge Companion to Arts Management* (1st ed., pp. 1–11). Routledge.

MacNeill, K., & Tonks, A. (2013). Leadership in Australian Arts Companies: One Size Does Not Fit All. In J. Caust (Ed.), *Arts Leadership: International Case Studies (*1st ed., pp. 69–82). Tilde University Press.

Magee, J. C., & Galinsky, A. D. (2008). Social hierarchy: The self-reinforcing nature of power and status. *Academy of Management Annals*, 2(1), 351–398. https://doi.org/10.1080/19416520802211628

Merton, R. K. (1957). The role-set: Problems in sociological theory. *The British Journal of Sociology, 8*(2), 106–120.

Möllering, G. (2006). *Trust: Reason, Routine, Reflexivity*. Elsevier.

Möllering, G. (2012). Trusting in art: Calling for empirical trust research in highly creative contexts. *Journal of Trust Research*, *2*(2), 203–210. https://doi.org/10.1080/21515581.2012.708509

Nisbett, M., & Walmsley, B. (2016). The romanticization of charismatic leadership in the arts. *The Journal of Arts Management, Law, and Society*, *46*(1), 2–12. https://doi.org/10.1080/10632921.2015.1131218

Offerman, L., & Scuderi, N. (2017). Sharing Leadership. In B. Shamir, R. Pillai, M. Bligh, & M. Uhl-Bien (Eds.), *Follower-centered Perspectives on Leadership: A Tribute to the Memory of James R. Meindl* (pp. 71–91). Information Age Publishing.

Ostrower, F. (2002). *Trustees of Culture: Power, Wealth, and Status on Elite Arts Boards*. University of Chicago Press.

Pearce, C. L. (2004). The future of leadership: Combining vertical and shared leadership to transform knowledge work. *Academy of Management Executive*, *18*(1), 47–57. https://doi.org/10.5465/ame.2004.12690298

Peterson, R. (1986). From Impresario to Arts Administrator: Formal Accountability in Nonprofit Cultural Organizations. In P. DiMaggio (Ed.), *Nonprofit Enterprise in the Arts: Studies in Mission and Constraint* (pp 161–183). Oxford University Press.

Quigg, A.-M. (2007). Bullying in theatres and arts centres in the United Kingdom. *International Journal of Arts Management*, *10*(1), 52–64.

Radaelli, E. (2012). American Cultural Policy and the Rise of Arts Management Programs: The Creation of a New Professional Identity. In J. Paquette (Ed.), *Cultural Policy, Work and Identity: The Creation, Renewal and Negotiation of Professional Subjectivities* (pp. 145–159). Ashgate.

Reid, W., & Karambayya, R. (2009). Impact of dual executive leadership dynamics in creative organizations. *Human Relations*, *62*(7), 1073–1112. https://doi.org/10.1177/0018726709335539

Reid, W., & Karambayya, R. (2016). The shadow of history: Situated dynamics of trust in dual executive leadership. *Leadership*, *12*(5), 609–631. https://doi.org/10.1177/1742715015579931

Rentschler, R. (2015). *Arts Governance: People, Passion, Performance* (1st ed.). Routledge.

Reynolds, S., Tonks, A., & MacNeill, K. (2017). Collaborative leadership in the arts as a unique form of dual leadership. *The Journal of Arts Management, Law, and Society*, *47*(2), 89–104. https://doi.org/10.1080/10632921.2016.1241968

Røyseng, S. (2008). Arts management and the autonomy of art. *International Journal of Cultural Policy*, *14*(1), 37–48. https://doi.org/10.1080/10286630701856484

Røyseng, S. (2019). The social contract of artists in the era of cultural industries. *International Journal of Cultural Policy*, *25*(2), 154–170. https://doi.org/10.1080/10286632.2016.1229313

Schmidt, T. (2016). *Theater, Krise Und Reform. Eine Kritik Des Deutschen Theatersystems*. Springer VS.

Schrauwen, J., Schramme, A., & Segers, J. (2016). Do Managers Run Cultural Institutions? The Practice of Shared Leadership in the Arts Sector. In K. Dalborg, & M. Löfgren (Eds.), *The FIKA Project: Perspectives on Cultural Leadership* (pp. 103–116). Nätverkstan Kultur.

Shamir, B., Pillai, R., Bligh, M., & Uhl-Bien, M. (Eds.). (2007). *Follower-centered Perspectives on Leadership: A Tribute to the Memory of James R. Meindl*. Information Age Publishing.

Shiner, L. (2001). *The Invention of Art: A Cultural History.* University of Chicago Press.

Stewart, R. (1991). Role Sharing at the Top: A Neglected Aspect of Studies of Managerial Behaviour. In S. Carlson, H. Mintzberg, & R. Stewart(Eds.), *Executive Behaviour* (pp. 120–136). Studia Oeconomiae Negotiorum.

Thornton, P. H., Ocasio, W., & Lounsbury, M. (2012). *The Institutional Logics Perspective: A New Approach to Culture, Structure, and Process.* Oxford University Press.

Tremblay, M. (2014). *Configurations et pratiques du leadership pluriel au sommet de compagnies théâtrale québécoise.* Master's thesis, Université du Québec à Montréal, Montréal.

Tschmuck, P. (2006). The budgetary effects of 'Privatizing' major cultural institutions in Austria. *The Journal of Arts Management, Law, and Society, 35*(4), 293–304. https://doi.org/10.3200/JAML.35.4.293-304

Zan, L., Bonini Baraldi, S., Ferri, P., Lusiani, M., & Mariani, M. M. (2012). Behind the scenes of public funding for performing arts in Italy: Hidden phenomena beyond the rhetoric of legislation. *International Journal of Cultural Policy, 18*(1), 76–92. https://doi.org/10.1080/10286632.2011.573849

Section I

Framing the research

2 Interpreting organizational context for arts co-leadership

> I realized you can't treat it like a bottom-line business because if we did there'd be a lot of things we wouldn't do. And if we didn't do them, then the patrons we have wouldn't come because they don't get any music they like to hear. So, there's a whole bunch of places where we're in a box - [that] we have to do. If we're going to aspire to be a world class orchestra, then we have to have musicians that are top quality, music directors that are top quality.
>
> Administrative director

Introduction

Arts organizations are pluralistic, as this administrative director from our research clearly explains to us. The triangle in Figure 1.1 (Chapter 1) portrays a meeting ground of multiple stakeholders whose many objectives and values shape arts organizations, sometimes producing tensions (Kraatz & Block, 2008, 2017). Co-leadership acts as an integrative mechanism that can address pluralism in arts organizations by joining a manager with a leading artist(s) as the executive co-leaders of the organization. In separate and relatively equal leadership roles, arts co-leaders "decouple" the artistic and commercial logics through their expertise and leadership of separate sides of the organization, establishing functional differentiation (Røyseng, 2008). But as co-leaders they are also called upon to integrate these perspectives collaboratively, to function jointly (Alvarez & Svejenova, 2005).

In the empirical data considered in our research here, the artistic director (AD) develops the program that draws an audience and often conceives of the art produced by the organization. The executive director (ED) is typically responsible for the administration, marketing, and funding of the organization. Social impact programs and audience education and development have become an extension of the organization's mission as well as part of the EDs audience relations responsibilities (Kawashima, 2006). These mandated responsibilities vary somewhat across funding and cultural policy contexts in parts of the world where co-leadership is practiced.

These dualistic and differentiated structures also respect the professional autonomy embedded in the defining logic of an organization's mission

DOI: 10.4324/9780429504259-3

(Battilana & Dorado, 2010; Battilana & Lee, 2014). In our case, that logic is the artistic imperative which can be in tension with the commercial imperative on the business side of the arts (Røyseng, 2008). However, in order to lead together as if they are one, and manage their differentiation, co-leaders in arts organizations attempt to integrate these logics in a "shared executive role space" (Gronn & Hamilton, 2004, p. 6) (Chapters 3 and 5).

In the arts, the pluralistic domains are personified by stakeholders like artists, audiences, funders, and boards of directors. Power is diffused across these stakeholders since art and audiences play equally important roles in orienting these organizations. Funders balance the equation and boards attempt to ensure the ongoing stability of the organization to support the production of art. Differing and divergent points of view result in a culture of ambiguity that co-leaders need to manage (Cohen & March, 1974; Denis et al., 2007; Greenwood et al., 2011).

Understanding organizational pluralism and multiple logics

Organizational pluralism is our anchor perspective in the book (Denis et al., 2007). However, this perspective interacts with several other theories. In the discussion that follows, we explain perspectives that seem to be the most pertinent to our study of pluralism in the arts. These include ontological explanations of societal and field influences (institutional logics and economies of worth) and theories or types of organizations that address reconciliation of tensions (paradox, complexity, and hybrid organizations). Internal organizational and individual concerns lead us to a discussion of professional identity and dynamics that focus on ambiguity.

To interpret the arts through these theories, we provide a short overview of pluralism and then we address each theoretical terrain in our list with illustrations from the arts. In the second section of this chapter, we deploy institutional logics to understand the multiple imperatives that drive pluralism in the arts. Drawing from the arts management literature, we see how legitimizing pressures affiliated with these logics manifest at different levels of analysis, creating dilemmas for arts leaders.

Pluralism

Organizational pluralism involves "multiple values and objectives, diffuse power, and knowledge-based work processes" (Denis et al., 2007, p. 180) resulting in a culture of goal ambiguity (Brès et al., 2018). In these organizations, groups of organizational members divide the work according to functional domains such as artistic professionals, financial services, or technical production – in the arts. Each group responds to certain imperatives, sharing values and goals to address a common set of problems, often in tension with other groups across the organization. Solutions are sought for these tensions. Executive co-leaders are coordinating mechanisms mandated to integrate these values and to solve the tensions to achieve cohesive action together as effective leaders (Denis et al., 2007, 2010). Shared understanding and decision-making must be negotiated continually throughout the organization because decisions are not always viewed as legitimate by a particular domain group's set of values. Later, we discuss logics and their interactive dynamics found in the arts management literature to explore issues around arts values and tensions.

Societal framing theories

Institutional logics theory is concerned with legitimacy of action and has evolved in reaction to institutional theory through explaining change (Friedland & Alford, 1991) largely in North America (Thornton et al., 2012). On the other hand, the theory of economies of worth was developed in the French Pragmatists sociology movement as a process view of change where values are debated, justified, and evaluated (Boltanski & Thevenot, 1991-2006; Cloutier et al., 2017). They are similarly structured.

Institutional logics theory

In institutional logics theory, scholars categorize the social environment according to seven institutional orders (Thornton et al., 2012): Family, community, religion, state, market, profession, and corporation. Logics embedded in each of these orders carry the norms and values of the institutions that the orders represent. A system of analysis identifies sources of legitimacy, authority, and identity for each order, as well as different types of mechanisms and forms of capital. The logics resident in the orders guide an understanding of what makes organizational action legitimate.

In the arts, the community and professional orders involve linked perspectives. Artists carry the professional order logics in arts organizations, but other technical and stage professionals partner with artists in that order, engaging with logics that support the creative process (Barkela, 2021). Community logics are informed by the artistic ideal as well, through its inspirational, transformational, and educational perspectives. Justified by these logics, arts organizations increasingly develop their community relationships for social impact and audience engagement. Of course, with many organizations, market and corporation orders are also at play, given the presence of the audience and funders in the triangle that we developed for arts organizations (Chapter 1).

Early scholarly research considered institutional logics to be quite static, and organizational change occurred by moving from one dominant logic to another (Fjellvær, 2010). However, more recently, actors from across different functional domains secure legitimacy by negotiating compromises between simultaneous and competing logics. For instance, Reay & Hinings (2009) explain how the medical profession and public funding authorities in Alberta, Canada, negotiated between profession and efficiency-related business logics, producing compromise practices and orientations. The logics manifest themselves in different ways according to the micro, macro, and meso levels of analysis. Levels are an important principle of analysis for understanding where managerial strategizing is targeted. For instance, stakeholders like funders, found at macro levels, typically guide institutionalized or socially constructed judgments about what is deemed to be legitimate behaviour undertaken by actors at meso (organizational) or micro (individual) levels. However, ambiguity occurs because of the presence of plural objectives. As a result, it is difficult to decide which strategy to adopt at a single point in time. Identity is affected.

To investigate the impact of pluralism on arts co-leadership, we mobilize institutional logics for its elaborated structure of theorizing to orient our research in this book. We illustrate the orders and system of analysis in the second half of this chapter to perceive how this theoretical approach helps to explain behavioural dynamics in the arts field. However, it is pertinent and useful to be aware of the other ontological theorizing frame that is economies of worth which provides alternative views of arts leadership.

Economies of worth

The worth or legitimacy of values also results from the ethical power of logics (Kraatz & Block, 2017), underpinning the economies of worth approach of the French Pragmatist Sociology movement (Boltanski & Thévenot, 1991-2006; Cloutier et al., 2017). This approach understands the social environment according to a different group of six worlds: Inspired, domestic, opinion (or fame), civic, market, and industrial. Later, a seventh world focused on projects (Boltanski & Chiapello, 2005). In these worlds, individual actors are legitimized by portraying qualities that respond to the principles of each world. In contrast to institutional logics where analysis of a situation is undertaken at a moment in time, this system is process-oriented, where "critique" is the first step in questioning standard practices and traditions in the logics situated in one of these worlds. Actors engage in debate, increasing information-sharing within the organization. A response to new possibilities resulting from the debate is called "justification". The outcome of the justification process is "evaluation" where new criteria are tested. This process accords agency and awareness to organizational actors who wish to make change happen, diversifying the logics in each world. In contrast to institutional logics theory, differences and debate are rarely seen as negative or dysfunctional (Cloutier et al., 2017) enabling change through the establishment of new conventions of practice (Denis et al., 2007).

Economies of worth comfortably invites the arts into its system through the world of "inspiration" (Boltanski & Thévenot, 1991-2006; Kleppe, 2018), focusing on creative work involving risk (Boltanski & Chiapello, 2005; Chiapello, 1998). Indeed, Chiapello (1998) conducted a major study of co-leadership constellations in five orchestras, an audio-visual production company and four publishers in France. Using the pragmatist frame as well as Bourdieu's understanding of the social role of art, she explores the artist-manager relationship processes in co-leadership. She observes that the resulting debate modifies management practice reducing artistic risk with compromise solutions that reduce artistic autonomy as well as their tradition of critique within society. There is less conflict in these organizations than expected, but the critique's societal value in a capitalist market economy is diminished (Chiapello, 2004). However, because of debate, Chiapello's observations may evolve over the long term.

Reconciling organizational pluralism

As we have pointed out, pluralism is a perspective that involves multiple objectives and values. Integration and reconciliation are necessary to find solutions to the organizational tensions that result. Co-leadership is viewed as a mechanism to accomplish this integration in the context of pluralism. We look at paradox, complexity, and hybrid organizations as lenses to observe organizational dynamics at different levels to supplement an understanding of pluralism. Paradox functions within the organization, and complexity and pluralism are influenced by environmental contexts, implicating institutional logics. Hybrid organizations are a type of organization found in complex environments where solutions are developed organizationally.

Paradox theory

Paradox has been evoked extensively in the arts management and creative industries literature (Defillippi & Arthur, 1998; Defillippi et al., 2007; Lampel et al., 2000; Wennes, 2002). Like institutional logics, paradox theory discusses competing and contradictory demands within organizations (Smith & Tracey, 2016). However, the two theories are independently conceived. Conflicting logics are guided by the legitimizing orders at a societal or field level (Thornton, 2004), typically focusing on two competing logics. On the other hand, paradox theory focuses on organizational and individual levels where two interdependent but opposing demands are at play, as illustrated in this citation from our research.

> It really is a dual, shared responsibility. You don't want an AD who makes all decisions based on art, because they will drive the company into financial ruin. You don't want someone who is so focussed on finance that they will sacrifice art to maintain the fiscal health of the company, which will destroy it anyway.
>
> Production director

The influence of these conflicting demands varies with context, but these demands do not stem from environmental legitimacy requirements. Paradoxes can never be resolved, hence the tensions require ongoing management and balancing (Smith & Tracey, 2016). This kind of tension may influence co-leadership dynamics in the shared role space.

Complexity

Complexity escalates the level of influence exerted on organizations beyond paradoxes by describing environments that generate "incompatible prescriptions of multiple institutional logics" (Greenwood et al., 2011, p. 317). Scholars of both institutional logics and complex organization theory view organizational operations through the lens of the legitimizing and prescriptive power of the institutional logics' orders (Thornton et al., 2012).

Organizational responses to complexity range from conformity and compromise through to defiance and manipulation (Greenwood et al., 2011; Oliver, 1991). How the organization and its leaders view these strategies is influenced by numerous dimensions. Two influences, among others, are suggested in the literature: The clarity and thickness of ties with external institutional influences and the centrality and compatibility of institutional logics (Besharov & Smith, 2014).

In the arts, numerous stakeholder relationships are influenced by the centralizing artistic ideal. For instance, professional ties among artists are guided by this artistic logic. However, market and corporation logics are also present in these organizations and can impact perspectives of public funders, boards of directors, and donors. These logics are often viewed as incompatible with the artistic ideal. Co-leaders are anchored in these divergent logics, individually responding to different stakeholders in their specialist leadership role. At the same time, they are required to navigate and respond jointly to the divergent logics in their mandated co-leadership role space to lead as one. Resolving the divergence in complexity generates change (Greenwood et al., 2011) and we discuss how that has occurred within the arts later in this chapter.

Hybrid organizations

Hybrid organizations are also pluralistic, but they describe organizations known as social enterprises who have specific issues around coherence between social mission and business objectives. These organizations are focused on social benefit, but are supported by the commercial base of the organization (Haigh et al., 2015). How these two organizational objectives are aligned determines the ease of managing these organizations (Battilana & Lee, 2014). For instance, microcredit banks are examples where alignment can be challenging. They may choose to finance a social purpose, while functioning with the logics of customer acquisition within a banking services company, creating tensions. Management solutions of these tensions at the organizational level of some social enterprises include hiring and socialization practices (Battilana & Dorado, 2010), different corporate structures to enable pertinent governance practices (Mair et al., 2015), and sensemaking of paradoxical outcomes over time (Jay, 2013).

Arts organizations are typically studied as public or non-profit which are primarily mission-based organizations, found in a different literature. In the arts, while funding of the artistic mission may be significant, commercial ticket revenue also provides market-based financing, thus introducing dynamics similar to hybrid organizations. The hybrid nature of the arts is often overlooked (Sgourev, 2011). The solutions and operating mechanisms mentioned in the hybrid literature may be helpful to co-leaders in the arts as they are confronted with the ticket revenue imperative in their organizations.

Coda

Other approaches to pluralism function at different levels of analysis. Heterogeneity, heteronomy, and ambidexterity are also concepts that describe aspects of pluralism in organizations with multiple objectives, but they are not treated extensively in the arts management literature. As well, there is a range of terminology that scholars deploy, suggesting a certain fragmentation regarding pluralistic organizations: Rationalities, social activity systems, frames and interpretive schemas, and meanings.

We have chosen to work with pluralism influenced by institutional logics given their relationship with legitimacy, and the structural theorizing system of institutional logics. The symbolic power of logics appears salient to the symbolic nature of artistic work.

In pluralistic organizations, the profession logic is key, integrating, and reconciling tensions between logics. The mission of these organizations is realized by pertinent professionals whose work carries the values of this logic. Artists adhere to these values and many of the traits of professionals. In co-leadership, these artists are partnered with executive managers to achieve the integration of logics. In the next section, we explore professional identities in a context of pluralism related to the arts.

Professional identity

Pluralistic organizations are typically identified as knowledge-based and professional (Denis et al., 2007; Denis et al., 2012; Gorman & Sandefur, 2011). These markers are typical of arts organizations. Professional status and self-identity are linked and anchored in a legitimizing profession logic at a societal level (Abbott, 1988). A respect for professional autonomy is reflected in how the profession shapes the organization's core mission and identity (Greenwood et al., 2002). A professional's individual identity is tied less to an organizational role and more to the insight they possess in their professional domain (Suddaby & Viale, 2011). The contrast between individual and organizational views of identity produces a tension around professional autonomy. The arts are particularly notable in this regard since artistic autonomy is characterized by individual vision and taste and is passionately linked with societal values around freedom of expression (Lampel et al., 2000). However, while professional identity is at the core of these organizations, markets, business, and community orders are also present, creating difficult choices when co-leaders negotiate priorities. This dynamic produces ambiguity, which we discuss in the next pages.

Professionals in most sectors undertake specialized training to acquire their designation. They are typically accredited or recognized by their peers in order to achieve and maintain a legitimized status (Abbott, 1988). This standardization is consistent with a profession logic that prioritizes quality, ethical standards, and an alignment of roles and responsibilities (Fjellvær, 2010; Ibarra, 1999). While artists have specialist training, professional artists are not necessarily accredited by peer associations in the same manner as other professionals like doctors and accountants (Bain, 2005). However, we suspect that peer evaluation in funding decisions may be a proxy for a parallel legitimacy marker.

Managers, on the other hand, are frequently viewed as preoccupied by efficiency and the financial sustainability of the pluralistic organization that they lead (Chiapello, 1998, 2004). Scholars often view the role of the managerial partner as less strategic than the professional executive, perhaps influenced by the analysis of professional service organizations (Mintzberg, 1979). However, in our research, the arts require a more strategic consideration of the managerial role in co-leadership in response to the important influence of market and business logics through audience and funding stakeholders (Kuesters, 2010; Peterson, 1986).

Artists' accomplishments establish a professional identity at field or community levels and build their career on the basis of this reputation (Lindqvist, 2017). Organizations hire artists as ADs to benefit from an affiliation with their reputations as well as their professional expertise, generating an organization-level identity of artistic quality and accomplishment (Glynn, 2006; Nisbett & Walmsley, 2016; Ostrower, 2002; Voss et al., 2006). The following comment reflects how artistic reputations and identities on an individual level translate into organizational-level identity.

> If the AD doesn't personify the company, we're missing something. He or she has to. It's an obligation.
>
> Production director

It also shows the importance given to the artistic imperative and how these professional leaders have power and influence in an organization and on its community or field-level reputation. However, the pluralism of this context can set up competition among the prevailing logics and hence generate ambiguous goals and challenges in making decisions, especially for co-leaders.

Exploring leadership in a culture of ambiguity in pluralistic organizations

Organizational leaders are carriers of the numerous institutional logics that are in play. To be accepted and effective in the various orders where they operate, leaders need to deliver symbolism and legitimacy associated with these logics. However, strategies that leaders develop may compete, and consequently become laden with tensions in the decision-making process (Greenwood et al., 2011; Smith & Tracey, 2016). Multiple objectives in pluralistic organizations can lead to a lack of clarity or ambiguity: Which issue to prioritize, how to balance the oppositional forces, what sequence of decisions to be followed over the short and long term, and who has the power or responsibility to decide. This ambiguity renders leadership strategically challenging (Cohen & March, 1974). Leader awareness about how ambiguity is present can help to manage the confusion.

Ambiguity can be understood in two ways: First, pluralistic organizations are inherently ambiguous, shaping the organizational culture and distinguishing one organization from another (Cohen & March, 1974; Cohen et al., 1972; Denis et al., 2001). Second, organizational members can intentionally cultivate ambiguity to achieve strategic decisions and action (Abdallah & Langley, 2014; Sillince et al., 2012).

An early understanding of ambiguous culture emerged in a study of an American university president (Cohen & March, 1974), and revealed three types of ambiguity that distinguish the organization. First, "goal" ambiguity arises from the plurality of interests and multiple meanings attributed to any goal. Second, "authority" is ambiguous when stakeholders and leaders are attributed with diffuse and equal sources of power that may not be tied to formal hierarchies. These sources of power serve particular organizational interests generating a political, dynamic organizational culture (Sillince et al., 2012). Finally, "technology" ambiguity occurs when there is an unclear relationship between goals and the diverging means or resources to achieve them.

Arts organizations experience both goal ambiguity and diffuse power that create ambiguity regarding priorities. The co-leaders are responsible for negotiating solutions in this difficult situation. But equal authority among co-leaders may create ambiguity about who is responsible (Chapter 6). This is the source of criticism from proponents of single leadership.

In the second understanding of ambiguity, an organization's strategy development processes are discovered typically through discourse analysis of key actors' organizational communications and their use of ambiguity

(Abdallah & Langley, 2014; Sillince et al., 2012). Three types of discourses are deployed: To protect a position, to invite participation in a decision, and to appeal to a particular point of view that requires strategic adaptation. Co-leaders' discourse may, for instance, introduce ambiguity in debates within their shared executive role space or together they may use ambiguity to influence organizational members. Managerial discourse and behaviour that mobilize ambiguity are important communication adaptive responses to difficult political situations (Empson, 2020).

A culture of ambiguity calls for structural and organizational responses, like co-leadership, to address the need for clarity. In the case of the arts, we observe that ambiguous authority can be solved by decoupling the co-leadership of AD and ED into their separate organizational hierarchies. The differentiation of expertise that underpins these separate leadership roles clarifies authority on each side of the organization (Røyseng, 2008).

> The skills are complementary, but they're not interchangeable. They serve very different needs.
>
> Board Chair

However, the combined leadership introduces the potential for ambiguous communications regarding both goals and means-end resources and mechanisms. Conflict can ensue. These forms of ambiguity require agility through differentiation and specialization but particularly complementarity within the co-leadership constellation and role space (Hodgson et al., 1965) (Chapter 3). We will reflect frequently on managing ambiguity and its implications for co-leadership in the arts.

Arts organizations have introduced co-leadership for several reasons: As a mechanism to manage tension and ambiguity (LeTheule & Fronda, 2005), as a means to establish legitimacy in response to pluralism and competing logics (Fjellvær, 2010), and as a conduit to satisfy stakeholders and accountability (Peterson, 1986) (Chapter 8). Functional differentiation across co-leadership appears necessary to preserve and even enhance artistic autonomy (Røyseng, 2008).

So far, in this chapter, we have outlined several inter-relating theoretical frames that can assist our understanding of the organizational context of co-leadership. These frames function as a prelude to the rest of the chapter. We investigate the multiple and divergent institutional logics resident in the arts that originate and manifest across levels of analysis (Thornton & Ocasio, 2008), and how they influence co-leaders in the arts.

While earlier explanations of these theoretical approaches related to pluralism included brief explanations of applications to the arts, our discussion below explores four dimensions of the artistic imperative in an investigation related to levels of analysis.

Analysing arts organization logics

In the sector, logics about art are very powerful, and they distinguish organizations, their leadership, and their environmental dynamics. In this section, using research focused on logics found in the arts field, we explore the mission-defining artistic imperative, which is rooted in the professions order of institutional logics (Thornton et al., 2012). This exploration of the imperative is accomplished through four dimensions: The artistic ideal, the social impact of art, the inspirational and educational impact of art, and artistic innovation. We use funding, marketing, and management to explore the competing logics embedded in the artistic imperative. At the end of the discussion of each dimension, the particular values and logics are summarized in one of Tables 2.1–2.4, highlighting the institutional orders and levels of analysis. We were inspired by Thornton et al. (2012) to shape these tables, providing further precision to the discussion that precedes each table.

It is worth noting that the competing logics found in communities, states, markets, and corporations often share a value with the artistic logic in the profession order. These competing logics are typically concerned with organizational viability and development compared with the creative and achievement orientation of artistic logics. Satisfying the artistic logic can test the organization's resources. Resolutions of the competition among logics are manifested in practices situated at organizational and individual levels, although arts management training texts explain these resolutions at a field-level. Unfortunately, the arts management literature has proven to be somewhat unclear at correlating the manifestation of logics with levels of analysis.

The artistic ideal

The profession logic in the arts originates with the Western notion of the Romantic ideal or the Liberal Humanist tradition of art (Kawashima, 2006; Shiner, 2001). Romanticism describes a changing moment in European history when artists no longer served as employees in aristocratic courts and churches or produced instrumentally commissioned works of visual art (Baxandall, 1972; DeNora, 1991; Shiner, 2001). These artists left behind an identity linked to the skill of craft, anchored in strongly institutionalized conventions, and in response to the political and social needs of their aristocratic employers (Shiner, 2001). Inspired by the flexibility of their new field-level identity, artists engaged in a freer expression of artistic imagination and emotions, in response to nature or in critique of society (Chiapello, 2004). Their artistic achievements were and still can be idealized by society as "art for art's sake" (Lee, 2005; Røyseng, 2008, p. 39; Shiner, 2001; Mansour, 2014). This ideal perceives artists as solo

Table 2.1 The artistic ideal

Primary value	*Logics*	*Orders*	*Levels*
Art for art's sake	Freedom of expression and liberation from craft identity (Belfiore, 2004; Lindqvist, 2017; Shiner, 2001, Mansour, 2014)	Prof	s f
	Independence from conventions (Lampel et al., 2000; Røyseng, 2008)	Prof	f i
	Natural and humanistic (Lindqvist, 2017)	Prof	s f
	Artist critique (Chiapello, 1998, 2004), political	Prof	s f
	Unique talent, solo genius (DeNora, 1991, 1995; Lampel & Germain, 2016; Shiner, 2001) versus collective creation (Becker, 2008)	Prof	s f o i
	Excellence (Fillis, 2006; Glynn, 2006)	Prof	f o i
	Sacrosanct and above law (Lee, 2005; Lindgren, 2009; Lindqvist, 2017; Quigg, 2007)	Prof	s f
	Non-rational mystique (Lampel & Germain, 2016),	Prof	f i
	Passionate commitment to artistic production (Rentschler, 2015)	Prof	o i
	Recognition, consecration, and prestige = artistic leadership (Fillis, 2006; Lindqvist, 2017; Nisbett & Walmsley, 2016; Røyseng, 2008)	Prof	f o i
	Intangible reputational source (Glynn, 2006; Ostrower, 2002)	Prof	f o
	Sacrifice (Wennes, 2002)	Prof Fam	i
Professional autonomy	Artists not viewed as professionals like accredited professionals (accountants and medical doctors) (Sapiro, 2019) but viewed as above law (Lindgren, 2009)	Prof	s f
	Professional identity or hybrid identity (Blomgren & Waks, 2015)	Prof	f i
Artistic and professional autonomy	Autonomy and differentiation (Røyseng et al., 2020; Sapiro, 2019; Stichweh, 2013)	Prof	s f o i
	Authority of artist and organization regarding programming vs audience input (Belfiore & Bennett, 2007; Glow, 2013; Kawashima, 2006; Lee, 2005; Walmsley, 2013)	Mkt Prof Comm	f o i
	Differentiation and dedifferentiation – hybrid individuals and organizations (Blomgren & Waks, 2015; Kleppe, 2018; Kuesters, 2010; Røyseng, 2008)	Prof	f o i
	Vertical and internal employment versus external contracting (Lampel et al., 2000)	Corp Prof	f o
	Arm's length funding: British arts council tradition in Anglo-Saxon countries (Upchurch, 2004, 2007, 2016) or separated direct funding mechanisms (Lindqvist, 2007)	Prof Comm	f o

Key to abbreviations:

Institutional world orders: Mkt = Markets, Corp = Corporations, Prof = Professions, St = States, Fam = Families, Rel = Christian religions, Comm = Communities.

Levels of analysis: s = societal, f = field, o = organization, i = individual.

geniuses (DeNora, 1995), although an understanding of how artistic work is collective has since been well articulated by numerous scholars (Becker, 2008). As well, increasingly, artists are seen as able managers and so may reflect a hybrid identity that tempers the exclusive focus of art and artistic achievement (Blomgren & Waks, 2015; Wu & Wu, 2016).

Devoted to excellence, consecrated, and prestigious (Fillis, 2006; Glynn, 2006; Ostrower, 2002), artists are endowed with a nonrational and passionate mystique through a vision of the artistic ideal (Lampel & Germain, 2016; Rentschler, 2015).

> It's almost religious, my fervour for this place, if not religious, spiritual, because I do believe in the communion with the audience... I keep saying, you are the word made flesh.
>
> AD

> You're not doing it for the money, for God's sake. Everyone in this office is grossly underpaid. ... Art is what drives people.
>
> AD

Their commitment and artistic achievements become a tangible reputational resource, generating field leadership and recognition (Glynn, 2006; Lindqvist, 2017; Nisbett & Walmsley, 2016), despite the personal and financial sacrifices that seem necessary on an individual level to pursue the ideal (Wennes, 2002).

> It's so odd that people say:" My job is not my life, that I don't want to be defined as a dancer". I can't imagine not wanting to be defined by your career, if your career is a definable interest of yours, more than anything else in the world.
>
> AD

However, based on the ideal and their commitment to art as a calling, ADs have been critiqued as believing that their autonomy places them outside the law (Lindgren, 2009; Quigg, 2007). Since the 19th century, the powerful logic of the artistic ideal has been linked at a societal level with freedom of expression (Belfiore & Bennett, 2007; Kawashima, 2006). Certain national jurisdictions have legislated freedom of expression in society, highlighting the role that artistic freedom of expression should play in democracy (Chapter 4).

At the field level, this logic is defined by professional autonomy and differentiation (Røyseng et al., 2020; Sapiro, 2019). Some scholars are concerned that managerial thinking interferes with artistic process in organizations (Beirne & Knight, 2002), suggesting that autonomy of art is reduced and dedifferentiation reduces the artist's critical perspective in society (Chiapello, 2004). Others, in different settings, have found that the clear differentiation between art and administrative management (Røyseng, 2008) strengthens artistic autonomy. As well, art-producing organizations engage with artists either by vertically integrating them in the organization or contracting them as independents suggesting organizational practices that respect artistic differentiation and professional autonomy (Lampel et al., 2000).

At the field and societal levels, government-funding structures reflect concerns about the autonomy of art. The arts council movement that originated in Britain just before World War II intended to separate art from political interests as a funding model, enabling independent organizational and artistic decision-making (Upchurch, 2004, 2007, 2016). In contrast, despite field-level efforts to structure direct funding through arm's length principles in Sweden, political interests and public decision-making processes appear to interfere with work in regional and municipal arts organizations (Lindqvist, 2007), reducing professional and artistic autonomy.

In Table 2.1, the logics found in the artistic ideal or imperative are analyzed according to the pertinent world order and levels of analysis.

The artistic ideal, situated in the institutional order of professions, strongly influences other competitive logics in the arts. In the next sections, we see how these competing logics are tempered by the artistic ideal and manifest adaptations.

The social impact of art

> And we have a conviction about the importance of this repertoire and what it can do for you, what it does for us, what it can do for human beings, what it means, and I think it makes the world a better place, and it makes a better artist and betters the people you are involved with; I think it's absolutely vital... part of our heritage.
>
> AD

> I believe the arts play a higher purpose in society and I have been incredibly lucky to live the life of an artist.
>
> AD

Philosophers and artists in the Romantic era articulated a socially conceived understanding of art that was humanistic, uplifting, and contributing to the betterment of humanity (Belfiore & Bennett, 2007). The above comments by artistic leaders demonstrate how they link their artistic work with an understanding of its inspirational role in society. Current research in art therapy, social inclusion, and social change reflects these social values featured in non-traditional programmes that reach out to new communities to enable benefits from the presence of art (Kawashima, 2006; Lindelof, 2014; Löfgren, 2016). For some time, these logics have encouraged cultural policy makers and private funders to support the use of art to solve health and social problems. This extension of the artistic ideal has generated a significant range of organizational and artistic practices that address these concerns (Belfiore & Bennett, 2007; Kawashima, 2006; Nijkamp et al., 2018). The citations below provide a sense of how people view the artistic imperative and its role in making change in society and reinforcing democracy:

> This aggressive, intellectual, challenging, issue-based theatre company is simply doing that work that was improving the quality of life in our community... sharing a vision of what the role of the organization should be in the community. What kind of space we should be occupying.
>
> Board member

> Art and culture have the power to build and develop society, and a rich and varied cultural field is a prerequisite for the freedom of speech and a functioning democracy. ... Cultural experiences introduce a diversity of meanings and expressions and ... promote tolerance and understanding for others, and reflection and insight about values, identities and society.
>
> Norwegian Ministry of Culture (2018)

Despite the field's respect for the artistic ideal, scholars critique this trend to social impact as justification for both public and private funding of the arts (Belfiore & Bennett, 2007; Saifer, 2020). This trend has raised some concerns. First, these activities may replace purely artistic work where resources for each objective depend on funders' interests; second, managerial logics respond to funding needs shifting the power balance, and threatening professional autonomy (Røyseng et al., 2020).

Since the 1990s, New Public Management (NPM) has been deployed aiming to develop the efficient realization of and accountability for government policies (Belfiore, 2004; Hood, 1991). This approach has embraced a quantitative and accounting logic that challenges the qualitative sensibilities and unpredictable creativity of the artistic imperative. Management and accounting practices impose organization-level evaluation measurement that provides the means to respond to field-level NPM funding requirements (Chiaravalloti, 2014; Herman, 2018; Loots, 2019). For the arts, governments have begun to consider return on investment through accountability. These systems may either produce conflict with artistic dynamics (Chiaravalloti, 2014; Townley, 2002) or solve the organizational dilemmas in evaluation (Knardal, 2020; Vermeulen & Maas, 2021).

Some scholars and practitioners argue that this logic and these social programs have become somewhat instrumental, diminishing funders' and organizations' focus on the primary value of art (Belfiore & Bennett, 2007; Fillis, 2006; Kawashima, 2006). This tension between the artistic imperative and measuring the impact of these social programs brings the institutional orders of communities and corporations into the portrait of organizational and field-level dynamics. Of course, communities reflect the social nature of the programs, but the impact evaluations relate to a business rationale as deployed in NPM. When this occurs, using social impact arguments to justify funding of the arts can disconnect the original affiliation of humanistic social objectives with the artistic ideal, unfortunately producing the possibility of more ambiguity and confusion in the field.

In Table 2.2, the value of the social imperative contrasts with funding policies and evaluation. Community and corporate orders play out across these themes, mainly at the field and organizational levels.

Table 2.2 The social impact of art

Primary value	*Logics*	*Orders*	*Levels*
Social imperative: Uplifting and humanistic	Social inclusion, art therapy, and solutions for societal problems (Kawashima, 2006; Lindelof, 2014)	Comm	s o i
Cultural funding policies of social initiatives	Funding support for art to solve health and social problems (Belfiore & Bennett, 2007)	Comm	s f o
	Art social impact activities (Belfiore & Bennett, 2007; Nijkamp et al., 2018)	Comm	s f o
	Social impact as funding justification or instrumental funding policies versus funding the value of art (Belfiore & Bennett, 2007; Fillis, 2006; Kawashima, 2006)	Prof Comm	s f o
Funding and performance evaluation of social initiatives	Development of NPM and performance evaluation (Belfiore, 2004; Hood, 1991)	Corp	s f o
	Accountability, impact evaluation, and statistical analysis (Belfiore, 2004; Chiaravalloti, 2014; Le Theule & Fronda, 2005; Loots, 2019)	Corp	f o
	Management accounting and auditing culture (Belfiore, 2004; Chiaravalloti, 2014)	Corp	f o
	Performance measures versus artistic process (Belfiore, 2004; Chiaravalloti, 2014; Herman, 2018; Townley, 2002; Vermeulen & Maas, 2021)	Corp	f o

Key to abbreviations:

Institutional world orders: Mkt = Markets, Corp = Corporations, Prof = Professions, St = States, Fam = Families, Rel = Christian religions, Comm = Communities.

Level of analysis: s = societal, f = field, o = organization, i = individual.

The inspirational and educational impact of art

Artistic innovation in the Romantic era explored freedom from conventions, but at the same time, art production was influenced by the tastes of the emerging bourgeois market (Mansour, 2014). Some current research provides insight into the co-creation of art by audience and artists during performance and exhibitions, building on the passionate and emotional elements of the experience (Boorsma, 2006; Ramsey White et al., 2009). Audience development that links to the inspirational and educational dimensions of the artistic ideal is a key addition to the relationship orientation of arts marketing (Kawashima, 2006; Lee, 2005). The symbiosis of democracy, audience engagement, and taste cultivation generates a service-dominant marketing logic (Kawashima, 2006; Ramsey White et al., 2009). The Romantic mystique supports artists as authorities to direct programming at the organizational level (Belfiore & Bennett, 2007; Lee, 2005). However, the traditional curatorial authority and autonomy of artists and their organizations is being questioned, valuing more audience participation and inclusiveness in arts organization strategies (Belfiore & Bennett, 2007; Glow, 2013; Kawashima, 2006). Implicating audiences in the programming and production of art is seen to strengthen the democratic facet of the artistic ideal (Glow, 2013), although others have observed that it is mainly art-educated audience members who participate in such experiments, thus contradicting this democratic intent (Walmsley, 2013). This inclusive experience could ironically render arts democracy as a form of audience-oriented marketing (Lee, 2005).

Contemporary arts marketing has been positioned in opposition to artistic autonomy (Lampel et al., 2000). However, other scholars argue that because respect for artistic autonomy and the artistic ideal is prioritized commercial, consumer-oriented marketing appears to be less applicable to the arts and cultural sectors (Boorsma, 2006; Lee, 2005). Textbooks typically suggest arts marketing strategies that avoid influencing the artistic product directly (Lee, 2005). Instead, marketers focus on managing the informational, social, and contextual experiences that surround the artistic presentation to remove barriers and establish a long-term relationship marketing approach (Boorsma, 2006; Lee, 2005; Lee & Lee, 2017). As a result, marketers act as important organizational intermediaries between audience members and artists' work (Colbert & Dantas, 2019; Lindelof, 2014).

In Table 2.3, the intersection of audience, democracy, and professional autonomy logics mingles markets, professions, and communities as institutional orders (Thornton et al., 2012) and the market logic adapts to the power of the artistic profession logic to avoid confrontation. The audience relationship dynamics of these logics are consistently manifested at the organizational level.

Table 2.3 The inspirational and educational impact of art

Primary value	*Logics*	*Arenas*	*Levels*
Relationship with audience	Market development opposing artistic autonomy (Lampel et al., 2000)	Mkt Prof	f o
	Institutional strength of artistic imperative prevents influence of art by commercial marketing perspectives (Belfiore & Bennett, 2007; Boorsma, 2006; Lee, 2005; Lee & Lee, 2017; Voss et al., 2006)	Mkt Prof	f o
	Customer satisfaction with informational, social, and contextual experiences = relationship marketing (Boorsma, 2006; Lee, 2005; Lee & Lee, 2017)	Mkt	o
	Marketers mediate development of audience-art relationship (Colbert & Dantas, 2019; Lindelof, 2014; Voss et al., 2006)	Mkt	o
	Co-creation of art between artist and audience = democracy, also audience engagement through service-dominant marketing relationship (Kawashima, 2006; Ramsey White et al., 2009)	Mkt Prof	o
Inspiration and educational impact of art	Artistic imperative suggests audience development: Taste cultivation and deepening arts engagement (Kawashima, 2006; Lindelof, 2014)	Prof Comm	f o
	Artistic imperative suggests audience outreach and development (Belfiore & Bennett, 2007; Kawashima, 2006; Lindelof, 2014; Voss et al., 2006)	Prof Comm	s f o
	Authority of organization and artists regarding programming vs audience input. (Belfiore & Bennett, 2007; Glow, 2013; Kawashima, 2006; Lee, 2005; Walmsley, 2013)	Prof Comm	o
	Democratic relationship with audience = audience-oriented marketing (Lee, 2005)	Mkt Comm	f o

Key to abbreviations:

Institutional world orders: Mkt = Markets, Corp = Corporations, Prof = Professions, St = States, Fam = Families, Rel = Christian religions, Comm = Communities.

Level of analysis: s = societal, f = field, o = organization, i = individual.

Artistic innovation

Another important dimension of the artistic ideal is creative innovation (Lampel & Germain, 2016; Lampel et al., 2000). By challenging artistic boundaries and conventions, or renewing the classical or traditional repertoire, artists generate novelty (Chiapello, 1998; Glynn, 2002;

Table 2.4 Artistic innovation

Primary value	*Logics*	*Orders*	*Levels*
Innovation	Drive for creativity and aestheticization (Lampel et al., 2000)	Mkt Corp Prof	s f o
	Challenging artistic boundaries (Chiapello, 1998; Voss et al., 2006),	Prof	f o i
	Renewing the tradition as a classical artist (Chiapello, 2004)	Prof	f o i
	Classic repertoire versus new work (Glynn, 2002; Glynn & Lounsbury, 2005; Herman, 2018)		
	Independent of tradition and conventions (Becker, 2008; Voss et al., 2006) – autonomous organization	Prof	f o i
	Provocation (Chiapello, 1998, 2004; Lampel et al., 2000)	Prof Comm	f o i
	Novelty (Lampel & Germain, 2016; Lampel et al., 2000)	Prof	o i
	Artistic creativity and experimentation (Wu & Wu, 2016),	Prof Comm	f o
	Avant-garde (Lindqvist, 2017)		
	Leadership in virtuosic performance and innovative creativity (Lindqvist, 2017)	Prof	f o i
	Recognition by boards and funders (Nisbett & Walmsley, 2016; Ostrower, 2002)		
Efficiency and managerialism	NPM logic and rational thinking produces tension in organizations (Beirne & Knight, 2002)	Mkt Prof Corp	s f o
	But differentiation enriches effective artistic autonomy (Røyseng, 2008; Røyseng et al., 2020)		
	Require plans and reports (Belfiore, 2004; Le Theule & Fronda, 2005; Townley, 2002)	Corp	f o

Key to abbreviations:

Institutional world orders: Mkt = Markets, Corp = Corporations, Prof = Professions, St = States, Fam = Families, Rel = Christian religions, Comm = Communities.

Level of analysis: s = societal, f = field, o = organization, i = individual.

Glynn & Lounsbury, 2005). If their artistic identity draws them to the avant-garde of their discipline, their experimentation may also appear artistically or socially provocative (Chiapello, 1998, 2004). Virtuosic accomplishments and innovation are often recognized as leadership in the field (Lindqvist, 2017).

> I have always put myself in danger in my work, … to really try to find new forms and to renew myself. I had to reveal myself, show myself.

> In fact, that's what being an artist is really about, that we do something personal that will reach people.
>
> AD

When artists are appointed to the role of AD, boards of directors and funders validate this stature as a benefit to organizations (Nisbett & Walmsley, 2016; Ostrower, 2002). This recognition is a significant motivator for artists and organizations but it is subjective and difficult to predict (Lampel et al., 2000). As a result, the ongoing development of original and promising talent to discover and promote innovation in the field is also an important responsibility within the logic.

> Because we're working on the art ... as well as the artists we were working with by really training them in the repertoire. .... we've really tried to expand the relationship with the orchestra beyond the simple sort of contractor for service kind of relationship.
>
> ED

Intuition and non-rational thinking have also been recognized as core to the artistic process (Lampel et al., 2000). However, aligning intuition with demands for rational planning and managerial thinking, as emphasized in NPM, has become a source of tension and conflict in arts organizations. Traditional managerial logic can constrain artistic accomplishment (Beirne & Knight, 2002), but scholars have also observed relationships within organizations that allow richer commitments to each side of the equation (Røyseng, 2008). As a structuring mechanism, the differentiation that co-leadership provides allows artistic autonomy to function effectively. Consequently, as found in Table 2.4, artistic achievements that relate to the professional order can benefit the artists (individual level), the organization, and the audience (field level).

Summary commentary

> I want to move people's hearts... to bring emotions to life.
>
> AD

Within the professions order, the Romantic-based artistic imperative dominates other logics that are present in the field. While some key logics do compete, field actors have found solutions to manage tensions with other logics. Competing logic relationships are not always consistent and may result in confusion and ambiguity.

Art may inspire, stimulate, and transform audiences in difficult circumstances. Many arts organizations have embraced social impact activities, extending the artistic ideal to justify public and private arts funding. However, performance evaluation using managerial accounting logics and practice has intervened, causing friction and frustration. Scholars and leaders in the field favour re-emphasizing the value of innovation and competence in artistic accomplishments.

Artistic autonomy and freedom of expression may appear oppositional to conventional marketing logics, but in field-level practice, arts marketers choose to prioritize audience development and relationship marketing, and generally shun the application of a commercial approach. Arts marketers focus on product extensions like social activities, service orientation, and facilitated logistics, rather than the artistic product itself.

When the artistic ideal is characterized as intuitively innovative and unpredictable, managerial logic, with its planning and reduction of public expense (NPM), is contrasted as competitive. However, some observers indicate that evaluation systems inherent in a managerial approach can align with and inform internal organizational systems. In fact, debate within the co-leadership can enhance differentiation and enrich the commitment to artistic achievement.

The dynamic co-habitation of artistic ideals with typically competitive logics produces unexpected results within these pluralistic and complex organizations in the arts. The power of the artistic ideal ensures compromises with seemingly significant opposing imperatives like accountability for funding and market logics, but extended applications of the ideal can result in ambiguous priorities, confusion, and frustration. Arts co-leaders are forced to decode counter-intuitive relationships among logics that operate at multiple levels to resolve challenging demands on their leadership.

Conclusion

In this chapter, we explored theories that provide understanding of the dynamism in pluralistic organizations. The wide variety of professional and functional domains in the arts led us to pluralism as our framing theory. These domains are anchored in values related to logics at the societal level. We also identified institutional logics theory as an appropriate lens since it brings insight on symbolic values and legitimizing. Logics may be divergent, and compete, and the arts field has witnessed the negotiation of numerous differences in logics since arts management became a legitimate function in the 1960s (Chapter 4). In the second half of this chapter, we drew a portrait of the artistic imperative in relation to competing logics such as marketing, social impact, and innovation. For arts co-leaders, debating competing logics structures organizational meaning.

Paradox theory also describes oppositional dynamics, but unlike logics, paradoxes function without resolution and without legitimizing importance. Several scholars have called on paradox to explain the dynamics of differences in the arts, such as rarefied versus broadly commercial art (Lampel et al., 2000). However, some paradoxes may actually be competing logics – polar ends of a continuum with affiliated legitimizing norms.

Managers may gain insight on organizational dynamics if they can discern the difference between paradox and competing logics.

Because of the box office income, arts organizations appear similar to hybrid organizations. However, the literature on hybrids often describes significant differences between the social mission and the commercial revenue source that require specific managerial practice to resolve. In the arts, commercial revenue is in response to the mission-based activities which is why this sector is more often studied through a non-profit lens rather than as hybrids.

Some scholars prefer the affinity between pluralism and the French pragmatists' economies of worth theory (Cloutier et al., 2017). Although similar in structure to the orders of institutional logics, the greater flexibility of this approach towards debate and change makes it attractive in a pluralistic environment. However, given that competing logics drive their organizational dynamics, pluralistic organizations inevitably function within a complex institutional environment. As a result, our analysis is oriented to institutional logics (Greenwood et al., 2011).

Professional identity is an important feature of the arts. It underpins co-leadership. The artistic imperative is at the core of these organizations, giving the profession order and its set of logics significant influence. As a result, its societal importance solves the competition with other logics, evolving at the organizational and leadership levels in the field of arts management studies. However, the kaleidoscope effect of logics in the arts and the lack of clarity about their levels of analysis can blur understanding, rendering analysis challenging. More research is needed to gain greater clarity.

References

Abbott, A. D. (1988). *The System of Professions: An Essay on the Division of Expert Labour.* University of Chicago Press.

Abdallah, C., & Langley, A. (2014). The double edge of ambiguity in strategic planning. *Journal of Management Studies*, *51*(2), 235–264. https://doi.org/10.1111/joms.12002

Alvarez, J. L., & Svejenova, S. (2005). *Sharing Executive Power: Roles and Relationships at the Top.* Cambridge University Press.

Bain, A. (2005). Constructing an artistic identity. *Work, Employment and Society*, *19*(1), 25–46. https://doi.org/10.1177/0950017005051280

Barkela, B. (2021). Leadership communication and knowledge integration across the artistic, technical and administration area in theaters. *Journal of Arts Management, Law and Society*, *51*(6), 393–409. https://doi.org/10.1080/10632921.2021.1974628

Battilana, J., & Dorado, S. (2010). Building sustainable hybrid organizations: The case of commercial microfinance organizations. *Academy of Management Journal*, *53*(6), 1419–1440. https://doi.org/10.5465/amj.2010.57318391

Battilana, J., & Lee, M. (2014). Advancing research on hybrid organizing – Insights from the study of social enterprises. *The Academy of Management Annals*, *8*(1), 397–441.

Baxandall, M. (1972). *Painting and Experience in 15th century Italy.* Oxford University Press.

Becker, H. S. (2008). *Arts Worlds. Updated and Expanded.* University of California Press.

Beirne, M., & Knight, S. (2002). Principles and consistent management in the arts: Lessons from British theatre. *International Journal of Cultural Policy, 8*(1), 75–89. https://doi.org/10.1080/10286630290032459

Belfiore, E. (2004). Auditing culture: The subsidised cultural sector in the new public management. *International Journal of Arts Management, 1*(2), 183–202.

Belfiore, E., & Bennett, O. (2007). Rethinking the social impact of the arts. *International Journal of Cultural Policy, 13*(2), 135–151. https://doi.org/10.1080/10286630701342741

Besharov, M. L., & Smith, W. K. (2014). Multiple institutional logics in organizations: Explaining their varied nature and implications. *The Academy of Management Review, 39*(3), 364–381. http://dx.doi.org/10.5465/amr.2011.0431

Blomgren, M., & Waks, C. (2015). Coping with contradictions: Hybrid professionals managing institutional complexity. *Journal of Professions and Organization, 2*(1), 78–102. https://doi-org.proxy2.hec.ca/10.1093/jpo/jou010

Boltanski, L., & Chiapello, È (2005). *The New Spirit of Capitalism.* Verso Press.

Boltanski, L., & Thévenot, L. (1991–2006). *On Justification: Economies of Worth.* (C. Porter, Trans.). Princeton University Press.

Boorsma, M. (2006). A strategic logic for arts marketing: Integrating customer value and artistic objectives. *International Journal of Cultural Policy, 12*(3), 73–92. https://doi-org.proxy2.hec.ca/10.1080/10286630600613333

Brès, L., Raufflet, E., & Boghossian, J. (2018). Pluralism in organizations: Learning from unconventional forms of organizations. *International Journal of Management Reviews, 20*(2), 364–386. https://doi.org/10.1111/ijmr.12136

Chiapello, È. (1998). *Artistes versus Managers: Le Management Culturel face à la Critique Artiste.* Éditions Métaillés.

Chiapello, È. (2004). Evolution and co-optation: The 'artist critique' of management and capitalism. *Third Text, 18*(6), 585–594. https://doi.org/10.1080/0952882042000284998

Chiaravalloti, F. (2014). Performance evaluation in the arts and cultural sector: A story of accounting at its margins. *The Journal of Arts Management, Law, and Society, 44*(2), 61–89. https://doi.org/10.1080/10632921.2014.905400

Cloutier, C., Gond, J.-P., & Leca, B. (2017). Justification, evaluation and critique in the study of organizations: Contributions from French pragmatist sociology. *Research in the Sociology of Organizations, 52*, 3–29. https://doi.org/10.1108/S0733-558X20170000052001

Cohen, M. D., & March, J. G. (1974). *Leadership and Ambiguity: The American College President* (2nd ed.). Harvard Business School Press.

Cohen, M. D., March, J. G., & Olsen, J. P. (1972). A garbage can model of organizational choice. *Administrative Science Quarterly, 17*(1), 1–25. https://doi.org/10.2307/2392088

Colbert, F., & Dantas, D. (2019). Customer relationships in arts marketing: A review of key dimensions in delivery by artistic and cultural organizations. *International Journal of Arts Management, 21*(2), 4–14.

Defillippi, R., Grabher, G., & Jones, C. (2007). Introduction to paradoxes of creativity: Managerial and organizational challenges in the cultural economy. *Journal of Organizational Behavior, 28*(5), 511–521. https://doi.org/10.1002/job.466.

Defillippi, R. J., & Arthur, M. B. (1998). Paradox in project-based enterprise: The case of film making. *California Management Review*, *40*(2), 125–139. https://doi.org/10.2307/41165936

Denis, J.-L., Lamothe, L., & Langley, A. (2001). The dynamics of collective leadership and strategic change in pluralistic organizations. *The Academy of Management Journal*, *44*(4), 809–837. https://doi.org/10.2307/3069417

Denis, J.-L., Langley, A., & Rouleau, L. (2007). Strategizing in pluralistic contexts: Rethinking theoretical frames. *Human Relations*, *60*(1), 179–215.

Denis, J.-L., Langley, A., & Rouleau, L. (2010). The practice of leadership in the messy world of organizations. *Leadership*, *6*(1), 67–88. https://doi.org/10.1177/1742715009354233

Denis, J.-L., Langley, A., & Sergi, V. (2012). Leadership in the plural. *The Academy of Management Annals*, *5*(1), 211–283. https://doi.org/10.1080/19416520.2012.667612

DeNora, T. (1991). Musical patronage and social change in Beethoven's Vienna. *American Journal of Sociology*, *97*(2), 310–346. https://doi.org/10.1086/229781

DeNora, T. (1995). *Beethoven and the Construction of Genius: Musical Politics in Vienna, 1792-1803*. University of California Press.

Empson, L. (2020). Ambiguous authority and hidden hierarchy: Collective leadership in an elite professional service firm. *Leadership*, *16*(1), 62–86. https://doi.org/10.1177/1742715019886769

Fillis, I. (2006). Art for art's sake or art for business sake: An exploration of artistic product orientation. *The Marketing Review*, *6*(1), 29–40, https://doiorg.proxy2.hec.ca/10.1362/146934706776861573

Fjellvær, H. (2010). *Dual and unitary leadership: managing ambiguity in pluralistic organizations* (Publication Number 2010/10). Doctoral dissertation, Norwegian School of Economics and Business Administration, Bergen. https://openaccess.nhh.no/nhh-xmlui/bitstream/handle/11250/164362/fjellver%20avh%202010.PDF?sequence=1

Friedland, R. A., & Alford, R. (1991). Bringing Society Back In: Symbols, Practices and Institutional Contradictions. In P. DiMaggio, & W. W. Powell (Eds.), *The New Institutionalism in Organizational Analysis* (pp. 232–263). University of Chicago Press.

Glow, H. (2013). Cultural Leadership and Audience Engagement: A Case Study of the Theatre Royal Stratford East. In J. Caust (Ed.), *Arts Leadership: International Case Studies* (1st ed., pp. 132–144). Tilde University Press.

Glynn, M. A. (2002). Chord and discord: Organizational crisis, institutional shifts, and the musical canon of the symphony. *Poetics*, *30*(1–2), 63–85.

Glynn, M.-A. (2006). Maestro or Manager? Examining the Role of the Music Director in a Symphony Orchestra. In J. Lampel, J. Shamsie, & T. K. Lant (Eds.), *The Business of Culture: Strategic Perspectives on Entertainment and Media* (1st ed., pp. 57–70). Routledge.

Glynn, M. A., & Lounsbury, M. (2005). From the critics' corner: Logic blending, discursive change and authenticity in a cultural production system. *Journal of Management Studies*, *42*(5), 1031–1055.

Gorman, E. H., & Sandefur, R. L. (2011). 'Golden age,' quiescence, and revival. *Work and Occupations*, *38*(3), 275–302. https://doi.org/10.1177/0730888411417565

Greenwood, R., Raynard, M., Kodeih, F., Micelotta, E. R., & Lounsbury, M. (2011). Institutional complexity and organizational responses. *The Academy of Management Annals*, *5*(1), 317–371. https://doi.org/10.1080/19416520.2011.590299

Greenwood, R., Suddaby, R., & Hinings, C. R. (2002). Theorizing change: The role of professional associations in the transformation of institutionalized fields. *Academy of Management Journal*, *45*(1), 58–80.

Gronn, P., & Hamilton, A. (2004). 'A bit more life in the leadership': Co-principalship as distributed leadership practice. *Leadership and Policy in Schools*, *3*(1), 3–35. https://doi.org/10.1076/lpos.3.1.3.27842

Haigh, N., Walker, J., Bacq, S., & Kickul, J. (2015). Hybrid organizations: Origins, strategies, impacts, and implications. *California Management Review*, *57*(3), 5–12. https://doi.org/10.1525/cmr.2015.57.3.5

Herman, A. (2018). Pragmatized aesthetics: The impact of legitimacy pressures in symphony orchestras. *Journal of Arts Management, Law and Society*, *49*(2), 136–150. https://doi.org/10.1080/10632921.2018.1473311

Hodgson, R. C., Levinson, D. J., & Zaleznik, A. (1965). *The Executive Role Constellation: An Analysis of Personality and Role Relations in Management*. Harvard University: Division of Research, Graduate School of Business Administration.

Hood, C. (1991). A public management for all seasons? *Public Administration*, *69*(1), 3–19. https://doi-org.proxy2.hec.ca/10.1111/j.1467-9299.1991.tb00779.x

Ibarra, H. (1999). Provisional selves: Experimenting with image and identity in professional adaptation. *Administrative Science Quarterly*, *44*(4), 764–791.

Jay, J. (2013). Navigating paradox as a mechanism of change and innovation in hybrid organizations. *Academy of Management Journal*, *56*(1), 137–159. https://doi.org/10.5465/amj.2010.0772

Kawashima, N. (2006). Audience development and social inclusion in Britain: Tensions, contradictions and paradoxes in policy and their implications for cultural management. *International Journal of Cultural Policy*, *12*(1), 55–72. https://doi.org/10.1080/10286630600613309

Kleppe, B. (2018). Managing autonomy: Analyzing arts management and artistic autonomy through the theory of justification. *Journal of Arts Management, Law, and Society*, *48*(3), 191–205. https://doi.org/10.1080/10632921.2017.1377661.

Knardal, P. S. (2020). Orchestrating institutional complexity and performance management in the performing arts. *Financial Accountability & Management*, *36*(3), 300–318. https://doi.org/10.1111/faam.12223

Kraatz, M. S., & Block, E. (2008). Organizational Implications of Institutional Pluralism. In R. Greenwood, C. Oliver, K. Sahlin-Andersson, & R. Suddaby (Eds.), *The SAGE Handbook of Organizational Institutionalism* (pp. 243–275). SAGE Publications Limited.

Kraatz, M. S., & Block, E. (2017). Institutional Pluralism Revisited. In R. Greenwood, C. Oliver, T. Lawrence, & R. E. Meyer (Eds.), *The SAGE Handbook of Organizational Institutionalism* (2nd ed., pp. 532–557). SAGE Publications.

Kuesters, I. (2010). Arts managers as liaisons between finance and art: A qualitative study inspired by the theory of functional differentiation. *The Journal of Arts Management, Law, and Society: Arts Management: A Sociological Inquiry*, *40*(1), 43–57. https://doi.org/10.1080/10632921003603976

Lampel, J., & Germain, O. (2016). Creative industries as hubs of new organizational and business practices. *Journal of Business Research*, *69*(7), 2327–2333. https://doi.org/10.1016/j.jbusres.2015.10.001.

Lampel, J., Lant, T., & Shamsie, J. (2000). Balancing act: Learning from organizing practices in cultural industries. *Organization Science*, *11*(3), 263–269. https://doi.org/10.1287/orsc.11.3.263.12503

Lee, H.-K. (2005). When arts met marketing. *International Journal of Cultural Policy*, *11*(3), 289–305. https://doi.org/10.1080/10286630500411309

Lee, J. W., & Lee, S. H. (2017). 'Marketing from the art world': A critical review of American research in arts marketing. *Journal of Arts Management, Law and Society*, *47*(1), 17–33. https://doi.org/10.1080/10632921.2016.1274698

LeTheule, M.-A., & Fronda, Y. (2005). The organization in tension between creation and rationalization: Facing management views to artistic and scientific creators. *Critical Perspectives on Accounting*, *16*(6), 749–786. https://doi.org/10.1016/j.cpa.2003.09.004

Lindelof, A. M. (2014). Audience development and its blind spot: A quest for pleasure and play in the discussion of performing arts institutions. *International Journal of Cultural Policy*, *21*(2), 200–218. https://doi.org/10.1080/10286632.2014.891585

Lindgren, A. C. (2009). The National Ballet of Canada and the Kimberly Glasco legal arbitration case. *The Journal of Arts Management, Law, and Society*, *39*(2), 101–116. https://doi.org/10.3200/JAML.39.2.101-116

Lindqvist, K. (2007). Public governance of arts organizations in Sweden: Strategic implications. *International Journal of Arts Management*, *13*(3), 303–317.

Lindqvist, K. (2017). Leadership in Art and Business. In E. Raviola & P. Zackariasson (Eds.), *Arts and Business: Building a Common Ground for Understanding Society* (pp.161–175). Routledge.

Löfgren, M. (2016). On the Public Value of Arts and Culture. In K. Dalborg, & M. Löfgren (Eds.), *The FIKA Project: Perspectives on Cultural Leadership* (pp. 75–99). Nätwerkstan Kultur.

Loots, E. (2019). Strings attached to arts funding: Panel assessments of theater organizations through the lens of agency theory. *The Journal of Arts Management, Law, and Society*, *49*(4), 274–290. https://doi.org/10.1080/10632921.2019.1617812

Mair, J., Mayer, J., & Lutz, E. (2015). Navigating institutional plurality: Organizational governance in hybrid organizations. *Organization Studies*, *36*(6), 713–739. https://doi.org/10.1177/0170840615580007

Mansour, C. (2014). Art, A Modern Phenomenon: An Interview with Larry Shiner. *The Platypus Review* 67 (June). Retrieved on August 13, 2022 from https://platypus1917.org/2014/06/01/art-modern-phenomenon-interview-larry-shiner/.

Mintzberg, H. (1979). *The Structuring of Organizations*. Prentice Hall.

Nijkamp, J., Burgers, J., & Kuiper, C. (2018). Toward social inclusion through connecting arts and crafts in Rotterdam. *The Journal of Arts Management, Law, and Society*, *48*(4), 259–272. https://doi.org/10.1080/10632921.2018.1494069.

Nisbett, M., & Walmsley, B. (2016). The romanticization of charismatic leadership in the arts. *The Journal of Arts Management, Law, and Society*, *46*(1), 2–12. https://doi.org/10.1080/10632921.2015.1131218

Norwegian Ministry of Culture. (2018). *Kulturens kraft: Kulturpolitikk for framtida.* (Meld. St. 8). Retrieved on August 13 2021, from https://www.regjeringen.no/no/dokumenter/meld.-st.-8-20182019/id2620206/.

Oliver, C. (1991). Strategic responses to institutional processes. *Academy of Management Review*, *16*(1), 145–171.

Ostrower, F. (2002). *Trustees of Culture: Power, Wealth, and Status on Elite Arts Boards.* University of Chicago Press.

Peterson, R. (1986). From Impresario to Arts Administrator: Formal Accountability in Nonprofit Cultural Organizations. In P. DiMaggio (Ed.), *Nonprofit Enterprise in the Arts: Studies in Mission and Constraint* (pp. 161–183). Oxford University Press.

Quigg, A.-M. (2007). Bullying in theatres and arts centres in the United Kingdom. *International Journal of Arts Management*, *10*(1), 52–64.

Ramsey White, T., Dennis, N., Hede, A. M., & Rentschler, R. (2009). Lessons from arts experiences for service-dominant logic. *Marketing Intelligence & Planning*, *27*(6), 775–788. https://doi.org/10.1108/02634500910988672

Reay, T. & Hinings, C.R. (2009). Managing the rivalry of competing institutional logics. *Organization Studies*, *30*(6), 629–632. https://doi.org/10.1177/0170840609104803

Rentschler, R. (2015). *Arts Governance: People, Passion, Performance* (1st ed.). Routledge.

Røyseng, S. (2008). Arts management and the autonomy of art. *International Journal of Cultural Policy*, *14*(1), 37–48. https://doi.org/10.1080/10286630701856484

Røyseng, S., Di Paolo, D., & Wennes, G. (2020). As you like it! How performance measurement affects professional autonomy in the Norwegian public theater sector. *Journal of Arts Management, Law and Society*, *50*(1), 52–66. https://doi.org/10.1080/10632921.2019.1693458

Saifer, A. (2020). Racial neoliberal philanthropy and the arts for social change. *Organization*. Online first, 1–21. https://doi.org/10.1177/1350508420973327

Sapiro, G. (2019). Rethinking the concept of autonomy for the sociology of symbolic goods. *Biens Symboliques/Symbolic Goods*, 4. https://doi.org/10.4000/bssg.334

Sgourev, S. (2011). 'Wall Street' meets Wagner: Harnessing institutional heterogeneity. *Theory and Society*, *40*(4), 385–416. https://doi.org/10.1007/s11186-011-9144-6

Shiner, L. (2001). *The Invention of Art: A Cultural History.* University of Chicago Press.

Sillince, J., Jarzabkowski, P., & Shaw, D. (2012). Shaping strategic action through the rhetorical construction and exploitation of ambiguity. *Organization Science*, *23*(3), 630–650. https://doi.org/10.1287/orsc.1110.0670

Smith, W. K., & Tracey, P. (2016). Institutional complexity and paradox theory: Complementarities of competing demands. *Strategic Organization*, *14*(4), 455–466. https://doi.org/10.1177/1476127016638565

Stichweh, R. (2013). The History and Systematics of Functional Differentiation in Sociology. In M. Albert, B. Buzan & M. Zürn (Eds.), *Bringing Sociology to International Relations: World Politics as Differentiation Theory* (pp. 50–70). Cambridge University Press.

Suddaby, R., & Viale, T. (2011). Professionals and field-level change: Institutional work and the professional project. *Current Sociology*, *59*(4), 423–442. https://doi.org/10.1177/0011392111402586

Thornton, P. (2004). *Markets from culture: Institutional logics and organizational decisions in higher education publishing*. Stanford University Press.

Thornton, P., & Ocasio, W. (2008). Institutional Logics. In R. Greenwood, C. Oliver, K. Sahlin, & R. Suddaby (Eds.), *The SAGE Handbook on Organizational Institutionalism* (pp. 99–129). Sage.

Thornton, P. H., Ocasio, W., & Lounsbury, M. (2012). *The Institutional Logics Perspective: A New Approach to Culture, Structure, and Process*. Oxford University Press.

Townley, B. (2002). The role of competing rationalities in institutional change. *Academy of Management Journal*, *45*(1), 163–179. https://doi.org/10.2307/3069290

Upchurch, A. (2004). John Maynard Keynes, the Bloomsbury group and the origins of the arts council movement. *International Journal of Cultural Policy*, *10*(2), 203–217. https://doi.org/10.1080/1028663042000255817

Upchurch, A. (2007). Linking cultural policy from Great Britain to Canada. *International Journal of Cultural Policy*, *13*(3), 239–254. https://doi.org/10.1080/10286630701556407

Upchurch, A. (2016). *The Origins of the Arts Council Movement: Philanthropy and Policy*. Palgrave Macmillan.

Vermeulen, M., & Maas, K. (2021). Building legitimacy and learning lessons: A framework for cultural organizations to manage and measure the social impact of their activities. *The Journal of Arts Management, Law, and Society*, *51*(2), 97–112. https://doi.org/10.1080/10632921.2020.1851839

Voss, Z. G., Cable, D. M., & Voss, G. B. (2006). Organizational identity and firm performance: What happens when leaders disagree about 'Who we are?' *Organization Science*, *17*(6), 741–755. https://doi.org/10.1287/orsc.1060.0218

Walmsley, B. (2013). Co-creating theatre: Authentic engagement or inter-legitimation? *Cultural Trends: Exploring Policies on Participation and Engagement in the Arts*, *22*(2), 108–118. https://doi.org/10.1080/09548963.2013.783176

Wennes, G. (2002). *Skjønnheten og udyret: Kunsten å lede kunstorganisasjonen*. Doctoral dissertation, Norwegian School of Economics and Business Administration, Bergen.

Wu, Y., & Wu, S. (2016). Managing ambidexterity in creative industries: A survey. *Journal of Business Research*, *69*(7), 2388–2396. https://doi.org/10.1016/j.jbusres.2015.10.008

3 Parsing co-leadership theory for the arts

Introduction

Co-leadership is one of the theoretical paths found in plural leadership literature in recent years. Pluralism and institutional logics theory describe the social context for co-leadership. Co-leadership is seen as an integrating mechanism in response to these environmental dynamics. Some logics in the arts have been somewhat integrated in the field at the micro and meso levels (Chapter 2). However, these logics continue to compete at the macro level, creating the tensions that co-leaders may face as they attempt to lead as one. In this chapter, we examine theorizing about plural leadership, specifically co-leadership, gaining insights into how scholars explain the challenges and solutions found in plural leadership research. Our study of arts co-leadership primarily uses theory from management and plural leadership, despite the rich range of other scholarly traditions that inform the arts management field (DeVereaux, 2020; Radaelli, 2012). Scholars increasingly study co-leadership in specific professional sectors. In fact, a significant body of co-leadership research has been set in the arts. The following review of plural leadership theory supports the empirical analysis on arts co-leadership in our book (Chapters 5 to 9).

The discussion for this chapter unfolds as follows:

- Categorizing plural leadership,
- Identifying founding concepts,
- Extending core issues through recent co-leadership research,
- Highlighting arts contributions to co-leadership research,
- Synthesizing key findings from the co-leadership literature, and
- Linking to the empirical chapters.

Categorizing plural leadership

Plural leadership contrasts with unitary or single leadership (Fjellvær, 2010; Locke, 2003) and describes a range of situations where multiple actors occupy formal and informal leadership roles in the same organization or team. The breadth of this research has changed the perspective on leadership

DOI: 10.4324/9780429504259-4

from individual to collective (Cullen-Lester & Yammarino, 2016). Plural leadership theorizing is now published with increasing frequency.

Variations of plural leadership carry numerous labels in the literature. Shared, distributed, collective, relational, co-leadership, dual executive leadership, and team leadership are terms that have been deployed to describe these formal and informal dynamics. Some of the different terms of plural leadership describe quite different phenomena while others overlap. Both positivist and constructivist epistemologies underlie leadership logics. Quantitative and qualitative methodologies are brought to bear (Denis et al., 2012). These contrasting approaches generate a certain tension in the literature. However, despite the differing perspectives (Sergi et al., 2012; Yammarino et al., 2012), scholars have also collaborated to bridge the epistemological divide (Sanchez et al., 2020; Uhl-Bien & Ospina, 2012).

Our research focuses on one type of plural leadership: Co-leadership. We deploy qualitative methods, and our data has been newly analysed for this book. Our current methodological approach has emerged abductively (Timmermans & Tavory, 2012).

Despite the recent suggestion that "managerial shared leadership" could serve as an organizing term for this field (Döös & Wilhelmson, 2021), we find that the typology described in an earlier plural leadership analysis by Denis et al. (2012) is more helpful to explain our work (Foreword). The typology links with pluralism, which is a theorizing frame for our work (Chapter 2).

In their field-structuring and sense-making review of the literature, Denis et al. (2012) suggest the use of "plural leadership" as an overview term, evoking the pluralistic context in which this leadership is usually situated (Chapter 2). They propose a useful four-part categorization to explain the full range of the collective phenomena:

- Sharing leadership for team effectiveness (shared leadership),
- Pooling leadership capacity at the top to direct others (co-leadership),
- Spreading leadership within and across levels over time (distributed leadership), and
- Producing leadership through interaction (relational leadership) (p. 215).

In the following discussion, we explain each plural leadership category, the research approach underpinning the related logics, and opportunities that arise for our research. We present the categories in a different sequence by placing the approach called "pooling leadership at the top" as our fourth category. It frames our book on co-leadership. The other three categories are: "Sharing, spreading, and producing" leadership and compared to co-leadership, they are characterized by emergent and more broadly attributed states of leadership, found throughout teams and organizations.

Many scholars intuitively refer to "shared leadership" to describe any kind of plural leadership. However, it is specifically deployed in team research to look at the process of leaders' emergence within organizational groups rather than executive-level leadership. As an expansionary tactic, scholars in shared leadership have recently added co-leadership at the group level to their definition (D'Innozenso et al., 2016). It is studied in a wide spectrum of sectors like high tech, surgical operating and emergency rooms, and corporate board rooms (Offerman & Scuderi, 2017). Scholars using this terminology rely on positivist epistemology and quantitative methods (Cox et al., 2003; Pearce & Conger, 2003; Yammarino et al., 2012). They find creative results and team coherence at this group level (Cox et al., 2003).

A single leader may facilitate the emergence of shared leadership within the organization (Pearce, 2004). This provokes us to consider how co-leaders at the top might also develop shared leadership at other organizational levels. The distribution of shared leadership across levels in the arts field is a possibility that we explore further in Chapter 9 (Schrauwen et al., 2016). Arts management scholars have expressed enthusiasm for developing a culture of sharing leadership that can counteract bureaucratic cultures found in direct funding contexts (Dragićević Šešić, 2020). Sharing leadership relates to an innovation logic typical in the arts (Chapter 2). More research of all kinds will be useful to understand how co-leadership, which is relatively hierarchical, and shared leadership, which is emergent within groups, may operate together in the arts for maximum effectiveness (Chapter 10).

"Distributed leadership" involves dispersing or relaying leadership responsibility (Gronn, 2002; Leithwood et al., 2009) broadly throughout the whole organization (Buchanan et al., 2007) and even across several organizations (Vangen & Huxham, 2003) over time (Bolden, 2011). Gronn and Hamilton (2004) described the choice and delegation of leadership responsibility as a spontaneous process. Distributed leadership has been frequently studied in education and health care in larger institutional and public contexts. Scholars' enthusiasm about the possibilities for improved democracy, access, and school performance convinced public policy authorities of its value, leading to frequent normative and institutionalized discourse applied to this approach, particularly in Britain (Bolden, 2011; Denis et al., 2012). During this institutionalization phase, the democratic logics of distributed leadership attracted British arts management scholars. A study of the Royal Shakespeare Company is an example of this focus (Hewison et al., 2013). On the other hand, research with a critical perspective has revealed an aspect of ambiguous authority in distributed leadership and, hence, risky accountability in large public institutions (Currie et al., 2009).

"Relational and interactional leadership" avoids attributing leadership to an individual, but embeds it in inter-relational, processual, and collective daily activity (Raelin, 2011; Uhl-Bien, 2006). Inspired by Mary Parker Follett (1924), as a socially constructed culture, this approach to leadership produces a wide-spread collaboration of actors without mandated authority (Follett, 1924; Hosking, 1988; Wood, 2005). This collectivist approach reflects the notion of post-heroic leadership, a descriptor that was coined by researchers in reaction to single leadership which they saw as centralized, charismatic, and inspiring, but leaving organizational members with little agency (Crevani et al., 2007).

This collectivist and occasionally normative orientation avoids discussion of issues of followers and power (Fleming & Spicer, 2014; Shamir et al., 2007), challenging the logics of hierarchy in leadership (Denis et al., 2012). Some arts researchers evoke interactional leadership without naming it in their theorizing on arts leaders. Ropo et al. (2013) explore the social construction of leadership in the performing arts as aesthetically materialized and embodied in a relational dynamic. Mintzberg (1998) studied a symphony orchestra's music director and coined the term "covert leadership" where professionals need inspiration, but not direction. In contrast, an artistic leader's celebrity and charisma have been found to enhance loyalty among followers and funding stakeholders (Nisbett & Walmsley, 2016). We raise this distinctive aspect of arts co-leadership throughout the book.

"Pooling leadership capacity at the top to direct others" is the fourth approach to plural leadership identified by Denis et al. (2012). It is distinct from other categories due to its organizational hierarchy and authority and is the focus of our book. Its presence has been observed as early as Ancient Rome (Sally, 2002) and in the US since the 1930s in the arts (Durham, 1986; London, 2013). Alvarez and Svejenova (2005) identified a list of over 60 examples from the financial and creative industries. In 2016, several arts interest groups in Canada confirmed that most theatres, dance companies, and symphony orchestras in the country were led by co-leaders (Gibeau et al., 2016).

Co-leadership involves a small number of executives whose joint leadership bridges the functional differentiation between business and profession logics (managers as opposed to artists, doctors, and lawyers) (Empson & Alvehus, 2020; Fjellvær, 2010; Gibeau et al., 2020; Kuesters, 2010; Reid & Karambayya, 2009). This type of leadership typically appears in pluralistic organizations where a culture of ambiguity exists (Cohen & March, 1974). Co-leadership is an attempt to integrate competing logics resident and hence address ambiguity. For instance, in Australia, researchers found that collaborative behaviour among co-leaders prioritized and enhanced the artistic mandate (MacNeill & Tonks, 2009; MacNeill et al., 2013; Reynolds et al., 2017). While co-leadership may often function well as a solution, it also creates dynamics that can lead to further confusion and problems. These difficulties are highlighted by scholars of single leadership.

"Single leadership" features one individual in the top executive role. This form is a traditional focus and dominant logic in leadership studies (Bass, 1990; Burns, 1978; Dionne et al., 2014). Scholars argue that single leaders' strategic view is often inspirational, influencing others to produce organizational effectiveness and achieve overall satisfaction (Locke, 2003). These scholars typically refute the legitimacy and value of co-leadership

(Fayol, 1949). They argue that assigning power equally among co-leaders renders decision-making inefficient, authority unclear, and strategic direction overly complex (Locke, 2003). Co-leadership studies are often preoccupied by how this leadership arrangement can function coherently and act as one to counter these criticisms.

These studies are largely focused on the strategic orientations and behavioural dynamics among executive level co-leaders. They explore organizational decision-making and strategizing (Alvarez & Svejenova, 2005; Bhansing et al., 2016), how logics and values are integrated (Fjellvær, 2010; Gibeau et al., 2020; Gronn & Hamilton, 2004), and how behavioural dynamics can impact the leadership of the organization (Reid & Karambayya, 2009; Reynolds et al., 2017). Much of the early research describes an emergent dynamic to establish the co-leadership constellation (Hodgson et al., 1965). Current researchers have confirmed that in smaller civil society or non-profit arts organizations, artists may emerge as self-selected co-leaders for their organizations (Dragićević-Šešić & Stefanović, 2017; Järvinen et al., 2015; Panctot & Lusiani, 2021). However, more frequently, these leadership roles are mandated by a third party as a governance decision (Alvarez & Svejenova, 2005).

Plural leadership is a multi-faceted phenomenon that has attracted researchers from different perspectives in management and plural leadership. It occurs in many arts disciplines and intensively in certain regions (Chapter 4). While we present co-leadership as a valuable means to lead and manage in the arts and cultural sector, we do not present an idealized portrait and we balance its positive impact with its challenges.

Identifying founding concepts

The thread of inquiry into co-leadership and plural leadership began in response to closely observed experiences (Gronn, 1999; Heenan & Bennis, 1999; Hodgson et al., 1965). Table 3.1 summarizes the four key concepts from the founding theoretical works about co-leadership. Table 3.2 appears later and outlines the issues that have been identified in further co-leadership research fields including the arts. This theoretical grounding frames the empirical chapters to come in the book.

Executive role constellation and shared role space

The foundational work on co-leadership by Hodgson et al. (1965) describes dynamics within a trio of executives who coalesced as a co-leadership unit in a psychiatric hospital. Their study is the earliest exploration of how a group can lead as one. It provides a significant counterargument to criticisms from single leadership scholars. The group's behaviour and leadership provide important insights into the separation, integration, and personal connection necessary for co-leadership success.

Table 3.1 Concepts from the founding literature

Concept	*Description*	*Key references*	*Other pertinent references*
Executive role constellation	Emergent trio of executives in psychiatric hospital. Provides insights on functional differentiation, overlap, and integration.	Hodgson et al., 1965	Denis et al., 2001; Fjellvær, 2010; Gibeau et al., 2016
Shared role space	Role theory to extend unit of analysis beyond single leadership role. Shared role space is completed through resources of co-leaders.	Gronn & Hamilton, 2004; Stewart, 1991b	Katz & Kahn, 1966; Merton, 1957
Specialization, differentiation, and complementarity	Specialization = individual professional expertise. Differentiation = division of labour. Complementarity = match of collective resources and environment to complete constellation and generate success.	Hodgson et al., 1965	Denis et al., 2001; Denis et al., 2010
Sharing executive power as corporate governance	Organizational design decision – governance mechanism in complex environments. Widespread in corporations and creative industries.	Alvarez & Svejenova, 2005	Cyert & March, 1963; Thompson, 1967
Stability versus fragility	Co-leadership is unstable and fragile with many powerful stakeholders and plurality of strongly held values.	Denis et al., 2001	Reid & Karambayya, 2016; Gibeau et al., 2020

The group members' positions in the organization were not formally equal, since one member of the trio reported to another, but they functioned in a collegial manner on an informally equal basis. "Executive role constellation" is the label chosen by Hodgson et al. (1965) to describe the separate professional expertise and personal social skills combined within the co-leadership. The coherence and effectiveness of the trio were exhibited across three dimensions: Specialization, differentiation, and complementarity. We will investigate these dimensions later in this discussion and return to these dimensions often in the discussions in our empirical chapters.

Another label appears in our discussion about co-leadership. "Constellation" implies individuals in different supervisory positions whose orbits are linked through behavioural ties. But we also use the term "configuration" to describe the co-leadership group, adding a more structural dimension to the executive leadership pool at the top. We make use of these two terms regularly but note the intended distinction between behavioural and structural relationships within the co-leadership.

A third term, "shared role space", conceptualizes the organization-level roles of co-leadership using role theory (Katz & Kahn, 1966; Stewart, 1991b). Role theory involves social construction and institutional expectations from the role and the different perspectives of role set and role space. Individuals in a role space are guided by legitimizing expectations from the role set to realize their role. A role set describes the interactive audience around the principal actor (e.g., followers and colleagues) (Merton, 1957). A role space describes the roles that the individual leader plays within their job and in relation to their audience (e.g., supervisor, mentor, and co-leader) (Stewart, 1991a, 1991b). A shared role space is occupied by two, three, or more individuals who work together within that space to lead the organization as an ensemble (Gronn & Hamilton, 2004). The realization of roles can involve conflict (many potentially competing expectations from the role set) and ambiguity (search for clarity of responsibilities) because of the pluralistic context. Like constellations, the actors in this shared role space are confronted by the need to negotiate their differences and to integrate their pluralistic objectives in order to lead with a singular vision (Fayol, 1949) – or with a shared cognition (Alvarez & Svejenova, 2005).

The literature about shared role space identifies two possible configurations of roles or jobs in education and health care. A third contrasting configuration occurs in the arts where role differentiation and autonomy are significant factors. Defining this third configuration is an important contribution of our research.

In the first configuration, Gronn and Hamilton (2004) conclude that co-principals jointly complete the shared role space of one job – that is principal for the school. They are similarly qualified in the role that provides pedagogical leadership. Occasionally, co-principals bridge administrative and pedagogical roles (Döös & Wilhelmson, 2021) which reflect the arts co-leadership configuration.

In the second configuration, Stewart (1991a, 1991b) analysed the inter-relational dynamics of chairs of governing boards and managers in regional districts in the British National Health System (NHS). She developed the notion of a shared role space and found that the two different jobs created a shared role space that is bigger than either individual job. Together, they provide leadership of the organization. Each job holder can complement the other's preference for tasks within the one leadership role space to complete that separate role. Compared to co-principals, who complete the one job as two similarly qualified actors in the leadership space, the British NHS study provides a perspective on two jobs and two different types and levels of actors who combine in the leadership role space. Stewart's identification of the leadership role space inspired Gronn and Hamilton (2004) to promote the notion of shared role space in their study of co-leadership.

In the arts, we have observed that co-leaders also hold two separate roles, but these roles are at the same top executive level, leading their respective artistic or managerial functions. These individuals also lead jointly in the executive role space, aspiring to lead as one. As a result, each leader holds two roles within the role space. Their joint leadership involves negotiation of competing values and integration of logics (Fjellvær, 2010; Kuesters, 2010) (Chapter 5). Despite their separate roles and the presence of competing logics, co-leaders also manage interdependence (Gronn & Hamilton, 2004). As a result, it becomes important to understand conflict, collaboration, and trust within the arts shared role space and the arts leadership constellation (Chapters 6 and 7). The interpersonal dynamics of co-leadership reveal how leading as one is difficult but also possible.

Specialization, differentiation, and complementarity

In the psychiatric hospital case analysed by Hodgson et al. (1965), a dynamic balance of three dimensions over time influenced either individual authority or collaborative and relational work within the professional trio. Specialization recognizes an individual's professional expertise and legitimacy as defined within the organizational context. Without a variety of specialized professional, organizational, and emotional skills, collaboration among the constellation members is limited. Differentiation in job responsibilities within the constellation is also necessary to avoid overlap, potential competition, and conflict. In the arts, functional differentiation is a key dimension, because of the two separately defined jobs within the role space or constellation. Separating the roles supports artistic autonomy, a concern related to liberty of expression (Røyseng, 2008), but it emphasizes the need for integration and collaboration in arts co-leadership.

Finally, complementarity considers the collective resources brought into the constellation by its members and the degree to which the combination of these resources responds to organizational needs by integrating logics. Therefore, the constellation's success is a function of completing the specific executive role space with expertise, reputation, and behaviour that convey legitimacy (Hodgson et al., 1965, pp. 284–285; Denis et al., 2010, p. 76). The well-being of the relationship is found in its degree of complementarity. For arts co-leaders, complementarity reflects their efforts to integrate logics across their specialized and differentiated organizational leadership roles to lead together as one. This is distinct from other constellations that are by nature more "conjoint" (Gronn, 2002). In Chapter 5, we analyse constellations according to the different degrees of logic integration and the resulting impact on these dimensions. In Chapter 6, we explore how a competitive, status-seeking conflict can block the joint leadership behaviour needed for complementarity.

Organizational design and governance

Alvarez and Svejenova (2005) reference configuration theory to demonstrate that executive co-leadership is an organizational design choice that acts as a corporate governance mechanism (Cyert & March, 1963; Thompson, 1967). In the context of the arts, leadership configuration may be a decision by the funder, the board of directors, or the leaders themselves who share the role space for a long or short period of time (De Voogt, 2006). In Chapter 4, we provide an overview of these variations by region and art discipline.

Agency theory dominates the study of governance in for-profit and non-profit. It is underpinned by distrust. Executive leaders are assumed to be economically self-interested and therefore need to be monitored (Jensen & Meckling, 1976). Alvarez and Svejenova (2005) explain that agency theorists would view trust within co-leadership as collusive, thereby undermining effective governance. However, many scholars indicate that trust is important for successful collaboration and longevity in joint ventures (Madhok, 1995, p. 2006) and in the constellation or role space for co-leaders (Gronn & Hamilton, 2004; Hodgson et al., 1965). In line with this reasoning, Alvarez and Svejenova (2005) theorize trust as an important relational mechanism in co-leadership that generates shared cognition and overcomes decision-making hurdles.

In many jurisdictions, regions, and sectors, the arts are structured as non-profit or civil society organizations governed by boards of directors (Chapter 4). There are three different views of how non-profit governance works. In one approach, governance theory involves tensions between internal and external perspectives (Cornforth, 2003). In another approach, governance influences on the organization are explained by stakeholder-board relationships (Coule, 2015). Finally, powerfulgovernance coalitions can develop across leadership, board, and stakeholder roles (Andersson & Renz, 2019; Willems et al., 2017). All three approaches underscore how power functions within and around the organization. Co-leaders may solve competing logics through their relationship with a board of directors, thus providing a dynamic view of how social hierarchy and governance logics interact (Chapter 8).

Stability versus fragility

Founding scholars, Denis and colleagues (1996, 2001, 2010) observed concerns about stability and fragility in their analysis of strategic decision-making in government-mandated hospital mergers in Québec. These are pluralistic organizations in demanding, changing environments with multiple and powerful stakeholders and plural leadership. A culture of ambiguity prevails. Organizational instability results from interpersonal values differences among the co-leaders and from environmental and political interference by stakeholders. Organizations are fragile because a constellation of leaders can only sporadically achieve integration of logics and alignment of interests to move the organization forward strategically (Denis et al., 2001). In the arts management literature, instability has been recognized when leadership transition or conflict and confrontation occurs. In Australia, when a new artistic director (AD) arrives, or when there are significant confrontations between these leaders, the norm suggests that the executive director (ED) may depart the organization (MacNeill et al., 2013; Reynolds et al., 2017).

The dark-side and inherent dilemmas of co-leadership in ambiguous, complex, and pluralistic environments are not often discussed (Denis et al., 2010). These less optimistic portraits contrast with the early co-leadership literature where scholars focused on ongoing positive relationships (Gronn, 1999; Gronn & Hamilton, 2004; Hodgson et al., 1965). As well, Alvarez and Svejenova (2005) describe life-long shared careers for co-leaders linked by family, like the Almodovar brothers (film producer and director of award-winning films from Spain), or by strong emotional ties, like environmental artist, Christo, and his wife, Jeanne-Claude (Svejenova et al., 2010). Such partnerships provide significant protection for idiosyncratic creative vision – necessary for realizing innovative objectives within the artistic ideal (Alvarez et al., 2005). As mutually chosen leaders with an equally deep commitment to their organizational purpose, they are distinctive in the landscape of co-leadership, but other research reflects the fragile nature of the relationship.

These founding concepts shape both relational and organizational dynamics related to co-leadership, and the perspectives and insights that emerge in the empirical chapters that follow.

Extending core issues through recent co-leadership research

In the following discussion, we pursue issues that provide theoretical foundations for our empirical studies of co-leaders in the arts. These issues build on theory that describes the environment (Chapter 2) and the founding literature of plural leadership (Chapter 3). They highlight the co-leadership relationship: Conflict or collaboration and trust reflect concerns about how to lead as one, equality versus hierarchy and celebrity and charisma all relate to the question of parity in co-leadership and its problem of ambiguous authority, and finally, ambiguous communications may enable political manoeuvring within parity and ambiguous authority. Table 3.2 provides a summary.

Table 3.2 Issues in the current co-leadership literature

Concept	*Description*	*Key references*	*Other pertinent references*
Conflict or collaboration	Range of conflict types affects interpersonal dynamics and collaboration, and hence, organization's functionality.	Reid & Karambayya, 2009; Reynolds et al., 2017	Bhansing et al., 2016; Cray et al., 2007
Trust	Trust facilitates the relationship, compensates for conflict, and enables collaboration.	Alvarez & Svejenova, 2005; Reid & Karambayya, 2016	Gronn, 2002; Reynolds et al., 2017
Parity versus hierarchy	Question formal parity of status and power in the relationship. Hybrid practices of co-leadership are observed.	Krause et al., 2015; Gronn, 2016	MacNeill & Tonks, 2013; Empson & Alvehus, 2020
Management versus leadership	Co-leadership structures vary. Management = assigned position. Leadership = individual attribution. In the arts, leadership attribution may differ between ED and AD.	Gronn, 1999, 2002; DeRue & Ashford, 2010; MacNeill & Tonks, 2013	Reynolds et al., 2017
Celebrity and charisma	Artists' celebrity and charisma as assets or challenge to arts leadership and organizational well-being.	Lindqvist, 2017; Nisbett & Walmsley, 2016; Ostrower, 2002; Quigg, 2007	Kleppe & Røyseng, 2016; Lindgren, 2009
Ambiguity strategies	Solutions to manage governance tensions and co-leadership relationships.	Alvarez & Svejenova, 2005; Denis et al., 1996; Empson, 2020	

Conflict and collaboration

Once the concepts of pluralism, competing logics, and ambiguity are deployed to understand the organizational context, the potential for conflict becomes clear. Role theory explains that multiple expectations from the role set can result in ambiguity and conflict for the role (Ebbers & Wijnberg, 2017). The ambiguity of multiple goals may encourage conflict in decision-making. Despite the largely positive outcomes for co-leadership reported by the founding scholars, the risk of conflict is an important element within these relationships, particularly in the arts (Reid & Karambayya, 2009). Integrating the logics of the different domains in an arts organization and fulfilling the separate and joint roles of co-leadership are difficult. Ambiguity and conflict can prevent the co-leaders from acting as one.

However, the absence of conflict is reported by some scholars. MacNeill and colleagues conclude that collaborative (Reynolds et al, 2017), authentic (2013), and feminist (2009) relationship behaviours were in evidence among the co-leaders in major cultural institutions in Australia. In this context, effective conflict management appears to have been in operation although Australian arts leaders characteristically seem to demonstrate leadership reluctance which may result in less conflict in parity leadership relationships like those in co-leadership (Goodwin, 2020). The founding research on co-leadership advocates humility (Gronn, 1999; Heenan & Bennis, 1999). In Finland, active collaboration is identified among co-artistic directors. In Québec, arts co-leaders demonstrate the positive use of ambiguity to aid role-sharing in theatre companies (Järvinen et al., 2015; Tremblay, 2014). Collaboration between Reubens and Brueghel, the Elder, two major visual art studios in 17th-century Belgium, has also been studied (De Voogt & Hommes, 2007).

Conflict management capabilities may vary in arts organizations depending on their size and funding system. In Anglo-Saxon countries, funding mechanisms like arts councils create an arm's length distance from the political process to allow for organizational and artistic autonomy (Upchurch, 2016). In this less directive context, the norm of co-leadership is more socially constructed than regulated by law or funding agreement as occurs in Europe (Fjellvær, 2010; Tschmuck, 2006), leaving these organizations open to socially constructed norms, competing logics, and more potential for conflict.

Research on groups in the social-psychology literature indicates that conflict can contribute to creativity (Tjosvold, 2006). However, conflict types can vary from constructive to toxic (Jehn & Mannix, 2001). The negative effects of conflict can be dissipated through conflict management skills and early intervention (Rahim, 2002). On the other hand, status conflict is a competitive attempt to influence social hierarchy without explicitly mobilizing the subject of the conflict. It can contribute to a toxic culture (Bendersky & Hays, 2012). In the arts, status and influence are linked to a high regard for art (Nisbett & Walmsley, 2016; Ostrower, 2002). We explore social hierarchy in the co-leadership role space by delving into status conflict (Chapter 6). We also suggest that future research compares variations in context in the cultural field in relation to different propensities for conflict (Chapter 10).

Trust

Trust operates in both intimate and work relationships (McAllister, 1995). In co-leadership's founding literature, many scholars emphasize the need for trust to avoid conflict and competition. For Hodgson et al. (1965), trust is embedded in complementarity. Gronn and Hamilton (2004, p. 6) uncovered trust in their study of the dynamic in "intuitive development" in co-principal roles in schools. Alvarez and Svejenova (2005) argue that trust is a key relational mechanism of executive co-leadership effective functioning (Madhok, 1995; Svejenova, 2006).

Reid and Karambayya (2016) observed how trust is facilitated by elements outside the relationship. New co-leaders' ability to trust was affected by the shadow of organizational history, such as past decisions by a board of directors or relationship dynamics with a previous executive.

Swift trust describes the potential for trust in short-term project relationships, like among film crew members (Meyerson et al., 1996). It relies on institutionalized, codified "ways of doing" to judge trustworthiness – predictable and reliable behaviour by another member of the team. Uncovering institutionalized expectations of what an artistic leader or manager "should do" in a long-term relationship may also be useful to enhance our understanding of the evolution of co-leadership relationships. We look at assumptions and expectations when a new co-leader is hired to partner with an incumbent (Chapter 7). In that process, "leap of faith" and "suspension of disbelief" are metaphors that demonstrate how initiating trust might involve the risk of decisional blind spots (Möllering, 2006).

Equality versus hierarchy

Equality is a contested consideration in co-leadership. Nonetheless, research shows that the majority of co-leadership configurations functions with a formally equal mandate (Döös & Wilhelmson, 2021). The co-leadership roles in the arts are usually considered formally equal in the shared role space (Reid & Karambayya, 2009), whereas other research reveals that not all roles may be equally mandated (Fjellvær, 2010; MacNeill & Tonks, 2013). Gronn's (1999) initial portrait of co-leadership may have idealized the impact of the co-leaders in the organization as informally equal, despite hierarchical differences. In later publications, Gronn (2016) distanced himself from these initial reflections on co-leadership, suggesting that informally equal status and impact are rarely realized. As a result, he revised his approach, calling co-leadership a "hybrid configuration", reflecting a range of relationships with formal and informal relative status.

Our research provides some useful evidence that recognizes the separate and joint roles of arts co-leaders. Boards of directors hire their co-leaders individually indicating separate roles are prioritized by boards (Chapter 8). However, the three different roles (AD, ED, and joint executive leaders) have been acknowledged formally in certain disciplines and regions in the arts (Chapter 4). A distinctive example is the National Theatre in Britain, where in 2019, the AD and ED were announced as co-CEOs (Snow, 2019) as well as being recognized with their functional titles. Other examples are found in Québec, Canada, where job titles and descriptions often indicate either an AD or ED responsibility plus that of the co-Director General (Lavoie, 2021). Job descriptions for the joint role involve responsibilities for developing the organization and special projects, as well as being equal spokespersons for the organization. Each is expected to respect the other's artistic vision or organizational strategic plan as well as collaborate where duties overlap. Hence, individual co-leaders undertake leadership responsibility for two roles. However, the exact shape of arts leadership configurations on the international stage varies in response to organizational needs (MacNeill & Tonks, 2013), to regional societal values, and to art disciplines (Chapter 4).

In northern Europe, government funders and legal structures that implant co-leadership in arts institutions often dictate that despite equal reporting to the board or to the government, the AD has the last word about artistic programming. This provision affirms the artist's professional judgment and aligns artistic freedom with democratic freedom of expression (Fjellvær, 2010; Tschmuck, 2006). However, it also suggests a form of inequality in the co-leadership. In fact, some scholars and practitioners consider that the ED's role functions only in a supportive manner to the AD, suggesting that the role is less strategic (Lapierre, 2001; MacNeill et al., 2013; Reynolds et al., 2017). However, EDs usually lead organizational development and functional equilibrium (Kuesters, 2010), as well as the organization's social role in the community (Löfgren, 2016).

In the private sector, Krause et al. (2015) tested the value of equal sharing of command in co-CEOs (Fayol, 1949). They found that, up to a limit, increasing power differences between these co-CEOs produced greater organizational performance. Extreme differences in power were problematic for firm performance. They concluded that equal co-leadership may be valuable, but for reasons other than performance (Krause et al., 2015).

Equality becomes a state of being that may be negotiated from moment to moment. Ambiguity of intention and imprecisely defined responsibilities may be strategic tools that enable the political manoeuvring necessary to function with the informal power differences in co-leadership (Alvarez & Svejenova, 2005; Empson, 2020; Empson & Alvehus, 2020). To explore these differences, we analyse status conflict found in our data, its impact on equality in the co-leadership configuration, and the power dynamics between the AD and ED leadership roles in the arts (Chapter 6). We also study co-leadership and board relationship patterns that attempt to solve the competing logics and ambiguous authority in non-profit governance (Chapter 8).

Celebrity and charisma

Artists personify the artistic ideal that is key among the logics in the arts field. Particularly talented artists manifest leadership through their performance achievements and their innovative ideas (Lindqvist, 2017). Innovations generate notoriety within the art world. Artistic leaders' celebrity and charisma garner funders' interest and media and public support for their organizations (Nisbett & Walmsley, 2016; Ostrower, 2002).

However, the legitimizing impact of being in service to art (René, 2018) can normalize abusive behaviour (Quigg, 2007), which undermines confidence and creative productivity within the artistic process (Abfalter,

2013; Auvinen, 2001). When abuse by artistic leaders is publicly exposed, controversy and organizational criticism arise (Kleppe & Røyseng, 2016; Lindgren, 2009). Intolerance for abusive behaviour within the performing arts and museum sectors has significantly increased as a result of new legal regulations and newly evolved social movements like #MeToo!, Black Lives Matter, and decolonizing advocates. Abuse masked by charisma has become a governance issue in the arts (Lederman, 2018). The COVID-19 pandemic period particularly intensified pressure on arts boards of directors to conduct a more critical evaluation of artistic directors' leadership skills and performance. However, the role of co-leadership in the evolving dilemma of artistic celebrity has yet to be examined.

This recent and public re-evaluation of the impact of celebrity linked with the importance of the artistic ideal influences our own reflections regarding power dynamics (Chapter 6) and governance issues for co-leadership and boards (Chapter 8). We suggest further research regarding these topics (Chapter 10).

Using ambiguity to manage executive relationships

In pluralistic organizations, intentionally ambiguous communication provides leaders with the flexibility to negotiate the power differences and politics inherent in their relationship (Abdallah & Langley, 2014). With ambiguity, an illusion of normalcy may prevail, but behind the scenes, manoeuvring occurs on the part of one or both co-leaders. Recent research on co-leadership in professional service firms reveals use of ambiguous communications and hidden political manoeuvring in times of crisis (Empson, 2020). On the other hand, ambiguity has been found to cushion and buffer the shared role space for teams of co-leaders in theatre organizations (Tremblay, 2014). These examples reveal that ambiguity transforms a situation with either positive or negative results and studying ambiguity in co-leadership situations reveals the informal power dynamics that underlie formal and official structures (Bolden, 2011; Collinson, 2005). We revisit ambiguity as an organizational culture when we investigate status conflict (Chapter 6).

Highlighting arts contributions to co-leadership research

Plural leadership research is multi-sectoral (Alvarez & Svejenova, 2005; Empson, 2017). Founding scholars in this literature were particularly interested in non-profit and public organizations where the context is pluralistic, and mission-carrying professionals like doctors and teachers are accompanied by managers (Döös & Wilhelmson, 2021; Gibeau et al., 2020). For-profit professional service firms also provide an important context for study of co-leadership (Empson, 2020), as home to respected professionals, such as lawyers and accountants.

Focusing on co-leadership in the non-profit arts, we identified 19 publications and three doctoral dissertations or masters theses (Antrobus, 2009;

Beard, 2012; Carneiro, 2019). Several of the scholarly publications began as dissertations or as research partnerships with professionals in the sector. Some scholars who study arts co-leadership come from within the arts sector while others bring views and theories from other fields. All but one of these publications appeared between 2006 and 2017 clustering around two co-leadership topics: One is strategic decision-making and the other is relational dynamics with organizational implications. Most of these publications appear in the sector's specialty journals and, as a result, are not widely known to other management scholars (Gibeau et al., 2016). We have threaded findings from this body of research through our discussion, confirming its place in the literature on co-leadership. These publications are summarized by topic in Table 3.3.

This research is often qualitative. Either one or both co-leaders together were interviewed. Occasionally, interviews were part of a larger research process throughout the organization but most frequently they focused specifically on the co-leaders themselves (Döös & Wilhelmson, 2021). The research is mainly descriptive and applies theory, but some studies are analytical and develop new theories (Denis et al., 2012). Some studies are analytically deductive and quantitative focusing on strategic decision-making (Beard, 2012; Bhansing et al., 2016; Voss et al., 2006). Australia, Canada, Scandinavia, Netherlands, and England are the main sites for research reflecting the geographic distribution of this leadership practice in the arts, but we investigate the extent of co-leadership practice in the arts around the globe (Chapter 4). This executive configuration is long-standing, especially in the US, but case studies have recently appeared in South-east Asia, India, and Latin America signaling the potential emergence of co-leadership practice in these regions (Caust, 2013, 2015; Ruiz-Gutiérrez et al., 2016).

As with other co-leadership research, the focus of research in the arts often centers on the relationship and how values and logics influence its functionality and the potential for conflict (Castañer, 1997). Other studies focus on how differing logics influence strategic decision-making (Bhansing et al., 2012; Bhansing et al., 2016; Cray et al., 2007). Given the authority of the artistic ideal in the arts sector and the pluralistic and ambiguous organizational goals (Chapter 2), balanced dynamics in co-leadership and effective strategic decision-making may appear difficult to achieve. Despite this, our data showed that co-leaders generally accomplished a balanced integration (Chapter 5). At the organizational level, we go on to consider co-leadership's influence on arts governance and boards of directors (Chapter 8) and co-leadership's interaction with other executive managers within the arts organization (Chapter 9).

Synthesizing key findings from the co-leadership literature

Theorizing about plural leadership began with close observations of newly discovered co-leadership situations (Gronn, 1999; Heenan & Bennis, 1999; Hodgson et al., 1965). These arrangements appeared intriguing but improbable when viewed through the lens of the extensive and institutionalized

Table 3.3 Research on arts co-leadership

Author(s)	*Location and data source*	*Methodology*	*Theoretical frame and issues*
Shared role space dynamics			
De Voogt & Hommes, 2007	Holland: Two art studios in the 16th century.	Art history texts, Anecdotal.	Organizational and leadership structure.
MacNeill & Tonks, 2009	Australia: Six performing organizations – executive duos.	Qualitative interviews analysed individually, Descriptive.	Gender studies and shared role space dynamics.
Reid & Karambayya, 2009	Canada: Eight performing organizations case studies.	Qualitative, 8–9 interviews per organization, Analytical.	Conflict: Shared role space dynamics and impact on organization.
Kuesters, 2010	Germany: Music production and presentation organizations, Individual managers interviewed for "code orientations".	Qualitative interviews, Descriptive.	Functional differentiation (Luhmann).
MacNeill & Tonks, 2013	Australia: Major performing arts and museums (28 possible cases).	Qualitative interviews with leaders, Analytical.	Management structures versus leadership and organizational success.
MacNeill et al., 2013	Australia: Six performing arts organizations, Duos interviewed.	Qualitative, Authentic leadership measure to match terminology in discrete duo interviews, Descriptive.	Authentic behaviour within duos.
Järvinen et al., 2015	Finland: Seven theatre director duos.	Qualitative, Pairs interviewed together, Analytical.	Self-chosen duos in shared role space.

(Continued)

Table 3.3 Research on arts co-leadership *(Continued)*

Author(s)	*Location and data source*	*Methodology*	*Theoretical frame and issues*
Reid & Karambayya, 2016	Canada: Eight performing arts case studies.	Qualitative, 8–9 interviews per organization, Analytical.	Trust influenced by previous relationships and impact on organization.
Schrauwen et al., 2016	Belgium, Holland, and France: Established performing arts institutions – 24 cases.	Qualitative, Interviews with senior admin and board chair plus documents, Analytical.	Distributed leadership in response to complex environment (called shared leadership), Extension of shared role space.
Reynolds et al., 2017	Australia: 28 performing arts organizations.	Qualitative, Interview analysis, Descriptive.	Collaborative leadership.
Ebbers & Wijnberg, 2017	The Netherlands: Project-based film production.	Qualitative but deductive, Analytical.	Role theory – conflict, ambiguity, and definition, Extension of shared role space.
Strategic decision-making and organizational impact			
Castañer, 1997	Spain (Barcelona): A symphony orchestra case study.	Qualitative archival documents, Analytical.	Organizational theory analysis of executive leader succession, tension between profession and business logics, and leadership stability.
Voss et al., 2006	US: Theatre companies.	Quantitative, Analytical.	Identity differences in shared role space with impact on the organization.

Table 3.3 Research on arts co-leadership *(Continued)*

Author(s)	*Location and data source*	*Methodology*	*Theoretical frame and issues*
Cray et al., 2007	Australia: Point of reference.	Theoretical. Development of hypotheses, Deduction.	Strategy: Four leadership styles applied to four decision processes, Strategic decision-making in complex organizations.
Antrobus, 2009 (thesis)	UK: Museums and theatre companies, 34 interviews.	Qualitative, Analytical and applied.	Strategy: Introduction of joint leadership to include management values and develop collaborative culture in leadership and the organization.
Cray & Inglis, 2011	Canada: Performing arts organizations – 14 cases, Variety of size.	Qualitative interviews with managerial side, Deductive.	Strategy: Decision-making influenced by logics.
Bhansing et al., 2012	The Netherlands: Performing arts 51 duos.	Quantitative survey, Deductive, Analytical, cause, and effect.	Strategy: Test cognitive heterogeneity (logics) on decision-making in equal executive duos.
Beard, 2012 (dissertation)	US: Performing arts, 117 organizations.	Quantitative survey, Deductive, Analytical, cause, and effect.	Test influence of leadership structure and budgeting effectiveness.

(Continued)

Table 3.3 Research on arts co-leadership *(Continued)*

Author(s)	*Location and data source*	*Methodology*	*Theoretical frame and issues*
Bhansing et al., 2016	UK: Performing arts organizations – 66 duos.	Quantitative, 132 individual responses to interviews, Analytical, cause, and effect.	Testing diversity of perspectives (logics) in duo leadership decision-making strategies.
Carneiro, 2019 (thesis)	Canada, India, and Portugal, Three theatre companies.	Qualitative, Interviews with each co-leader independently.	Explore how co-leadership contributes to support of art across stages of organizational development.
Governance			
De Voogt, 2006	The Netherlands: Two museums.	Journalistic reports of a specific moment, Anecdotal.	Financial crisis management.
Power			
Auvinen, 2001	Europe: Six major opera houses.	Qualitative, Descriptive.	Habermas, Nielson: Civil society, economy, and state.

perspective of single executive leadership (Fayol, 1949). They provoked exploration of both relationship and organizational dynamics to explain their continued functionality (Gibeau et al., 2016). Founding scholars called on contingency theory, strategic decision-making practice, and role theory for sensemaking about the phenomena (Alvarez & Svejenova, 2005; Denis et al., 2001; Gronn, 1999, 2002; Hodgson et al., 1965). The organizational context for co-leadership has been defined as pluralistic, professional, and ambiguous (Cohen & March, 1974; Denis et al., 1996; Denis et al., 2012). In the arts, the logics revolve around four distinctive themes related to the artistic ideal (Chapter 2).

Scholars of co-leadership developed the idea of the shared role space, looking at the relationship dynamics but also how leadership is manifested by a collective voice. Gronn and Hamilton (2004) and Stewart (1991b) mobilized role theory to construct the concept of role space; Gibeau et al. (2020), Fjellvær (2010), and Empson (2020) made use of competing logics to investigate the collective voice; and Bhansing et al. (2016) and Cray et al. (2007) engaged with strategic orientations to describe the challenges of decision-making. Politics and power embedded in co-leadership have been the focus of study in the context of professional service firms, where ambiguous leadership authority pervades (Empson, 2020; Empson & Alvehus, 2020). Formal structural differences in the leadership configuration have been observed in the arts (Järvinen et al., 2015; MacNeill & Tonks, 2013). However, informal power differences within co-leadership and the impact on the organization's functionality have been little studied either in the arts or across the co-leadership field.

Linking to the empirical chapters

Our initial research focused on the relationship and how it functions in a context of competing logics (Fjellvær, 2010; Reid & Karambayya, 2009, 2016). Through an abductive process with our data, we gain new insight on the integration of competing logics within the co-leadership (Chapter 5). We examine conflict and its effect on status differences (Chapter 6), and we analyse how the risks related to leaps of faith influence trust and its role in decision-making. Many scholars have continued to explore the relationship and strategic decision-making dynamics within pluralism, but research on the impact on follower satisfaction and organizational performance has been limited (Döös & Wilhelmson, 2021). To extend the study of co-leadership's organizational impact, we examine the co-leadership's influence both above, with the board of directors, and below into the organization (Denis et al., 2012) (Chapters 8 and 9).

Throughout this discussion of the literature, we have indicated the relevant chapters in which we plan to develop the issues. Table 3.4 provides a summary that links these concepts and issues to upcoming chapters.

Table 3.4 Links to upcoming chapters

Chapter topic	• *Concept or issue* • *Specific aspect*

4 – Practice of co-leadership	• Context
	  • Understanding of co-leadership presence and practice in the arts globally,
	• Governance
	  • Policy and funding variations determine co-leadership mandating practices.

5 – Logics	• Competing logics
	  • Foundational theorizing for chapter,
	• Executive role constellations and shared role space
	  • Individual co-leader cognition determines logic integration and how role space responsibilities are fulfilled,
	• Specialization, differentiation, and complementarity
	  • Integration of logics influences how these dimensions are realized,
	• Ambiguity
	  • Ambiguity dominates organizational culture because of pluralistic goals.

6 – Status conflict	• Status conflict
	  • Foundational theorizing for chapter,
	• Authority
	  • Each individual co-leader is professional expert on their side of the organization,
	• Ambiguity
	  • Ambiguity results from pluralistic goals, influencing decision-making in the shared role space,
	• Parity versus hierarchy
	  • Mandated parity may be confusing, rendering the shared role space vulnerable to competition for hierarchical power, frequently mobilizing the artistic imperative,
	• Charisma and celebrity
	  • Charisma and celebrity support status and may be mobilized in status conflict,
	• Power
	  • Status conflict may lead to changes in informal power.

7 – Trust	• Trust
	  • Foundational theorizing for chapter,
	• Swift trust
	  • How trust relies on early compliance with institutionalized practices,
	• Familiarity and artistic imperative
	  • Familiarity with artistic knowledge to make leaps of faith in relationships.

(Continued)

Table 3.4 Links to upcoming chapters *(Continued)*

Chapter topic	• *Concept or issue* • *Specific aspect*

8 – Governance and boards	• Non-profit governance logics
	  • Foundational theorizing for chapter,
	• Governance and trust
	  • Arising from agency theory with implications for co-leadership functionality,
	• Board-staff relations
	  • Expert professionals as co-leaders, plus the power of the artistic imperative – information asymmetry influences board governance practices,
	• Celebrity and charisma
	  • Boards avoid a governance surveillance posture with ADs, using the co-leadership to solve resulting ambiguity.

9 – Co-leadership and followers	• Follower theorizing
	  • Co-leadership directs from the top,
	  • In middle of continuum of leader-follower theories,
	• Role theory
	  • Role crafting occurs when co-leader relationship is distanced,
	  • Boundaries of shared role space are dynamic,
	• Distributed leadership culture
	  • Occurs by invitation or by failure of co-leader relationship,
	• Fragility
	  • Co-leadership fragility influences distributed leadership practices.

Our research on this phenomenon is situated in Anglo-Saxon countries and Northern Europe. We have discovered that this reflects its practice geographically. The plural leadership literature would benefit from more perspectives beyond these regions. For this reason, Chapter 4 becomes important, as we undertake an initial analysis of executive leadership configurations practiced in the arts globally, informed by experts and senior managers.

References

Abdallah, C., & Langley, A. (2014). The double edge of ambiguity in strategic planning. *Journal of Management Studies*, *51*(2), 235–264. https://doi.org/10.1111/joms.12002

Abfalter, D. (2013). Authenticity and respect: Leading creative teams in the performing arts. *Creativity and Innovation Management*, *22*(3), 295–306.

Alvarez, J. L., Mazza, C., Pederson, J. S., & Svejenova, S. (2005). Shielding idiosyncrasy from isomorphic pressures: Towards optimal distinctiveness in European filmmaking. *Organization*, *12*(6), 863–888. https://doi.org/10.1177/1350508405057474

Alvarez, J. L., & Svejenova, S. (2005). *Sharing Executive Power: Roles and Relationships at the Top*. Cambridge University Press.

Andersson, F. O., & Renz, D. (2019). Who really governs and how: Considering the impact of the dominant coalition. *Nonprofit Quarterly, Fall*.

Antrobus, C. (2009). *Two heads are better than one: what art galleries and museums can learn from the joint leadership model in theatre*. NESTA Innovation Fellowship study at Clore Leadership London.

Auvinen, T. (2001). Why is it difficult to manage an opera house? The artistic-economic dichotomy and its manifestations in the organizational structures of five opera organizations. *Journal of Arts Management, Law and Society*, *30*(4), 268–282. https://doi.org/10.1080/10632920109597317

Bass, B. M. (1990). *Handbook of Leadership* (3rd ed.). Free Press.

Beard, A. (2012). *'No money, no mission' - Financial performance, leadership structure and budgeting in nonprofit and performing arts organizations*. Doctoral dissertation, New York University, New York.

Bendersky, C., & Hays, N. (2012). Status conflict in groups. *Organization Science*, *23*(2), 323–340. https://doi.org/10.1287/orsc.1110.0734.

Bhansing, P., Leenders, M., & Wijnberg, N. (2012). Performance effects of cognitive heterogeneity in dual leadership structures in the arts: The role of selection system orientations. *European Management Journal*, *30*(6), 523–534. https://doi.org/10.1016/j.emj.2012.04.002

Bhansing, P., Leenders, M., & Wijnberg, N. (2016). Selection system orientations as an explanation for the differences between dual leaders of the same organization in their perception of organizational performance. *Journal of Management & Governance*, *20*(4), 907–933. https://doi.org/10.1007/s10997-015-9330-4

Bolden, R. (2011). Distributed leadership in organizations: A review of theory and research. *International Journal of Management Reviews*, *13*(3), 251–269. https://doi.org/10.1111/j.1468-2370.2011.00306.x

Buchanan, D. A., Addicott, R., Fitzgerald, L., Ferlie, E., & Baeza, J. I. (2007). Nobody in charge: Distributed change agency in healthcare. *Human Relations*, *60*(7), 1065–1090. https://doi.org/10.1177/0018726707081158

Burns, J. M. (1978). *Leadership*. Harper & Row.

Carneiro, M. (2019). *How do dual executive leadership practices of theatre production companies around the world make decisions for their artistic and organizational wellbeing?*, Master's thesis. HEC Montréal, Montréal.

Castañer, X. (1997). The Tension between Artistic Leaders and Management in Arts Organizations: The Case of the Barcelona Symphony Orchestra. In M. Fitzgibbon & A. Kelly (Eds.), *From Maestro to Manager: Critical Issues in Arts and Culture Management (pp.* 379–416). Oak Tree Press.

Caust, J. (Ed.). (2013). *Arts Leadership - International Case Studies* (1st ed.). Tilde University Press.

Caust, J. (Ed.). (2015). *Arts and Cultural Leadership in Asia*. Routledge.

Cohen, M. D., & March, J. G. (1974). *Leadership and Ambiguity: The American College President* (2nd ed.). Harvard Business School Press.

Collinson, D. (2005). Dialectics of leadership. *Human Relations*, *58*(11), 1419–1442. https://doi.org/10.1177/0018726705060902

Cornforth, C. (Ed.). (2003). Conclusion: Contextualising and Managing the Paradoxes of Governance. *The Governance of Public and Non-profit Organisations: What Do Boards Do?* (pp. 237–253). Routledge.

Coule, T. M. (2015). Nonprofit governance and accountability: Broadening the theoretical perspective. *Nonprofit and Voluntary Sector Quarterly*, *44*(1), 75–97. https://doi.org/10.1177/0899764013503906

Cox, J. F., Pearce, C., & Perry, M. (2003). Toward a Model of Shared Leadership and Distributed Influence in the Innovation Process: How Shared Leadership Can Enhance New Product Development Team Dynamics and Effectiveness. In C. Pearce, & J. Conger (Eds.), *Shared Leadership: Reframing the How's and Why's of Leadership* (pp. 48–68). Sage.

Cray, D. & Inglis, L. (2011) Strategic Decision Making in Arts Organizations. *The Journal of Arts Management, Law, and Society*, *41*(2), 84–102. https://doi.org/10.1080/10632921.2011.573444

Cray, D., Inglis, L., & Freeman, S. (2007). Managing the arts: Leadership and decision making under dual rationalities. *Journal of Arts Management, Law and Society*, *36*(4), 295–313. https://doi.org/10.3200/JAML.36.4.295-314

Crevani, L., Lindgren, M., & Packendorff, J. (2007). Shared leadership: A post-heroic perspective on leadership as a collective construction. *International Journal of Leadership Studies*, *3*(1), 40–67.

Cullen-Lester, K., & Yammarino, F. (2016). Collective and network approaches to leadership: Special issue introduction. *The Leadership Quarterly*, *27*(2), 173–180. https://doi.org/10.1016/j.leaqua.2016.02.001

Currie, G., Lockett, A., & Suhomlinova, O. (2009). The institutionalization of distributed leadership: A 'Catch-22' in English public services. *Human Relations*, *62*(11), 1735–1761. https://doi.org/10.1177/0018726709346378

Cyert, R. M., & March, J. G. (1963). *A Behavioral Theory of the Firm*. Prentice-Hall.

D'Innozenso, L., Mathieu, J., & Kukenberger, M. (2016). A meta-analysis of different forms of shared leadership–team performance relations. *Journal of Management*, *42*(7), 1964–1991. https://doi.org/10.1177/0149206314525205

De Voogt, A. (2006). Dual leadership as a problem-solving tool in arts organizations. *International Journal of Arts Management*, *9*(1), 17–22.

De Voogt, A., & Hommes, K. (2007). The signature of leadership: Artistic freedom in shared leadership practice. *The John Ben Shepperd Journal of Practical Leadership*, *2*(1), 1–6.

Denis, J.-L., Langley, A., & Cazale, L. (1996). Leadership and strategic change under ambiguity. *Organization Studies*, *17*(4), 673–699. https://doi-org.proxy2.hec.ca/10.1177/017084069601700406

Denis, J.-L., Lamothe, L., & Langley, A. (2001). The dynamics of collective leadership and strategic change in pluralistic organizations. *The Academy of Management Journal*, *44*(4), 809–837. https://doi.org/10.2307/3069417

Denis, J.-L., Langley, A., & Rouleau, L. (2010). The practice of leadership in the messy world of organizations. *Leadership*, *6*(1), 67–88. https://doi.org/10.1177/1742715009354233

Denis, J.-L., Langley, A., & Sergi, V. (2012). Leadership in the plural. *The Academy of Management Annals*, *5*(1), 211–283. https://doi.org/10.1080/19416520.2012.667612

DeRue, D. S., & Ashford, S. J. (2010). Who will lead and who will follow? A social process of leadership identity construction in organizations. *Academy of Management Review*, 35(4), 627–647. https://doi.org/10.5465/amr.35.4.zok627

DeVereaux, C. (2020). Arts Management: Reflections on Role, Purpose, and the Complications of Existence. In W. J. Byrnes & A. Brkić (Eds.), *The Routledge Companion to Arts Management* (1st ed., pp. 12–22). Routledge.

Dionne, S., Gupta, A., Sotak, K., Shirreffs, K., Serban, A., Hao, C., Kim, D., & Yammarino, F. (2014). A 25-year perspective on levels of analysis in leadership research. *Leadership Quarterly*, *25*(1), 6–35. https://doi.org/10.1016/j.leaqua.2013.11.002

Döös, M., & Wilhelmson, L. (2021). Fifty-five years of managerial shared leadership research: A review of an empirical field. *Leadership*, *17*(6), 715–746. https://doi.org/10.1177/17427150211037809

Dragićević-Šešić, M., & Stefanović, M. (2017). Leadership styles and values: The case of independent cultural organizations. *Cultural Management: Science and Education*, *1*(1), 29–37. https://doi.org/10.30819/cmse.1-1.03

Dragićević Šešić, M. (2020). Contemporary Arts in Adaptable Quality Management: Questioning Entrepreneurialism as a Panacea in Europe. In W. J. Byrnes & A. Brkić (Eds.), *The Routledge Companion to Arts Management* (1st ed., pp. 39–54). Routledge. https://doi.org/10.4324/9781351030861

Durham, W. (1986). *American Theatre Companies, 1931-1986*. Greenwood Press.

Ebbers, J., & Wijnberg, N. (2017). Betwixt and between: Role conflict, role ambiguity and role definition in project-based dual-leadership structures. *Human Relations*, *70*(11), 1342–1365. https://doi.org/10.1177/0018726717692852

Empson, L. (2017). *Leading Professionals: Power, Politics, and Prima Donnas*. Oxford University Press.

Empson, L. (2020). Ambiguous authority and hidden hierarchy: Collective leadership in an elite professional service firm. *Leadership*, *16*(1), 62–86. https://doi.org/10.1177/1742715019886769

Empson, L., & Alvehus, J. (2020). Collective leadership dynamics among professional peers: Co-constructing an unstable equilibrium. *Organization Studies*, *41*(9), 1234–1256. https://doi.org/10.1177/0170840619844291

Fayol, H. (1949). *General and Industrial Management*. Isaac Pitman.

Fjellvær, H. (2010). *Dual and unitary leadership: managing ambiguity in pluralistic organizations* (Publication Number 2010/10). Doctoral dissertation, Norwegian School of Economics and Business Administration, Bergen. https://openaccess.nhh.no/nhh-xmlui/bitstream/handle/11250/164362/fjellver%20avh%202010.PDF?sequence=1

Fleming, P., & Spicer, A. (2014). Power in management and organization studies. *Academy of Management Annals*, *8*(1), 237–298. https://doi.org/10.1080/19416520.2014.875671

Follett, M. P. (1924). *Creative Experience*. Longmans Green.

Gibeau, É, Langley, A., Denis, J.-L., & van Schendel, N. (2020). Bridging competing demands through co-leadership? Potential and limitations. *Human Relations*, *73*(4), 464–489. https://doi.org/10.1177/0018726719888145

Gibeau, É, Reid, W., & Langley, A. (2016). Co-leadership: Contexts, Configurations and Conditions. In J. Storey, J. Hartley, J.-L. Denis, P. 't Hart, & D. Ulrich (Eds.), *Routledge Companion to Leadership* (pp. 225–240). Routledge.

Goodwin, K. (2020). Leadership reluctance in the Australian arts and cultural sector. *The Journal of Arts Management, Law, and Society, 50*(3), 169–183. https://doi.org/10.1080/10632921.2020.1739184

Gronn, P. (1999). Substituting for leadership: The neglected role of the leadership couple. *The Leadership Quarterly, 10*(1), 41–62. https://doi.org/10.1016/S1048-9843(99)80008-3

Gronn, P. (2002). Distributed leadership as a unit of analysis. *The Leadership Quarterly, 13*(4), 423–451. https://doi.org/10.1016/S1048-9843(02)00120-0

Gronn, P. (2016). Fit for purpose no more? *Management in Education, 30*(4), 168–172. https://doi.org/10.1177/0892020616665062.

Gronn, P., & Hamilton, A. (2004). 'A bit more life in the leadership': Co-principalship as distributed leadership practice. *Leadership and Policy in Schools, 3*(1), 3–35. https://doi.org/10.1076/lpos.3.1.3.27842

Heenan, D. A., & Bennis, W. G. (1999). *Co-leaders: The Power of Great Partnerships*. John Wiley & Sons.

Hewison, R., Holden, J., & Jones, S. (2013). Leadership and Transformation at the Royal Shakespeare Company. In J. Caust (Ed.), *Arts Leadership: International Case Studies,* (1st ed., pp. 141–160). Tilde University Press.

Hodgson, R. C., Levinson, D. J., & Zaleznik, A. (1965). *The Executive Role Constellation: An Analysis of Personality and Role Relations in Management.* Harvard University, Division of Research, Graduate School of Business Administration.

Hosking, D. M. (1988). Organizing, leadership and skilful process. *Journal of Management Studies, 25*(2), 147–166.

Järvinen, M., Ansio, H., & Houni, P. (2015). New variations of dual leadership: Insights from Finnish theatre. *International Journal of Arts Management, 17*(3), 16–27.

Jehn, K. A., & Mannix, E. A. (2001). The dynamic nature of conflict: A longitudinal study of intragroup conflict and group performance. *Academy of Management Journal, 44*(2), 238–251. https://doi.org/10.2307/3069453

Jensen, M., & Meckling, W. (1976). Theory of the firm - managerial behavior, agency costs and ownership structure. *Journal of Financial Economics, 3*(4), 305–360.

Katz, D., & Kahn, R. L. (1966). *The Social Psychology of Organizations.* Wiley.

Kleppe, B., & Røyseng, S. (2016). Sexual harassment in the Norwegian theatre world. *The Journal of Arts Management, Law, and Society, 46*(5), 282–296. https://doi.org/10.1080/10632921.2016.1231645

Krause, R., Priem, R., & Love, L. (2015). Who's in charge here? Co-CEOs, power gaps, and firm performance. *Strategic Management Journal, 36*(13), 2099–2110. https://doi.org/10.1002/smj.2325

Kuesters, I. (2010). Arts managers as liaisons between finance and art: A qualitative study inspired by the theory of functional differentiation. *The Journal of Arts Management, Law, and Society: Arts Management: A Sociological Inquiry, 40*(1), 43–57. https://doi.org/10.1080/10632921003603976

Lapierre, L. (2001). Leadership and arts management. *International Journal of Arts Management, 3*(3), 4–12.

Lavoie, D. (2021). Administrative director and director general, Montréal, Canada: Festival TransAmériques (FTA). Interview.

Lederman, M. (2018). When the #MeToo reckoning came for Canadian arts. The Globe and Mail.

Leithwood, K., Mascall, B., & Strauss, T. (Eds.). (2009). *Distributed Leadership According to the Evidence*. Routledge.

Lindgren, A. C. (2009). The National Ballet of Canada and the Kimberly Glasco legal arbitration case. *The Journal of Arts Management, Law, and Society, 39*(2), 101–116. https://doi.org/10.3200/JAML.39.2.101-116

Lindqvist, K. (2017). Leadership in Art and Business. In E. Raviola & P. Zackariasson (Eds.), *Arts and Business: Building a Common Ground for Understanding Society* (pp. 135–147). Routledge.

Locke, E. A. (2003). Leadership: Starting at the Top. In C. L. Pearce, & J. A. Conger (Eds.), *Shared Leadership: Reframing the Hows and Whys of Leadership* (pp. 271–284). Sage.

Löfgren, M. (2016). On the Public Value of Arts and Culture. In K. Dalborg, & M. Löfgren (Eds.), *The FIKA Project: Perspectives on Cultural Leadership* (pp. 75–99). Nätwerkstan Kultur.

London, T. (Ed.). (2013). *An Ideal Theater: Founding Visions for a New American Art*. Theatre Communications Group.

MacNeill, K., & Tonks, A. (2009). Co-leadership and gender in the performing arts. *Asia Pacific Journal of Arts and Cultural Management*, 6(1), 391–404.

MacNeill, K., & Tonks, A. (2013). Leadership in Australian Arts Companies: One Size Does Not Fit All. In J. Caust (Ed.), *Arts Leadership: International Case Studies* (1st ed., pp. 69–82). Tilde University Press.

MacNeill, K., Tonks, A., & Reynolds, S. (2013). Authenticity and the other: Co-leadership in arts organisations. *Journal of Leadership Studies*, 6(3), 6–16. https://doi.org/10.1002/jls.21252

Madhok, A. (1995). Revisiting multinational firm' tolerance for joint ventures: A trust-based approach. *Journal of International Business Studies*, 26(1), 117–137.

McAllister, D. J. (1995). Affect - and - cognition - based trust as foundations for interpersonal cooperation in organizations. *Academy of Management Journal, 38*(1), 24–59. https://doi.org/10.2307/256727

Merton, R. K. (1957). The role-set: Problems in sociological theory. *The British Journal of Sociology*, *8*(2), 106–120.

Meyerson, D., Weick, K., & Kramer, R. M. (1996). Swift Trust and Temporary Groups. In R. M. Kramer & T. R. Tyler (Eds.), *Trust in Organizations: Frontiers of Theory and Research*. Sage Publications.

Mintzberg, H. (1998). Covert leadership: Notes on managing professionals. *Harvard Business Review*, 1998 November–December, 140–147.

Möllering, G. (2006). *Trust: Reason, Routine, Reflexivity*. Elsevier.

Nisbett, M., & Walmsley, B. (2016). The romanticization of charismatic leadership in the arts. *The Journal of Arts Management, Law, and Society*, *46*(1), 2–12. https://doi.org/10.1080/10632921.2015.1131218

Offerman, L., & Scuderi, N. (2017). Sharing Leadership. In B. Shamir, R. Pillai, M. Bligh, & M. Uhl-Bien (Eds.), *Follower-centered Perspectives on Leadership: A Tribute to the Memory of James R. Meindl*. Information Age Publishing.

Ostrower, F. (2002). *Trustees of Culture: Power, Wealth, and Status on Elite Arts Boards*. University of Chicago Press.

Panctot, C., & Lusiani, M. (2021). Beyond dualism? Exploring the polyphonic dimension of cultural productions. *Journal of Arts Management, Law and Society*. https://doi.org/10.1080/10632921.2020.1851837

Pearce, C. (2004). The future of leadership: Combining vertical and shared leadership to transform knowledge work. *The Academy of Management Executive, 18*(1), 47–57. https://doi.org/10.5465/ame.2004.12690298

Pearce, C., & Conger, J. A. (2003). All Those Years Ago: The Historical Underpinnings of Shared Leadership. In C. Pearce, & A. Conger (Eds.), *Shared Leadership: Reframing the Hows and Whys of Leadership* (pp. 1–18). Wiley.

Quigg, A.-M. (2007). Bullying in theatres and arts centres in the United Kingdom. *International Journal of Arts Management, 10*(1), 52–64.

Radaelli, E. (2012). American Cultural Policy and the Rise of Arts Management Programs: The Creation of a New Professional Identity. In J. Paquette (Ed.), *Cultural Policy, Work and Identity: The Creation, Renewal and Negotiation of Professional Subjectivities (pp. 145-159).* Ashgate.

Raelin, J. A. (2011). From leadership-as-practice to leaderful practice. *Leadership,* 7(2), 195–211. https://doi.org/10.1177/1742715010394808

Rahim, M. A. (2002). Toward a theory of managing organizational conflict. *International Journal of Conflict Management, 13*(3), 206–235.

Reid, W., & Karambayya, R. (2009). Impact of dual executive leadership dynamics in creative organizations. *Human Relations, 62*(7), 1073–1112. https://doi.org/10.1177/0018726709335539

Reid, W., & Karambayya, R. (2016). The shadow of history: Situated dynamics of trust in dual executive leadership. *Leadership, 12*(5), 609–631. https://doi.org/10.1177/1742715015579931

René, V. V. (2018). *L'influence du sens de responsabilité sur la motivation de diriger: étude de la direction artistique.* Master's thesis, Montréal: HEC Montréal.

Reynolds, S., Tonks, A., & MacNeill, K. (2017). Collaborative leadership in the arts as a unique form of dual leadership. *The Journal of Arts Management, Law, and Society, 47*(2), 89–104. https://doi.org/10.1080/10632921.2016.1241968

Ropo, A., Sauer, E., & Salovaara, P. (2013). Embodiment of leadership through material place. *Leadership, 9*(3), 378–395. https://doi.org/10.1177/1742715013485858

Røyseng, S. (2008). Arts management and the autonomy of art. *International Journal of Cultural Policy, 14*(1), 37–48. https://doi.org/10.1080/10286630701856484

Ruiz-Gutiérrez, J., Grant, P., & Colbert, F. (2016). Arts management in developing countries: A Latin American perspective. *International Journal of Arts Management, 18*(Special Edition Latin America Spring 2016), 6–31.

Sally, D. (2002). Co-leadership: Lessons from Republican Rome. *California Management Review, 44*(4), 84–99. https://doi.org/10.2307/41166144

Sanchez, I. D., Ospina, S., & Salgado, E. (2020). Advancing constructionist leadership research through paradigm interplay: An application in the leadership-trust domain. *Leadership, 16*(6), 683–711. https://doi.org/10.1177/1742715020919226

Schrauwen, J., Schramme, A., & Segers, J. (2016). Do Managers Run Cultural Institutions? The Practice of Shared Leadership in the Arts Sector. In K. Dalborg, & M. Löfgren (Eds.), *The FIKA Project: Perspectives on Cultural Leadership* (pp. 103–116). Nätverkstan Kultur.

Sergi, V., Denis, J. L., & Langley, A. (2012). Opening up perspectives on plural leadership. *Industrial and Organizational Psychology, 5*(4), 403–407. https://doi.org/10.1111/j.1754-9434.2012.01468.x

Shamir, B., Pillai, R., Bligh, M., & Uhl-Bien, M. (Eds.). (2007). *Follower-centered Perspectives on Leadership: A Tribute to the Memory of James R. Meindl.* Information Age Publishing.

Snow, G. (2019). Rufus Norris and Lisa Burger to become joint chief executives of the National Theatre. The Stage.

Stewart, R. (1991a). Chairmen and chief executives: An exploration of their relationship. *The Journal of Management Studies*, *28*(5), 511–528.

Stewart, R. (1991b). Role Sharing at the Top: A Neglected Aspect of Studies of Managerial Behaviour. In S. Carlson, H. Mintzberg, & R. Stewart (Eds.), *Executive Behaviour* (pp. 120–136). Studia Oeconomiae Negotiorum.

Svejenova, S. (2006). How much does trust really matter? Some reflections on the significance and implications of Madhok's trust-based approach. *Journal of International Business Studies*, *37*(1), 12–20.

Svejenova, S., Vives, L., & Alvarez, J. L. (2010). At the crossroads of agency and communion: Defining the shared career. *Journal of Organizational Behavior*, *31*(5), 707–725. https://doi.org/10.1002/job.702

Thompson, J. D. (1967). *Organizations in Action. Social Sciences Bases of Administrative Theory*. McGraw Hill.

Timmermans, S., & Tavory, I. (2012). Theory construction in qualitative research: From grounded theory to abductive analysis. *Sociological Theory*, *30*(3), 167–186. https://doi.org/10.1177/0735275112457914

Tjosvold, D. (2006). Defining conflict and making choices about its management: Lighting the dark side of organizational life. *International Journal of Conflict Management*, *17*(2), 87–95. https://doi.org/10.1108/10444060610736585

Tremblay, M. (2014). *Configurations et pratiques du leadership pluriel au sommet de compagnies théâtrale québécoise*. Master's thesis, Université du Québec à Montréal, Montréal.

Tschmuck, P. (2006). The budgetary effects of 'Privatizing' major cultural Institutions in Austria. *The Journal of Arts Management, Law, and Society*, *35*(4), 293–304. https://doi.org/10.3200/JAML.35.4.293-304

Uhl-Bien, M. (2006). Relational leadership theory: Exploring the social processes of leadership and organizing. *The Leadership Quarterly*, *17*(6), 654–676. https://doi.org/10.1016/j.leaqua.2006.10.007

Uhl-Bien, M., & Ospina, S. (Eds.). (2012). *Advancing Relational Leadership Research: A Dialogue Among Perspectives* (Vol. 6). Information Age Publishing.

Upchurch, A. (2016). *The Origins of the Arts Council Movement: Philanthropy and Policy*. Palgrave Macmillan.

Vangen, S., & Huxham, C. (2003). Enacting leadership for collaborative advantage: Dilemmas of ideology and pragmatism in the activities of partnership managers. *British Journal of Management*, *14*(s1), S61–S76.

Voss, Z. G., Cable, D. M., & Voss, G. B. (2006). Organizational identity and firm performance: What happens when leaders disagree about 'Who we are?' *Organization Science*, *17*(6), 741–755. https://doi.org/10.1287/orsc.1060.0218

Willems, J., Andersson, F., Jegers, M., & Renz, D. (2017). A coalition perspective on nonprofit governance quality: Analyzing dimensions of influence in an exploratory comparative case analysis. *Voluntas* *28*(4), 1422–1447. https://doi.org/10.1007/s11266-016-9683-6

Wood, M. (2005). The fallacy of misplaced leadership. *Journal of Management Studies*, *42*(6), 1101–1121.

Yammarino, F., Salas, E., Serban, A., Shirreffs, K., & Shuffler, M. (2012). Collectivist leadership processes: Putting the 'we' in leadership science and practice. *Industrial and Organizational Psychology*, *5*(4), 382–402. https://doi.org/10.1111/j.1754-9434.2012.01467.x

4 Situating co-leadership in the arts globally

Introduction

Organizations and their leadership configurations vary in response to social and symbolic contextual influences (Denis et al., 2010). Given variations in the symbolic value of art in many societies, leadership in this sector differs globally. In our research for this book, we have discovered that co-leadership is well-established in the West, particularly in countries with Anglo-Saxon traditions as well as Northern Europe and Scandinavia (Bhansing et al., 2016; Järvinen et al., 2015; Reynolds et al., 2017). However, it is rarely found in many parts of the Global South despite suggestions in the plural leadership literature that co-leadership is widespread (Alvarez & Svejenova, 2005; Denis et al., 2012; Gibeau et al., 2016). Occasional examples are scattered, and its presence may be emerging beyond the West. Other leadership configurations in the arts include variations of single leadership as well as collectives. Hence, the global field reflects a hybrid perspective on leadership structures (Gronn, 2009, 2015).

This concentrated geographic distribution of co-leadership piqued our curiosity about the variety of executive leadership practices elsewhere in the arts. Some scholars in the arts have begun the conversation through case studies of leadership or in-depth research of leadership practice in specific regions (Caust, 2013, 2015; Dragićević Šešić & Stefanović, 2017). In this chapter, we expand beyond the West to undertake a more global analysis of international leadership practices in the arts and their organizational implications (Henze, 2021).

Scholars of plural leadership argue that co-leadership is pertinent in a professional context, where mission-oriented professionals and managers share the executive leadership role space (Denis et al., 2012). These executive relationships negotiate pluralism and competing logics typical of these professional organizations (Fjellvær, 2010; Gibeau et al., 2016). Cultural context plays a role in configuring pluralistic values and also how co-leadership is shaped. So, we investigate the contextual specifics to understand the global practice of executive leadership in the arts.

DOI: 10.4324/9780429504259-5

To do this, we consulted the literature and spoke with over 25 scholars, experts, and senior managers around the world (see Table 4.1 at end of chapter). Four explanatory themes shape our observations providing relevant illustrations in the global context. Later in this chapter, we explore organizational influences on arts co-leadership variations, resulting in three ideal types. This typology normalizes the different means of arts co-leadership development found in the literature to date.

The sectoral context for this book is non-profit or civil society arts as well as public and government organizations. We have excluded the commercial and for-profit cultural industries, but as Alvarez and Svejenova (2005) explain, co-leadership is also quite present in this sector.

Expert observers offered us an understanding of leadership configurations in their region and their assessment of influences on practice (Table 4.1). We studied research that highlight cases situated outside of Western Europe and the Anglo-Saxon tradition (Carneiro, 2019; Caust, 2013, 2015; Rånlund et al., 2016; Ross, 2017; Ruiz-Gutiérrez et al., 2016). We sought out historical accounts of the arts (Dizikes, 1993; Durham, 1986; London, 2013) and regionally focused explanations of the history of arts management training (Radaelli, 2012; Şuteu, 2006). Instructional texts also offered regional perceptions of optimal executive leadership practices in the arts (Bonet Agustí & Schargorodsky, 2018; Dragićević Šešić & Dragojević, 2005; Evrard, 2004; Montanari, 2018; Radbourne & Fraser, 1996; Stein & Bathurst, 2008).

Of course, there are two comprehensive references about leadership in general, using social values studied by national context (Hofstede, 1983; House et al., 2004). These are substantial global studies about leadership in general, but the role of co-leadership in such research is not considered. We have chosen, instead, to focus our research on factors that weigh significantly within the arts management field and that link with institutional logics theory (Thornton et al., 2012).

We organize our discussion in this chapter as follows:

The first section covers four contextual influences on arts leadership structures around the world that we have identified. These influences reflect important societal and field-level logics related to the arts.

- The role of art and artists in society,
- The presence of formal cultural policy and funding,
- An appreciation of arts management training,
- Institutionalized art discipline practices.

The first three influences vary geographically. The fourth pertains to specific art disciplines and does not change appreciably across regional cultures.

In the second section, we contribute the ideal-type typology of co-leadership according to two axes: Size, from small organizations to large institutions, and external funding dynamics, from private to public.

- Sharing responsibilities and work in start-ups,
- Formally dividing the roles among themselves,
- Mandating the roles from above.

Exploring the contextual influences

The role of art and artists in society

An artist is a key player in the executive leadership configuration because artists are the professionals central to the mission of the organization. However, the particular position that the artist occupies in the leadership configuration appears influenced by societal priorities about artistic expression around the world.

A study commissioned by the United Nations in 2013 articulates the link between artistic expression and the democratic principles of freedom of speech (Shaheed, 2013). This report found that artistic creation, production, and dissemination have been censored, licensed, and restrained for political, religious, and economic reasons in numerous contexts. Policies in other regions support the inclusion of art in the right to liberty of expression: The First Amendment of the US Constitution (1791) and the European Convention of Human Rights (2012). Article 10, in the latter, designates artistic expression as a priority. Recently, this principle was extended to protect artistic expression on the internet (Andel et al., 2020).

Variations in freedom of artistic expression are reflected in different leadership configurations. Vertically shaped co-leadership can prioritize either an artistic director (AD) or an executive director (ED). As well, an individual charismatic and politically engaged artist-entrepreneur or a work-sharing collective can ensure security of expression in threatening political environments. Finally, a seemingly equal AD-ED co-leadership can address artistic autonomy.

Vertical co-leadership

To begin with contrasting examples, we compare vertical co-leadership configurations in France and China. France is a historically important democracy in the modern world where the arts are a hallmark of international leadership, including art experimentation and social criticism (Chiapello, 2004). As independent legal entities, national cultural institutions are typically led by an artist appointed by the Minister of Culture or even by the President of the Republic (Jocelyn, Table 4.1). In this context, appointing an artist as the senior executive leader suggests a high respect for artists' ability to fulfil and inspire the organization's mission and manage the demands of institutional leadership (Chiapello, 2004; Jocelyn, Table 4.1).

In contrast, since the declaration of the People's Republic of China in 1949, communism has been the political system in Chinese society. An "independent watchdog" organization based in the US rates China very poorly regarding freedom of expression (Freedom House, 2021). Reports suggest that China's artists are increasingly called upon to reflect the country's socialist political culture and Chinese values (Ramzy, 2014). Artistic autonomy and an artist's right to critique do not appear to be a priority. Arts institutions are part of the government, and the single executive "head" of the organization is a government employee and the administrative manager for the organization (Liu, Table 4.1).

In each situation, a second individual is appointed to support the primary leader. In France, the AD typically chooses an administrative colleague in a reporting relationship (Jocelyn, Table 4.1). In China, the government also appoints the AD, but this person reports to the managerial head (Liu, Table 4.1). Furthermore, in China, the government appoints a Communist Party observer as a guide to ensure that artistic production reflects government policy. The relative status of the AD in each of these executive leadership configurations appears to reflect contrasting priorities about artistic expression.

Single leadership

Strong solo leadership in arts organizations has been noted in some regions with hierarchical and controlling political leadership. One expert suggested that a history of political and military dictatorships in Latin America modelled a single leadership culture (Bonet Agustí, Table 4.1), realizing one-on-one hierarchical connections with government authorities. In the arts, political navigation to ensure organizational sustainability was privileged over artistic autonomy and expression, seen as threatening to the regime in power.

With a different history, Brazilian artistic institutions also function with a single leadership structure. They were founded in the early 19th century when the Portuguese royal court was displaced from Lisbon to Rio de Janeiro where an aristocratic authority prevailed (Baiocchi, Table 4.1). Subsequently, the country was declared an independent democratic empire, but a hierarchical and, recently, a managerial mindset within single leadership has predominated. MBA graduates may hold positions as single-leader arts CEOs. Artistic and music leaders are credited just below the CEO in organizational lists of personnel.

Serbia has experienced significantly contested political dynamics in the late 20th century. Charismatic single leaders have proved useful for galvanizing followers, giving voice to new ideas and political opposition (Dragićević Šešić & Stefanović, 2017).

In India, charismatic artistic leadership appears to have parallels with the guru culture of the classical arts (Ross, Table 4.1) and the artistic heritage of Rabindranath Tagore and the teachings of political and philosophical leaders like Mahatma Gandhi. Our experts noted that a vast number and variety of small and entrepreneurial contemporary arts organizations are led by single artistic leaders with important ideas (Rao, Table 4.1; Ross, Table 4.1). These entrepreneurial organizations typically operate with a culture of trust, surrounded by family and friends for support. While there is little societal recognition of the symbolic value of contemporary art current in India (British Council, 2020), the economic value of film production in the region is well-recognized and promoted (Kamineni & Rentschler, 2021; Rao, Table 4.1).

Collectives

Collectives reflect democratic values and objectives, so they may provide protection from controlling interventions like arduous licensing procedures and censorship found in high-control political contexts. While collectives contrast with charismatic leaders noted above, both approaches appeared successful in the struggle for legitimacy and recognition in politically charged contexts.

Contemporary theatre in Chile originated with artist collectives embedded in universities. The protection offered by this academic environment enabled them to express their social and political criticisms through art during the authoritarian military regime of the 1970s and 1980s (Lopez Rodriguez, 2016). Collectives are also a feature of artistic organizations in South-East Asia (Janamohanan et al., 2021) where authoritarian governments have and still do exist. Similarly, in Serbia, art collectives have provided leadership in community-based political and social change movements (Dragićević Šešić & Stefanović, 2017).

Artistic autonomy and co-leadership

Co-leadership presents a conundrum regarding artistic autonomy and freedom of expression despite its predominance in largely democratic countries. Such a leadership configuration introduces managerial values into the organizational culture (Beirne & Knight, 2002; Røyseng, 2008). In the UN study on artistic expression, Shaheed (2013) indicates that the power of corporate sponsorship and pressures to increase audiences may act as a constraint on freedom of artistic expression. In some regions in Northern Europe, this problem is addressed by legislating or designating the AD as having the ultimate decision-making power regarding artistic creation and programming (Austrian Federal Republic, 1999).

In Britain, where co-leadership is increasingly practiced (Carreiro, Table 4.1; Morland, Table 4.1), the CEO role designates greater power within the co-leadership. This allocation varies, sometimes added to the AD title, at other times related to the ED, and occasionally added to both roles (Dickson, 2018; Snow, 2019). As well, the ADs photo is featured on UK websites, but in North America, both the AD and the ED are featured. In Australia, an informal practice has been observed where an ED offers their resignation upon the arrival of a new AD. This gesture ensures the ADs freedom to choose a collaborative managerial partner, suggesting a more supportive, and perhaps informally subordinate, role for the ED (Reynolds et al., 2017). It could also be a reticence in the leadership culture by the ED to continue to take charge (Goodwin, 2020).

Like Britain, boards of directors in Québec often formally attribute two roles held by the co-leaders – either AD or administrative director and then co-CEO (co-director general). This recognizes the individual expertise and responsibilities of each leader as well as the joint role that they develop together (Lavoie, Table 4.1).

While symphony orchestras appoint both an AD (music director) and ED or CEO who are equally responsible for the organization, ADs are often absent as they travel to guest conducting contracts and other leadership roles. They are typically contracted for 12–15 weeks in the year despite their ongoing presence on season brochures and other organizational materials. The regular presence of the ED or, increasingly, CEO provides a platform for a more significant executive role with the board as well as the community. The informal equality of the co-leadership is quite contested in practice (Bennett, Table 4.1).

Executive leadership configurations in the arts vary, seemingly in conjunction with socially held values of art and freedom of expression. In the next discussion, we explore a related theme regarding cultural policy and funding structure for the arts.

The presence of cultural policy and funding

In this section, we outline three different ecosystems for public funding of the arts: Arts councils, direct funding, and limited funding. We link these to leadership configuration practices.

Arts council funding

The Anglo-Saxon arts council form of public funding is notable for the arm's-length principle, which establishes autonomy from the political process for funding recipients. Funding allocations are recommended by juries of artistic peers (Upchurch, 2016). This autonomy sets up boards of directors as the formal and independent governance authority for the organization. Hence, the decisions about configuration and personnel for executive leadership are normally made by an organization's board of directors rather than by the government. American and Canadian arts organizations have a long-established tradition of co-leadership anchored in the market and funder accountability needs (Peterson, 1986). Co-leadership is a manifestation of artistic autonomy and differentiation. In these regions, a significant portion of organizational budgets depends on market-based income. This requires financial risks to be managed. Employing knowledgeable artistic and managerial specialists makes co-leadership a practical choice for these boards (Chapter 8). Organizations in Britain and Australia-New Zealand adopted the co-leadership practice somewhat later, as market and funding accountability influences grew (Alexander, 2018).

Direct funding

In European examples, direct and significant government funding of independent arts institutions typically involves public regulations or funding agreements that mandate the configuration of executive leadership (Austrian Federal Republic, 1999; Fjellvær, 2010). Executives may be hired by the board of directors or a committee designated by the government. Co-leadership has been well-established and legitimized in German-speaking and Scandinavian countries as a risk management mechanism (Abfalter, Table 4.1). However, as we mentioned, ADs are given the right of final decisions about artistic programs (Abfalter, Table 4.1; Fjellvær, 2010). As well, in German-speaking countries, the "intendant" is the AD of major institutions that often include theatre, opera, dance, and, sometimes, symphony orchestras. A commercial or managing director is typically appointed alongside this executive artistic leader. But the intendant has significant symbolic and political power (Konrad, Table 4.1; Schmidt, 2016) and often has greater practical power as a result of flexibility gained through employment regulations (Heskia, 2021).

In South Korea and Southern Europe (Italy, Spain, and Portugal), major arts institutions were part of the government, but in certain countries, they have recently been made independent entities (Carneiro, Table 4.1; Park, Table 4.1; Zan et al., 2012). Single artists are appointed by the government to lead most of these institutions. In Italy, the senior artistic leader is typically accompanied by a lawyer as the managerial executive (Donelli, Table 4.1). Their professional skills enable them to navigate particularly bureaucratic environments. However, in Portugal, co-leadership is found in publicly funded municipal theatres, some privately funded theatres, as well as smaller dance and transdisciplinary companies with positive results (Carneiro, Table 4.1). In Spain, the practice of co-leadership is varied, but there is no overview study of the practice of leadership structures. Some publicly owned theatres are under government administration, and others are publicly owned but privately managed. Co-leadership is found in a number of important public theatres and festivals (Swayne Obregón, Table 4.1).

In Russia and South-East Europe (SEE), extensive government funding generated a pervasive bureaucratic political culture, and single charismatic arts leadership grew in response (Cameron & Lapierre, 2013; Dragićević Šešić, 2013). However, over the last ten years, the rise of authoritarianism in many of these countries has resulted in dismissal or silencing of these arts leaders to demonstrate loyalty to the regime (Dragićević Šešić, Table 4.1). Historically, in the former Yugoslavia, the socialist tradition of self-management and governance often resulted in co-leadership. The government would appoint the director for an independent arts organization, but internal self-management processes would also produce a leader of the employees. This person would be recommended and appointed as a co-leader with the government appointee (Jakovljević, 2016). Despite its success, this self-management system was viewed as inefficient and has been discouraged by advocates of the new public management movement (NPM) since the return to peace after the Yugoslav wars. Consequently, single leadership has been observed (Dragićević-Šešić, Table 4.1).

Limited cultural policy and funding

The absence of systematic and reliable government cultural policies and funding can generate instability and may limit resources in such regions as India, Africa, South-East Asia, and Latin America. Cultural policies and government funding that would lead to accountability, and potentially to co-leadership configurations, remain unstructured and limited (Rao, Table 4.1; Ruiz-Gutierrez, Table 4.1; Janamohanan, Table 4.1; Darkwa Asare, Table 4.1). Single leaders or collectives appear to predominate.

Independent civil society arts organizations in these regions depend on a variety of private funding sources, frequently private international funding, and different types of earned revenue, sometimes unrelated to their mission. As well, ticket revenue is not reliable, constraining them to small operating budgets (Janamohanan et al., 2021; Rao, Table 4.1; Ruiz-Gutiérrez, Table 4.1). In India, single founding leaders function as artistic entrepreneurs by attracting the moral and financial support of a strong network of trusting friends and family in lieu of external boards of directors (Rao, Table 4.1; Ross, 2017). However, the loss or retirement of these strong but solo leaders typically leads to the closure of the organization (Ross, 2017).

In many countries in Africa, there is one major cultural centre that is affiliated with or part of the government. These institutions typically have a single leader who is appointed politically (Darkwa Asare, Table 4.1). Within the institution, artists lead each disciplinary unit. In Ghana, the current director of the national cultural centre was trained in arts management in the US at the University of Minnesota. Outside of these national institutions, art is largely produced on a project-by-project basis by an entrepreneurial individual working as a volunteer. The revenue from performing is distributed among the participating artists (Darkwa Asare, Table 4.1). In South Africa, arts management is more developed, with an arts council in place, but cultural institutions appear to function with single CEOs.

In India, South-East Asia, and Africa, support from international diplomacy organizations like the British Council and international development foundations is important (Abou al Aazm, Table 4.1; Dhanwani & Shetty, 2019; Janowicz-Panjaitan & Noorderhaven, 2009; Rao, Table 4.1). These remotely based funders have their own mandates and investment criteria, but their support is much appreciated (Janamohanan et al., 2021). Their distance allows grant recipients more artistic autonomy from legitimizing conformity and reduced accountability reports that would be required by a local government funder (Peterson, 1986). This flexibility permits artists to respond to specific environmental conditions and their own objectives for leadership structure. Leadership structures are quite variable.

Few South-East Asian (SEA) countries have national cultural policies or related government structuring or funding. Different organizational forms operate with volunteers or partially paid employees. Sometimes funded by an artist's family, small organizations are unable to afford the addition of a managerial co-leader (Janamohanan et al., 2021). Ironically, in both Austria and Québec, Canada, smaller organizations have also questioned the affordability of co-leadership (Abfalter, Table 4.1) despite the substantial funding system for larger organizations in each of these environments. Artists in start-up organizations with little access to the public funding system collectively evolve their own managerial capacity.

In summary, identifying three different funding contexts reveals different patterns of leadership configurations. Each funding system changes provisions for organizational governance, artistic resources, and dominant logics that influence the structure of leadership. In a context of little government funding, practice is very entrepreneurial and individual, with personal relationships supporting the project-based work. Direct government funding appears to have encouraged single leadership or has structured as co-leadership, where a type of top management team includes an AD. Arts councils enable agency for governance and leadership choices in each organization although institutionalized logics inspire conforming practices.

The application and value of arts management training

Arts management training demystifies the application of management in the sector, demonstrating how it has a separate role and function in art-producing organizations (Peterson, 1986; Radaelli, 2012). Its presence as an institutional logic in both the field and within arts organizations encourages the inclusion of managerial roles particularly at the executive leadership level of these organizations. Tracing the development of arts management training programs in the following section provides insights about its influence on leadership practice and structures in specific regions.

Post-World War II with the development of arts funding in North America and in Europe, concerns arose regarding organizational stability of arts and efficiency. It was felt that an understanding of arts management and its training would solve these problems. Hence, the Rockefeller Foundation and other major US foundations, UNESCO, and the Council of Europe played active and early roles in the creation of training programs, the development of network associations, and the funding of research chairs (Peterson, 1986; Radaelli, 2012; Şuteu, 2006). As well, NPM shaped thinking about generating more efficient arts funding and management practice in Europe (Hood, 1991). Co-leadership has been practiced extensively in many of the regions targeted by these private and public funders. This pre-occupation by funders provides the co-leadership structure with much legitimization.

Today's US arts organizations continue to depend on a combination of earned revenue and private funding (Caust, 2018; Laughlin, 2019) and while European arts organizations are substantially funded by the government, their environment has grown increasingly complex as they become independent of government. The field requires sophisticated organizational capacity, suggesting the strategic need for managerial training alongside professional artistic training (Dragićević Šešić & Dragojević, 2005; Şuteu, 2006).

Early arts management programs in the US began in prestigious universities like Harvard and Yale in the late 1960s. The Association of Arts Administration Educators (AAAE) was founded in 1975, and in 2021 included 95 member programs largely based in the US and Canada. Co-leadership by an AD and ED has become institutionalized as a common practice in North America. EDs in major American performing arts organizations frequently list business or arts management degrees as part of their experience. The Canadian Association of Arts Administration Educators (CAAAE) was founded including 12 members across the country in 2021 with the objective of sharing information.

In Europe, the first program in sectoral management was launched in 1960, in Belgrade, Serbia (Dragićević Šešić, 2009). The dean of the Faculty of Arts, Vjikoslav Afrić, wanted students in theatre and film to benefit from production and management training to accompany their projects. The program continues today. City University in London and Paris-Dauphine (Paris VIII) in France founded their programs respectively in 1971 and the late 1980s (Şuteu, 2006). Founded in 1988, the European network on cultural management and policy (ENCATC) is supported by UNESCO with 151 members in April 2021. The network functions in partnership with the European Union, UNESCO and is an observer to the Council of Europe. These programs support the establishment of separate management and leadership roles in arts organizations throughout the region. While this recognition occurred later in Europe than in the US (Røyseng, 2008), co-leadership exists in the northern regions and in a few organizations in Southern Europe. Vertical co-leadership also calls on this training when the artistic leadership has a secondary role in the organization. This is rarely found in Northern Europe and Britain.

ENCATC is both international and European, but German-speaking countries within Europe have established their own but similar association called Association for Cultural Management (*Fachverband Kulturmanagement e.V.*) with 80 members that include both institutions and individuals (Abfalter, Table 4.1). Co-leadership is common in these countries (Abfalter, Table 4.1; Heskia, Table 4.1; Schmidt, Table 4.1) but requires business managers to possess adept political skills for organizational impact.

In China, arts institutions are structured with a vertical leadership configuration with artistic leadership roles separated from managerial roles that are more senior, organizationally. As a result, a need for people who have management training was created in China's arts ecosystem, and specific training in arts management training began in the early millennium.

The Chinese government has recognized that developing creative industries' organizational capacities can stimulate economic growth that comes with creative industry development. Consequently, since 2016, it has been accrediting university programs: 34 programs with an arts management major and another 63 with a cultural industry management major – with significant growth expected through to 2035. There are two associations to support networking among these management training programs: The China Arts Administration Education Association (CAAAEA) and the China Arts Management Professional Committee (Zhang, Table 4.1).

Another support group is evolving among South-East Asian (SEA) countries to support leadership and organizational development in arts organizations in the region. Founded in 2011, ANCER is an open network anchored in Singapore but linking to institutional representatives from the other countries in the region. ANCER is initiating shared knowledge and developing links with the emerging arts management programs in the region. A recent UNESCO study of nine countries reveals a large number of very small and recently established arts organizations in the region (Janamohanan et al., 2021) with informal and limited managerial functions. In countries like Cambodia, there remains little civic infrastructure after a period of destructive control by a genocidal regime and foreign invasion during the 1970s and 1980s. Artistic founders and volunteers share production tasks, but a separate organizational role for managers has not yet been recognized (Janamohanan et al., 2021). Some consulting scholars suggest innovating partnerships between NGOs and local citizens as the country reconstructs itself, thus pushing the solutions beyond institutions in the public and private spheres (Čopič & Dragićević Šešić, 2018). Organizational development of the arts remains difficult to predict, and management training in many SEA countries needs to be sensitive and locally appropriate.

In Taiwan, another network has been founded with an initial meeting in November 2018, coordinated by the Taiwan Association of Cultural Policy Studies and affiliated with the National Taiwan University of the Arts in Panchiao, New Taipei City. Like ANCER, in SEA, the intention of the Taiwan association is to develop a conversation about management and organizational practice and cultural policy among different cultural actors in the country. We have little insight into the leadership practices and structures in Taiwan, but the emergence of this organization reflects a field concern in that regard.

India and Brazil are both regions where scholars and consultants report limited availability of management training to support the large ecosystem of arts organizations (Baiocchi, Table 4.1; Costa, 2018; Dhanwani & Shetty, 2019). Arts management training is in a very nascent stage in India (Rao, Table 4.1; Ross, 2017) and is limited or quite recent in Latin America (Costa, 2018; Ponte, 2021; Ruiz-Gutiérrez et al., 2016). As we have seen in India and in Latin America, many arts organizations are led by single charismatic artistic leaders and large arts institutions are led by managerial leaders. For more sophisticated arts management development, reflection on training and practice will make a difference.

Commissioned studies, workshops, and consulting projects in India, subsidized by the British Council in partnership with European universities, are expanding an awareness of the value of arts management training to stabilize organizations (Dhanwani & Shetty, 2019). As well, capacity building in Indian theatre has been undertaken with Serbian consultants who have developed knowledge on how to manage minimally resourced organizations led by socially and politically engaged artists (Dragićević Šešić, 2014). Pressure for arts management training has recently increased because of the global pandemic and the resulting fragility of the sector (British Council, 2020). In India, management roles and careers are found in the larger and more commercial cultural industries. Similar management jobs and career paths do not exist in the NGO arts sector (Rao, Table 4.1). As a result, it is rare for entrepreneurial artists in NGOs to separate the roles and partner with trained management professionals. Only two cases of co-leadership have been documented in India (Carneiro, 2019; Khorshed, 2015).

In certain countries in SEE, local arts management training is well-established (Dragićević Šešić, 2009). However, due to economic and political turbulence in the late 20th century, this context requires perspectives, priorities, and processes that differ from a Western view of the role of arts management (Dragićević Šešić & Dragojević, 2005). Managerial leadership roles in major arts institutions are perceived as bureaucratic links to government. They have abandoned the earlier collective approach to management from the socialist era in the 1960s through to the 1980s. Smaller civil society organizations function more organically (Dragićević Šešić & Stefanović, 2017), sometimes with single leaders and others as collectives. Despite the changes, the arts management training has been very important for the role that these organizations play in this society.

The utility of separating training in management from art and liberal arts for future arts leaders is debated (Şuteu, 2006). In Europe, professional artistic training programs have begun to include management as part of the curriculum, suggesting the possibility that artists can combine both artistic and managerial roles as leaders (Abfalter, Table 4.1; Järvinen et al., 2015). In contrast, many American arts management training programs assume a concurrent or prior artistic training, even in undergraduate programs. While there is still a preference for field experience among US organizational managers, there is a growing appreciation for MBA or arts management training (Rhine & Pension, 2021). In fact, some ADs in major performing companies have diplomas in arts management (MacNeill & Tonks, 2013). Hence, the separation of art and management is not always needed or appropriate, depending on the region, stakeholder involvement, and the vision for the place of management in an arts organization.

Finally, research also reveals that graduates of arts management programs display little diversity, calling on leaders of these programs to sensitize students about diversity, equity, and inclusion. Reflecting the larger population in the region (Cuyler et al., 2019) strengthens the legitimacy of the leadership in arts organizations.

To summarize this first part of the chapter, we have illustrated three environmental influences on co-leadership practice – the role of art in society, the presence of cultural policy and funding, and the appreciation of arts management research and training. These are the themes that seem to vary arts leadership configurations around the world. We have also identified several types of executive leadership configurations that range from a charismatic solo leader through vertical or horizontal co-leadership to collectives. Our report on these international variations is tentative and needs further research. But this initial effort enriches the understanding on co-leadership practice within the plural leadership literature. The traditional focus on co-leadership is anchored in the West. However, a fourth understanding of leadership configurations cuts across regional views, defining the structure by discipline.

Institutionalized art discipline practices

There are two disciplines where a single executive leader heads up the organization regardless of regional influences: Visual art (museums and art galleries) and large opera companies. These are typically large institutions where the single executive leader reports to the board or government and a functionally diverse management team reports to this executive leader. This leader may also have some experience in and training about organizations and management. However, in the discussion that follows, we also note several exceptions to the solo leader model in North America.

Museums and art galleries

Art museums and non-profit galleries typically have facilities and collections to maintain and operate. Some are part of the government, particularly in Europe, but increasingly, they have become independent government agencies (Tschmuck, 2006). Generally, they are better resourced than companies in the performing arts in order to support an art collection. While important exhibitions often attract significant attendance, their ticket revenue is a smaller proportion of their overall budget than in the performing arts (Ingram, Table 4.1; McCaffery, Table 4.1).

In most of these large institutions, a single leader is the ultimate executive authority reporting to the board or government ministry. However, below this single director, responsibilities are divided and typically assigned to artistic and administrative specialists. This leadership configuration is similar to a top management team in the private sector where decisions are ultimately made or endorsed by the organizational leader in consultation with functional specialists (Hambrick & Mason, 1984). In contrast to an equal-status co-leadership configuration, this single executive leadership structure may reduce the extent of internal negotiation necessary over resource allocation.

In our interviews, experts justified how a single-director configuration prevails in museums (Ingram, Table 4.1; McCaffery, Table 4.1). They argue that since performing ADs are involved in the creation and performance activities of their organizations, they need managing partners to ensure that the executive leadership responsibilities are fulfilled. Museum directors are less involved in the artistic production of the organization and have the resources to hire specialists to support their leadership. Even smaller galleries maintain the single leader tradition.

Despite these explanations, observers have questioned whether single art museum directors really can balance the different imperatives (Antrobus, 2009; Donnelly, 2010), proposing that co-leadership and the necessary collaboration may also be useful in museums. As Denis et al. (2001) suggest, in the hospital field, managing extremely complex institutions requires plural solutions. While the museum world has largely resisted the co-leadership configuration, some notable exceptions stand out: The Metropolitan Museum of Art in New York (President and CEO, and Director) and The Philadelphia Museum (Director and CEO and President and COO) and briefly, the Museum of Modern Art in Los Angeles (Gelt, 2021). In Canada, the Museum of Contemporary Art in Toronto also had dual executives for a short period (McCaffery, Table 4.1). In Europe, at Vienna's Kunsthalle, a trio of women called WHW (a Marxist reference to What? How? And for Whom?) has become collective curatorial directors of the contemporary arts presentation venue (Bailey, 2020). Finally, Tate Liverpool and Tate St-Ives were led by co-leaders from 2006 or 2007 to 2018 (Antrobus, Table 4.1), but the structure was abandoned as a cost-saving strategy with the arrival of a new CEO of the Tate overall in 2017. However, recently, Birmingham Museums, a collection of several museums in Birmingham, England, appointed two individuals in a shared CEO position. Finally, early in the millennium, in two museums in the Netherlands (the Stedelijk Museum and the Bojimans Van Beuningen Museum), co-leadership appeared briefly as a solution to financial issues (De Voogt, 2006). Despite these examples, single-leader CEO-led museums in the US, Canada, and Britain are well-institutionalized. There is little evidence of co-leadership in most other regions in our research.

Opera

European opera has a long tradition of impresario leaders who mounted individual productions or privately owned companies that frequently toured in North America (Dizikes, 1993; Peterson, 1986). This tradition of a single producing leadership appears to have been transplanted and institutionalized in large opera companies in North America (Corrigan, Table 4.1). In these North American companies, a general director is typically the sole executive reporting to the board. While very often this individual has artistic training and experience, they lead with their management training and skills in response to the financial risk related to the audience imperative at the box office (Corrigan, Table 4.1). North American public funding is not as munificent as in Europe. As in museums, these single leaders have a top management team of functional specialists leading the organization's activities. This team typically includes a music director AD who functions like a chief curator in museums working at a slightly more senior level than others in the team. On the other hand, smaller companies in North America have adopted co-leadership, following decisions by their boards of directors.

Opera institutions in Europe have retained a tradition of "intendants" as the primary artistic leader of a multi-disciplinary institution. Websites indicate that some intendants have management training as well as their artistic credentials. These institutions are generally larger than their North American analogue, attracting significant public funding, reducing box office pressures, and prioritizing the intendant as the ultimate executive leader. The ADs of the individual resident disciplines are also important leaders in the organization. A managing or commercial director works with and for the intendant (Auvinen, 2001; Konrad,

Table 4.1). Intendants are exceptionally powerful and managing directors need to develop their relationship with their colleagues to ensure that their contributions to decisions are respected (Heskia, Table 4.1; Konrad, Table 4.1, Schmidt, Table 4.1). Boards of directors seem less powerful in major institutions in Europe, particularly in German-speaking countries (Heskia, 2021).

Hence, while executive leadership structures vary globally, we found two disciplines that were institutionally linked to single leadership regardless of their location. We next focus exclusively on co-leadership to understand different organizational contexts for this configuration.

Conceptualizing variations of co-leadership practice: Developing a typology

Much co-leadership research takes place in large professional institutions like hospitals, schools, universities, and international professional service firms (Chapter 3) (Döös & Wilhelmson, 2021; Pancot & Lusiani, 2021) as well as large business corporations (Alvarez & Svejenova, 2005; Arnone & Stumpf, 2010; Heenan & Bennis, 1999). But, while the practice is well-established in larger arts organizations and institutions in the West, researchers have also published international stories of co-leadership dynamics in small, entrepreneurial, and project-based artistic organizations (Järvinen et al., 2015; Leung & Tung, 2015; Pancot & Lusiani, 2021; Rånlund et al., 2016). We discovered early evidence of the practice in US resident theatres founded before World War II (Durham, 1986; London, 2013), despite claims by Peterson (1986) that it began in the late 1960s in response to accountability for arts council funding (Kleppe, 2018).

To structure our sense of the practice from our reading and consultations, and to consolidate our global findings, in Figure 4.1, we developed a typology of arts co-leadership practice according to two dimensions: Funding and organization size. For funding, there is a continuum of sources from public, to a hybrid of public and private, to mainly private in the US (Laughlin, 2019). For organizations, we consider the difference between institutional and entrepreneurial types, largely related to size. The typology reflects a behavioural perspective of executive co-leadership (Järvinen et al., 2015; Tremblay, 2014), contrasting an emergent or bottom-up approach with a top-down mandated configuration. Despite this, the larger and more established the organization becomes, the more co-leadership has symbolic and practical importance.

The typology in Figure 4.1 normalizes and contextualizes variations in practice that scholars have previously identified as being new or exceptional (Järvinen et al., 2015; Reynolds et al., 2017). It also demonstrates a variety of practical responses to organizational needs, especially in start-ups. The typology reveals the value of co-leadership, where a partnering

Large and well-established institution

Independent

Private funding or Arm's-length public funding: Arts council with some private funding

Large non-profit with major donors and foundations AD involved in fundraising with CEO-ED (US)	Large non-profit with hybrid funding-some public funding at arm's length AD involved in fundraising with ED	Government department or mandated agency with direct funding Regulations for executive structure or government employees
Medium-sized non-profit privately funded AD involved in some fundraising	Medium-sized non-profit but mixed funding at arm's length AD exclusively involved in art	Medium organization with large proportion government funding AD exclusively involved in art
Small entrepreneurships Private funding Share the work informally	Entrepreneurial Some government funding at arm's length (Anglo-Saxon tradition) Share the work with some structure	Independent and entrepreneurial with public funding Structured with two or three executives Civil society (non-profit)

Direct and extensive public funding

Small and-or young entrepreneurship

Figure 4.1 Typology of co-leadership by organization size and funding context.

manager protects the autonomy of the artistic leader, and realization of their artistic vision effectively (Alvarez et al., 2005). This view of co-leadership as a strategic partnership counteracts the criticism that co-leadership imposes traditional managerial thinking on artists (Beirne & Knight, 2002; Macdonnell & Bereson, 2019). However, experts explained how a mandated approach to co-leadership is motivated by risk management – the "four eyes" principle that may be constraining (Abfalter, Table 4.1).

There are three ideal types that appear in Figure 4.1. The first type involves a collegial approach to the work that emerges in artistic start-ups. Sharing jobs and filling in gaps prevail. This mode of functioning may continue well after the founding of the organization, depending on funding. A second type occurs because of structural change within the organization, following events such as leadership succession, major artistic and marketing success, or new funding. Organizations appear to formalize the leadership configuration with titles and perhaps job descriptions that are typically negotiated within a founders' group or the current leadership group. There may be a board of directors, probably including the founders, but the key actors make the decision themselves. Funding may still be informal and unpredictable (Leung & Tung, 2015; London, 2013; Rånlund et al., 2016).

The third type is found in medium to large, institutionalized situations with an established board and formalized and ongoing funding (Reid & Karambayya, 2009; Tschmuck, 2006). The leadership configuration and choice of personnel are typically mandated by the board or the funder who appoints a selection committee. While an evolution from the entrepreneurial status to institution might appear as a natural progression, changes in leadership structures have rarely been documented (Reid & Karambayya, 2016). Normally the case or the research focuses on one type of configuration.

In the following discussion, we illustrate these different types of co-leadership with examples from around the world.

Sharing responsibilities and work in start-ups

Creator-led and founded companies in dance and theatre are a significant component of the arts community (Recaman & Colbert, 2016). The creators may seek out managerial partners early in the development of their company. But, for other organizations in the arts, the start-up activities often involve several people (London, 2013; Tremblay, 2014), many of them artists (Järvinen et al., 2015). According to accounts, the founders may share a common background at a school or previous professional work experience (Blasko, 2016; Carneiro, 2019; Järvinen et al., 2015). They may have different talents, interests, and craft skills. The following examples illustrate how entrepreneurial collaborators with complementary expertise founded artistic companies.

The celebrated choreographer and dancer, Akram Khan, worked with Farooq Chaudhry from early days of his company in London, England. According to the company's website, Chaudhry had been a successful dancer and newly trained as an arts manager when he met Khan in 1999 in the foyer of the Queen Elizabeth Hall in London. These entrepreneurial co-leaders are reported to have shared a deep knowledge of the art of dance and a desire to collaborate on a new language for dance. Equally motivated, they created the Akram Khan Company one year later (Akram Khan Company, 2022). Currently called Executive Producer, Chaudhry facilitated Khan's successful creation and early performing career in dance-theatre inspired by Kathak, the traditional classical dance form of his cultural community originating in Pakistan and India.

Tremblay (2014) researched eight theatre companies in Montréal, Canada, founded by groups of two to six artists and production artisans. She studied the practices used to combine tasks and roles, discovering how the members of the companies use ambiguity to manage tensions and potential conflict. Each company has a common vision of their art, identifies tasks related to the production of the art, and shares the management of producing art, often on an ad hoc basis.

London (2013) assembled historic documents produced by important pioneers in the regional theatre movement in the US. These documents reveal how entrepreneurial theatre artists partnered with donors and investors to finance their projects, largely with private share capital. Acquiring and managing this financial support required the founding artists to partner with producers who were often close friends or life partners. Several examples are noteworthy. Provincetown Players was founded by a group of artists in the 1920s. The key leaders who emerged were George Cram Cook, an economist and his partner, Susan Glaspell, a playwright. This was an important platform for launching Eugene O'Neill's early career with productions developed both in Cape Cod and New York. Arena Stage was founded in Washington, DC, in 1950 by AD Zelda Fichandler, initially with a volunteer partner, her husband, the economist, Thomas Fichandler. The organization became a non-profit in 1959. Mr Fichandler filled the role of ED for twenty years. In the late 1930s, actor and director, Orson Welles and John Houseman, producer, met through a production of Shakespeare's Macbeth, later developing Project 891, the classical theatre unit in the Federal Theatre Project in New York. In 1937, they founded the Mercury Theater, and their tempestuous professional partnership developed several successful Broadway productions and radio broadcasts, particularly "War of the Worlds" in 1938. Their theatrical partnership was short-lived, but legendary.

These new arts ventures illustrate a common theme. Each artistic entrepreneur benefitted from complementary and empathetic expertise to share the organizational development of the initial vision. Informality predominated and leadership was emergent. Some organizations were founded as collectives, but leadership was assumed as a result of individual expertise and often in collaboration with another key member of the organization. Sharing the work was accomplished informally and sometimes ambiguously, responding to the needs and vision of the moment. Most administrative partners in this early stage were not "EDs", but producers who managed logistics and money to realize the artists' ideas. Spontaneity may be practical for a time but may eventually stop functioning.

Formally dividing the roles from within the organization

In this second type of arts co-leadership, the separation of executive roles occurs consciously and somewhat analytically as people recognize that the roles involve different types of work and experience. The decision to formally designate responsibilities is made within the organization. Roles evolve, relying on specialized skills and aptitudes, but with some residual overlap. Job descriptions and contracts that establish greater structure at the executive level may be part of this process.

A collective of seven circus artists, Les 7 doigts de la main, came to this realization. Quite early in their development, they were confronted with the management of costs and logistics for their first tour. They concluded that they needed someone apart from themselves to play a role as ED and to manage the business of their organization, starting with someone related to a member of the troupe. They later accepted an offer from Nassib El-Husseini to become their President-ED. In this structured partnership with the co-ADs, he has enabled them to undertake extensive touring, significant international partnerships, financial stability, and a purpose-built facility in Montréal (Leroux-Côté, 2015).

Another example comes from Rabat, in Morocco, North Africa. The theatre company "Dabateatr" was founded in 2004 by Jaouad Essouanni with the goal of becoming a leading institution to express a national theatrical style and ideas as well as to employ local professionals, trained at the national school. As the second employee of the company, Selwa Abou el Aazm was hired by the founder to develop the administrative side of the company with him. Two years later she accepted the offer to become ED in a formal co-leadership. She stayed a further three years in that role. The company grew to seven people and organizational structuring occurred. However, after five years of working together, limited resources and impatience to achieve the ideal wore down the relationship. A new ED was needed. The company continues to operate with a co-leadership configuration (Abou al Aazm, Table 4.1).

Finally, a pair of theatre artists in India founded their company "Indian Ensemble". After some time together, they realized that they needed to upgrade a project manager to an ED role to satisfy several organizational needs: Support of touring, organizing training affiliated with the company, and fundraising. Without a board, the co-ADs assumed the responsibility for leadership succession from one generation of artists to another and the ED supported the transition (Carneiro, 2019, Table 4.1).

In all cases in this section, formalizing roles typically emanate from incumbent AD(s). The company has either been founded by a solo artist or a group of artists, or an AD has been functioning alone for several years. The AD(s) chose to promote internally or to bring in someone that they knew to help realize their organizational ambitions. In the three examples, a board did not exist to confirm the separation of roles. However, in other situations, a board may be added, or the existing board may become more formal by partnering with the ED in a more fiduciary role. In this fashion, the governance dynamic becomes more ordered and formal, and it grows into a mandating responsibility, as we see in the following section.

Mandating the roles

In the settings examined in the previous sections, executive co-leaders choose each other to accomplish the work of producing art. The relationships and configurations may be informal and ambiguous or formalized, in clearly defined separate roles. However, in larger and more established organizations, continuity, stability, and risk management become important governance issues. Consequently, boards of directors or government funders mandate the specialized and separate co-leadership roles to balance and manage these issues. In these organizations, mandated co-leadership becomes a governance mechanism.

In Reid's (2007) original research in Canada, boards made decisions to re-configure leadership. In four of eight arts organizations, they decided to change from a single artist as executive leader to a co-leadership arrangement. Governance control became important to them in situations where the financial dynamics of the organization had become risky (Chapter 8). These boards hired an ED to report to them and to partner with the founding or long-time AD who continued reporting to them. Board decisions were made independently, responding to specific organizational needs. However, they also appeared to be aware of an institutionalized practice of co-leadership in the field.

> We looked around at what a lot of other organizations were doing and said that seems to make sense. We just knew that when we were going to become that much bigger, that it would be way too much to ask of one man, or one woman.
>
> Board president

In three other cases, despite some history of co-leader conflict, boards chose to continue the practice, reflecting their perception of the governance and legitimizing the value of the co-leadership configuration. These cases are situated in North America financed by a mixture of private and arts council funding.

In many northern European countries, the executive co-leadership configuration is decided by the government while boards often recommend the choice of individuals who fill the co-leadership roles. Co-leadership has been a common practice in the arts for some time in the German-speaking countries (Abfalter, Table 4.1). This institutionalized practice was attractive for public funders, concerned about efficiency and stability. In the late 1990s and early 2000s, throughout Europe, arts organizations were moved from within the government and given independent status, often governed by boards of directors (Heskia, 2021; Tschmuck, 2006; Zan et al., 2012). The change was underpinned by the NPM reform philosophy, which has since become an institutionalized logic (Hood, 1991). The approach intends to render government and public organizations more efficient, managerial, and market oriented. While these artistic institutions are organizationally independent, they still receive extensive funding directly from their relevant Ministries or Departments of Culture and other public funders, ensuring resource dependence on several levels of government.

In Germany and Austria, the leadership and board structure are determined by government legislation or regulation and in Scandinavia, by letters of agreement for each arts organization (Austrian Federal Republic, 1999; Fjellvær, 2010; Tschmuck, 2006). Like in Anglo-Saxon traditions, the boards of these organizations are mandated by the government to oversee the organization's financial stability and fulfilment of the mission. However, in Austria, boards would be involved in the recruitment and appointment of leadership candidates but do not have the choice of executive configuration.

Regardless of many funders' concerns for managerial competence, artistic expertise and creative voice are important considerations in public and private sector funding that reflects the legitimizing influence of the artistic imperative (Nisbett & Walmsley, 2016; Ostrower, 2002) (Chapter 2). In recognition of and to protect this priority in Europe, public governance mandates often establish that the AD has the last word on programming and artistic ideas (Tschmuck, 2006). However, this practice can contribute to co-leadership tensions about budgeting and financial results that can ultimately impact artistic well-being (Beirne & Knight, 2002; Fjellvær, 2010).

Another governance concern about art's pre-eminence that might be addressed by co-leadership has become more public since the #MeToo Movement in 2017. Scholars have documented the influence of the romantic artistic imperative, generating an attitude of entitlement and abuse of power by artistic leaders in Britain (Quigg, 2007), Norway (Kleppe & Røyseng, 2016), Germany (Schmidt, 2016), and Canada (Lindgren, 2009) (Chapter 2). Arts boards, in addition to fiscal responsibilities, have been newly confronted with human resource and ethical issues, in their relationship with executive leaders (Lederman, 2018). In the past, the support of an artistic ideal and vision may have taken precedence over governance concerns about executive leadership behaviour (Lindgren, 2009). An ED may choose to be loyal to their AD to ensure collaboration (Goodwin, 2020; Reynolds et al., 2017), but co-leaders are also being called on to assess the impact of ethical behaviours on organizational reputation and stability, their relationship with boards, and with each other. In certain jurisdictions, managing this behaviour has legal implications for everyone at the executive and board level.

We have portrayed three ideal types of co-leadership, first synthesized in Figure 4.1. The first two suggest either an informal or formal collegial sharing of expertise to ensure that the production of artistic work is achieved. The third involves mandating the co-leadership for the purposes of governance risk management undertaken by boards or funders. In Anglo-Saxon regions, in more established organizations, it is more likely that boards are involved in the configuration decision. As Peterson (1986) has observed, the formal differentiation of the two logics of art and management inherent in co-leadership configurations have been institutionalized in these regions. In Europe, NPM logic has been an equally institutionalizing force (Hood, 1991).

Conclusion: Environments for single and co-leadership

Our polling of experts about co-leadership worldwide reveals that it is not universal in the arts. Observers of co-leadership suggest that logic integration is a key organizational reason for co-leadership in pluralistic organizations. We found that social values and logics also create the institutionalized executive leadership practice dominant in a region. As well, the practice of co-leadership occurs in different types of organizations and varies by organizational size and funding context. Our analysis demonstrates that one practice does not fit all. Following this initial effort to map leadership practices, we encourage colleagues to become sensitized to cultural differences in further research on arts leadership structure.

Single leadership is a more institutionalized practice, and scholars have traditionally focused on this approach. It is not surprising to find that single leadership in the arts is common in parts of the world or specific disciplines. However, for the purposes of artistic autonomy and differentiation, there are good reasons to separate the professional leadership on the art side from the managerial functions of the organization. But not all contexts are conducive to or supportive of co-leadership. Understanding of leadership needs to evolve and debate will be useful.

Dispersed examples of co-leadership around the world might be an indication that interest is evolving by artists who wish to partner with supportive and developmental colleagues. A collaborative culture may ensue. But the practice's institutionalized status may also be a reason for its presence. Cultural policy, funding, and arts management training are increasingly present internationally, perhaps influencing co-leadership adoption. Hence, understanding its dynamics and strategic potential becomes important. Our research addresses standard practices found in certain parts of the world, and this chapter has put those practices into regional perspective. We hope it will extend horizons and possibilities for scholars, managers, and governance authorities.

Table 4.1 International experts and their key insights

Dagmar Abfalter (interview, 2019 and 2022) Universität für Musik und darstellende Kunst, Vienna, Austria *The "four-eyes" principle – risk management.*
Selwa Abou el Aazm (interview, 2019) Cultural worker, Montréal, Canada *Significant leadership role in founding of a national theatre in Morocco.*
Claire Antrobus (interview, 2022) Coach, facilitator, trainer, and consultant *Collaboration possibilities in co-leadership are beneficial for museums.*
Alessandra Baiocchi (interview, 2021) Escola de negocios PUC-Rio, Brazil *Historical and current perspective on arts leadership in Brazil. Well-established organizations with single leader and top management teams that include the AD.*
Andrew Bennett (interview, 2019) Cultural worker, Ontario, Canada, and formerly Britain and Portugal *Symphony orchestras are different as performing organizations. The CEO is always present and more influential, organizationally.*
Luis Bonet Agustí (interview, 2019) Universidad de Barcelona, Spain *Influence of military dictatorships in Latin America has led to single leadership in the arts. More control.*
Maria Carneiro (interview, 2019 and 2022) Teatro da Trindade Inatel, Lisbon, Portugal (newly, Teatromosca) *Co-leadership created a more open and supportive culture.*
Assis Carreiro (information exchange, 2019) Agent in dance, Britain *Co-leadership is growing in Britain, but each organization has its history.*
Patrick Corrigan (interview, 2021) General Director, Opéra de Montréal, Canada *History of impresario in opera leads to single leadership, but with senior AD.*
Amos Darkwa Asare (interview, 2021) University of Cape Coast, Ghana *Arts practice is entrepreneurial with little organizational structure outside of National Theatres.*
Chiara Carolina Donelli (interview, 2021) University of Parma, Italy *Since institutional independence from the government, single leader with an accompanying lawyer in response to bureaucratic culture.*

(Continued)

Table 4.1 International experts and their key insights *(Continued)*

Milena Dragićević Šešić (interview, 2022) Faculty of Dramatic Arts, University of Arts in Belgrade *Arts leadership and management in crisis and political dictatorships require particular and unconventional perspectives. A socialist tradition of self-governance in former Yugoslavia shaped the emergence of co-leadership.*
Thomas Heskia (interview, 2021) Leuphana University, Germany *Commercial director has less formal power and needs to navigate carefully and politically.*
Sharilyn Ingram (interview, 2019) Executive cultural worker in museum sector, Canada *Museum directors are single leaders working with more resources and a top management team. Museum directors are not involved in art creation compared to most performing ADs.*
Sunitha Janamohanan (interview, 2021) LASALLE College of the Arts, Singapore *As former British colony, Singapore has established arts organizations, but other SEA countries have informal and variable organizational structures. Young sector. Collectives are notable.*
Matthew Jocelyn (interview, 2021) Cultural worker and artistic director, France and Canada *In France, an artist as an executive leader is valued and recognized as being capable as a manager.*
David Lavoie (information exchange, 2021) Festival TransAmériques (FTA), Montréal, Canada *Job descriptions recognize differences between a co-CEO role and an artistic director and administrative director roles.*
Suzie Jiazin Liu (interview. 2021) University of South Australia *In China, an executive manager is appointed first by the government with an artist as second. Then a guide is appointed to ensure adherence to government policies.*
Elmar Konrad (interview, 2021) Hochschule Mainz, Germany *Intendants are extremely powerful in major cultural institutions (opera, theatre, dance, and music). They have other senior managers around them in each discipline.*
Moira McCaffery (interview, 2019) (Formerly) Canadian Art Museum Directors' Organization *Co-leadership is rarely seen in museums with some notable exceptions.*
Rebecca Morland (information exchange, 2019) Cultural worker in theatre, Britain *Co-leadership in the performing arts is growing in Britain, and how it works is being revealed in the press.*

(Continued)

Table 4.1 International experts and their key insights *(Continued)*

Shin-Eui Park (information exchange, 2019) Kyun Hee University, South Korea *In South Korea, there is a vertical co-leadership structure with an artist appointed and then a government manager hired by the government.*
Dipti Rao (interview, 2019) The Art X Company, India *No arts management training and orientation in independent NGO arts community in India. Entrepreneurial artistic leaders, rarely with independent boards. Rare examples of co-leadership. Vast and very diverse country.*
Ina Ross (interview, 2019) Saar University of Fine Arts, Germany *In India, high degree of diversity and variety of practice. Charismatic individual founder is reliant on family and friends for support and funding.*
Jaime Ruiz-Gutiérrez (interview in 2019) Universidad de los Andes, Colombia *Very little arts management training and many arts organizations are social enterprises.*
Ulrike Schmidt (interview, 2020) (Formerly) Hamburg Ballett, Germany *Need to be very agile personally and politically to sustain the relationship with the AD and manage from below.*
Tania Swayne Obregón (information exchange, 2022) FAETEDA (Federation of Associations of Performing Arts Companies – Spain) *Some presence of co-leadership but variable, often related to being a public organization or part of the government. Very little consolidated information.*
Beili Zhang (information exchange, 2021) Tianjin Conservatory of Music, China *Government recognition of arts and cultural management training to support extensive sectorial growth through the next decade or two.*

References

Akram Khan Company (2022). Retrieved April 9, 2022 from https://www.akramkhancompany.net/about-us/

Alexander, V. D. (2018). Heteronomy in the arts field: State funding and British arts organizations. *British Journal of Sociology*, *69*(1), 23–43. https://doi.org/10.1111/1468-4446.12283

Alvarez, J. L., Mazza, C., Pederson, J. S., & Svejenova, S. (2005). Shielding idiosyncrasy from isomorphic pressures: Towards optimal distinctiveness in European filmmaking. *Organization*, *12*(6), 863–888. https://doi.org/10.1177/1350508405057474

Alvarez, J. L., & Svejenova, S. (2005). *Sharing Executive Power: Roles and Relationships at the Top*. Cambridge University Press.

Andel, J., Francesco, G. D., Krasznahorkai, K., DeVlieg, M. A., & Whyatt, S. (supported by Levan Kharatishvili). (2020). *Manifesto on the Freedom of Expression of Arts and Culture in the Digital Era: For the Council of Europe in the framework of the 70th anniversary of the European convention on human rights*. Retrieved August 13 2022 from https://rm.coe.int/manifesto-on-the-freedom-of-expression-of-arts-and-culture-in-the-digi/1680a056a2

Antrobus, C. (2009). *Two heads are better than one: what art galleries and museums can learn from the joint leadership model in theatre*. NESTA Innovation Fellow study at Clore Leadership, London.

Arnone, M., & Stumpf, S. A. (2010). Shared leadership: From rivals to co-CEOs. *Strategy & Leadership*, *38*(2), 15–21. https://doi.org/10.1108/10878571011029019

Austrian Federal Republic (1999). *Bundestheaterorganisationsgesetz* – representation of the companies. Retrieved August 15, 2022 from https://www.ris.bka.gv.at/GeltendeFassung.wxe?Abfrage=Bundesnormen&Gesetzesnummer=10010085

Auvinen, T. (2001). Why is it difficult to manage an opera house? The artistic-economic dichotomy and its manifestations in the organizational structures of five opera organizations. *Journal of Arts Management, Law and Society*, *30*(4), 268–282. https://doi.org/10.1080/10632920109597317

Bailey, M. (2020). Are three heads better than one? How to run a museum as a collective. *The Art Newspaper*. Retrieved February 20, 2022 from https://www.theartnewspaper.com/news/new-direction-for-vienna-s-kunsthalle

Beirne, M., & Knight, S. (2002). Principles and consistent management in the arts: Lessons from British theatre. *International Journal of Cultural Policy*, *8*(1), 75–89. https://doi.org/10.1080/10286630290032459

Bhansing, P., Leenders, M., & Wijnberg, N. (2016). Selection system orientations as an explanation for the differences between dual leaders of the same organization in their perception of organizational performance. *Journal of Management & Governance*, *20*(4), 907–933. https://doi.org/10.1007/s10997-015-9330-4

Blasko, R. (2016). Stanica and New Synagogue, Zilina, Slovakia. In S. Ranlund, K. Dalborg, & M. Löfgren (Eds.), *Narratives by Cultural Change Makers*. (pp. 124–136). Nätversktan Kultur.

Bonet Agustí, L., & Schargorodsky, H. (2018). *Theatre Management: Models and Strategies for Cultural Venues*. Knowledge Works. National Centre for Cultural Industries.

British Council (2020). *Taking the temperature report 2: The deepening impact of COVID 19 on India's creative economy*. Federation of Indian Chambers of Commerce and Industry (FICCI) and the Art X Company.

Cameron, S., & Lapierre, L. (2013). Mikhail Piotrovsky and the State Hermitage Museum. In J. Caust (Ed.), *Arts Leadership: International Case Studies* (1st ed., pp. 3–18). Tilde University Press.

Carneiro, M. (2019). *How do dual executive leadership practices of theatre production companies around the world make decisions for their artistic and organizational wellbeing?* Master's thesis, HEC Montréal.

Caust, J. (Ed.). (2013). *Arts Leadership - International Case Studies* (1st ed.). Tilde University Press.

Caust, J. (Ed.). (2015). *Arts and Cultural Leadership in Asia*. Routledge.

Caust, J. (2018). *Arts Leadership in Contemporary Contexts* (1st ed.). Routledge.

Chiapello, È. (2004). Evolution and co-optation: The 'artist critique' of management and capitalism. *Third Text*, *18*(6), 585–594. https://doi.org/10.1080/0952882042000284998

Čopič, V., & Dragićević Šešić, M. (2018). Challenges of public-civic partnership in Cambodia's cultural policy development. *ENCATC Journal of Cultural Management & Policy*, *8*(1), 4–15.

Costa, L. F. (2018). Training for cultural production and management in Brazil. *The Journal of Arts Management, Law, and Society*, *48*(1), 70–79. https://doi.org/10.1080/10632921.2017.1366378

Cuyler, A., Durrer, V., & Nisbett, M. (2019). Steadfastly white, female, hetero and able-bodied: An international survey on the motivations and experiences of arts management graduates. *International Journal of Arts Management*, 22(3), 5–16.

De Voogt, A. (2006). Dual leadership as a problem-solving tool in arts organizations. *International Journal of Arts Management*, *9*(1), 17–22.

Denis, J.-L., Lamothe, L., & Langley, A. (2001). The dynamics of collective leadership and strategic change in pluralistic organizations. *The Academy of Management Journal*, 44(4), 809–837. https://doi.org/10.2307/3069417

Denis, J.-L., Langley, A., & Rouleau, L. (2010). The practice of leadership in the messy world of organizations. *Leadership*, *6*(1), 67–88. https://doi.org/10.1177/1742715009354233

Denis, J.-L., Langley, A., & Sergi, V. (2012). Leadership in the plural. *The Academy of Management Annals*, *5*(1), 211–283. https://doi.org/10.1080/19416520.2012.667612

Dhanwani, R., & Shetty, S. (2019). *Arts Management in India: A first-of-its-kind study addressing challenges in formal education for arts management in India*. SDA Bocconi Asia Center, Mumbai, and The Art X Company.

Dickson, A. (2018). 'Don't screw it up!' Artistic directors on the perils of regime change. *The Guardian*.

Dizikes, J. (1993). *Opera in America, A Cultural History*. Yale University Press.

Donnelly, J. A. (2010). The CEO art museum director: Business as usual? *Transatlantica: Revue d'études Américaines. American Studies Journal*, 2(The Businessman as Artist). https://doi.org/10.4000/transatlantica.5044

Döös, M., & Wilhelmson, L. (2021). Fifty-five years of managerial shared leadership research: A review of an empirical field. *Leadership*, 17(6), 715–745. https://doi.org/10.1177/17427150211037809

Dragićević Šešić, M. (2009). Educational Programs in Strategic Cultural Management within the Regional Context. *Cultural Policy and Management Yearbook (KPY)*, 1, 99–107.

Dragićević Šešić, M. (2013). The Leadership Style of Mira Trailovic: An Entrepreneurial Spirit in a Bureaucratic World. In J. Caust (Ed.), *Arts Leadership; International Case Studies* (1st ed., pp. 19–34). Tilde University Press.

Dragićević Šešić, M. (2014). Diary from India: Meeting with remarkable women. *Blog: Mediantrop, Regionalni casopis media i kulturu*. Retrieved October 14, 2021 from https://www.mediantrop.rankomunitic.org/milena-dragicevic-sesic-diary-from-india-meeting-with-remarkable-women.

Dragićević Šešić, M., & Dragojević, S. (2005). *Arts Management in Turbulent Times - Adaptable Quality Management: Navigating the Arts through the Winds of Change*. Boekmanstudies.

Dragićević Šešić, M., & Stefanović, M. (2017). Leadership styles and values: The case of independent cultural organizations. *Cultural Management: Science and Education*, *1*(1), 29–37. https://doi.org/10.30819/cmse.1-1.03

Durham, W. (1986). *American Theatre Companies, 1931–1986*. Greenwood Press.

Evrard, Y. (Ed.). (2004). *Le Management des Entreprises Artistiques et Culturelles* (2e éd). Economica.

Fjellvær, H. (2010). *Dual and unitary leadership: managing ambiguity in pluralistic organizations* (Publication Number 2010/10). Doctoral dissertation, Norwegian School of Economics and Business Administration, Bergen. https://openaccess.nhh.no/nhh-xmlui/bitstream/handle/11250/164362/fjellver%20avh%202010.PDF?sequence=1

Freedom House (2021). *Global Freedom Scores*. Freedom House. Retrieved August 13, 2022 from https://freedomhouse.org/.

Gelt, J. (2021). Well, that didn't last long. Klaus Biesenbach is out at MOCA, days after new hire. *Los Angeles Times*.

Gibeau, É, Reid, W., & Langley, A. (2016). Co-leadership: Contexts, Configurations and Conditions. In J. Storey, J. Hartley, J.-L. Denis, P. 't Hart, & D. Ulrich (Eds.), *Routledge Companion to Leadership* (pp. 225–240). Routledge.

Goodwin, K. (2020). Leadership reluctance in the Australian arts and cultural sector. *The Journal of Arts Management, Law, and Society*, *50*(3), 169–183. https://doi.org/10.1080/10632921.2020.1739184

Gronn, P. (2009). Leadership configurations. *Leadership*, *5*(3), 381–394. https://doi.org/10.1177/1742715009337770

Gronn, P. (2015). The view from inside leadership configurations. *Human Relations*, *68*(4), 545–560. https://doi.org/10.1177/0018726714563811

Hambrick, D. C., & Mason, P. (1984). Upper echelons: The organization as a reflection of its top managers. *Academy of Management Review*, *9*(2), 193–206.

Heenan, D. A., & Bennis, W. G. (1999). *Co-leaders: The Power of Great Partnerships*. John Wiley & Sons.

Henze, R. (2021). Thinking Cultural Management from the South: New Frames for the 'Western' Discourse Informed by Latin America. In R. Raphaela Henze & F. Escribal (Eds.), *Cultural Management and Policy in Latin America* (pp. 3–21). Routledge.

Heskia, T. (2021). Public boards; Questions of representation in supervisory boards of German, Austrian and Swiss theatres. *International Journal of Arts Management*, *24*(1), 32–47.

Hofstede, G. (1983). National cultures in four dimensions: A research-based theory of cultural differences among nations. *International Studies of Management & Organization*, *XIII*(1–2), 46–74.

Hood, C. (1991). A public management for all seasons? *Public Administration*, *69*, 3–19.

House, R. J., Hanges, P. J., Javidan, M., Dorfman, P. W., & Gupta, V. (Eds.). (2004). *Culture, Leadership, and Organizations: The Global Leadership and Organizational Effectiveness (GLOBE) Study of 62 Societies*. Sage Publications.

Jakovljević, B. (2016). *Alienation Effects: Performance and Self-management in Yugoslavia, 1945–91*. University of Michigan Press.

Janamohanan, S., Sasaki, S., & Wong Wai Yen, A. (2021). *Managing Creativity and the Arts in South-East Asia*. UNESCO, Paris & Bangkok.

Janowicz-Panjaitan, M. K., & Noorderhaven, N. G. (2009). Trust, calculation and interorganizational learning of tacit knowledge: An organizational roles perspective. *Organization Studies*, *30*(10), 1021–1044. https://doi.org/10.1177/0170840609337933

Järvinen, M., Ansio, H., & Houni, P. (2015). New variations of dual leadership: Insights from Finnish theatre. *International Journal of Arts Management*, *17*(3), 16–27.

Kamineni, R., & Rentschler, R. (2021). *Indian Movie Entrepreneurship: Not Just Song and Dance*. Routledge.

Khorshed, A. (2015). A New Concept of Organizational Structure and Leadership Practice at Bishaud Bangla in Chittagong. In J. Caust (Ed.), *Arts and Cultural Leadership in Asia* (pp. 86–92). Routledge.

Kleppe, B. (2018). Managing autonomy: Analyzing arts management and artistic autonomy through the theory of justification. *Journal of Arts Management, Law, and Society*, *48*(3), 191–205. https://doi.org/10.1080/10632921.2017.1377661

Kleppe, B., & Røyseng, S. (2016). Sexual harassment in the Norwegian theatre world. *The Journal of Arts Management, Law, and Society*, *46*(5), 282–296. https://doi.org/10.1080/10632921.2016.1231645

Laughlin, S. (2019). USA. In I. King, & A. Schramme (Eds.), *Cultural Governance in a Global Context: An International Perspective on Art Organizations* (pp. 267–300). Palgrave MacMillan.

Lederman, M. (2018). When the #MeToo reckoning came for Canadian arts. *The Globe and Mail*.

Leroux-Côté, J. (2015). *Les 7 doigts de la main: Un collectif qui repousse les frontières. Projet d'intégration*. HEC Montréal, Montréal.

Leung, C. C., & Tung, K. Y. (2015). Dual Roles: Collaborative Leadership in a Newly Developed Music Ensemble: A Case Study from Hong Kong. In J. Caust (Ed.), *Arts and Cultural Leadership in Asia* (pp. 105–120). Routledge.

Lindgren, A. C. (2009). The National Ballet of Canada and the Kimberly Glasco legal arbitration case. *The Journal of Arts Management, Law, and Society*, *39*(2), 101–116. https://doi.org/10.3200/JAML.39.2.101-116

London, T. (Ed.). (2013). *An Ideal Theater: Founding Visions for a New American Art*. Theatre Communications Group.

Lopez Rodriguez, P. (2016). Management practices in theater: A diagnosis of Chilean independent companies and their operating models. *International Journal of Arts Management*, *18*(3 – special issue), 173–182.

Macdonnell, J., & Bereson, R. (2019). Arts Management and Its Contradictions. In W. J. Byrnes, & A. Brkić (Eds.), *The Routledge Companion to Arts Management* (1st ed., p. 1–11).. Routledge.

MacNeill, K., & Tonks, A. (2013). Leadership in Australian Arts Companies: One Size Does Not Fit All. In J. Caust (Ed.), *Arts Leadership: International Case Studies* (1st ed., pp. 69–82). Tilde University Press.

Montanari, F. (2018). Organizational Design and People Management. In P. Dubini, F. Montanari, & A. Cirrincioni (Eds.), *Management of Cultural Firms* (pp. 257–289). Bocconi University Press.

Nisbett, M., & Walmsley, B. (2016). The romanticization of charismatic leadership in the arts. *The Journal of Arts Management, Law, and Society*, *46*(1), 2–12. https://doi.org/10.1080/10632921.2015.1131218

Ostrower, F. (2002). *Trustees of Culture: Power, Wealth, and Status on Elite Arts Boards*. University of Chicago Press.

Pancot, C., & Lusiani, M. (2021). Beyond dualism? Exploring the polyphonic dimension of cultural productions. *Journal of Arts Management, Law and Society*, *51*(1), 73–91. https://doi.org/10.1080/10632921.2020.1851837

Peterson, R. (1986). From Impresario to Arts Administrator: Formal Accountability in Nonprofit Cultural Organizations. In P. DiMaggio (Ed.), *Nonprofit Enterprise in the Arts: Studies in Mission and Constraint* (pp. 161–183). Oxford University Press.

Ponte, B. (2021). Cultural Management in Latin America and Europe: Between the Ashes and the Flame. In R. Henze & F. Escribal (Eds.), *Cultural Management and Policy in Latin America* (pp. 22–33). Routledge.

Quigg, A.-M. (2007). Bullying in theatres and arts centres in the United Kingdom. *International Journal of Arts Management*, *10*(1), 52–64.

Radaelli, E. (2012). American Cultural Policy and the Rise of Arts Management Programs: The Creation of a New Professional Identity. In J. Paquette (Ed.), *Cultural Policy, Work and Identity: The Creation, Renewal and Negotiation of Professional Subjectivities* (pp. 145–159). Ashgate.

Radbourne, J. & Fraser, M. (1996). *Arts Management: A Practical Guide*. Allen & Unwin.

Ramzy, A. (2014). Xi Jinping Calls for Artists to Spread 'Chinese Values'. *New York Times*.

Rånlund, S., Dalborg, K., & Löfgren, M. (Eds.). (2016). *The FIKA* Project: *Narratives by Cultural Change Makers*. Nätverkstan Culture.

Recaman, A.-L., & Colbert, F. (2016). Tania Pérez-Salas, dancer and choreographer: From artistic creation to management of a cultural enterprise. *International Journal of Arts Management*, 18(Special edition), 232–260.

Reid, W. (2007). *Conflict and trust in dual executive leadership*. Doctoral dissertation, York University.

Reid, W., & Karambayya, R. (2009). Impact of dual executive leadership dynamics in creative organizations. *Human Relations*, *62*(7), 1073–1112. https://doi.org/10.1177/0018726709335539

Reid, W., & Karambayya, R. (2016). The shadow of history: Situated dynamics of trust in dual executive leadership. *Leadership*, *12*(5), 609–631. https://doi.org/10.1177/1742715015579931

Reynolds, S., Tonks, A., & MacNeill, K. (2017). Collaborative leadership in the arts as a unique form of dual leadership. *The Journal of Arts Management, Law, and Society*, *47*(2), 89–104. https://doi.org/10.1080/10632921.2016.1241968

Rhine, A. S., & Pension, J. (2021). The MFA in theater management and the MBA: A replicative study of perspectives of decision-makers at theaters in the United States. *Journal of Arts Management, Law and Society*, *51*(6), 351–364. https://doi.org/10.1080/10632921.2021.1925192

Ross, I. (2017). Arts management the Indian way: Bangalore's Ranga Shankara theatre. *International Journal of Arts Management*, *19*(2), 59–68.

Røyseng, S. (2008). Arts management and the autonomy of art. *International Journal of Cultural Policy*, *14*(1), 37–48. https://doi.org/10.1080/10286630701856484

Ruiz-Gutiérrez, J., Grant, P., & Colbert, F. (2016). Arts management in developing countries: A Latin American perspective. *International Journal of Arts Management*, *18*(Special edition), 6–31.

Schmidt, T. (2016). *Theater, Krise und Reform. Eine Kritik Des Deutschen Theatersystems*. Springer VS.

Shaheed, F. (2013). *Report of the Special Rapporteur in the field of cultural rights: The right to freedom of artistic expression and creativity*. Human Rights Council, United Nations General Assembly.

Snow, G. (2019). Rufus Norris and Lisa Burger to become joint chief executives of the National Theatre. *The Stage*.

Stein, T. S., & Bathurst, J. (2008). *Performing Arts Management: A Handbook of Professional Practices*. Allworth.

Şuteu, C. (2006). *Another Brick in the Wall: A Critical Review of Cultural Management Education in Europe*. Boekmanstudies.

Thornton, P. H., Ocasio, W., & Lounsbury, M. (2012). *The Institutional Logics Perspective: A New Approach to Culture, Structure, and Process*. Oxford University Press.

Tremblay, M. (2014). *Configurations et pratiques du leadership pluriel au sommet de compagnies théâtrale québécoise*. Master's thesis, Université du Québec à Montréal, Montréal.

Tschmuck, P. (2006). The budgetary effects of 'Privatizing' major cultural institutions in Austria. *The Journal of Arts Management, Law, and Society*, *35*(4), 293–304. https://doi.org/10.3200/JAML.35.4.293-304

Upchurch, A. (2016). *The Origins of the Arts Council Movement: Philanthropy and Policy*. Palgrave Macmillan.

Zan, L., Bonini Baraldi, S., Ferri, P., Lusiani, M., & Mariani, M. M. (2012). Behind the scenes of public funding for performing arts in Italy: Hidden phenomena beyond the rhetoric of legislation. *International Journal of Cultural Policy*, *2012*(18), 1. https://doi.org/10.1080/10286632.2011.573849

Section II

Theorizing relational dynamics in arts co-leadership

5 Working with interdependence

Logics, values, and the shared role space

> Well, the natural kind of frisson between two competing views, one being artistic and one being basically business - that if you can coalesce the views, then that's fine, but if the artistic is trying to go in one direction and the business has decided it wants to go in a different direction, then the potential for conflict is quite strong.
>
> Artistic director (AD)

An executive role space in arts organizations is inhabited by functionally different co-leaders. However, as we have heard in the comment above, their interaction within that space is key to understanding how adequately the responsibilities within the role space are covered, how they integrate the logics inherent in their respective roles and the potential for conflict. These leadership roles are typically differentiated, anchored in either the artistic or the managerial sides of the organization. In a situation characterized by multiple demands, co-leaders face a constant challenge of integrating co-existing and sometimes competing demands.

Understanding dimensions of co-leadership and the shared role space

For all pluralistic organizations, the integration of multiple logics is a core challenge (Fjellvær, 2010; Gibeau et al., 2020). As we described in Chapter 2, logics are the values, beliefs, and assumptions held by groups of organizational actors that guide their actions and practices (Gibeau et al., 2020; Thornton & Ocasio, 2008). Each group of actors occupies a certain domain or sphere of activity in the organization (Dowling & Pfeffer, 1975; Thompson, 1967) and maintains a high degree of control over the specific activities in the domain. The organization as a whole consists of multiple domains with their related goals and in a pluralistic organization, domains may be grouped together. In our context, groups such as creation, design, direction, performance, and production are typically collected within the artistic domain. Promotion and marketing, financial administration,

DOI: 10.4324/9780429504259-7

fundraising, and facilities management are typically grouped within the management domain (Kuesters, 2010; Reid & Karambayya, 2009). In a pluralistic organization, each group of domains normally has a co-leader at the top of their side of the organization. In each organizational context, the combination of responsibilities, expectations, and limitations for the co-leaders will create a shared leadership role space that they inhabit together (Gronn & Hamilton, 2004; Stewart, 1991). They can negotiate how much of the shared role space each of them should or can occupy; how much their roles should or will overlap; and how and to what degree they will be able to coordinate their work within that shared role space (Fjellvær, 2010; Hodgson et al., 1965).

Managing co-existing and competing logics

Several methods for managing competing logics in organizations have been identified. Structural separation compartmentalizes logics in different parts of the organization (Thornton et al., 2012). Temporal separation allows them to take precedence at different points in time (Kraatz & Block, 2008; Le Theule & Fronda, 2005; Thacher & Rein, 2004). Organizations have also been found to rely on recruiting, socialization, or third-party intervention to navigate between competing logics (Battilana & Dorado, 2010; Le Theule & Fronda, 2005). These studies of reconciliation of competing logics are mostly analysed at the individual co-leader or organizational level. However, the combined efforts of the co-leaders in the shared role space have rarely been analysed considering implications for the organization.

Exceptionally, Fjellvær (2010) and Gibeau et al. (2020) have in fact studied co-leadership integration of multiple logics. For example, Fjellvær (2010) found that an individual co-leader either followed a *dominant* logic, or simultaneously considered multiple underlying logics which was called a *balanced* integration of logics. A leader who follows a balanced integration of logics is able and willing to integrate professional and managerial logics (in our case, artistic and financial or market logics). On the other hand, a leader may pursue a dominant or priority logic, either managerial, professional, or social (Fjellvær, 2010; Gibeau et al., 2020; Löfgren, 2016). This leader follows a set of goals associated with a particular professional domain rather than search for or develop a combined logic. In co-leadership constellations of two individuals, the generic logic integration combinations could be either: Dominant-dominant, dominant-balancing, or balancing-balancing. If both co-leaders follow a balanced integration of logics, then the possibility of generating an over-arching goal set for the organization exists (Gibeau et al., 2020; Thacher & Rein, 2004). This higher-level goal encompasses all logics and informs the activity of each domain. The goal can be interpreted according to the values of each professional domain as well as inter-domain values.

By adopting an overarching perspective to integrate multiple logics, the co-leaders identify shared values that transcend potentially competing logics (Gibeau et al., 2020). This higher level of integration may result in innovative strategies for the organization.

Sharing the role space

Our investigation was guided by the following questions:

> How do arts co-leader constellations fill their shared role space?
> How do they approach the integration of multiple coexisting logics?

Answering these questions mobilizes perspectives developed by Gronn (2002) and Hodgson et al. (1965). To compare different co-leadership constellations, we first considered the division of technological and social labour (Gronn, 2002), what Hodgson et al. (1965) called specialization. These are the specific tasks and functions that are distinct for each co-leader (Fjellvær, 2010).

Second, the degree of differentiation involves how much of the shared role space each co-leader occupies and whether or not their roles overlap and by how much. A high degree of overlap or low differentiation may create a zone of mutual substitution or duplication which can simplify decision-making by reducing options and points of view (Gibeau et al., 2016). However, low differentiation may also create tension and conflict because responsibility for control becomes ambiguous.

The third dimension, complementarity, is strongly tied to both specialization and differentiation. This last dimension is the key to understanding the potential for co-leaders to manage co-existing and competing logics (Hodgson et al., 1965). Co-leaders with a clear understanding of the interdependencies between distinct professional domains can serve in a bridging function by developing their personal relationships to link their respective domains (Fjellvær, 2010). Too much specialization or too much overlap may create tension and conflict within the relationship. Coordination of the work in the shared role space reduces these excesses. High complementarity will be achieved if co-leaders establish a relationship that enables them to coordinate their work within the shared role space so that the jointly held responsibilities within the role space are adequately fulfilled.

In addition to this structural side of the co-leadership (specialization, differentiation, and complementarity), we also introduce and illustrate the cognitive aspect of logic integration. A conscious understanding of the need for managing different logics and objectives enables co-leaders to engage in integration. Overall, we found that co-leaders in the arts agree on the need to integrate co-existing logics, but how they do this depends on their complementarity within the shared role space. Their approach to co-existing logics is the foundation for their relationship. Each co-leader negotiates with the other the importance of any logic or set of logics within the constellation.

Stewart (1991) points out that in situations with two leaders, how they negotiate the division of roles described above will be influenced by the mandated functions of the position, any external constraints on what is achievable (e.g., resources) as well as aspects of the work that one executive may take on while another may not (Stewart, 1991, p. 126). The amount of the space that the individual co-leader occupies in the shared role space does not necessarily reflect the balance of power among the co-leaders, either formally or informally. We have assumed so far that they are formally equal because they have been mandated to jointly undertake the responsibilities of co-leadership by a board of directors or government-funding authority. However, intuitively, we know that informally this equality may not necessarily be the case. Nor is the relationship necessarily static. It may be fluid over time (Schreyögg & Sydow, 2010).

In this investigation, we analyse how co-leaders fulfil the responsibilities found in the shared role space: How they integrate co-existing logics; how specialized they are in their work functions; and the degree that roles overlap or are differentiated. We study how co-leaders are able to coordinate their work and through this we can gain an understanding of their role complementarity (Hodgson et al., 1965). Co-leaders with comprehensive coordination and an ability to fulfil the responsibilities within the shared role space achieve high complementarity. As a result, we see the degree of complementarity as a proxy for how co-leaders approach the integration of logics.

We outline seven different types among a total of 13 cases that illustrate how the dynamics of shared role space are managed. Commensurate with previous work (Gibeau et al., 2016), we found that constellation types vary along a spectrum of types from integrated through distributed to disconnected (Gibeau et al., 2020). The types are presented in Figure 5.1 as graphic representations. We have separated those cases with balanced integration of logics on the left and cases with at least one co-leader pursuing dominant logic on the right. Role dominance in the relationship is suggested by the size of the role circle and the amount of surface both circles cover within the ellipse represents the shared role space. The specifics of each type are discussed with illustrative quotes from organizational participants in our research.

Type A: Overarching integration of logics

This first type includes two organizations whose co-leaders fully integrate logics. In both organizations, functions are clearly divided between the AD and executive director (ED). Their respective expertise and collaborative relationship ensure that the needs of the whole leadership role space are

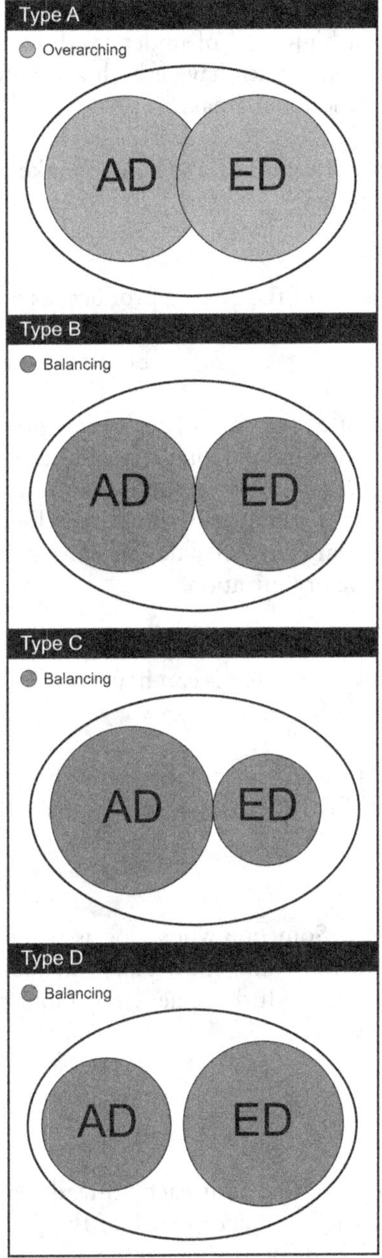

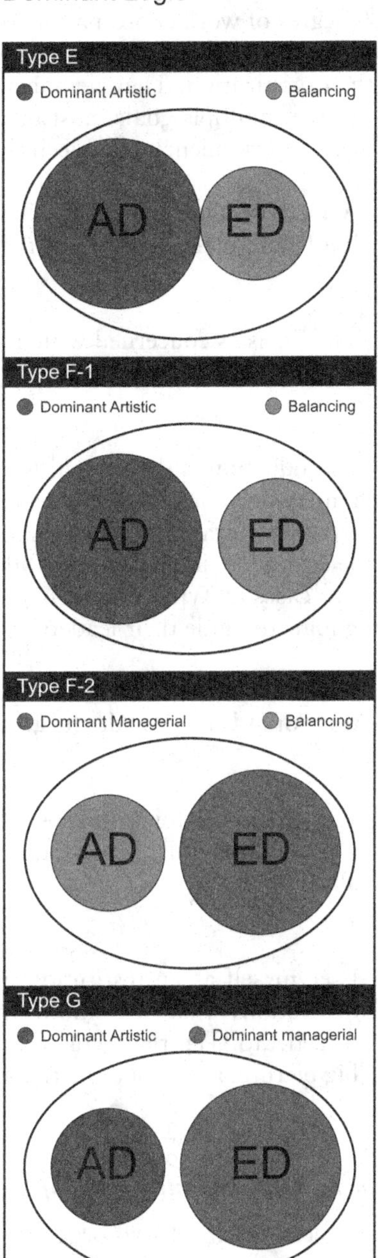

Figure 5.1 Types of role integration.

addressed. Figure 5.1 shows that there is some overlap in roles. There is a high degree of work coordination as the co-leaders engage in collegial decision-making, and both relate to members from all professional domains of the organization. They demonstrate a high level of understanding and accept that multiple goals must be addressed. Both have a high awareness of the interdependencies between their functional areas.

> Art is very subjective, but the balance sheet is not. I'm here to make art, but I can't make art unless I make money.
>
> AD

> The ED is as concerned with excellence of the artistic product, as with excellence on the service side.
>
> Board president

Art production is the mutual motivator at the core of the organization. Such integrated constellations engage in forward and long-term planning of the artistic program in order to manage any short-term financial variance. While co-leaders in all our cases address the integration of multiple logics, the two cases in Type A reach beyond balancing. They develop an overarching logic to guide their leadership of the organization.

> ...fulfilment, that is what people want, so the leaders have to provide that, or at least provide the groundwork so that it can happen.
>
> ED

> We're doing it for a purpose that I believe in, to share insights into this very humanizing art form. And ED believes in that. We share this absolutely.
>
> AD

> I see myself as an institution builder. Someone whose job is to build institutions that are more important than individuals including myself...to keep the whole forest in view all the time... it's about the big picture, not about one tree in the forest.
>
> AD

Type B: Balanced integration of logics

In the next group of two organizations, we find that each co-leader also shows an explicit awareness, understanding, and acceptance of the "other side" logic. In this constellation, co-leaders demonstrate balancing of multiple logics: ADs adjust repertoire to market conditions and EDs accept artistic idiosyncrasies.

However, functions are highly specialized with limited role overlap. Responsibilities and formal authority are clearly divided. This specialization ensures stability in times of succession. In one case, co-leaders explicitly agree to ensure that there is little role overlap. In the other case, co-leaders are mandated independently by the board of directors; ADs are hired on four-year contracts, whereas the ED is on a permanent basis. High coordination and ongoing consultation ensure that responsibilities in the shared role space are adequately covered. Including the entire staff in program and production presentations is an example of an ADs awareness of the interdependence of logics.

> AD asks me for advice, I ask AD for advice. I will not answer for example about the artistic quality of a dancer or a choreographer project…I wouldn't know how to say that. But I'm going to answer in terms of marketing, in terms of communication…it helps cross the bridge between the art world and the administrative world.
>
> ED

> For the whole range of leadership issues, we talk if we need to…even if the ED formally has more staff than I do, we talk. ED will talk about administrative challenges – or I will ask about an actor "how do you think I should handle this?" ED knows more about labour laws and collective agreements and a lot of things that are outside my domain. So, I ask for advice. So, this partnership works well the way it is.
>
> AD

Compared to the Type A cases, there is high differentiation. While there is a mutual respect and understanding of interdependencies, we found no evidence that these co-leaders actively use the shared role space to confront, explore, and negotiate ideas. They do not innovate by creating another logic and constructing an overarching common goal as Type A did. In comparison, Type B demonstrates adequate but not extraordinary complementarity.

Type C: Moderately balanced integration of logics – uneven occupation of role space

In this type, co-leaders feature high specialization and differentiation, with no overlap between roles. The cases of Type C are different from Types A and B because one of the co-leaders in Type C occupies a larger part of the shared role space and there is less coordination between the co-leaders. Nonetheless, in both cases of this type, co-leaders use a balanced integration of multiple logics. Despite low coordination and lack of an overarching goal, these cases were able to negotiate a stable working relationship.

> I have to be able to describe the situation so that the AD understands what situation we are in. If I cannot, then it is hard to move on...The artistic side, they have a voice inside that has to come out and they have to share that voice. This creates energy, so we may have conflicts, but they need to become positive conflicts – that something positive comes out of it.
>
> ED

Type D: Balanced integration of logics – disconnected in the role space

Type D involves one case, a symphony orchestra. Both co-leaders of this case are willing to integrate artistic and financial logics, and at the time of our investigation, both co-leaders claimed to have adopted a balancing approach to the integration of logics. Both were motivated by the role of art in society and the artistic ideal, and both recognized their mutual dependence. There was a clear division of functions, high specialization, and equally high differentiation with no overlap between roles.

Since this is a symphony orchestra, the ED is more present in the organization, occupying more of the shared role space than the AD. At the same time, the AD is the organization's public face, generating power and an ability to connect with the board directly, leveraging requests.

From the co-leader interviews, we understood that they can coordinate their work within the shared role space, but others in the organization who we interviewed suggested that tensions and significant differences in values and priorities exist compared with previous types of co-leader cases discussed here. These unresolved differences in approach to multiple logics indicate a case of disconnection in the shared role space. An example of disconnection was the ED's conscious abstention from coordinating projects that could have generated improved community relations for the organization or developed further legitimacy and credibility for the AD.

> So, two smart people together isn't a bad thing. But they're very different characters. I really think they're going to have to work some things out.
>
> Artistic administrator

This case as Type D demonstrates that even if both co-leaders have a balanced approach to the integration of multiple logics, their lack of complementarity seriously hampers their ability to adequately fulfil the obligations of co-leadership and cover the shared role space.

Types A to D all describe situations where co-leaders have a balanced integration of logics. The different types vary in co-leaders specialization and role differentiation, but they have a degree of complementarity and fulfil the shared role space. Types E to G represent cases where one or both co-leaders follow a dominant logic, and their occupation of the shared role space is uneven.

Type E: Conditional dominant and balanced integration of logics – living well together

The co-leaders in the two cases of Type E have specialized functions with little overlap between roles. They are able to coordinate their work well, but there is an imbalance in how much of the shared role space they cover and most importantly, a lack of clarity about whether it is all covered. The AD in one case follows a conditional dominant artistic logic, but still recognizing the strong interdependencies involved. Through including all members of the organization when articulating the pursuit of the mission, AD is strongly committed to protecting and developing the artistic vision.

> I fight for the artistic ideas. At the same time, it is my responsibility of course to keep the finances in order. And the artistic staff… the artistic staff, the actors, they want me to program things that include them on the cast list. Obviously - if you go by that alone, it will limit what artistic ideas you can realize.
>
> AD

> But someone who knows about theatre – they know that there is nothing more detailed than running a theatre. If we don't have systematic people – then we cannot be artists: Cannot be as spontaneous and crazy as we are supposed to be. We need someone to keep us under control.
>
> AD

The ED in this case focuses on the managerial and particularly financial support system for the art and has no interest in taking a more prominent role. Hence, although this is a case of a dominant role pursuing a quite dominant logic, at the time of study, this case was not characterized by ambiguity and tension over competing logics. The marketing and production directors worked directly with the AD, and if the ED had expected to occupy more of the shared role space, this arrangement could have presented challenges, but it did not due to this particular EDs approach.

> The ED is so good at the job, you know. There is always a nest egg fund – to everyone's annoyance really, but we have never seen a deficit thanks to ED. But ED doesn't want to be in charge – doesn't care about that. ED has been offered a bigger position and is not interested. Works way too much, is very conscientious.
>
> Marketing director

For the other case in Type E, the AD displays a dominant artistic logic and demonstrates a very strong commitment to the specific artistic vision, yet also explicitly expresses an awareness and acceptance of the interdependencies involved. With the EDs accommodating style, they are able to coordinate their work by negotiating a rigid allocation of responsibility.

> They certainly weren't totally siloed, but they...thought they were on the same page, but each had different interpretations. It can't be siloed. It has to be divided with clear and distinct accountabilities because both of them are accountable to the board. There are pieces where they need to be continuously collaborative...so they've adopted the "balanced scorecard" -written agreements that express mutual accountability between job functions which are reviewed regularly.
>
> Board president

Type F: Dominant logic – dominant role meets balancing co-leader

Type F includes three organizations, where it is even more clear that the co-leaders do not adopt the same approaches to integrating logics. One logic dominates and there is uneven role space coverage. In two of the cases, the AD pursues a dominant artistic logic and in the third case, the ED pursues a dominant market logic, whereas the other co-leader tries to balance the integration of co-existing logics. In Figure 5.1, both versions of Type F are illustrated. We found high specialization in all three, but there was an uneven distribution of functions where one leader takes on a larger part of the shared role space including encroaching on the other's areas of responsibility. A disconnection in the role space is evidenced through a low ability to coordinate their work, even if this is somewhat alleviated in one of the cases by the balancing ED who becomes a strategic allocator of energy and resources.

Another characteristic about the three Type F cases is that the co-leaders who follow a dominant logic also take on a dominant role.

> AD is more grandiose than ever in terms of expectations... someone who feels that this organization is their domain, is their stomping ground, and that they are, to a certain extent, entitled to do whatever they might want to do....
>
> ED

> That is a pure dictatorship, because when AD says this is how it's going to be, nobody questions it and nobody changes it.
>
> Board member

The person in the dominant role is unwilling to coordinate the work, ignoring the inherent interdependencies in the organization by focusing primarily on their own role.

> I want an audience. I want people to listen to what I have to say. No way am I going to compromise my stuff anymore... That vibrancy can only happen with a person like me who has a vision and a passion and a drive.
>
> AD

> The marketing budget is the money that's left after AD's paid for the scenery, that's the priority ... they would never think that from a marketing point of view the names of the shows are a drawback.
>
> Marketing director

Intrusive behaviour is a symptom of uneven role space coverage.

> I insist on imaging the company at all times. And I'm really adamant about this, I step on people's toes about it, I won't let letters go out unless I've looked at them, ED writes horribly ... it's just appalling.
>
> AD

In the third case of Type F, the ED was trying to move into artistic domains, such as participating in the selection of artists and repertoire. A stressed and uncomfortable AD recruited the board's formal authority to establish written agreements about what the ED could and could not do regarding the artistic decisions. The ED retaliated by changing budget allocations, which seriously diminished the artistic program. The number of musicians and administrative personnel on sick leave increased, symptomatic of leadership dysfunction.

Type G: Dominant-dominant integration of logics – quiet resistance

In Type G, co-leaders were highly disconnected, each following separate dominant logics – market and managerial for the ED and artistic logic for the AD. Functions were highly specialized with no overlap between roles. Their ability to coordinate the work was low and sometimes the ED used formal power to enforce compliance by the AD. Consequently, there was an uneven and inadequate coverage of the responsibilities within the role space.

In meetings, the AD tried to avoid open conflict with the ED, but simultaneously acted to protect the artistic staff, and proposed an expansion of the AD role space by taking over functions from other departments.

The ED explicitly invoked a higher formal authority, ignored or ridiculed symbols of artistic identity, and used formal power to control rather than coordinate.

> I gathered the leaders again and said that – I demand loyalty to my vision – and to this idea – and as long as I have the support of the government and the board in what I am doing – then you must accept it.
>
> ED

> I have always emphasized that the only thing that can save us is that we respect the formal hierarchy – that we follow it strictly. Both down – decisions filter down – but also criticism from below and up through the ranks. You do not get to go to someone other than your immediate supervisor.
>
> ED

Integrating multiple logics within a shared role space

In our study, nine out of 13 cases represented co-leaders' balanced integration (Types A to D). Only two cases involved a dominant managerial logic (in Types F and G). Overall, there was a prevailing acceptance by ADs and EDs of the presence, importance, and need for a strong artistic logic, despite its interdependence and coexistence with financial or managerial logics. This may reflect an expectation of high quality of art from government and private funders, but also a recognition of the significant role of box office and other market-oriented projects.

> It's a collaborative job and involves respect for each other's skill. ED consults me for the artistic side, and I consult ED for the administration component.
>
> AD

> The bottom line is that the last word in terms of artistic decision has to be made by me, and the last word in terms of administration has to be made by ED. But understanding that one goes with the other. I mean there's no brick wall between the two, it's like the two hemispheres of the same brain. They have to work in conjunction.
>
> AD

> The success of the company really depends on this synergy between the two directors.
>
> AD

Previous research investigating co-leadership constellations has focused on task functions and role overlap (Gibeau et al., 2016) and how co-leaders manage the integration of logics (Gibeau et al., 2020). This reflects a preoccupation with differentiation and specialization (Hodgson et al., 1965). We propose that the dimension of complementarity can explain much of the difference between constellations that initially look quite similar such as A and B or E and F. This dimension most reflects the cognitive approach used to solve the problem of competing logics (Hodgson et al., 1965). Complementarity also refers to the scope and appropriateness of the resources (expertise, legitimacy, and relationships) that a constellation has available to solve the challenges faced by the organization. If co-leaders adequately cover the responsibilities of the shared role space and can coordinate their work, then co-leadership works quite well, even if one logic is dominant in the constellation. While this dynamic appears paradoxical, each co-leader has different needs and expectations about how much of the shared role space they want to occupy, as in Types C and E (Stewart, 1991). The combination of their approaches within the constellation fundamentally determines what kind of working relationship they will have. For those who can coordinate this work, the needs within the shared role space can be covered and the relationship may become innovative as they lead the organization together.

In addition to the snapshots of constellations already presented in our discussion, we were subsequently able to follow several of these organizations over time. We found that integration of logics and complementarity are fluid dynamics among co-leaders (Alvehus, 2019). Co-leaders occupy the shared role space and manage co-existing logics, evolving as the executive relationship develops and with phases in organizational development. For example, in one of our Type C cases, at the time of the initial interviews, we saw that the co-leaders both adopted a balanced integration of logics although the AD took a larger part of the role space. Three years later, the situation had slowly changed to the point where each was siloed into their own side of the organization, communicating less, demonstrating significant differentiation (Hodgson et al., 1965). The ED had shifted to a dominant managerial logic. Thus, we propose that there is a temporal dimension to co-leadership constellations that practitioners and academics alike should consider.

Comparing with other contexts

Arts co-leadership constellations appear to provide adequate coverage of the shared role space. There are few cases of role overlap. In contrast, co-principals in schools (Gronn & Hamilton, 2004) and co-leaders in professional service firms (Empson, 2017) and health organizations (Gibeau et al., 2020) are less diverse and roles are not as clearly differentiated. While more arts co-leaders have a balanced approach to logic integration, we also find higher specialization of functions and high differentiation. Table 5.1 compares

Table 5.1 Patterns of integration and differentiation across sectors

Sector	*Illustrative study*	*Empirical context*	*Integration of logics*	*Differentiation*
Education	Gronn & Hamilton, 2004	Schools with co-principals. Common objective.	High. Same logic, not competing.	Very low. In fact, each could do the other's job. Negotiated division of labour.
Health care	Gibeau et al., 2020	Health institutions. Co-leaders in clinics and centres within a larger institution.	Low. Dominant managerial. No cases of dominant professional. One case of balanced.	Quite low in most cases. Focus on managerial job in co-leadership. Professional medical practice outside of co-leadership.
Professional service firms	Empson, 2017	Law, accounting, and consulting partnerships. Co-leadership reconciles ambiguity due to individual versus collective goals.	High. Same professional logic.	Low to medium. Each could do the other's job with formal training. By preference and/ or peer appointment. Emphasis on distinct roles.
Newspapers	Fjellvær, 2010	Journalistic publications. Co-leaders are top management team.	Medium to high. Strong freedom of the press logic contrasts with commercial.	High differentiation in most cases. Separate leadership functions plus joint role as co-leaders.
Arts and cultural organizations	Reid & Karambayya, 2009; Fjellvær, 2010	Small to medium organizations. Co-leaders are top management team.	Medium to high. Strong artistic logic needs to co-exist with managerial, marketing, or financial logic.	High differentiation in most cases. Separate leadership functions plus joint role as co-leaders.

typical arts organization profiles compared to illustrative empirical studies of co-leadership constellations in education (Gronn & Hamilton, 2004), health (Gibeau et al., 2020), professional service firms (Empson, 2017), and newspapers (Fjellvær, 2010).

Table 5.1 suggests that arts organizations are distinctive compared with other contexts, except perhaps newspapers. First, in the arts, there is high functional specialization, and two separate leadership roles need to work together. Second, the profession logic, which is the artistic logic, is present and accepted across all cases. This is similar for the education and professional service firm examples, but those examples are found in organizations where the presence of multiple domains is not as evident. In education organizations, the focus is on sharing the workload (Gronn, 1999), and in professional service firms, leadership in the plural is often introduced to balance the objective of the individual and the collective (Empson, 2017). However, Fjellvær (2010) found that newspapers with editorial and managerial co-leaders displayed high specialization and high differentiation similar to our findings in the arts. Finally, for the majority of cases, arts co-leaders adopt a balanced integration of logics. In the health care examples, Gibeau et al. (2020) found this balanced integration in only one constellation.

Arts organizations are generally smaller organizations independent of large systems. Education organizations are part of a larger institutional field with a strong influence from the prevailing education logic (Gronn & Hamilton, 2004). The health care cases are also part of larger institutions, and these co-leadership constellations are situated in middle management. They do not report directly to a board of directors. Co-leaders in professional service firms are mandated by their peers and Empson (2017) describes how they navigate depending on their relationship and negotiated co-habitation of the shared role space. In comparison, our co-leaders constitute the top management and report to a board of directors, reflecting a structural differentiation that is more pronounced in the arts (Kleppe, 2017, 2018).

Finally, with the exception of professional service firms that are for-profit and strongly revenue-oriented, organizations in the three other fields experience financial constraints. But unique in the arts is a hybrid revenue model, where both market and funders of the mission share the financial burden of the organization. The box office may influence ADs choices, forcing a consideration of multiple objectives and logics. In one of our cases, the co-leaders' attention was focused on reducing a significant accumulated deficit so market response to future programming was a major consideration for the AD. In another, the risk of producing over-budget major productions without assurance of box office return was a source of much tension within the co-leadership. In this case, the AD did not consider the market concerns and the relationship suffered.

It seems that in health care organizations, for example, a person using managerial logics can play a large role and even duplicate or substitute for a medical co-manager in the co-leadership. This replacement capability from managerial to artistic task rarely happens in arts co-leadership. We propose that this difference is a consequence of the power of the artistic imperative. In the performing arts, each role has distinctly different skill sets and aptitudes, and together with the expected autonomy of the AD (Røyseng, 2008), this leads to high levels of specialization.

Gibeau et al. (2020) observed co-leadership in health care institutions, introduced as a pilot project to improve communications between staff and professionals. A medical doctor was added to an incumbent administrator to form the co-leadership of a unit in the hospital. In North America, doctors function as autonomous professionals, and appear uncomfortable as managers, lacking connection to the organization. In certain regions in the arts, there is a different commitment to and understanding of this type of leadership constellation (Chapter 4). Artists and cultural workers in Western and Anglo-Saxon arts organizations are well aware of co-leadership as an institutionalized practice before they enter the field.

Challenging the achievement of innovation

Gibeau et al. (2020) suggest that true bridging occurs when organizations capitalize on tensions to innovate and create new opportunities. They suggest that for an organization to achieve and follow an overarching logic that successfully guides development, co-leaders surpass a combination of their individual logics. In such cases, co-leaders bridge logics, change perspectives, and develop a new overall mission. We concur with Gibeau et al. (2020). To accomplish innovation and an over-arching integration of logics, co-leaders need to be aware of and accept the ongoing tensions inherent in the pluralism of these organizations. Ideally, these leaders would be confidently competent in their own professional domain, share a common understanding, respect each other's professional domains and their interdependencies, and engage in a balancing approach. They would both contribute equally to organizational strategy, so that the ED is not considered a servant in deference to art and to the AD (MacNeill et al., 2013; Reynolds et al., 2017). They adopt a repertoire of relationship and trust building practices including regular communication, and a capacity and willingness to negotiate solutions that integrate the organization's underlying common interests. When the shared leadership role space is focused in such a way, the stage is set for developmental innovation.

As an example, the specific repertoire of one of our case organizations is a hallmark of its identity and for its audience. Senior actors in this company who were experienced interpreters of the repertoire were retiring.

The theatre's co-leaders realized that young actors in the country were not receiving this specific knowledge and skill elsewhere, and that the company's prime resource was not being renewed. As a result, the co-leaders acknowledged an expensive responsibility to preserve and re-vitalize the art. They founded and funded an ongoing in-house specialist training program, which provides two-year paid opportunities to early and mid-career actors to upgrade their craft in this specific repertoire and to join the company. The co-leaders convinced the government and private donors for additional funds for this initiative, which maintains the viability of the company's artistic mission.

However, stakeholders in the arts may want to consider whether innovation is the fundamental goal that should underpin the decision to establish co-leadership. Co-leadership may be ideally situated to confront the inherent ambiguities due to multiple objectives and capitalize on this tension to develop something new (Fjellvær, 2010). Yet as we have seen, this also involves a central challenge of developing a constructive working relationship between the co-leaders. As a result, we question the idea that the core purpose of co-leadership is to bridge logics to achieve innovation, something that leads to more than one plus one being two (Gibeau et al., 2020).

Political scientist, Johan Galtung introduced the idea of a negative peace – the absence of open conflict (Gleditsch et al., 2014). In contrast, positive peace is an active state, integrating ideas and action through cooperation (Galtung & Fischer, 2013; van Hoef & Oelsner, 2018). While we agree with Gibeau et al. (2020) that a bridging practice should be productive and useful, it is the equivalent of positive peace. Negative peace is perhaps a more realistic goal for co-leaders in the arts who must manage the ambiguities and tensions to fulfil the artistic mission. A negative peace in the arts can justify pooling leadership at the top (Gibeau et al., 2016) in order to cope with complexity (Arnone & Stumpf, 2010) (albeit not necessarily in large organizations), manage continuity and change during transitions (O'Toole et al., 2002), share the workload (Gronn & Hamilton, 2004), and accommodate co-founders (Alvarez et al., 2007). Obstacles to innovative performance can be many and a dominant approach does not necessarily impede the achievement of the ultimate balancing act.

Conclusion

Our investigation shows that co-leaders vary in what they do to manage their shared role space and the demands arising from multiple logics. However, most of the constellations we studied balance the integration of logics. To a large degree, they are also able to coordinate their work and adequately cover the requirements of the shared role space.

As we shall see in chapters 6, 7, 8, and 9, this does not imply that the working relationships are without tension or conflict, but we find that most artistic leaders and executive leaders acknowledge the mutual dependencies inherent in their organizations. Considering the power of the artistic imperative, in our research, arts co-leaders show a surprisingly high level of awareness and willingness to integrate and adapt other logics (Chapter 2).

References

Alvarez, J. L., Svejenova, S., & Vives, L. (2007). Leading in pairs. *Sloan Management Review*, *48*(4), 10–14.

Alvehus, J. (2019). Emergent, distributed, and orchestrated: Understanding leadership through frame analysis. *Leadership*, *15*(5), 535–554. https://doi.org/10.1177/1742715018773832

Arnone, M., & Stumpf, S. A. (2010). Shared leadership: From rivals to co-CEOs. *Strategy & Leadership*, *38*(2), 15–21. https://doi.org/10.1108/10878571011029019

Battilana, J., & Dorado, S. (2010). Building sustainable hybrid organizations: The case of commercial microfinance organizations. *Academy of Management Journal*, *53*(6), 1419–1440. https://doi.org/10.5465/amj.2010.57318391

Dowling, J., & Pfeffer, J. (1975). Organizational legitimacy: Social values and organizational behavior. *Pacific Sociological Review*, *18*(1), 122–136.

Empson, L. (2017). Leading Professionals: Power, Politics, and Prima Donnas. Oxford University Press.

Fjellvær, H. (2010). *Dual and unitary leadership: managing ambiguity in pluralistic organizations* (Publication Number 2010/10). Doctoral dissertation, Norwegian School of Economics and Business Administration, Bergen. https://openaccess.nhh.no/nhh-xmlui/bitstream/handle/11250/164362/fjellver%20avh%202010.PDF?sequence=1

Galtung, J., & Fischer, D. (2013). Johan Galtung: Pioneer of Peace Research. Springer.

Gibeau, É, Langley, A., Denis, J.-L., & van Schendel, N. (2020). Bridging competing demands through co-leadership? Potential and limitations. *Human Relations*, *73*(4), 464–489. https://doi.org/10.1177/0018726719888145

Gibeau, É, Reid, W., & Langley, A. (2016). Co-leadership: Contexts, Configurations and Conditions. In J. Storey, J. Hartley, J.-L. Denis, P. 't Hart, & D. Ulrich (Eds.), *Routledge Companion to Leadership* (pp. 225–240). Routledge.

Gleditsch, K. S., Metternich, N. W., & Ruggeri, A. (2014). Data and progress in peace and conflict research. *Journal of Peace Research*, *51*(2), 301–314. https://doi.org/10.1177/0022343313496803

Gronn, P. (1999). Substituting for leadership: The neglected role of the leadership couple. *The Leadership Quarterly*, *10*(1), 41–62. https://doi.org/10.1016/S1048-9843(99)80008-3

Gronn, P. (2002). Distributed leadership as a unit of analysis. *The Leadership Quarterly*, *13*(4), 423–451. https://doi.org/10.1016/S1048-9843(02)00120-0

Gronn, P., & Hamilton, A. (2004). 'A bit more life in the leadership': Co-principalship as distributed leadership practice. *Leadership and Policy in Schools*, *3*(1), 3–35. https://doi.org/10.1076/lpos.3.1.3.27842

Hodgson, R. C., Levinson, D. J., & Zaleznik, A. (1965). *The Executive Role Constellation: An Analysis of Personality and Role Relations in Management.* Harvard University: Division of Research, Graduate School of Business Administration.

Kleppe, B. (2017). Theatres as risk societies: Performing artists balancing between artistic and economic risk. *Poetics*, *64*, 53–62. https://doi.org/10.1016/j.poetic.2017.08.002

Kleppe, B. (2018). Managing autonomy: Analyzing arts management and artistic autonomy through the theory of justification. *Journal of Arts Management, Law, and Society*, *48*(3), 191–205. https://doi.org/10.1080/10632921.2017.1377661

Kraatz, M. S., & Block, E. (2008). Organizational Implications of Institutional Pluralism. In R. Greenwood, C. Oliver, K. Sahlin-Andersson, & R. Suddaby (Eds.), *The SAGE Handbook of Organizational Institutionalism* (pp. 243–275). SAGE Publications Limited.

Kuesters, I. (2010). Arts managers as liaisons between finance and art: A qualitative study inspired by the theory of functional differentiation. *The Journal of Arts Management, Law, and Society: Arts Management: A Sociological Inquiry*, *40*(1), 43–57. https://doi.org/10.1080/10632921003603976

Le Theule, M.-A., & Fronda, Y. (2005). The organization in tension between creation and rationalization: Facing management views to artistic and scientific creators. *Critical Perspectives on Accounting*, *16*(6), 749–786. https://doi.org/10.1016/j.cpa.2003.09.004

Löfgren, M. (2016). On the Public Value of Arts and Culture. In K. Dalborg, & M. Löfgren (Eds.), *The FIKA Project: Perspectives on Cultural Leadership* (pp. 75–99). Nätwerkstan Kultur.

MacNeill, K., Tonks, A., & Reynolds, S. (2013). Authenticity and the other: Co-leadership in arts organisations. *Journal of Leadership Studies*, *6*(3), 6–16. https://doi.org/10.1002/jls.21252

O'Toole, J., Galbraith, J., & Lawler, E. E. (2002). When two (or more) heads are better than one: The promise and pitfalls of shared leadership. *California Management Review*, *44*(4), 65–83. https://doi.org/10.2307/41166143

Reid, W., & Karambayya, R. (2009). Impact of dual executive leadership dynamics in creative organizations [article]. *Human Relations*, *62*(7), 1073–1112. https://doi.org/10.1177/0018726709335539

Reynolds, S., Tonks, A., & MacNeill, K. (2017). Collaborative leadership in the arts as a unique form of dual leadership. *The Journal of Arts Management, Law, and Society*, *47*(2), 89–104. https://doi.org/10.1080/10632921.2016.1241968

Røyseng, S. (2008). Arts management and the autonomy of art. *International Journal of Cultural Policy*, *14*(1), 37–48. https://doi.org/10.1080/10286630701856484

Schreyögg, G., & Sydow, J. (2010). CROSSROADS—organizing for fluidity? Dilemmas of new organizational forms. *Organization Science*, *21*(6), 1251–1262. https://doi.org/10.1287/orsc.1100.0561

Stewart, R. (1991). Role Sharing at the Top: A Neglected Aspect of Studies of Managerial Behaviour. In S. Carlson, H. Mintzberg, & R. Stewart (Eds.), *Executive Behaviour* (pp. 120–136). Studia Oeconomiae Negotiorum.

Thacher, D., & Rein, M. (2004). Managing value conflict in public policy. *Governance: An International Journal of Policy, Administration and Institutions*, *17*(4), 457–486. https://doi.org/10.1111/j.0952-1895.2004.00254.x

Thompson, J. D. (1967). *Organizations in Action: Social Science Bases of Administrative Theory*. McGraw-Hill.

Thornton, P., & Ocasio, W. (2008). Institutional Logics. In R. Greenwood, C. Oliver, K. Sahlin, & R. Suddaby (Eds.), *The SAGE Handbook on Organizational Institutionalism* (pp. 99–129). Sage.

Thornton, P. H., Ocasio, W., & Lounsbury, M. (2012). *The Institutional Logics Perspective: A New Approach to Culture, Structure, and Process*. Oxford University Press.

van Hoef, Y., & Oelsner, A. (2018). Friendship and positive peace: Conceptualising friendship in politics and international relations. *Politics and Governance*, 6(4), 115–124. https://doi.org/10.17645/pag.v6i4.1728

6 Challenging equality

Pluralism, competitive conflict, and social hierarchy

> I was in a very dysfunctional relationship with the Managing Director... It was pretty nasty actually. I remember we tried to fire each other once. You're fired. No, you're fired. You can't fire me. You can't fire me.
>
> Artistic director (AD)

> If ... conflict ever surfaced in a two-headed organization such as ours it would impact the staff and to some extent the board and then you just wouldn't be as cohesive, effective a unit and it would hurt you in that way.
>
> Board president

Introduction

Mandated joint responsibility for co-leadership at the top of an organization proposes formal status equality (Alvarez & Svejenova, 2005; Reid & Karambayya, 2009). The AD in the first citation recalls the ambiguity that formal parity poses. This lack of clarity about decision-making authority can lead to conflict in an effort to break the decisional paralysis. However, as one of our respondent board presidents confirmed (above), conflict can unsettle the whole organization by undermining the co-leaders' relationship and their ability to integrate pluralistic goals (Chapter 5). This is why traditional leadership scholars advocate single leadership for vision clarity and employee motivation (Locke, 2003). Scholars observe that a social hierarchy of ranked status stabilizes an organization. It promotes a clear system of order and shared expectations about authority and decision-making responsibilities (Magee & Galinsky, 2008).

Research to understand the impact of single versus co-leadership perspectives found that moderate power differences between co-CEOs appear to generate more effective performance in for-profit organizations (Krause et al., 2015). Neither parity nor strongly hierarchical co-leaders produce the same positive performance as a small power gap. Power indicators in this research involved salary, tenure, and share capital ownership, as well as appointments to board chair. In the non-profit sector, while some power indicators like salary and tenure are similar, other very potent sources of

DOI: 10.4324/9780429504259-8

power like ownership do not exist. However, in the arts, symbolic and cultural factors contribute to power differences. The artistic ideal is a leading logic for arts organizations. This ideal enhances the ADs public profile, celebrity, and status, possibly overshadowing the other leaders, sometimes diminishing the intention of the co-leadership's formal parity.

Scholars argue that for success in co-leadership relationships, shared cognition, trust, and collaboration in the relationship at the top are key as a peer-based alternative to hierarchical stabilization of these relationships (Alvarez & Svejenova, 2005; Reynolds et al., 2017). We explore trust and its influence on co-leadership in Chapter 7. However, in this chapter, we investigate status conflict to study social hierarchy dynamics in arts co-leadership. In our data, these co-leaders were mandated equally. But the dilemma of status parity in arts co-leadership sometimes served as a springboard for competition and status conflict, perhaps in an effort to achieve the comfort of some social hierarchy for co-leaders (Krause et al., 2015).

Attributing co-leadership status

Leadership is understood as an attributed status (Yukl, 2012). DeRue and Ashford (2010) explain the hierarchy of leadership as a social process of attribution. They outline how leader and follower identities are acknowledged and adopted in groups through a recursive and fluid social dynamic of "claiming and granting" (p. 631). When a leader claims this role, followers grant it and a positive cycle of social recognition of hierarchy occurs across levels of analysis.

DeRue and Ashford (2010) also nuance their model of vertical dynamics to include shared and distributed forms of plural leadership in their model (Chapter 3). Their theory shows how group members smoothly alternate leader and follower roles over time in an emergent fashion (p. 634). This alternating ebb and flow of leader-follower identity development contrasts with co-leadership. Mutual attribution of co-leadership with parity status is not addressed by these scholars. Balancing the organization's leadership equally across the differentiated artistic-administrative divide in the arts may be more complex than implied by DeRue and Ashford (2010), Hodgson et al. (1965), or Gronn and Hamilton (2004). As well, DeRue and Ashford (2010) have overlooked the potential for conflict that occurs when a leadership claim is not granted but blocked through resistance and competitive conflict, especially within a peer-based dynamic like that found in co-leadership.

Scholarly advocates of plural leadership demonstrate values of collectivity and democracy (Gronn & Hamilton, 2004), rarely addressing status and power dynamics that construct informal social hierarchy (Bolden, 2011; Denis et al., 2012). Exceptions include work by Denis and colleagues (1996, 2001) and Empson (2020). Formal parity among co-leadership members is often illusory. Our research in this chapter addresses issues of social hierarchy that arise in co-leadership status conflict.

While collaboration does exist within arts co-leadership (Reid & Karambayya, 2009; Reynolds et al., 2017), multiple goals and ambiguous priorities also render co-leadership ripe for political maneuvering and, ultimately, conflict to gain influence. Because of its focus on social hierarchy, status conflict becomes a pertinent lens to study these dynamics (Bendersky & Hays, 2012).

The following question guides our investigation:

How does status conflict influence status parity and social hierarchy among arts co-leaders, their relationship, and their leadership attribution?

In the following discussion, after applying the notions of social hierarchy and conflict to the sector, we investigate five practices of status conflict from our case research on co-leaders in the arts. Insights are gained regarding types of status conflict, status acquisition, and its impact in co-leadership decision-making. The challenges for achieving complementarity in the shared role space and positive functioning of the co-leadership are better understood (Hodgson et al., 1965).

Social hierarchy differences and logics within arts co-leadership

Important social values shape an individual's status in a group (Magee & Galinsky, 2008, p. 354). These social values can be implicit or explicit, changing over time, suggesting the influence of legitimizing institutional logics to reinforce this ranking process (Bendersky & Pai, 2018; DeRue & Ashford, 2010; Magee & Galinsky, 2008). Power is a more static construct of acquired resources deployed with the purpose to influence others' behaviour and organizational strategy (Fleming & Spicer, 2014; Magee & Galinsky, 2008). Status and power are distinct constructs that dynamically intertwine to shape social hierarchy.

Discussion of hierarchy in arts co-leadership has been limited to descriptions of formal management structures (Alvarez & Svejenova, 2005; Döös & Wilhelmson, 2021; MacNeill & Tonks, 2013). Missing from the discussion to date is an understanding of the social process of establishing status through contextual legitimacy (Denis et al., 2010). Arts co-leadership with formal parity and informal power differences is a useful context to investigate status contests. However, before reporting our empirical analysis, we illustrate co-leaders' power sources and status attribution.

Power sources

French and Raven (1959) and Raven (1965) categorized six different power sources (referent, legitimate, expert, reputational, coercive, and informational power) that are useful for our purposes. Bass (1990) further categorized these ideas as either formal position power or personal power.

In the cultural field, each co-leader typically has legitimate and formal power as the top authority on their side of the organization. In the formal management structure, the co-leaders also jointly hold legitimate power as the jointly mandated leadership constellation. However, variations in individual informal power sources exist that contribute to the lack of clarity about equal and joint decision-making in the shared role space.

As individuals, ADs typically have significant expert and reputation power in recognition of an accomplished artistic practice (Lindqvist, 2017). Their charisma accords very public referent power. Recognition of their mastery of the creative and programming process is informed by the culture of the artistic ideal (Nisbett & Walmsley, 2016; Rentschler, 2015) (Chapter 2). Their reward power consists of their ability to hire and promote artists who depend on performing opportunities to build careers. This latter power unfortunately was disrupted with the global pandemic in the 2020s and has been questioned by the #MeToo! and other social justice movements. ADs formal and informal power vary depending on the competition between arts or business logics that are shaped by funding structure, regional culture, and arts discipline (Chapter 4).

For executive directors (EDs), their core activities are based in expert and referent power. Their responsibilities for the organization's financial and market well-being link them strategically with governing boards of directors and funders, giving them influence regarding organizational strategies (Chapter 8). They are also involved in government lobbying with peers and in donor relationships, guided by corporation and market logics (Chapter 2). As arts organizations increasingly add a social orientation to their mission, these responsibilities may extend the EDs presence more broadly into their community through an alignment with community logics (Kawashima, 2006; Löfgren, 2016; Thornton et al., 2012). However, compared to ADs, these leaders are much less public. Of course, EDs also have reward power for staff on their side of the organization, although in some regions like Europe, employment laws reduce this power (Heskia, 2021). EDs informal power differential with the AD varies by funding structure, regional culture, and discipline (Chapter 4).

Status

Arts organizations provide a particularly public platform for attributions of status. Service to art is seen as a calling to the artistic ideal, motivating artists to high achievement and to ascend to an AD role (René, 2018) (Chapter 2). A company's identity is informed by the ADs creative or performance work, linking to personal taste (Lampel et al., 2000). So organization and AD identities co-mingle. This co-mingling is enhanced when artists have founder status. AD leadership can inspire and attract other collaborating artists, board members, public and private funders, and an audience to their organization (Nisbett & Walmsley, 2016;

Ostrower, 2002). Especially in larger institutions, many ADs are celebrity art makers whose status draws media attention (Lindqvist, 2017). As a result, they may acquire a higher public leadership attribution and status than their managerial partner.

But EDs also gain legitimacy and status according to their previous organizational accomplishments and demonstrations of expertise through market and corporation or business logics (Chapter 2). However, their profile is anchored within their organizations and may not be as public as ADs (Reid & Karambayya, 2009). Each leader's individual reputation and status evolve as artistic and organizational processes develop.

The mandate of formal parity and leading as one is a demanding task for co-leaders to undertake. As mentioned earlier, research demonstrates that effectiveness is improved with differences in power within the shared role space (Krause et al., 2015). Status conflict makes sense as a means of establishing or increasing power differentiation within the shared role space, congruent with this research. The resulting informal social hierarchy helps to overcome the decision-making ambiguity of parity in the shared role space.

Conflict

Status conflict is a recently defined conflict type that introduces a competitive approach to rankings in a group, arising from an attempt to change relative status (Bendersky & Hays, 2012). Status conflict is not directly concerned with the substance (what, who, how, when, and why) of a conflict as other forms of conflict are. Status conflict can occur independently or co-occur with task conflict. Status and values conflict have not been linked. However, status conflict promotes hoarding of information and political engagement with bystanders or allies to take sides to further fuel negative conflict (Bendersky, 1998; Bendersky & Pai, 2018; Cronin & Besrukova, 2019; Magee & Galinsky, 2008). It attempts to legitimize and increase the status of the originating actor in the conflict or reduce the status of the other. When this occurs in co-leadership, it can detract from organizational well-being and development.

Nonetheless, without debate and occasional conflict, co-leadership can lose its purpose to span logics and innovate for a more effective organization (Gibeau et al., 2020). In fact, constructive conflict, usually task conflict, can contribute positively to organizational well-being, allowing for information exchange and strategically beneficial and productive solutions (Bendersky & Hays, 2012; Bendersky & Hays, 2017; Jehn & Mannix, 2001; Tjosvold & Wisse, 2009). Nonetheless, task conflict appears to shift into more destructive forms – process and, particularly, relationship conflict (Amason, 1996; Jehn & Mannix, 2001). Process conflict considers how to undertake the task. But relationship or values conflict concerns differences in personal values where identity and a sense of belonging may be challenged (Jehn, 1997). These latter forms of conflict engage the emotions and can negatively impact performance and attributions of legitimacy. The influence of competing logics and pluralism in the arts can contribute to this escalation of conflict types.

The existence of co-leadership conflict in the cultural field is debated. Some arts management scholars have found only collaborative relationships among co-leaders who solve tensions effectively without negative conflict (Järvinen et al., 2015; Reynolds et al., 2017). Others acknowledge that conflict exists by presenting conflict management as key to success in the sector (Montanari, 2018; Schrauwen et al., 2016). Finally, some have reported that conflict can be very disturbing, rendering co-leadership fragile and organizations unstable (Bhansing et al., 2012; Bhansing et al., 2016; Castañer, 1997; Reid & Karambayya, 2009). Different theoretical lenses have enabled cultural co-leadership scholars to explain differences in perspective that might lead to conflict: Competing values and logics, differing mental mindsets and orientations (Bhansing et al., 2012; Cray et al., 2007; Fjellvær, 2010; Reid & Karambayya, 2009). Exploring status conflict practices further grounds co-leadership research in political and social realities, providing useful theoretical insights and helpful lessons for practitioners (Bolden, 2011; Collinson, 2005; Denis et al., 2012).

Researching co-leadership status conflict in the arts

In this section of the chapter, we explore how changes in social hierarchy may occur in arts co-leadership through status conflict dynamics. Collaborative practices may also influence status and we have identified instances of collaborative relationships in our data. However, we reserve this orientation for future research in order to focus on the learning that status conflict provides in a formal parity co-leadership context. We analyse each co-leader according to dominant or deferential behaviour (Bendersky & Hays, 2012; Collinson, 2005).

We define dominant roles as those associated with seniority attributed through founder-status, tenure and incumbency role, career experience, previous co-leadership experience, significant external or internal recognition, and linkage with the artistic mission and the artistic ideal. This is different from dominance discussed in Chapter 5 where we observe dominant logics advocated by a particular co-leader member in the role space. Based on these power differences, there are three possible relationship types in these co-leadership configurations: AD-dominant, ED-dominant, and AD-ED parity. Table 6.1 provides a portrait of the distribution of cases across the types at the time of the interviews.

Of the 18 cases analysed in our research, 11 AD dominant status cases were identified, divided almost equally between competitive and collaborative modes. In the competitive cases, only two ADs embodied the stereotype of a charismatic and sometimes difficult artist (Abfalter, 2013;

Table 6.1 Collaborative and competitive cases in our data

	Prior relationship	*Incumbent's role, status, and seniority*	*Incoming member's role, status, and seniority*
AD dominant			
5 Collaborative	3 Conflict, 1 Ethics, 3 Weak expertise. (some descriptions overlap)	4 ADs prior 2–10 years in organization, 1 AD arrived at same time as ED.	4 EDs junior, 1 ED mid-career arriving concurrent with AD.
6 Competitive	3 Conflict, 1 Conflict with board, 1 Ethics, 1 Unknown.	2 ADs were founder, 3 ADs with 5–10 years in organization, 1 AD hired at same time as ED.	3 EDs first time plus specialty experience, 3 EDs mid-career, in another discipline.
AD-ED equal status			
3 Collaborative	2 Conflict, 1 Board strategy.	1 ED with 5 years, 2 Co-leaders hired at same time.	1 AD career transition, 2 Co-leaders with parallel experience and similar status.
2 Competitive	1 Conflict, 1 unstable leadership over time.	1 ED chose AD, 1 AD one year and first-time.	1 AD career transition, 1 ED mid-career executive.
ED dominant			
2 Collaborative	1 Conflict in past, 1 Organizational evolution.	1 ED senior experience, 1–3 AD founders.	1 AD first time junior, 1 ED mid-career.

Chiapello, 2004; Nisbett & Walmsley, 2016). None of the ED dominant cases involved competition.

In the cases with dominant ADs, their status had been claimed and granted frequently over time often through their artistic accomplishments, but sometimes through conflict with previous EDs. These conflicts were resolved either by ED departures or board intervention (Reid & Karambayya, 2016). The quality of the prior relationship is also documented in the table.

In the two competitive AD-ED equal status cases, the leaders had engaged in ongoing status contests attempting to gain greater power. Ironically, they maintained the status balance within the relationship since neither of the partners submitted to the other's claims for dominance nor attributed leadership identity.

Status conflict practices

In the competitive cases, we have identified a spectrum of five status conflict practices: (1) Being silent or absent, (2) testing and insisting, (3) competing about expertise, (4) intimidating, and (5) co-opting powerful allies. The conscious intention to undertake status conflict is revealed incrementally across the spectrum.

Although status conflict often occurred on its own, it also appeared to be linked with other forms of conflict before, or after the initiation of status conflict. In some instances, the organization's previous co-leadership had experienced negative conflict, and this history appears to cast a shadow on the relationship under study. This observation parallels other findings about the shadow of past trust experiences (Reid & Karambayya, 2016), especially in the more emotionally difficult relationships. One case with a history of conflict reveals a process of escalation across the status conflict practice types.

Being silent or absent

Rich and regular communication affirms the existence and importance of the other person or people in the shared leadership role space (Alvarez & Svejenova, 2005; Gronn & Hamilton, 2004). However, being silent in response to a leadership claim eliminates voice, diminishing the status of others as co-leadership partners (Bendersky & Hays, 2012). This practice also prevents information exchange and logic integration, and thus degenerates effective decision-making for the organization. In three of the four cases of being silent, the ADs were dominant.

Being silent or absent involves limited or no response to the need for conversation even when the person is present in the offices and studios of the arts organization. Being silent or absent may also involve missing staff meetings or working from home. Touring to other cities or pursuing other guest artist activities elsewhere may also result in a break in communication. In organizations like symphony orchestras, the music director is often absent from the organization, guest conducting elsewhere. Other types of organizations tour and so may draw the AD away from the office. These situations require determined efforts to communicate, although our recent pandemic experience has demonstrated that distanced communication can be more easily accomplished than we previously thought. However, even with audio-visual facility on the internet, a lack of effort to communicate with the distant partner was occasionally used to impart a less strategic status in the organization.

A first example of this practice was found in an organization where the long-tenured AD communicated senior status by arriving late at or by not attending staff meetings convened by the new ED. The ADs behaviour was noted by the ED but never contested, reflecting a deferential approach.

This contrasted with the ADs relationship with the previous ED who had initiated extreme conflict. With the new ED, the AD appeared to engage in subtle status dynamics – communicating that information coming from the EDs side of the organization was of limited value and generating questions about the equality of the co-leadership and the organizational status of the ED.

> where I see some problems ... is ADs sincerity at a senior management meeting. AD walks in late and looks disengaged, these kinds of things, and everyone can see it and they kind of accept it. Pisses me off, and I've never confronted AD about it as to why ... I think it is viewed as my meeting. ... it filters down into some of the direct reports ... but I've got other fish to fry so I just go on to something else.
>
> ED

In a second case, there was no response to proposed strategic ideas from one co-leader to the other. In this situation, the board had approved a change to co-leadership requested by the newly appointed single artistic producer. They recognized that the organization needed this kind of collegial approach after the previous dictatorial single leader. However, despite this offer of equal collaboration by the AD to the ED, the ED was disappointed that proposals for production and organizational innovations did not elicit a response. Communication between the AD and the ED settled into email or exchanged comments on draft grant applications, despite the regular presence of both in the offices. This limited their potential for strategic information exchange and limited the development of complementarity within the co-leadership.

> Q: How frequently do the two of you talk, like face to face? A: Alone? If it's once a week? Once a month probably.
>
> ED

An informal status differential already existed between the two executives. The ED was new to this level of responsibility, in contrast to the ADs previous experience as an AD elsewhere. The AD also had a longer tenure in the organization. The ADs silence and lack of engagement in organizational issues further diminished the EDs sense of leadership in the organization, stunting a newly established legitimate power. ED reflected an attitude of respect by beginning the relationship with a deferential approach, normally adopted with ADs. However, realizing that a reduced status and submissive mode was being imposed through the ADs silence, EDs sensed that a strategic contribution to the organization was being limited (Bendersky & Hays, 2012). Whether this lack of attention was purposeful was not revealed in the interviews with the AD, but other staff noticed and confirmed its impact, creating ambiguity about leadership authority and identity.

ED decided to challenge the silence in order to change status and experience more agency, but the initiative was unsuccessful.

> ED: … the usual assembling of the season and a budget. A level of frustration on my part just building and building and building until I wrote a letter about all the things that were just driving me crazy, and what AD needed to do to make it better and that would affect me in a positive way. And AD had a great reaction: "let's talk about this." And that was great, that there was the will … but then we didn't talk further.

The third case was more obviously conflicted. The AD was a creative artist and had worked with two EDs in the same organization over the previous 10 years. The new ED had never worked at that level. In this situation, physical absence initiated the silence. The AD had difficulty coordinating meetings with the ED during normal office hours, only appearing at the end of the day after finishing rehearsals in the studio. AD assumed that the ED would accommodate by working late into the evening as previous EDs had done. Subsequently, instead of submitting, the ED contested the ADs behaviour by working from home and taking days off, contributing to the conflict and organizational distress. The AD criticized the ED to employees for this lack of presence, thus recruiting staff as allies in the conflict (DeRue & Ashford, 2010). But ultimately, personal face-to-face silence also occurred. The situation escalated further into a multitude of silenced and silencing ruptures that communicated the ADs personal conflict with the ED, linking personal conflict with status conflict.

> And AD went through a period of literally ignoring me. [Not] looking at me in the eye, not saying hello to me when he came in, not coming to any staff meetings, just generally not communicating whatsoever.
>
> ED

In this case, retaliatory silence was used to compete for status dominance but also reduced the EDs status and degraded the organizational situation over time.

Finally, one of our symphony orchestras provides an example of being silent resulting from very limited distance communication. The incumbent ED began the job with a default superior status, lacking a full-time music director (AD). As CEO, leadership status had been granted by the board of directors and musicians, acknowledging sorely needed stabilization work during the two years prior to the new ADs arrival. As well, the ED was able to claim leadership status with the board by chairing a small board committee to select and hire the new AD. The ED claimed senior status as being the executive solely in charge of the strategic direction of the organization. The AD however claimed equal status in the interview.

As the relationship unfolded, the ED rarely acknowledged the ADs international artistic status which would have involved travelling to attend concerts conducted elsewhere to discuss organizational plans in person. Others in the organization considered it the EDs responsibility to initiate communication.

> If the ED is not picking up the phone and hasn't spoken to the AD at least once every 10 days, then things break down. And in a way, it's probably EDs responsibility to find the AD, because the AD is not in residence the same way an ED is.
>
> Artistic administrator

To maintain dominant status with the board, the ED further silenced the AD by rarely extending an invitation to board meetings or by carefully shaping the messages that were communicated when AD or the artistic administrator attended board meetings.

> ED would like to be the total face to the board of everything to do with the organization. ... obviously AD wants to be with the board too. So, ED tries to have AD present [at board meetings] only when ED is present to control that, and AD doesn't like that. And we give AD the opportunity because we think it's important. ...
>
> President, board of directors

> But ED has been very jealous, that's the only word that I can use, about being the only person. ED doesn't really want the board to have that much of a relationship with AD and that is a tension.
>
> President, board of directors

Ironically, the EDs dominating and competitive practices in this case kept the status parity in balance rather than increasing the EDs status. The ADs public celebrity and mission-linked profile also influenced the board.

In a collaborative case, a theatre company provides a useful contrasting example where the use of task conflict without status conflict was productive for the organization. While the AD had much seniority through tenure and celebrity, the relationship with the individual who was to become ED was well established. Prior to appointment, the ED had undertaken some project development in another role in the organization. As co-leaders, their frequent daily communication generated much sharing of perspectives and information. They were able to debate programming choices, then deferentially acknowledge how the other was ultimately right, moving the organization forward. The ADs generous affirmation of the EDs judgment raised the EDs status for future program discussions.

> And we're on the same page, and because we've known each other for so long we can talk about things ... there's something really important here. ED believes in my vision.
>
> AD

> We're not stepping on each other's toes – I'm also able to carry some of the weight for AD. So, there are times when I'm able to cross the line a bit, and be in a quasi-artistic mode, and of course AD is positive enough to let that happen.
>
> ED

Commentary

Being silent is a common practice. It was found in four of the eight cases of competitive relationships with varying impact. The practice has a significant impact on the other's power and status, and the complementarity of the role space. This potent practice subtly destabilizes the formal parity within the relationship of a jointly mandated co-leadership. The lack of active participation in a relationship shuts down information sharing, limits work coordination, refuses reciprocal attribution of leadership claims, and thus diminishes the status of the claiming partner. This behaviour frees the silent member to distance themselves from fulfilling the joint leadership responsibilities in the shared role space. While being silent avoids overt conflict, it expands ambiguity in the role space by reducing negotiation of a clear understanding. When used by ADs, being silent is a particularly compelling status conflict practice. When being silent, the ADs mission-related identity takes over the role space, covertly disturbing the joint leadership balance. Co-leadership effectiveness can be significantly undermined.

Testing and insisting

Both testing and insisting were practices which affirmed a superior status related to both expert (artistic competence) and referent power (celebrity). Both sources of power were linked to the artistic logic, conferring greater legitimacy to the AD within the co-leadership dynamic.

In one company, the AD had long been the single leader and stage director. The board appointed an ED as co-leader, but this person left after 18 months of contested authority with the AD. The second ED came from a different art discipline. When this new ED arrived in the organization, the AD presented the new ED with a script and asked for an opinion. The ED initially deferred but recognized this as a test of artistic competence and possible ambitions to participate in programming content that would meet market expectations. ED had been hired to bring peace to the organization and chose a deferential way to negotiate with the AD:

> The second week here, the AD gave me a test... it was a play [script]. What do I know about plays? And AD said, well why don't you read it and see what you think. And I thumbed through it, it was more edgy than anything else, and it was [going to be] a part of our season subscription ... and AD positioned it as something that was really wanted. I found a way to say no, and AD dropped it and we went on.
>
> ED

In arts organizations, goal ambiguity between artistic autonomy and positive market response induces tension in the leadership role space (Lampel et al., 2000). The testing experience was memorable and uncomfortable for the ED, reinforcing the AD's dominant status and ultimate control in artistic matters. But it also recognized the EDs responsibility for marketing.

In another more conflicted case of testing, an openly aggressive AD claimed superior status by acting as the employer and setting an objective that challenged the new ED to meet.

> I do recognize that it is a huge challenge for someone coming in with no experience, but I remember saying, part of the reason you're getting this job is because [of your past experience in the discipline]. We are producing a certain type of work. If you're able to get this organization on the road, you will have succeeded, and along the way you probably will learn an enormous amount.
>
> AD

With no previous experience at the executive level, the ED deferentially accepted the challenge.

> And AD always said: You have a year. So, I invested time and energy in the organization.
>
> ED

The ADs vigilant dominance and the EDs lack of experience resulted in some very difficult exchanges, escalating to extremely negative conflict later in the relationship. We will return to this case.

In a third case, insisting occurred. The relationship between the charismatic artistic co-founders and their first ED ended in acrimony, rooted in task and values conflict about the risk of growing the company beyond its financial means to meet artistic aspirations. Their new ED faced the co-ADs renewed insistence for growth that required a deferential but strategically collaborative response. When confronted with a refusal, the consistently present AD persisted with other solutions to gain EDs agreement with his strategy.

> AD is a negotiator by personality type. So, if not achieved one way, AD will come back at it from another direction, you know, AD will just keep coming at it until we find a resolution. AD is creative around problem-solving as well, when given the challenge to solve.
>
> ED

Commentary

In all three cases of testing or insisting, the AD was dominant, and their competitive practice maintained this status. They had accumulated attributed informal status as the senior leader with long tenure in the organization and in the artistic discipline as well as being founder in one case. The EDs were new to the job, and in some cases, new to the discipline, with less expert and referent power than their partners who were linked to the artistic logic and mission. Testing generates a subtly coercive atmosphere and insisting undermines and eliminates the conversation and debate necessary to explore and integrate the perspectives in a shared role space (Gronn & Hamilton, 2004).

Although testing and insisting practices appear somewhat benign, and the relationship is not ruptured by them, they contest the parity in the relationship, rendering fulfilment of the joint status and its responsibilities more ambiguous and the role space as less intuitively complementary. These practices imply decisional seniority for the AD and the dominant influence of the artistic logic and artistic autonomy. However, the EDs were deferential and accepted this implied seniority and for some time, the co-leadership was effective. Conflict in one of the cases escalated and in another, the ED eventually left. In the third, the relationship appeared to work well, but senior managers were quite involved in negotiating the balance (Chapter 9). While we found no EDs engaging in this testing and insisting practice, that may be the result of ADs being incumbents in these cases as well as being personally linked with the organizational mission (Lampel et al., 2000). Further research observing other co-leaders might provide more nuances to the insight.

Competing expertise

Typically, in the arts, each leader is responsible for separate functional areas whose work is coordinated in the shared role space. But concerns about public image and marketing in an arts organization, for instance, can overlap between AD and ED fields of expertise. Two cases of this overlap illustrate status conflict, in addition to task or process conflict, and thus, impact on complementarity in the shared role space (Hodgson et al., 1965).

In one case, the board appointed a new AD to revitalize the programming vision for the company. AD was given significant public recognition as an artist and as a youthful visionary for the future. The organization had been previously riven by toxic conflict, but soon after the ADs arrival, the incumbent ED who had participated in that conflict departed abruptly. The AD was left as a single leader for some time, having to crisis-manage across the whole organization and plan the upcoming season. This process included conceiving the season brochure and staging the photo shoot for marketing materials for ADs first season.

> For my first season, I want to infuse an image that is more personal. That is more poetic, and I want the images to be works of art as such.
>
> AD

For the ADs second season, the preparation of the brochure was reclaimed by the newly appointed ED on the basis of role responsibility and marketing expertise. The ADs involvement was not welcome. Feeling hurt, the AD argued for the necessity of having the artistic vision and graphic judgment present as the season image was developed. The ED responded:

> When I arrived, the attendance rate [for the ADs first season] was very low, compared to our usual … So, for the next season's brochure, we used a company that has communication strategy expertise …This created – which I never imagined, - very strong tensions. AD kept asking "But what's wrong with last year's brochure?" My response was: the images "don't tell us what the show is about. It doesn't sell the shows".

While this appears to be process conflict, there was competitive status conflict about whose voice was the legitimate authority concerning issues that engaged both market and artistic logics.

> AD told me several times that it was an ADs job to do this, and I had to say: "Well yes, but it's also mine, it's a collaboration … I'm responsible for all the marketing aspects. In the end, I have to fill the seats."
>
> ED

Despite this conflict, the AD and ED maintained parity in the company's social hierarchy, but 18 months after this incident, the ED left. Complementarity had become less effective, and the co-leadership was fragile.

In the second case, a small symphony orchestra, the EDs experience with the region's cabaret and jazz scene led to a proposal that programming should become more accessible and community-based to include local soloists and amateurs. The music director (AD), who had international classical music training, resisted this change and continued to program classical repertoire, setting up task conflict. Each claimed to be responding to mission-driven imperatives, community or artistic, justified according to their experience and expertise. An appeal to the board resulted in a decision that excluded the ED from all programming decisions, reconfirmed the expertise of the AD, and the primacy of the artistic logic. To compensate for this status reduction, the ED used other competitive tactics within the administrative jurisdiction to reduce the impact of the ADs vision of purely classical programming. Mid-year, the budget was suddenly and significantly reduced, and the AD was forced to use community talent and amateurs to balance financially.

> ... And I have always tried to balance the recruitment of musicians but still keep enough money to do everything you would want to do. But now that production budget has crumbled away. Maybe find other collaborations where there are others who pay – Let's say you play with a church choir and the organist conducts. Maybe an incompetent conductor [but] it doesn't cost us anything to play with them.
>
> AD

The ADs ability to program according to expertise and vision was constrained, reducing ADs status anchored in the artistic ideal and an international reputation. In later years, this AD left. The organization had become much less recognized for its competence in classical music.

Commentary

In both cases of competing expertise, the ED and AD maintained an equal status, but the relationship was not long-lasting, reflecting disturbance of the relationship. Other forms of conflict were present. Co-leadership shared role space may include overlapping responsibilities despite the differentiation of the separate responsibilities. A perceived transgression of a boundary challenging the other's professional identity seems to have resulted in task and process conflict. While status conflict does not appear to upset the formal equal status of the partners in the co-leadership, it undermined the ability to lead as one, rendering it fragile. Status conflict appears to engage in the relevant competing logics to establish legitimacy claims to a dominant status. As competitive behaviour, this conflict contributes to a culture of ambiguity and organizational instability (Denis et al., 2001; Dickson, 2018).

Intimidating

Direct and aggressive behaviour occurred in only one case. Traditionally, the AD had worked with limited resources for new creations. The previous ED had refused the budget for a new and larger production, but it was ultimately approved by the board president after that EDs departure. The critical and financial success of this novel production was a breakthrough for the company, providing some financial breathing room for the successor ED.

The situation also confirmed the ADs sense of legitimacy as an important innovative artist.

> When the company is perceived as something that is vibrant and alive, that can only happen with a person like me who has a vision and a passion and a drive. Now I've reached the point where...I want an audience. I want people to listen to what I have to say.
>
> AD

This elevated status would have been compromised if AD accepted reduced budgets in the future. In the next year, another new production of the same type was not as well received. Financial issues returned and pressure mounted. Testing and eliminating voice through silence eventually intensified to direct confrontation. The very charismatic AD became increasingly aggressive and intimidating to retain gains in resources and status.

> And when I would try to speak to AD, I would get glared at. Long, long silences, long glares. Just made to feel like I was the enemy. It was very tough. ... AD has an ability to make people feel very uncomfortable very easily.
>
> ED

The ED was forced to defer to the AD. To avoid cutting the ADs budget or other resources, the ED looked to other solutions, including donations of large sums from EDs own salary and reduction of administrative budgets.

> At times, AD would talk about compromise, but it was a game, a face-off, a stand-off, a game of poker. Who was going to crumble first? And on occasion, I set up the expectations and rules of the game by crumbling myself. ... First of all I kept increasing my personal contribution.
>
> ED

A powerful stakeholder, the board treasurer, observed and questioned the EDs inability to control the ADs spending. This treasurer doubted the efficacy of the equally mandated status. Despite voicing this opinion sympathetically, this perspective further reduced the EDs leadership status with other organizational actors, questioning parity in the co-leadership arrangement in the arts.

> What are you doing all this for? You're not doing this because it's a model example of a budgetary process. You are running an organization because you've got an art form that you want to produce and show to the public. So, if that's where it tilts a little bit more in favour of the AD then I think that's my conclusion as to why you have got to give greater power to that person, because they have got that unique thing.

Commentary

In this single case, intimidation becomes a point of no return in a very conflicted relationship – the brink of rupture in the relationship. Although the ED expressed a desire for collaboration, the AD defaulted to a single leadership command style, claiming dominant status as the artistic professional and exclusive adherence to the artistic ideal. Values conflict and related toxic status conflict evolved together to diminish the EDs power (Bendersky & Hays, 2012) more than other status conflict practices described in this chapter, confirming suggestions that status conflict is relationship conflict. Certainly, in this case, any distinction is difficult to discern. Aggressive demands for status affirmation by one actor that diminishes the other undermine the joint leadership in an equally mandated role space. A compromise that balanced the company's artistic achievement and financial stability would not be easily achieved in these circumstances (Chapter 5).

Co-opting a superior authority

Another significant competitive gesture to claim dominant status mobilizes an alliance with a superior authority, such as the board of directors or a major public funder (DeRue & Ashford, 2010). In one case, the new AD of a symphony orchestra wanted to add two projects to supplement the regular season. The impact of these projects would add public attribution to ADs status as an important institutional leader. Unfortunately, the orchestra was in a precarious financial situation. The first project was a documentary film for television about the new artistic leadership intended to enhance the organization's visibility, thanks to ADs international renown. At the ADs request, the board approved the additional expense of the documentary, leaving the ED no choice but to look for more revenue, very late in the financial cycle.

The board chair also supported the ADs other project. This was a special concert that would strategically position the organization in the community and actively engage other board members to assist. However, the concert relied on the EDs collaboration to make other staff resources available. Powerful allies do not always provide an advantage.

> The AD decided that we should do something for [disaster] relief. I thought it was absolutely right. ED didn't agree and basically did nothing to support the process. We even got the [artists'] unions to throw in everything for free. The newspapers [were convinced] to give us free ads but in the end, because not enough staff resources were thrown in [by the ED] to make this happen, so I killed it.
>
> Board chair

Several years later, the same AD felt threatened by a subsequent ED and twice negotiated directly with the board to have the contract extended. This pattern of AD dominance is perhaps surprising in a symphony orchestra in which the ED is the more resident executive of the organization. However, it confirms the power of the artistic ideal and the tenacity of artistic status once dominance has been affirmed (Chapter 2).

In the second case, we return to the situation where the AD had intimidated the ED, and values and status conflict flared into an impasse because of financial issues.

> The budget was going off the rails in terms of expenses once again... without getting any sense of partnership from AD, ... I decided to bring it to the executive and finance committees and identify it as an issue and ask AD to attend.
>
> ED

By co-opting the board to accept and share the responsibility of managing the ADs ambition, the ED undertook a risky move that significantly reduced leadership attribution, organizational status, and power. Effectively, ED abdicated to the board the integrating role in the shared role space.

> I knew that it would perhaps be a way of solving the problem for the organization, and that it might cost me my job. But I believed strongly that my relationship with the AD had deteriorated to such an extent that it was no longer a life that I wanted to be a part of. I felt this need for objectivity in order to stop this cycle of overspending with no consequences.
>
> ED

The board chair acceded to the EDs request to intervene, and in fact, the ED chose to depart, the ultimate deferential gesture in this case.

> ...that relationship was already so impaired that there was no salvaging it ...You can't make people respect each other, and you can't make people work well together. That's impossible... The board has been doing a lot of what I would consider to be staff level work and has been making sure that things are happening.
>
> President, board of directors

The board treasurer took over interim budget management and began a program of sensitizing the AD to the responsibility for relationship dynamics of formal parity with the next ED.

Commentary

Co-opting the board was found in two cases. One was undertaken by an AD in an equal situation. The AD did not always win. The other was instigated by an ED dominated by an AD.

In these cases, the practice overwhelmed the competition through alignment with a more powerful collective actor (DeRue & Ashford, 2010). This practice invites external stakeholders into the role space, changing the power differential. This gesture confuses the fulfilment of responsibilities in the role space, creates conflicting alliances for stakeholders, results in organizational inefficiencies, and demoralizes other members of the organization (Reid & Karambayya, 2009). As a result, the actor seeking support may win the battle but lose the war because their leadership status attribution diminishes significantly through the alignment. This relationship no longer engages just with the one individual. This would be particularly true of an ED who lacked the mission-related affiliation with the artistic ideal.

Conclusion

In this study of status conflict in arts co-leadership, our research objectives were to understand its impact on the co-leadership's mutual attribution, social hierarchy, and relationship. Formal parity is a common feature of mandated co-leadership. In a recent census of the co-leadership literature, equal status appeared in 69% of the publications (Döös & Wilhelmson, 2021) suggesting that an investigation of contesting dynamics and their impact on this equality might be valuable.

Criticisms of co-leadership touch on problems of ambiguity in the formally mandated parity that make reaching agreement on a single strategic vision difficult (Locke, 2003). This ambiguity results from a lack of clarity regarding decision-making authority over a plurality of objectives. Plurality is typical of professional organizations. In the arts, the criticism is complicated by concerns about the need to preserve artistic autonomy in this type of pluralistic context. Co-leaders who are equally empowered are vulnerable to status competition in the role space to gain relative power and influence. In fact, as research in the private sector has shown, some power differences render co-leadership more effective (Krause et al., 2015).

However, other more comfortable solutions have been proposed to dispel the ambiguity of co-leadership: Shared cognition and trust (Alvarez & Svejenova, 2005) as well as voluntary and mutual attribution of leadership which may be mutually accomplished in co-leadership (DeRue & Ashford, 2010). However, shared cognition and trust need ongoing attention and may not always be attainable because of competing logics and individual ambitions at play in the arts (Chapter 7). The power of the artistic ideal at the core of the arts mission can undermine attribution of non-arts leadership. In addition, memories of past conflict may block reciprocal attribution of joint executive leadership in new relationships.

In our study of co-leadership status conflict, we identified a spectrum of five practices. In this conclusion, we categorize these practices into two types according to the co-leaders' approach to the relationship. In the first, a co-leader attempts to deny the relationship, while in the second, co-leaders each work to create informal status differences within the relationship.

In the first type, being silent or co-opting a powerful ally have parallel aims. In each, the contested other is distanced from decision-making. Mutual attributions of partnership in the joint leadership role are thwarted (DeRue & Ashford, 2010). Being silent ignores and diminishes the other while co-opting bypasses and betrays the other. In some cases of being silent, the relationship continued when the power differential was relatively balanced and if some compensating behaviour occurred. However, the co-leaders typically lose access to information and expertise, which reduces complementarity (Hodgson et al., 1965). Increasing expertise is, of course, one of the reasons to put co-leadership in place. The responsibilities in the role space may not be completely fulfilled because one person is absent for short or long periods of time. These practices compromise joint leadership for the organization.

Co-opting is a more aggressive practice than the passivity of being silent. Co-opting power resources from outside the shared role space changes the ecosystem of power differential in the space. It excludes the other person from decision-making, eliminating the complementarity of the co-leadership. Both practices in this first theme refute the parity within the relationship and attempt to obviate the need for a relationship.

In the second type, status conflict involves face-to-face interaction and stays within the relationship. Nonetheless, these practices appear to range from minor irritation to abuse. Testing and insisting reinforce the status of the dominant partner. Testing appears to occur at the beginning of a new relationship, undertaken by the incumbent to clarify power differences or to understand how the new relationship may be different from a past acrimonious situation. With insisting, the desired decisions are made jointly although the difference in status is reinforced. Competition about expertise does not necessarily result in a change in status. However, the competition introduces tension in the relationship. Differentiation is confirmed but complementarity and trust are reduced. The co-leadership remains functional, perhaps an expression of negative peace, as described in Chapter 5. Finally, intimidation is extremely toxic to the relationship, seriously affecting complementarity producing personal conflict.

Research shows that status conflict can co-occur with task conflict and moderate the relationship with group performance (Bendersky & Hays, 2012). Status conflict also has a direct and negative effect on performance because of reduced information sharing. The relationship between status conflict and values conflict has not been clarified in the literature. From our research, we suggest that, within co-leadership, values conflict can be present prior to status conflict and interact with it. Values conflict may be recalled from previous conflictual relationships that replicate current differences (Reid & Karambayya, 2016). It may also have already settled into the relationship arising from competing logics and values that arise during difficult decision-making. Certain practices in our research demonstrate how values and status conflict combine to generate particularly toxic situations. These situations damage role complementarity and render decision-making difficult if not paralyzed. However, despite the negativity, status conflict may generate a change in power differential that can solve the decision-making stasis.

One case demonstrates this cumulative and interactive dynamic between values and status conflict. The ADs relationship with the previous ED broke down through the process of political manoeuvring and values conflict about funding for a new artistic initiative. The ED left and the board of directors approved the finances for the ADs new production (Reid & Karambayya, 2016). With the ADs status confirmed as a senior artist, the relationship with the subsequent ED carried forward the memory of the conflict. Adopting an employer stance, as opposed to a peer perspective, the AD challenged the ED to learn the job within a year, recognizing the new EDs lack of general management experience. While this appears to be status conflict, the AD was also projecting the previous regime's values conflict onto this relationship. Over time, market response to the artistic product and mixed financial and management results required a return to constrained budgeting. These circumstances forced AD and ED to replicate the same values conflict from the past. A blame culture ensued within the relationship. As well, both leaders practiced being silent, avoiding each other and being absent. Status conflict superimposed on values conflict escalated the negativity of the situation. At the same time, the AD refused to compromise on production expenses that were exceeding budget. Intimidation of the ED was an extreme status response to the threatened loss of resources and artistic identity. The ED acknowledged an impasse in the relationship. To regain power for budget control and establish decision-making authority, the ED appealed to the board, successfully co-opting their support in negotiating a compromise with the AD to stabilize the organization. The EDs gesture ceded control to the board in the shared role space and he left the organization. The gravity of the status conflict escalated throughout the relationship interacting with the already present values conflict carried forward from the previous relationship. These dynamics eliminate mutual leadership attribution within the co-leadership shared role space. They degenerate complementarity.

DeRue and Ashford's (2010) interpretation of shared and distributed leadership suggests a seamless process of claiming and granting leadership among individuals in a group. For co-leadership parity to work effectively, this same collegial dynamic is necessary within the shared role space. However, when status conflict arises, one co-leader appears to block another's claim to equal co-leadership. We suggest that DeRue and Ashford's view of collegial leadership-granting relationships requires further insights to fully explain leadership status attribution, especially if applied to co-leadership with mandated parity.

Not all co-leaders experience status or substantive conflict. Some benign task conflict can be productive for information sharing and debate for integrating logics (Gibeau et al., 2020; Reid & Karambayya, 2009). In our research and in published cases of co-leadership, we found that many role spaces do function well with collaboration and high complementarity (Hodgson et al., 1965) (Chapter 5). In these cases, the distinct artistic and managerial leadership roles provide sufficient differentiation and specialization with minimal to no negative conflict despite the dominant status of one or the other leader (Reid & Karambayya, 2009; Reynolds et al., 2017). The complicated challenges of role conflict and ambiguity in co-leadership appear to be reduced through shared cognition and trust (Alvarez & Svejenova, 2005; Biddle, 1986). Each leader needs to understand the other's logics and objectives, making decisions with a balanced approach (Chapter 5). A comment from one board president concludes our reflections on how these parity relationships may work with informal status differences.

I think *primus inter pares* is a much better focus than a junior-senior relationship.

References

Abfalter, D. (2013). Authenticity and respect: Leading creative teams in the performing arts. *Creativity and Innovation Management*, *12*(3), 295–306.

Alvarez, J. L., & Svejenova, S. (2005). *Sharing Executive Power: Roles and Relationships at the Top*. Cambridge University Press.

Amason, A. C. (1996). Distinguishing the effects of functional and dysfunctional conflict on strategic decision making: Resolving a paradox for top management teams. *The Academy of Management Journal*, *39*(1), 123–148. https://doi.org/10.2307/256633

Bass, B.M. (1990). *Handbook of Leadership* (3rd edition). Free Press.

Bendersky, C. (1998). Culture: The missing link in dispute systems design. *Negotiation Journal*, *14*(4), 307–311. https://doi.org/10.1111/j.1571-9979.1998.tb00168.x

Bendersky, C., & Hays, N. (2012). Status conflict in groups. *Organization Science*, *23*(2), 323–340. https://doi.org/10.1287/orsc.1110.0734

Bendersky, C., & Hays, N. A. (2017). The positive effects of status conflicts in teams where members perceive status hierarchies differently. *Social Psychological and Personality Science*, *8*(2), 124–132. https://doi.org/10.1177/1948550616667614

Bendersky, C., & Pai, J. (2018). Status dynamics. *Annual Review of Organizational Psychology and Organizational Behavior*, *5*, 183–199. https://doi.org/032117-104602

Bhansing, P., Leenders, M., & Wijnberg, N. (2012). Performance effects of cognitive heterogeneity in dual leadership structures in the arts: The role of selection system orientations [article]. *European Management Journal*, *30*(6), 523–534. https://doi.org/10.1016/j.emj.2012.04.002

Bhansing, P., Leenders, M., & Wijnberg, N. (2016). Selection system orientations as an explanation for the differences between dual leaders of the same organization in their perception of organizational performance. *Journal of Management & Governance*, *20*(4), 907–933. https://doi.org/10.1007/s10997-015-9330-4

Biddle, R. J. (1986). Recent developments in role theory. *Annual Review of Sociology*, *12*, 67–92.

Bolden, R. (2011). Distributed leadership in organizations: A review of theory and research. *International Journal of Management Reviews*, *13*(3), 251–269. https://doi.org/10.1111/j.1468-2370.2011.00306.x

Castañer, X. (1997). The Tension between Artistic Leaders and Management in Arts Organizations: The Case of the Barcelona Symphony Orchestra. In M. Fitzgibbon & A. Kelly (Eds.), *From Maestro to Manager: Critical Issues in Arts and Culture Management (pp.* 379–416). Oak Tree Press.

Chiapello, E. (2004). Evolution and co-optation: The 'artist critique' of management and capitalism. *Third Text*, *18*(6), 585–594. https://doi.org/10.1080/0952882042000284998

Collinson, D. (2005). Dialectics of leadership. *Human Relations*, *58*(11), 1419–1442. https://doi.org/10.1177/0018726705060902

Cray, D., Inglis, L., & Freeman, S. (2007). Managing the arts: Leadership and decision making under dual rationalities. *Journal of Arts Management, Law and Society*, *36*(4), 295–313. https://doi.org/10.3200/JAML.36.4.295-314

Cronin, M. A., & Besrukova, K. (2019). Conflict management through the lens of system dynamics. *Academy of Management Annals*, *13*(2), 770–806. https://doi.org/10.5465/annals.2017.0021

Denis, J.-L., Langley, A., & Cazale, L. (1996). Leadership and strategic change under ambiguity. *Organization Studies*, 17(4), 673–699. https://doi-org.proxy2.hec.ca/10.1177/017084069601700406

Denis, J.-L., Lamothe, L., & Langley, A. (2001). The dynamics of collective leadership and strategic change in pluralistic organizations. *The Academy of Management Journal*, *44*(4), 809–837. https://doi.org/10.2307/3069417

Denis, J.-L., Langley, A., & Rouleau, L. (2010). The practice of leadership in the messy world of organizations. *Leadership*, *6*(1), 67–88. https://doi.org/10.1177/1742715009354233

Denis, J.-L., Langley, A., & Sergi, V. (2012). Leadership in the plural. *The Academy of Management Annals*, *5*(1), 211–283. https://doi.org/10.1080/19416520.2012.667612

DeRue, D. S., & Ashford, S. J. (2010). Who will lead and who will follow? A social process of leadership identity construction in organizations. *Academy of Management Review*, *35*(4), 627–647. https://doi.org/10.5465/amr.35.4.zok627

Dickson, A. (2018). 'Don't screw it up!' Artistic directors on the perils of regime change. *The Guardian*.

Döös, M., & Wilhelmson, L. (2021). Fifty-five years of managerial shared leadership research: A review of an empirical field. *Leadership*, *17*(6), 715–746. https://doi.org/10.1177/17427150211037809

Empson, L. (2020). Ambiguous authority and hidden hierarchy: Collective leadership in an elite professional service firm. *Leadership*, 16(1), 62–86. https://doi.org/10.1177/1742715019886769

Fjellvær, H. (2010). *Dual and unitary leadership: managing ambiguity in pluralistic organizations* (Publication Number 2010/10). Doctoral dissertation, Norwegian School of Economics and Business Administration, Bergen. https://openaccess.nhh.no/nhh-xmlui/bitstream/handle/11250/164362/fjellver%20avh%202010.PDF?sequence=1

Fleming, P., & Spicer, A. (2014). Power in management and organization studies. *Academy of Management Annals*, *8*(1), 237–298. https://doi.org/10.1080/19416520.2014.875671

French, J. and Raven, B. (1959). The Bases of Social Power. In D. Cartwright (Ed.), *Studies in Social Power* (pp. 150–167). Institute for Social Research.

Gibeau, É., Langley, A., Denis, J.-L., & van Schendel, N. (2020). Bridging competing demands through co-leadership? Potential and limitations. *Human Relations*, *73*(4), 464–489. https://doi.org/10.1177/001872671988814

Gronn, P., & Hamilton, A. (2004). 'A bit more life in the leadership': Co-principalship as distributed leadership practice. *Leadership and Policy in Schools*, *3*(1), 3–35. https://doi.org/10.1076/lpos.3.1.3.27842

Heskia, T. (2021). Academic and cultural worker. Leuphana University. Interview.

Hodgson, R. C., Levinson, D. J., & Zaleznik, A. (1965). *The Executive Role Constellation: An Analysis of Personality and Role Relations in Management.* Harvard University: Division of Research, Graduate School of Business Administration.

Järvinen, M., Ansio, H., & Houni, P. (2015). New variations of dual leadership: Insights from Finnish theatre. *International Journal of Arts Management*, *17*(3), 16–27.

Jehn, K. A. (1997). A qualitative analysis of conflict types and dimensions in organizational groups. *Administrative Science Quarterly*, 42(3), 530–557.

Jehn, K. A., & Mannix, E. A. (2001). The dynamic nature of conflict: A longitudinal study of intragroup conflict and group performance. *Academy of Management Journal*, *44*(2), 238–251. https://doi.org/10.2307/3069453

Kawashima, N. (2006). Audience development and social inclusion in Britain: Tensions, contradictions and paradoxes in policy and their implications for cultural management. *International Journal of Cultural Policy*, *12*(1), 55–72. https://doi.org/10.1080/10286630600613309

Krause, R., Priem, R., & Love, L. (2015). Who's in charge here? Co-CEOs, power gaps, and firm performance. *Strategic Management Journal*, *36*(13), 2099–2110. https://doi.org/10.1002/smj.2325

Lampel, J., Lant, T., & Shamsie, J. (2000). Balancing act: Learning from organizing practices in cultural industries. *Organization Science*, *11*(3), 263–269. https://doi.org/10.1287/orsc.11.3.263.12503

Lindqvist, K. (2017). Leadership in Art and Business. In E. Raviola & P. Zackariasson (Eds.), *Arts and Business: Building a Common Ground for Understanding Society (pp.* 404–422). Routledge.

Locke, E. A. (2003). Leadership: Starting at the Top. In C. L. Pearce, & J. A. Conger (Eds.), *Shared Leadership: Reframing the Hows and Whys of Leadership* (pp. 271–284). Sage.

Löfgren, M. (2016). On the Public Value of Arts and Culture. In K. Dalborg, & M. Löfgren (Eds.), *The FIKA Project: Perspectives on Cultural Leadership* (pp. 75–99). Nätwerkstan Kultur.

MacNeill, K., & Tonks, A. (2013). Leadership in Australian Arts Companies: One Size Does Not Fit All. In J. Caust (Ed.), *Arts Leadership: International Case Studies* (1st ed., pp. 69–82). Tilde University Press.

Magee, J. C., & Galinsky, A. D. (2008). Social hierarchy: The self-reinforcing nature of power and status. *Academy of Management Annals*, *2*(1), 351–398. https://doi.org/10.1080/19416520802211628

Montanari, F. (2018). Organizational Design and People Management. In P. Dubini, F. Montanari, & A. Cirrincioni (Eds.), *Management of Cultural Firms* (pp. 257–289). Bocconi University Press.

Nisbett, M., & Walmsley, B. (2016). The romanticization of charismatic leadership in the arts. *The Journal of Arts Management, Law, and Society*, *46*(1), 2–12. https://doi.org/10.1080/10632921.2015.1131218

Ostrower, F. (2002). *Trustees of Culture: Power, Wealth, and Status on Elite Arts Boards.* University of Chicago Press.

Raven, B. H. (1965). Social Influence and Power. In I. D. Steiner, & M. Fishbien (Eds.), *Current Studies in Social Psychology* (pp. 371–382). Holt, Rinehart, Winston.

Reid, W., & Karambayya, R. (2009). Impact of dual executive leadership dynamics in creative organizations [article]. *Human Relations*, *62*(7), 1073–1112. https://doi.org/10.1177/0018726709335539

Reid, W., & Karambayya, R. (2016). The shadow of history: Situated dynamics of trust in dual executive leadership. *Leadership*, *12*(5), 609–631. https://doi.org/10.1177/1742715015579931

René, V. V. (2018). *L'influence du sens de responsabilité sur la motivation de diriger: Étude de la direction artistique.* Master's thesis, HEC Montréal, Montréal.

Rentschler, R. (2015). *Arts Governance: People, Passion, Performance* (1st ed.). Routledge.

Reynolds, S., Tonks, A., & MacNeill, K. (2017). Collaborative leadership in the arts as a unique form of dual leadership. *The Journal of Arts Management, Law, and Society*, *47*(2), 89–104. https://doi.org/10.1080/10632921.2016.1241968

Schrauwen, J., Schramme, A., & Segers, J. (2016). Do Managers Run Cultural Institutions? The Practice of Shared Leadership in the Arts Sector. In K. Dalborg, & M. Löfgren (Eds.), *The FIKA Project: Perspectives on Cultural Leadership* (pp. 103–116). Nätverkstan Kultur.

Thornton, P. H., Ocasio, W., & Lounsbury, M. (2012). *The Institutional Logics Perspective: A New Approach to Culture, Structure, and Process.* Oxford University Press.

Tjosvold, D., & Wisse, B. (Eds.). (2009). *Power and Interdependence in Organizations.* Cambridge University Press.

Yukl, G. A. (2012). Effective leadership behavior: What we know and what questions need more attention. *Academy of Management Perspectives*, *26*(4), 66–85. https://doi.org/10.5465/amp.2012.0088

7 Contending with ambiguity and vulnerability

Leaps of faith and mechanisms of trust

> You know, I see these relationships ... as a marriage. There's got to be the ability to be painfully honest with one another. You've got to have absolute trust. You are there for each other all of the time.
>
> Artistic director (AD)

> I'm quite willing to be in harness with you, ...as long as I know we're going in the same direction.
>
> Executive director (ED)

> So you need that tension, you need that respect, that distance, yet you are connected; you have to genuinely like one another because you give each other a certain latitude at times. Yet you've got to know that person is in your corner.
>
> AD

> You can do five times as much when there's trust because you don't have to run back and check with the other person. You can just go ahead.
>
> ED

Introduction

The future of organisational life is uncertain, especially in the arts (Lampel et al., 2000; Mandel, 2017). Uncertainty renders individuals and organizations vulnerable. To counter this vulnerability and potential paralysis, trust enables collaborative work and decision-making, as we understand from the comments made by the participants in our research at the beginning of this chapter. These participants claim that it solves tensions, enables honesty and information exchange, and contributes to efficiency. Founding scholars of co-leadership identify trust as an essential integrative lubricant in these executive relationships (Alvarez & Svejenova, 2005; Denis et al., 2012; Gronn, 2002). Combined with shared cognition, trust is a mechanism that enables role and task integration for co-leaders (Alvarez & Svejenova, 2005). Recognizing the uncertainty and vulnerability that co-leaders in the arts face, we were motivated to investigate the role of trust.

DOI: 10.4324/9780429504259-9

An initial platform for launching trust in a relationship involves imagining an optimistic "as if" scenario about outcomes, suspending doubt (Lewis & Weigert, 1985; Möllering, 2006). Some scholars call this suspension a "leap of faith", which generates a positive regard of the "other", thus enabling relationships to work with confidence and efficiency for a time (Möllering, 2005, 2006, p. 11). But suspension of doubt may be short-lived and requires either in-depth trust development or additional and periodically recurring leaps of faith. This could be particularly disquieting in a context of ambiguity where priorities are unclear, exacerbating uncertainty (Chapter 2). When trust is disappointed, the hopeful effect of "as if" scenarios is undermined.

In this chapter, we set out to explore two questions that enable insights into the process of trust development in an arts co-leadership relationship.

When a leap of faith is deployed to begin arts co-leadership, what does it reveal about preferences for successful co-leadership relationships?

What are the key mechanisms and dynamics that facilitate the process of trust development in arts co-leadership?

Before we discuss how trust might occur in our research, we briefly summarize aspects of trust theory. Familiarity is a key concept (Gulati, 1995) and we use it to study executive hiring decisions that involve leaps of faith and the use of trust mechanisms in the development of arts co-leadership relationships in our data. To conclude, we explore implications of these insights for researchers and practitioners.

Explaining trust theory

Research on trust in general suggests that the dynamic usually starts with the vulnerable partner (trustor) who focuses their trust on another partner (trustee) with reciprocal effect (Rousseau et al., 1998). A great deal of trust research assumes a pristine beginning for the relationship and scholars suggest that with time and familiarity in the relationship, trust either grows or spirals down (Ferrin et al., 2008). Researchers in the social psychology literature place emphasis on identifying categories of trust that reflect levels of commitment (Ferrin et al., 2008; Lewicki & Bunker, 1996). Möllering (2006), on the other hand, challenges us to explore trust through process: Initially through leaps of faith and then a subsequent construction of trust via conscious and unconscious mechanisms.

Suspension of doubt may be required when undertaking major decisions within the ambiguous cultures that result from differences of logics across stakeholders (Chapters 1, 2, and 5). Competition among these perspectives and legitimizing pressures produces a lack of clarity over priorities within the co-leadership shared role space (Gronn & Hamilton, 2004; Hodgson et al., 1965) (Chapter 2). A leap of faith brackets out or bypasses ambiguity and confusion.

Apart from the assumptions that support the suspension of doubt, Möllering (2006) identifies three mechanisms that develop trust past those initial leaps of faith: Rational decision-making, routines, and reflexivity. As a cognitive mechanism, rational decision-making shares information and perspectives. The process typically questions underlying assumptions, assesses alternatives, and formulates justifications (McNight et al., 1998).

Routines are grounded in automatic assumptions based on roles, rules, and systems (Zucker, 1986). Routines involve taken-for-granted attitudes, subconsciously following regular patterns and socially accepted institutions, suggesting that logics may be at play. Assumptions that support leaps of faith (Möllering, 2006) or presumptive trust (Meyerson et al., 1996) can also be the basis of routines that help develop trust.

Reflexivity evolves trust through active exploration of a relationship, seeking evidence to establish and support a mutual commitment to unguarded vulnerability. It functions through openness to continuous communication, familiarity expressed through mutual experiences, and the negotiation of joint expectations (Möllering, 2006).

The three mechanisms can work separately or together but in themselves are considered insufficient to induce trust (Möllering, 2005). They cannot eliminate doubt completely; uncertainty and vulnerability persist. As a result, to "bracket out" doubt, the creation of favourable "as if" fictions and leaps of faith remains necessary (Möllering, 2006, p. 111). The legitimacy of these fictions seems to be judged according to their congruence with prevailing logics. In the case of the arts, artistic autonomy together with competing logics like social impact, audience development, marketing, and managerialism will influence the development of these fictions (Chapter 2). As these fictions are realized or disappointed, ongoing trust development is promoted or inhibited. This approach to trust development is process-based, proceeding incrementally through positive or negative spirals, requiring further leaps of faith (Ferrin et al., 2008) in partnership with the trust mechanisms.

Understanding trust in the arts context

Despite their professional training and extensive rehearsals, performing artists live in the uncertainty of the moment as they interact with the artistic material, with each other and with spectators' response in each performance (Goffman, 1959). Both audience and performers must suspend for themselves the possibility that the illusion within the performance may be broken, dispelling the magic of the artistic experience (Möllering, 2012).

Much work in arts and culture is project-based involving creators, performers, and production professionals each working with aspects of the aesthetic logic. Work relationships in short-term projects use swift trust (Meyerson et al., 1996) where team members presume that an individual's reputation for consistent past performance in a well-defined role will be a dependable predictor for positive outcomes in a similar situation. Studies of film (Meyerson et al., 1996) and stage productions

(Goodman & Goodman, 1976) suggest that such presumptive trust or leaps of faith makes interdependent action possible in temporary situations.

Over time, they are typically confronted with uncertainty when making decisions. For instance, as a curator, producer, performer, or creator, the AD partners with the ED to anticipate uncertain audience responses to programming. Personal taste and opinion about quality and success vary widely, contributing to the difficulty in predicting audience interest and peer assessments (Lampel et al., 2000). The result is that "nobody knows" (Caves, 2000, p. 3) and "all hits are flukes" (Bielby & Bielby, 1994, p. 1287), so an ongoing suspension of doubt is necessarily an organizational practicality throughout the arts and creative industries.

Artists are frequently project leaders, so they are accustomed to practicing swift trust. When a new partner joins the co-leadership configuration, the familiarity with the short-hand mechanisms of swift trust may prevail. However, unlike workers in temporary projects, co-leaders in the arts inhabit their roles and the role space over several years and multiple organizational cycles. Co-leaders in arts and culture are not typically hired in tandem. While reputations exist within relatively small networks in the arts, the co-leaders do not necessarily know each other's work first-hand prior to their engagement as co-leaders (Reid & Karambayya, 2009). As a result, the hiring of a co-leader partner entails risk and vulnerability since relationships need to be functional within short order (Gronn & Hamilton, 2004). A gradual evolution of trust may not be possible or practical in the circumstances of arts co-leadership given the dynamic nature of most arts organizations (Lewicki & Bunker, 1996; Möllering, 2006). An initial suspension of doubt in these hiring situations relies on commonly accepted proxies that can serve as evidence for dependability, such as professional expertise that corresponds to a well-defined role and a fit with the mission (Gulati, 1995). We have chosen to explore the process of trust construction in the arts by analysing decisions about hiring an executive leader in the co-leadership, theorizing the co-leadership relationship dynamic through the lens of leaps of faith and trust mechanisms (Möllering, 2006).

However, trusting the other partner over the long run involves continued risk of vulnerability. Trust disruption may occur because of the difficulty of navigating across concurrent and competing logics. In addition to a leap of faith, mechanisms that build trust over the long term are required (Lewicki & Bunker, 1996; Möllering, 2006; Thornton & Ocasio, 2008). These mechanisms operate in synchrony with underlying logics that enable the participants to make sense of the context (Chapter 2). As a result of maintaining trust, complementarity can develop and co-leaders can achieve success as collaborative leaders of productive organizations (Hodgson et al., 1965). Because of its intuitively natural fit with the artistic process (Möllering, 2012), the study of trust initiation and development within arts co-leadership can be informative to researchers investigating similar high-risk circumstances. Familiarity (Gulati, 1995) provides a platform for the leaps of faith in these hiring decisions. The unpredictability that is typical in the arts provides an exceptional terrain to understand vulnerability and the use of trust in executive leadership and organizations (Denis et al., 2010; Eisenhardt, 1989; Eisenhardt & Graebner, 2007; Möllering, 2006).

Making sense of the data

In earlier research on trust in co-leadership in the arts, we found that the memory of experiences with previous leadership in the organization shapes the fragile dynamics of trust (Reid & Karambayya, 2016). The mandated introduction of a new partner into a co-leadership role space offered the incumbent an opportunity to re-establish trust within the executive leadership relationship, potentially re-making the role space functional and hopefully enabling complementarity.

Leadership succession history and hiring criteria surfaced in our data collection process. In 19 of the 20 cases referenced for this chapter, the prior co-leadership situation was problematic, involving serious negative conflict in the relationship with the co-leader or with the board where incompetence or even fraud occurred. In 18 cases, the ED left and the AD was incumbent. For those who experience difficult relationships in the arts, ED turnover was considered normal (Reynolds et al., 2017). Ironically, this frequent ED turnover provides coherence for our analysis across cases since incumbency involved the AD in almost every case.

Further study will be necessary to understand trust dynamics during the reverse case of hiring and integrating a new AD with an incumbent ED. There is opportunity to do so since between 2017 and 2020, many ADs in North American symphony orchestras and theatre companies departed and were replaced due to generational succession or fallout from the #MeToo! Movement.

Using familiar criteria for decision-making can be an important part of developing trust (Gulati, 1995). The comfort of familiarity counteracts the anxiety of vulnerability and uncertainty. In a hiring context, familiar features can function as proxies for trustworthiness and as a basis for a leap of faith when deciding among potential candidates for the ED position. For the majority of decisions made in our cases, a candidate's knowledge of the organization's art discipline was a priority. This priority aligns with an ADs need for an informed mutual perspective in the role space to realize their vision and support their professional autonomy. The artistic ideal is at the core of the mission of the organization. In 12 cases, candidates were chosen with training in the art discipline regardless of executive experience, often in reaction to previous EDs who lacked this artistic knowledge. However, in six cases, the candidate's experience as an executive leader in another arts discipline provided familiarity with the role. Four cases managed the knowledge risk further by choosing candidates from within the organization. These four candidates were familiar with both the organization and the discipline while not directly familiar with the role.

In summary, for our study, we discuss three familiarity dimensions that act as proxies for the suspension of doubt: Knowledge of the art discipline, prior experience as a cultural executive, and familiarity with the organization. With each dimension, we chose both a typical trust-positive case and a trust-negative case to provide a balanced understanding of the possibilities and uncertainty of the arts. As a result, we observed how the trust development process can spiral up or down. Trust is fragile and requires effort. In each story of co-leadership, we were able to identify the impact of investing in these mechanisms over time.

Proxy 1: Knowledge of the art discipline

Besides ED familiarity with the art discipline itself, the two cases in this category illustrate how the trust building dynamic with the ED may be influenced by the ADs relationship with the organizational mission. In the first case, the organization had diverged from its mission under a previous AD, and after the mission was re-established, it framed the new ADs programming and creative work and the organization's identity. In the second case, the ADs work as a creative artist personified the mission of the organization.

Mission-respecting: A trust-positive relationship

In this case, fidelity to the theatre company's mission became the key to trust and relationship building. The previous executive duo was in conflict over the eminent ADs repertoire choices that satisfied creative ambitions but departed from the company's mission, limiting its appeal to its specific market. By not renewing that ADs contract, the board created a controversy about artistic freedom in the local press. Both ED and AD left, a large deficit remained in place, and the board took steps to re-establish the company's original educational mission.

The board hired a new ED first – known to them from a previous executive search. Trained as an actor, this new ED was experienced at senior management levels in production and administration in theatre and dance. Having demonstrated an interest in the mission and with a background rooted in the art discipline, the board felt comfortable with the new EDs fit in the organization.

Partnering with the board to seek a new AD who would be committed to the particular mission, they identified a candidate trained as an actor, but who had management experience in the sector-wide professional association. The ideas of the organization's mission had been this person's focus both in the association and at the local arts council. As a stage director, the new AD was not well-known.

Given a lack of star status, the potential AD doubted the legitimacy of the candidacy. Both individuals were concerned about the financial well-being of the organization and their ability to work with the board. The ED provided a positive but honest assessment of the organization, the board, and how the AD would fit into the theatre's future, emphasizing the organization's mission. Consequently, each executive relied on the importance of the organization's mission as the basis for their leap of faith to join the organization.

> We lead together. It is not our company. We are trying to make the best decision for the company without a personal interest.
>
> AD

It was a self-directed co-leadership. The board hired each with a letter of employment but without detailed job descriptions. When they were challenged by strikes in their market and substantial theatre renovations, few normal routines were available to them to support trust development. Their familiarity with the discipline allowed them to work closely to find unconventional compromises and to deliver their joint leadership.

> The reason that it works so well is that ED knows what it's like to be in a show and I know what a budget is.
>
> AD

> For us it was clear, they were destined to get along.
>
> Board president

While not personal friends, they communicated regularly with much open reflection. The pair honestly expressed their mutual concerns and found solutions amicably.

> AD and I are not in conflict when it comes to making a decision.
>
> ED

> When difficulties arise, they tend to stick together rather than confront each other.
>
> Administrative director

Their joint tenure was lengthy and productive. The theatre renovation was a success, their audiences were appreciative, and the finances were stabilized. After 20 years, the AD retired and a new AD took over.

Commentary on proxy 1 – Trust-positive

As a mission-focused case, this co-leadership provides insights on all trust-building mechanisms. The development and use of an institutional mission is a foundational routine in many organizations and this organization had a social and artistic mission. It framed their co-leadership and their relationship. The duo became increasingly reflexive over time, making their decisions by sharing perspectives, mutual learning, and engaging in joint introspection that led to acceptable compromises. Ultimately, regular reflexivity along with occasional rational decision-making were at play. With continued communication, this process enabled the co-leaders to overcome any shared doubts and establish long-term trust. While compromises by the AD occasionally required leaps of faith, they were accomplished without tension or extended doubt, given the base of trust and honest reflection within the relationship.

Personifying the mission: A trust-negative relationship

In a second case, the AD was the leading creator for the organization. The ADs early years with the company were marked by a unique approach and a new audience. The prior ED was trained in another art discipline and had been in an executive role elsewhere in the arts, with sophisticated expertise in marketing and fundraising. EDs leadership was appreciated by several board members, but the co-leadership relationship was somewhat strained.

Encouraged by colleagues' advice about evolving into creative maturity, AD took a big step and developed a large and lavish production as the anchor for the upcoming season. The budget was stretched, so other programming was reduced. However, the company's accountant expressed concerns to the prior ED while still in the organization and together they spoke to the president of the board about the risks involved in this new approach. The AD felt betrayed because this communication took place without consultation. While there had been hard work to build trust in the co-leadership, the relationship was ruptured. The ED left.

> I truly believe there was a breakdown in the relationship between ED and I – we reached a point we were going two separate ways. ... Did I trust? I didn't assume that ED would go behind my back.
>
> AD

The AD championed the hiring of a new ED who came from the same art discipline and had special skills arranging tours, aligning with the ADs ambitions to extend touring for the new production. But a suspension of doubt was necessary, given this EDs lack of executive experience in revenue development and board management. The AD acknowledged that the ED had much to learn, transferring responsibility to the ED to validate the suspension of doubt and setting a trajectory for the relationship.

The new production was well received, appreciated by audiences and critics alike. The ED had time to observe and learn through this success. By mobilized grant writing skills successfully and producing a well-received strategic plan, ED engaged in legitimizing routines. On the other hand, the choice of fundraising professionals was problematic, creating budgetary pressure after the financial success of year one. The ADs ambitions surpassed the company resources. Demands for future production budgets created significant conflict and a mutually descending spiral in trust (Ferrin et al., 2008).

> And so, as we went into year three, we started to have better checks and balances ... but it became apparent that spending overages weren't so much a question of ignorance as a question of insolence. Willful negligence. "I need to do this, it's what it's going to cost. ..." So very, very passive aggressive, very disrespectful.
>
> ED

> AD had lost respect for ED. ED felt that and felt that it couldn't be gained back. There you had a recipe for disaster.
>
> Board president

Similar to the previous ED, this ED informed the board executive of the challenges in negotiating the program and budget. Open conflict overwhelmed the organization. Morale was low. The ED accepted a position elsewhere.

Commentary on proxy 1 – Trust-negative

In this case, there were a number of attempts to use trust-building mechanisms. Early conversations about art had reinforced the base of familiarity between the two leaders. The success of the ADs new production project generated confidence and assurance regarding professional accomplishments. But the EDs limited experience at the executive level left little capacity for honest or challenging exchange with the AD about the organization. The AD did not perceive the ED as an equal partner for reflection. So, the ED produced a strategic plan alone, a routine that excluded the ADs personalized vision for the organization. Rationally based financial and control mechanisms were put in place by the ED in partnership with the board treasurer. Finally, AD felt betrayed by ED to the board; a repetition of the previous relationship; and the AD viewed this act as dishonest. These experiences erased any residual suspension of doubt for the AD, who was unable to extend hope for trust and collaboration. The ED was defensive as a result, and equally lacking in trust. Efforts to gain ADs confidence failed. The mechanisms were ineffective. Rationality was overcome by emotions and routines and reflexivity were not shared. As a result, a spiral of negative trust and oppositional behaviour disintegrated their relationship. Decision-making in the executive role space became paralyzed and dysfunctional because the responsibilities were not jointly fulfilled.

Proxy 2: Experience in an executive role

Candidates with any executive role experience would probably be attractive to a board of directors. However, for ADs to suspend doubt, experience in the arts, even in another discipline, appeared necessary, manifesting the priority that ADs grant to the professional artistic logic. We explore this criterion for selection in two contrasting cases. Once again, the contrast relates to the ADs relationship to or identification with the mission. While both organizational missions were focused on creation, the first company involved three ADs who also undertook artistic work outside the organization. In the second company, there were two ADs, but they were exclusively invested in the aesthetic and creative purpose of the company.

Ironic twist: A trust-positive relationship

This company was founded by several ADs. Three remained, working part-time, taking turns mounting productions for the company as well as pursuing their careers elsewhere as performing and creative artists. During the early development of the company, they worked without an ED and acted as their own board of directors. Eventually, to professionalize their operation and to free them to pursue more creative projects outside of the company, they chose to hire a full-time ED. This person was a producer from the local public broadcaster. Instead of looking for someone who knew their art, the ADs leap of faith was based on the similarity of the role as an executive who managed creative talent in another performance medium.

From funding agencies, the newly arrived ED learned that external board members and a chair were needed to legitimize the organization's governance practice. The ADs were concerned about the potential loss of control in such a reconfigured board, expanded with unfamiliar members. Through frequent communication and patient reflection, the ED developed the ADs trust and convinced them to embark in a new strategic project of board membership. They remained as members of the board but accepted the routine of appointing additional and external board members, including an external chair.

The ADs were involved in the company to create their own productions, but their trust with the ED led them to depend on sophisticated managerial capabilities. The ADs suspended their concern about control. They became somewhat passive in the presence of competence, conferring increased authority to ED in decision-making. The ED expressed concerns that the company needed greater implication by the ADs to grow and sustain its distinctive aesthetic.

> I often told them that the space you don't take, I will fill. But you should be careful with that. …
>
> ED

ED discussed this autonomy with a long-standing board member.

> Beyond the productions, who provides the vision for this company? We questioned the involvement of the ADs in the company. Not in the context of their productions. They were completely invested. ... But in everything else, we seemed to be responsible for the art discipline, the development of this discipline. How do they gain back [their involvement in the development of the company]?
>
> ED

Ultimately, the ED left to follow a career opportunity, but also, feeling overburdened by the responsibility of a surplus of trust from the ADs. This generated an opportunity for reflection on co-leadership balance in this organization.

Commentary on proxy 2 – Trust-positive

Two mechanisms helped build on the ADs leap of faith. First was early reflexivity and information sharing among the ADs and ED about the risks of outside board members. The ED rendered the process respectful so confidence in these ideas was constructed among the ADs. Second was the newly configured board – a routine legitimizing and trust-building practice made successful through the chair's respectful leadership and new board members' commitment to provide expert and financial support to the organization. The board's partnership with the ED developed organizational objectives effectively without interfering in the ADs realization of their aesthetic. But the shared role space was not complete without full engagement by the ADs. The necessity to find the next ED was a useful opportunity to renew this engagement.

Distrusting visionary: A trust-negative relationship

This organization was founded by two artists who were a couple in life, with one acting as the most visible AD in company decision-making. AD was also the lead creator. Their original and distinctive vision gained significant international recognition for their company. The board of directors chose to add an ED to manage the finances and logistics, reporting directly to the board. While active in the cultural field, the first ED had no experience with musical production nor tolerance for deficits in this start-up organization. The relationship with the AD ended in toxic conflict about solutions to financial problems when a hiatus was imposed on performances. The AD felt betrayed and the ED left.

In the search for a replacement, the AD and several board members were convinced of the need for an appreciation of the specific style and art discipline to avoid repetition of the past. They discovered an ED with management experience in a different art discipline but who was familiar with their business model and had a collaborative personality. As a result, the board and AD rationalized their choice of ED and suspended their doubt. They hoped that the new ED would learn about their art practice quickly. A board member commented:

> I said, well you know we're lucky to have this manager. ED can develop cash flow models … personality is pretty good … is the [administrative] face of the company … presents well … we just had a real gem …
>
> Board member

A financially imposed performance hiatus inherited from the previous ED focused the AD on planning activities which allowed the new ED to become familiar with the company and its singular artistic vision through daily discussions with the AD and the marketing director. The ED also hired a production director, a routine solution, to help with logistical control and to connect budgets with artistic ambitions.

The ADs ambition was an increase to two annual productions. The ED suspended doubts about marketing and financial concerns and agreed. As a result of this decision early in their relationship, the AD, in turn, further suspended doubts about the EDs loyalty.

> They'd always wanted to do two shows a year, and I did it within the first year and a half I was here. And so in a way I sort of realized their dream. Now, three years later I don't know if it was the right thing to do.
>
> ED

Despite extensive daily social communications between the two, the AD made small operational decisions without consulting the ED. The ED chose not to challenge the AD to avoid trust disruption. The ED gained deeper insights on the ADs leadership of the organization through discussions with the marketing and production directors. The ADs proprietary approach to the organization limited questioning and reflection about the company's way of functioning.

> I can't leave ED alone with everything … I trust ED more than I've trusted anybody, and I don't trust anybody. I don't trust that anyone is going to work as hard as I am. … No, that's a fact!. Because this IS my life.
>
> AD

The protracted negotiation by the ED of a particularly appreciated performer's contract revealed the ADs ongoing doubt and tenacious approach to relationships. Despite the EDs appeal for trust that a time-based negotiation strategy would result in lower fees, the AD shared doubt about the strategy with other employees.

> I don't trust ED entirely because there are times I think that agents should be gone after more aggressively.
>
> AD

The ADs perspective was revealed to the ED, who felt that after five years of some success, the relationship was still influenced by the ADs inability to suspend and manage doubts. While the decision did not appear to be exclusively a result of the complaint, the ED was open to new opportunities, and left for another job.

Commentary on proxy 2 – Trust-negative

Two trust-building mechanisms were attempted in this case (Möllering, 2006). First, the addition of the institutionalized role of production manager was a routine that could facilitate AD-ED interdependence and mutual integration. Second, extensive communication appeared to support the relationship for the ED. While the first mechanism worked well, the second was limited by the inability to exchange honestly. The authority of the ADs founding and creative status allowed little space for more intimate sharing and contesting of assumptions, and the ED only undertook reflexive discussions about the organization with the marketing and production directors. This dynamic is similar to the trust-negative case in proxy 1. In both cases, the ADs engagement with the aesthetic logic was a personal vision that identified their company to the public. As a result, full reflexivity as an AD-ED trust-building mechanism in both relationships was not realistic. In this case, no other mechanisms were attempted.

Proxy 3: Promotion from within the organization

When organizations fill a new or vacated executive role, an internal candidate may appear as more trustworthy than external candidates. Through their continued affiliation with the organization, they are familiar to its members and have demonstrated loyalty (Gulati, 1995). On the other hand, moving up from within an organization may be risky since the person does not have senior executive-level experience. These two cases provide insights about how both personal and organizational familiarity appear as a useful trigger for initial suspension of doubt for trust development. However, the outcome may vary. In one, the AD was following in a tradition of senior and high-profile ADs who had always worked with an ED and in the second, the AD succeeded a charismatic unitary leader. The ED was the latter organization's first in that role.

Internally developed trust: A trust-positive relationship

In this trust-positive case, the previous ED had come from a non-arts executive position to replace a long-standing, retiring ED. AD attempted to facilitate this prior EDs insertion into the organization. But this ED did not adapt well and appeared decreasingly competent.

After 18 months, the board of directors concluded that a replacement was necessary. In consultation with the AD, the board chair identified an internal candidate. This person was a performing artist who had been assisting AD in developing artistic projects for several years, negotiating the business side and gaining familiarity with organizational routines. The board saw the candidate's knowledge of the discipline and familiarity with the large and complex organization as an advantage for the role. ED appeared committed to the institution's mission. The board chair, who was the president of a large corporation, proposed to mentor the artist as ED, to alleviate and suspend doubts about the artist's lack of executive experience. The chair's leap of faith paid off. Despite scepticism by some in the organization, ED proved to be well suited to the job.

> Coming from an … [artistic] background, there was huge speculation whether ED could make it work as a finance person, a boss. ED has never been a General Manager before. But ED has made it work by working very hard at making it work.
>
> Production Director

ED established priorities with the AD that were coherent with a shared understanding of the mission and with the ADs interpretation of that mission. ED reliably delivered support in a manner consistent with institutional traditions, ensuring ADs comfort with the co-leadership relationship.

> The understanding between the two of them, that if AD wants to do it, ED will find the money to make sure we can do it. That kind of success can help strengthen a relationship.
>
> Marketing director

The relationship evolved positively with open and regular communication.

> Oh my God, ED phones me three times a day, beginning at eight usually… What I like is ED will give me feedback but isn't overburdened with opinions as to what we should do.
>
> AD

Their regular communication reinforced the validity of the initial leap of faith and their mutual respect of the mission as a framing routine allowed them to air and resolve differences without strain. Occasionally, a leap of faith was required by the AD in some key programming decisions to overcome the financial insecurity of box-office predictions. They deployed predictive models provided by the marketing department as rational decision-making mechanisms.

> I sometimes have disagreements about programming with ED. For example, one year we got the rights to a well-known musical, and ED said let's do it, and I said "The Broadway revival didn't work, the

> national tour died, and there was a bad local production recently. Let me suggest something else." and ED said, "No I think this will work," I said "fine" and it did work. I was wrong. At the end of the day, I don't want to have red ink and I don't want to have bad art and nor does ED. So, we're on the same page.
>
> AD

ED gained internal and external respect, and financial stability was sustained over successive seasons responding well to institutional expectations of the role. Little suspension of doubt was required by the AD and the board.

Eventually, however, the board felt that the organization needed to be refreshed artistically so they concluded ADs tenure with a final fixed term contract. At the same time, the board extended the EDs contract for a much longer term, thus changing the context and dynamics of the relationship.

> When ED got the contract renewed ... EDs vision just totally opened up. But ... we've got a bit of a rocky road [because] AD is only in for a few more years, so AD is not as interested in thinking ten years out from now.
>
> Marketing director

Outside of programming routines they had less in common about the future. Trust-building reached a plateau through to the end of the formal relationship.

Commentary on proxy 3 – Trust-positive

The trust mechanisms that made this relationship a success evolved from positive and long-standing familiarity with each other and the organization. While the AD shaped the annual programming formula with some new ideas, ADs vision did not change the mission as a well-established framing routine. Communication and reflection within the co-leadership were constructive, based on the AD-ED mentoring relationship from the past and their joint commitment to a routine that balanced financial stability with the mission. Programming decisions integrated rational predictive routines that were developed by the marketing department and that worked well for the organization. Trust in the legitimacy of the mission enabled trust within the relationship.

However, the board decided to renew executive contracts for asymmetric end-dates. For the AD, this was the last contract. On the other hand, the longer contract for the ED was a rational decision to provide continuity. This decision proposed a future leap of faith by the ED about how future programming by the next AD would link with fidelity to the mission.

Passive engagement: A trust-negative relationship

In a less positive case, the prior single leader was highly regarded by the arts community but was financially chaotic and difficult for the board and organization members to follow.

> They were trained to work in ADs thinking pattern, because if you didn't you were probably going to lose your place.
>
> Board member

This leader was asked to retire after a sabbatical. The board found a more collegial replacement from within the artistic side of the organization.

After a short time, this newly appointed single leader found that sharing the executive role would facilitate the artistic work. AD asked the board to promote the organization's administrative director to ED, producing an internally sourced co-leadership. The two had previously worked towards solving financial problems together during the prior ADs sabbatical.

> We would have just been employees, but in the ADs absence … that is probably a factor in what started us off together in a dual relationship.
>
> ED

The organization was being monitored and coached through a five-year government-funded stabilization program. This required importing numerous rational business management routines like planning and budgeting exercises. The program's significant financial and legitimacy rewards would solve the company's major, accumulated deficit. The board suspended doubt about co-leadership and embraced the marriage of skills that would bring more expertise to the executive leadership role. They also recognized the potential tensions between the logics embedded in co-leadership. But given the new ADs collegial approach, they were hopeful that the arrangement would work well.

The administrative director had a great deal of experience in the routines of artistic production and financial planning in the same art discipline in several organizations. The ADs familiarity with ED and competence in administrative skills enabled a suspension of doubt concerning EDs lack of executive leadership experience. But for the ED, being promoted meant working with external stakeholders and the board, which was a new role.

The pressure of the financial crisis distracted this executive duo from establishing a close relationship. Each managed the situation from their particular point of view.

> There wasn't much of a relationship. There was a problem, and everybody had to go for it, chip away at it, but to actually have sat down and talked about what our situation was, no we were too busy bailing the boat to be talking about it or analysing it.
>
> ED

> Both of them hate conflict. Both of them hate having to talk about the 'f' word, you know "feelings" and they won't. But if they can problem-solve it in a logical way that seems to be the way that they handle it, so they have figured out their own processes.
>
> Board member

There was little reflexive communication. The standard routines of writing funding proposals and continuing to function in their previous manner from a distance across the office were perceived as sufficient.

> It's all very polite, and that's what collegiality is being interpreted as, we're not going to scream at each other, and maybe we're getting to the point where we would actually solve a few things if we start to scream at each other.
>
> ED

Further rational decision-making was added to the culture of the organization through an accountability exercise. Annual agreements were negotiated among senior staff about mutual responsibilities, organizing relationships with contracts instead of trust. As a result, while the ED had ideas for the organization that supported the artistic activities, ED waited for the AD to articulate artistic strategies anchored in the responsibility contract. This stalemate left the company's artistic identity in a vacuum.

Commentary on proxy 3 – Trust-negative

Before the co-leadership was established, the AD, ED, and organization were familiar with each other. However, trust never really developed in the relationship. The organization's new culture of rational decision-making solved its financial crisis becoming the norm in the co-leadership relationship. The leaders avoided the vulnerability that results from confrontational communication and information sharing. Negotiated accountability and routines like written grant applications supplanted reflexivity, resulting in isolation. The lack of shared critical thinking prevented the fulfilment of the strategic potential of the co-leadership relationship for the organization. Development of the relationship and the organization was stalled without a replacement for the mission that the previous charismatic leader personified.

Contributing to trust in co-leadership

In this chapter, we chose to investigate solutions for uncertainty in co-leadership in response to two questions. The first explored the presumptions of a leap of faith to begin a co-leadership relationship. The second investigated the process of trust development in the co-leadership relationships. Given our choice of six different cases from our data, the insights are illustrative, suggesting a need for further investigation on a broader basis.

We began with the role that familiarity plays in a leap of faith when an arts organization hires a new member into a co-leadership shared role space – a key moment of risky and strategic decision-making for the organization. As a result, boards and ADs find that someone with knowledge of the arts presents a reassuring profile as a solution for integration across the roles in the arts. We then followed the co-leaders in order to understand how trust evolved in the relationship through trust-development mechanisms (Möllering, 2006). We uncovered different AD perspectives about the mission and how that possibly produced shared cognition and developed trust. The use of a process orientation to identify these mechanisms in the arts expands trust research in a pluralistic and complex context (Kraatz & Block, 2008, 2017) (Chapter 2).

Leaps of faith

The hiring decision for the ED position in our data was made by the board of directors, but in all but one of the cases, ADs were incumbent and typically influenced this hiring decision. ADs seem to look for a partner with whom they can exchange ideas about artistic plans and develop their ideas to realize projects in support of the artistic mission. ADs assumed that familiarity with an art discipline would support this process (Gulati, 1995). On the other hand, board members in the hiring process in our data seem to look for candidates with management knowledge or evidence of significant potential to grow into this area. This combination of artistic and management knowledge can balance logics suggesting a hybrid professional as an ideal ED profile in these relationships (Chapter 5).

The candidates' combined knowledge was manifested in three different career trajectories that were used as a proxy in the hiring decision. We observed two career trajectories in our study where managers or potential managers worked or had been trained in a similar art discipline. One trajectory was from inside and the other was from outside the organization. A third and separate trajectory involved managers who worked in the arts but with a different art discipline. For each of the three proxies, a trust-positive case and a trust-negative case were investigated providing different outcome possibilities across the cases.

It seems that for boards of directors and ADs, an ideal co-leadership in the arts involves more than one dominant logic per person (Chapter 5). The ED is expected to be able to balance their own management and marketing logics with the artistic logic, suggesting that hiring committees sought hybrid professionals for the ED role (Blomgren & Waks, 2015; Gibeau et al., 2020). Typically, legitimacy gained from past experience promotes respect for these hybrid professionals' ability to make effective organizational decisions. Their hybridity appeared to enable certain of these managers to share cognition and to be trusted (Alvarez & Svejenova, 2005). The hiring committees aspired to extend the co-leadership beyond the division of professional and management logics. Embedding several logics in a role may serve the integration needs of the co-leadership role space more effectively (Alvarez & Svejenova, 2005) (Chapter 5).

Trust-building mechanisms

Möllering (2006) suggests that trust scholars consider three mechanisms in order to study the development of trust and the process of trusting: Rational decision-making, routines, and reflexivity.

In our research, we found that routines were the dominant mechanism mobilized for trust development in co-leadership in the arts. This reliance on routine parallels the general practice in the field where repetition of shared routines builds trust in professional practice such as occurs in swift trust (Meyerson et al., 1996). Innovations in the artistic process are rendered legitimate because the novelty evolves from routines ingrained in the craft of artistic performance (Payne, 2018; Pettinger, 2015). These routines and their underlying logics help counteract the goal ambiguity and the pluralistic culture of the context.

Recognizing and building on the organization's mission was the most valuable routine available to the co-leaders in our cases. However, the ADs vision of how to fulfil the mission of the organization had a significant impact on trust building in the relationship. The profession logic was manifested differently in the trust-positive and the trust-negative cases. In the latter, the ADs artistic practice personified the organization's mission, sometimes over-riding managerial logics. In the trust-positive cases, ADs served the organizationally defined mission in partnership with the EDs.

Shared responsibility for and to the mission was seen to be the fulcrum for trust-positive relationships. The mission focuses individual passions and innovations around the artistic ideal generating shared cognition and serving to anchor organizational development and unconventional decision-making. In these cases, co-leaders found authentic ways to interpret and advance their established organizational mission.

In contrast, in two trust-negative examples, we found that ADs as founders or as long-tenure creative artists demonstrated a proprietary need to control the mission instead of sharing its conception within the joint role space. In another example, the previous ADs personal mission appropriated the mission and left a void that successors failed to fill after ADs departure. This control reduces individual agency of other partner(s) and joint participation in the routines of the mission. It also constrains deeper reflexivity and shared cognition. Boards may need to be aware that attaining a certain balance of logics in a co-leadership requires an ED who is hybrid but is also politically adept at managing a relationship with an AD who takes a dominant view of logic integration (Chapter 5). Negotiating with ADs who define the mission through their own creative work may raise the need for negative peace as the achievable relationship, as discussed in Chapter 5. Avoiding conflict but maintaining a differentiated relationship ensures a level of stability for the organization.

The second mechanism of note is reflexivity. Artists feel vulnerable in their art, given their sense of calling to art and high standards of performance (Chapters 1 and 2) (Chiapello, 1998). In order for artists to undertake the vulnerability of innovation, honesty within and loyalty to the relationship appear to be necessary (Möllering, 2012). For the AD to realize coherent leadership in the role space with the incoming ED, there is an urgent need to move beyond swift trust to develop a deeper trusting relationship. Getting to know the other partner(s) at this deeper level appears important to achieve a shared cognition, to motivate and generate insights that support the creative process for artists (Alvarez & Svejenova, 2005; Gronn & Hamilton, 2004). Such reflexivity requires extensive and honest communication and loyalty (Möllering, 2006). These are significant concerns throughout the cases, and in their absence, disappointment was common.

Rational mechanisms proved to be the least supportive in trust development in the relationships in these cases. Ambiguous goals in this context (Lampel et al., 2000) make it difficult to undertake clearly reasoned rational decision-making (Cohen & March, 1974). Aesthetic judgment is at the core of realizing the organization's mission and is exercised in a culture of intuitive and institutionalized assessment. For instance, we saw that the external imposition of very rational managerial thinking undermined possibilities for relationship building and decision-making in one organization. Artists are passionate people and prediction is difficult (Bielby & Bielby, 1994; Lampel et al., 2000). Business logic commitments and polite collegiality significantly reduced the emotional stake in the executive relationship. When other rational decision-making was reported, it was largely informed by experience and judgment that was accessed intuitively.

As a result of this research, we also see how these relationships are fragile (Denis et al., 2001; Reid & Karambayya, 2016). Trust is a daring leap of faith by willing but vulnerable partners (Möllering, 2006; Rousseau et al., 1998). Despite the typical use of suspension of doubt in the arts for the purposes of swift trust, long-term trust is hard to achieve in the arts (Möllering, 2012). The vulnerable nature of the process of artistic risk characterizes the sector (Lampel et al., 2000) and predictions are regularly thwarted. Trust is a rare state.

Practical learning

There were several smaller but practical lessons in our study of trust. AD incumbents who focus mainly on art knowledge may undervalue the need for organizational and managerial role knowledge. Differentiation that supports the managerial logic may be lost in favour of the artistic logic (Chapter 2). As well, ADs may confuse a candidate's technical competence or knowledge of organizational routines for art knowledge. Similar to swift trust, these assumptions that are embedded in leaps of faith may be too reductive to sustain long-term relationships in the arts.

Promoting candidates from within can be very successful, since familiarity with the person provides a strong basis for a leap of faith, but the familiar context can also be challenging for both candidates and incumbents. The need to learn new routines because of a change in role may be refreshing but can also present new problems. Routines embedded in earlier relationships may need adjustment or some new routines may be needed. This may also involve reprioritizing the logic integration within the role space. The ambiguity of decision-making situated in the shared role space is a new experience that involves difficult learning (Chapter 2). The move to a position of authority may be a significant change in identity rendering the person vulnerable (Ibarra, 1999) and perhaps less open to reflection in the co-leadership relationship.

In summary, hybrid professionals have traditionally been studied as single leaders, particularly in healthcare environments (Blomgren & Waks, 2015). In the arts' setting, we found that a hybrid professional was desired by an AD as a co-leader, enabling the possibility for shared cognition and possibly trust (Alvarez & Svejenova, 2005). As well, some ADs define the organization's mission in terms of their own creative practice. Our data are not unusual, since many creative artists are founders of their own company. Co-leaders for these ADs appear to need well-honed political competencies. For those situations where the mission has been shaped by the history of the organization, co-leaders appeared to make use of the mission as a routine that enabled further shared cognition and trust. However, the notion of shared cognition raises concerns about artistic autonomy and the loss of differentiation. Scholars and arts professionals have expressed concern that autonomy and differentiation may be at risk when there is a managerial presence in an arts organization (Chiapello, 2004; Røyseng, 2008). Reflexivity is another mechanism that can encourage trust (Möllering, 2006), enhance complementarity, and support artistic autonomy (Hodgson et al., 1965). Since our analysis is illustrative, we suggest that further exploration of these observations may be useful for scholars and co-leaders alike.

References

Alvarez, J. L., & Svejenova, S. (2005). *Sharing Executive Power: Roles and Relationships at the Top*. Cambridge University Press.

Bielby, W. T., & Bielby, D. D. (1994). 'All hits are flukes': Institutionalized decision making and the rhetoric of network prime-time program development. *American Journal of Sociology*, *99*(5), 1287–1313.

Blomgren, M., & Waks, C. (2015). Coping with contradictions: Hybrid professionals managing institutional complexity. *Journal of Professions and Organization*, 2(1), 78–102. https://doi-org.proxy2.hec.ca/10.1093/jpo/jou010

Caves, R. E. (2000). *Creative Industries: Contracts between Art and Commerce*. Harvard University Press.

Chiapello, È. (1998). *Artistes Versus Managers: Le Management Culturel face à la Critique Artiste*. Éditions Métaillés.

Chiapello, È. (2004). Evolution and co-optation: The 'artist critique' of management and capitalism. *Third Text*, *18*(6), 585–594. https://doi.org/10.1080/0952882042000284998

Cohen, M. D., & March, J. G. (1974). *Leadership and Ambiguity: The American College President* (2nd ed.). Harvard Business School Press.

Denis, J.-L., Lamothe, L., & Langley, A. (2001). The dynamics of collective leadership and strategic change in pluralistic organizations. *The Academy of Management Journal*, *44*(4), 809–837. https://doi.org/10.2307/3069417

Denis, J.-L., Langley, A., & Rouleau, L. (2010). The practice of leadership in the messy world of organizations. *Leadership*, *6*(1), 67–88. https://doi.org/10.1177/1742715009354233

Denis, J.-L., Langley, A., & Sergi, V. (2012). Leadership in the plural. *The Academy of Management Annals*, *5*(1), 211–283. https://doi.org/10.1080/19416520.2012.667612

Eisenhardt, K. (1989). Building theories from case study research. *Academy of Management Review*, *14*(4), 532–550.

Eisenhardt, K., & Graebner, M. E. (2007). Theory building from cases: Opportunities and challenges. *Academy of Management Journal*, *50*(1), 25–32. https://doi.org/10.5465/AMJ.2007.2416088

Ferrin, D. L., Bligh, M. C., & Kohles, J. C. (2008). It takes two to tango: An interdependence analysis of the spiralling of perceived trustworthiness and cooperation in interpersonal and intergroup relationships. *Organizational Behavior and Human Decision Processes*, *107*(2), 161–178. https://doi.org/10.1016/j.obhdp.2008.02.012

Gibeau, É, Langley, A., Denis, J.-L., & van Schendel, N. (2020). Bridging competing demands through co-leadership? Potential and limitations. *Human Relations*, *73*(4), 464–489. https://doi.org/10.1177/0018726719888145.

Goffman, E. (1959). *The Presentation of Self in Everyday Life*. Doubleday.

Goodman, R. A., & Goodman, L. P. (1976). Some management issues in temporary systems: A study of professional development and manpower - the theater case. *Administrative Science Quarterly*, *21*(3), 494–501.

Gronn, P. (2002). Distributed leadership as a unit of analysis. *The Leadership Quarterly*, *13*(4), 423–451. https://doi.org/10.1016/S1048-9843(02)00120-0

Gronn, P., & Hamilton, A. (2004). 'A bit more life in the leadership': Co-principalship as distributed leadership practice. *Leadership and Policy in Schools*, *3*(1), 3–35. https://doi.org/10.1076/lpos.3.1.3.27842

Gulati, R. (1995). Does familiarity breed trust? The implications of repeated ties for contractual choice in alliances. *Academy of Management Journal*, *38*(1), 85–112. https://doi.org/10.2307/256729

Hodgson, R. C., Levinson, D. J., & Zaleznik, A. (1965). *The Executive Role Constellation: An Analysis of Personality and Role Relations in Management*. Harvard University: Division of Research, Graduate School of Business Administration.

Ibarra, H. (1999). Provisional selves: Experimenting with image and identity in professional adaptation. *Administrative Science Quarterly*, *44*(4), 764–791.

Kraatz, M. S., & Block, E. (2008). Organizational Implications of Institutional Pluralism. In R. Greenwood, C. Oliver, K. Sahlin-Andersson, & R. Suddaby (Eds.), *The SAGE Handbook of Organizational Institutionalism* (pp. 243–275). SAGE Publications Limited.

Kraatz, M. S., & Block, E. (2017). Institutional Pluralism Revisited. In R. Greenwood, C. Oliver, T. Lawrence, & R. E. Meyer (Eds.), *The SAGE Handbook of Organizational Institutionalism* (2nd ed. pp. 532–557). SAGE Publications.

Lampel, J., Lant, T., & Shamsie, J. (2000). Balancing act: Learning from organizing practices in cultural industries. *Organization Science*, *11*(3), 263–269. https://doi.org/10.1287/orsc.11.3.263.12503

Lewicki, R., & Bunker, B. B. (1996). Developing and Maintaining Trust in Work Relationships. In R. M. Kramer, & T. R. Tyler (Eds.), *Trust in Organizations: Frontiers of Theory and Research* (pp. 114–139). Sage Publications.

Lewis, J. D., & Weigert, A. (1985). Trust as a social reality. *Social Forces*, *63*(4), 967–985. https://doi.org/10.2307/2578601

Mandel, B. (2017). *Arts/Cultural Management in International Contexts*. Georg Olms Verlag.

McNight, D. H., Cummings, L. L., & Chervany, N. (1998). Initial trust development in new organizational development. *The Academy of Management Review*, *23*(3), 473–490.

Meyerson, D., Weick, K., & Kramer, R. M. (1996). Swift Trust and Temporary Groups. In R. M. Kramer & T. R. Tyler (Eds.), *Trust in Organizations: Frontiers of Theory and Research* (pp. 166–195). Sage Publications.

Möllering, G. (2005). The trust/control duality: An integrative perspective on positive expectations of others. *International Sociology*, *20*(2), 259–282. https://doi.org/10.1177/0268580905055478

Möllering, G. (2006). *Trust: Reason, Routine, Reflexivity*. Elsevier.

Möllering, G. (2012). Trusting in art: Calling for empirical trust research in highly creative contexts. *Journal of Trust Research*, *2*(2), 203–210. https://doi.org/10.1080/21515581.2012.708509

Payne, E. (2018). The craft of musical performance: Skilled practice in collaboration. *Cultural Geographies*, *25*(1), 107–122. https://doi.org/10.1177/1474474016684126

Pettinger, L. (2015). Embodied labour in music work. *The British Journal of Sociology*, *66*(2), 282–300. https://doi.org/10.1111/1468-4446.12123

Reid, W., & Karambayya, R. (2009). Impact of dual executive leadership dynamics in creative organizations. *Human Relations*, *62*(7), 1073–1112. https://doi.org/10.1177/0018726709335539

Reid, W., & Karambayya, R. (2016). The shadow of history: Situated dynamics of trust in dual executive leadership. *Leadership*, *12*(5), 609–631. https://doi.org/10.1177/1742715015579931

Reynolds, S., Tonks, A., & MacNeill, K. (2017). Collaborative leadership in the arts as a unique form of dual leadership. *The Journal of Arts Management, Law, and Society*, *47*(2), 89–104. https://doi.org/10.1080/10632921.2016.1241968

Rousseau, D. M., Sitkin, S. B., & Burt, R. S. (1998). Not so different after all: A cross-discipline view of trust. *Academy of Management Review*, *23*(3), 393–404. https://doi.org/10.5465/amr.1998.926617

Røyseng, S. (2008). Arts management and the autonomy of art. *International Journal of Cultural Policy*, *14*(1), 37–48. https://doi.org/10.1080/10286630701856484

Thornton, P., & Ocasio, W. (2008). Institutional Logics. In R. Greenwood, C. Oliver, K. Sahlin, & R. Suddaby (Eds.), *The SAGE Handbook on Organizational Institutionalism* (pp. 99–129). Sage.

Zucker, L. G. (1986). Production of trust: Institutional sources of economic structure, 1840–1920. *Research in Organizational Behavior*, *8*, 53–111.

Section III

Theorizing organizational dynamics with arts co-leadership

8 Managing risk

Board-staff relations, co-leadership, and information asymmetry

> We have a fiduciary responsibility here and a governance responsibility. We have less responsibility for the artistic ... Board Members who said, "I can't put myself in this kind of risk".
>
> Board chair

> The Executive Director (ED) has the ear of the board more than the Artistic Director (AD).
>
> Board member

> AD knows [that] if the process is working well between ED and the board, ADs life is a whole lot easier.
>
> Board member

> They accept that it's two individuals that have to make their way together ...but they choose to react to those two individuals instead of saying, "come up with a unified position".
>
> ED

Introduction

The relationship between a non-profit board of directors and executive co-leaders provides useful organizational terrain to extend our study of the shared leadership role space in the arts. It also enables a broader investigation of pluralism in the arts with the addition of non-profit governance logics (Cornforth, 2003b). The board-staff relationship in the arts is complex. This chapter's opening comments from participants in our research suggest some of the complications present in this relationship. They reflect the balance needed between artistic and managerial logics as well as different governance perspectives such as accountability and responsibility. They also reflect a hands-off approach to an ADs responsibility that may suggest a concern about artistic autonomy (Røyseng, 2008). This combination of logics generates possibilities for confusion and an additional culture of ambiguity for the board to navigate (Cohen & March, 1974; Cornforth, 2003b; Denis et al., 1996). Boards of directors typically

DOI: 10.4324/9780429504259-11

mandate co-leaders in recognition of the different expertise required to lead these profession-based organizations and thus as a solution to ambiguity. Co-leaders partner with a board to collectively provide strategic organizational leadership and performance that is accountable to stakeholders (King & Schramme, 2019).

Our investigation is informed by inter-related theories that explain non-profit board-staff relations that shape governance (Cornforth, 2003a, 2003b). Our analysis reveals unusual patterns of practice that are reflected in Figures 8.1–8.3 (later in this chapter). These practices may solve certain governance dilemmas and competing institutional logics, as well as facilitate the co-leaders' relationships with the board. But we also found that these practices have inherent risks. Our study of the nexus between co-leadership in the arts and their boards is unique in plural leadership research (Denis et al., 2010; Denis et al., 2012). We produce new insights into sharing the role space of co-leadership in the arts (Gronn & Hamilton, 2004; Stewart, 1991) and extend the dimensions of organizational ambiguity into the study of non-profit governance (Cohen & March, 1974).

Governance logics in the non-profit sector

Cornforth (2003a, 2003b) suggests a paradox lens to describe the dynamics of board-staff relations in non-profit organizations. However, we propose that these dynamics can be studied through the frame of competing logics which enables the introduction of legitimacy as a contextual pressure on relational behaviour, connecting to our use of institutional logics for the study of co-leadership (Thornton et al., 2012)(Chapter 5). Cornforth's analysis demonstrates how these dynamics create tensions, but they also guide a board's relationship with executive leaders and other organizational stakeholders. In response to governance scholars who have expressed interest in research beyond the board (Cornforth, 2012), our focus in this chapter is on co-leadership and its relationship with those who mandate and monitor the leaders' performance, that is, the board of directors. As a result, Cornforth's (2003a, 2003b) earlier theorizing of board-staff relations provides an interesting platform for our purposes. We briefly outline the competition among these governance logics in Cornforth's analysis, first examining the more internal board-staff relationship theories and then stakeholder perspectives.

Board-staff relations

Agency theory is a touchstone frame for governance studies in both for-profit and non-profit sectors. Rooted in the institutional order of business logics, it describes how for-profit boards represent owners to set policy and use that policy to assess decisions and ensure a CEO's adherence to organizational goals (Fama & Jensen, 1983; Jensen & Meckling, 1976). For-profit boards include internal executives and external experts rendering the board relatively well-informed about the organization's risks. However, distrust is a feature of this approach to CEO accountability.

In the non-profit sector, volunteer boards often lack professional knowledge of the mission, particularly regarding the mission-related practice that is at the core of the organization. Increasingly, non-profits have become professionalized in managerial terms (Hwang & Powell, 2009), but executive leaders are typically drawn from the professional corps, including artists. Expertise and legitimacy derive from the professional status in society (Abbott, 1988). The lack of board members' professional knowledge in the non-profit results in what agency thinking describes as information asymmetry raising questions about a board's ability to monitor and assess risk (Jensen & Meckling, 1976). This concern is evoked in the opening comments from participants at the top of the chapter. Pluralistic and ambiguous goals also contribute to this difficulty (Cornforth, 2004; Lampel et al., 2000) (Chapter 2).

Stewardship theory (Hernandez, 2012) is another board-staff perspective that contrasts with agency theory (Jegers, 2009). It conceives of horizontal and trusting partnerships where board members contribute collaboratively with executive leadership and other stakeholders to develop organizational strategies. Information asymmetry may play a role here, but collaboration and information sharing in a trusting relationship may reduce this problem. On the other hand, it may be difficult for board members to both trust and assess artists as executive leaders at the same time (Reid & Turbide, 2012). Scholars argue that the concurrent presence of agency and stewardship logics in board-staff relations sets up a tension (Cornforth, 2004; Coule, 2015; Sundaramurthy & Lewis, 2003).

Cornforth offers managerial hegemony as a further dynamic in board-staff relationships, extending the board's trust to a high degree. He portrays a single executive leader as all-powerful, where the board serves to rubber-stamp CEO ideas (Lorsch & MacIver, 1989). Linked with the artistic ideal, and hence the need for artistic autonomy, an ADs professional status, knowledge, and public notoriety may discourage a board from assessing the ADs work (Reid & Turbide, 2012) suggesting the possibility for managerial hegemony in the arts context. Researchers confirm that assessment of programming and collection decisions in performing and museum organizations appears to be off-limits to board members (Bieber, 2003; Kushner & Poole, 1996) according decisional autonomy to these artistic leaders (Abzug & Simonoff, 2004; Ostrower, 2002). Elite status board members in large arts institutions are attracted to the widely recognized professional leaders of their organizations and benefit from class cohesion through affiliation with these cultural leaders. A board's blind trust of executive leadership has resulted in financial or mission crises, thus justifying the concerns of proponents of agency theory (Reid & Turbide, 2012, 2013).

Stakeholder perspectives

Cornforth (2003a) also examines the influence of stakeholder and resource dependence theories on board responsibilities (Freeman, 1994; Pfeffer & Salancik, 1978). As community-based volunteers, board members negotiate access to funding stakeholders to generate resources for the organization (Brown et al., 2012; Laughlin, 2019), placing them and their organizations in accountability relationships with these stakeholders.

In the arts, board members may experience discomfort from the tension between this external role and that assessment role embedded in the board-staff relationship explained earlier. First, board members' passionate adoption of a vision that they promote to funders and donors may also inhibit their ability to monitor and critique the AD who developed that same vision (Brown et al., 2012; Cornforth, 2004; Rentschler, 2015). Second, board members may feel personally vulnerable to criticism of the AD and the organization from certain stakeholders with whom the member associates (Rentschler, 2015). This is particularly true if the organization's AD has a significant international reputation or is identified with a particular community (Reid & Turbide, 2012; Rentschler, 2015) (Chapter 2).

The democratic approach to stakeholder management is linked to the practice of representation on the board. In the non-profit or civil society arts in Europe, boards may include artists and funders (Tschmuck, 2006), and recently, in North America, members from under-represented communities (Laughlin, 2019). Certainly, donors are part of the mix, bringing passion for the art and veneration of artistic leaders (Rentschler, 2015). In response to information asymmetry, some boards choose to include individuals with artistic or arts management knowledge to facilitate evaluation and stewardship of executive leaders (Cornforth, 2004) replicating a for-profit approach that invites expertise onto the board.

Arts non-profit governance context

Boards of directors of non-profit or independent civil society arts organizations are typically elected or appointed to oversee both the mission and financial well-being of the organization. Wherever these sectors exist in the world, these governance responsibilities focus on several objectives: Respect for and promotion of the mission, assessment of organizational risks, and thoughtful choice of executive leaders (King & Schramme, 2019). When fully implicated, passionate and enthusiastic members of the board contribute value to the organization (Chait et al., 2005; King & Schramme, 2019; Rentschler, 2015). However, the ambiguity of multiple goals in these pluralistic organizations can result in lack of clarity and may challenge volunteer board members' motivation (Rentschler, 2015). The legitimacy accorded to celebrity artistic leaders appears to attract funders and professional collaborators, but it also protects these ADs from board assessment and questioning (Nisbett & Walmsley, 2016; Quigg, 2007).

This chapter's data are drawn from North American companies, where government funding is less generous than in Europe and Asia, but more structured than in much of the Global South (Chapter 4). Arts institutions and organizations in North America are mainly private non-profits, funded by their ticket-purchasing and donor communities (Hambrick & Mason, 1984; Laughlin, 2019). In Canada, more public funding is available than in the US, mainly through arts council grants. In North America, the state is rarely represented on boards, and board membership is emergent and bottom-up through a pervasive philanthropic culture that is distinctive in this region's arts sector (Laughlin, 2019).

In Europe, the New Public Management (NPM) movement from the 1980s and 1990s (Hood, 1991) influenced the transformation of state arts institutions into independent agencies (Tschmuck, 2006; Zan et al., 2012). Public funders now provide about 80–85% of the organization's budget. State control has been replaced by boards of directors, whose membership is sometimes shaped by public regulation. Board members may be designated representatives of specific institutional and corporate stakeholders and they may be called on to manage relationships with public or private institutional funders (Fanelli et al., 2019; Lindqvist, 2007). For instance, we found that between 60 and 70% of board members across major Scandinavian arts organizations were political or government appointees and the chair and deputy chairs were politicians or former politicians (Fjellvær, 2019). Other studies demonstrate similar membership in German-speaking countries (Heskia, 2021) and former arts executives in France affirm board membership by politicians and government bureaucrats (Jocelyn, 2021). Inspired by collaborative governance theory (Fanelli et al., 2019), the representation by institutional and public stakeholders reflects public-private engagement in the governance process, promotes democratic principles and cross-sector collaboration (Ansell & Gash, 2007). However, this type of board membership may still create issues of information asymmetry like those described in the North American non-profit context.

Neither stakeholder nor collaborative governance theories have considered the implications of a co-leadership executive configuration as an organizing and governance mechanism (Alvarez & Svejenova, 2005). Arts non-profit governance literature only makes passing reference to this leadership configuration, specifically in the US (Laughlin, 2019). To complete this gap in the literature, we focus here on co-leadership board relationship dynamics, revealing unusual patterns of practice. We investigate how co-leadership may solve the tensions inherent in board-staff relationships (Cornforth, 2003a, 2003b) and reduce board members' concerns about knowledge differential in the realization of their responsibilities.

The following questions serve as guides for this chapter.

How do boards and co-leadership work together in the non-profit arts?
In seeking solutions for competing logics in this relationship, what impact do boards have on the dynamics of the role space shared by co-leaders in the non-profit arts?

Researching arts governance with co-leadership

In each of eight cases in Canada, we interviewed several members of the board, including the board chair in all but one case. These board members had either a financial and internal organizational perspective or a market-donor and environmental perspective. Other than the board chair, specific roles included: past chair, treasurer, fundraising chair, connection with corporate sponsors, foundations and government, donor, artist, art connoisseur, management consultant, and lawyer. In seven additional cases, we interviewed one board member, usually the board chair. These latter cases provide some cross references for insights, but for this chapter, we concentrate on the eight cases where we had access to a significant range of board perspectives on co-leadership and board interactions.

In interviews, board members answered questions about their ability to undertake their responsibilities in response to the co-leadership presence and relationship. Both of the co-leaders also talked about their relations with the board. We were struck by the coherent repetition of similar perspectives across cases, generating confidence in our conclusions.

Also in the interviews, board decision-making processes were explained, particularly in terms of risk management concerning financial issues. Those members with a treasury or internal perspective including the board chair were most concerned with financial monitoring, whereas those aligned with a fundraising role were more engaged with their ability to support the artistic mission. Some board members highlighted their experiences with a co-leadership compared with that of a single leader elsewhere. Certain cases involved negative conflict within the co-leadership, particularly impacting the board's relationship with the AD. These cases were especially insightful.

Patterns of practice

In our analysis, three patterns of board practice with co-leaders emerged: (1) Establishing unique board member relationships with each leader (Figure 8.1); (2) delegating to the ED a monitoring relationship with the AD (Figure 8.2); and (3) intervening and managing problematic co-leadership relationships (Figure 8.3 [a and b]). The text outlines each set of behaviours, illustrated by citations from the cases. It is important to note that some cases appear across patterns suggesting relatedness from one pattern to another. Insights about the impact of arts co-leadership and their board relationships on non-profit governance are discussed.

Pattern 1: Unique board member relationships with each co-leader

In Figure 8.1, we illustrate how boards established separate relationships with each co-leader, rather than with the co-leadership as an integrated unit. Boards normally hired the co-leaders separately at different times, using different criteria regarding professional expertise for each role and different contract duration. They deployed different governance logics to justify their relationship with each of the AD and the ED.

On the other hand, the literature views co-leadership as a unit of plural leadership (Denis et al., 2012; Döös & Wilhelmson, 2021; Döös et al., 2019). Gronn and Hamilton (2004) conceive the shared role space within which co-leadership is realized and from which the organization is jointly managed. Boards in our data do not appear to recognize or assess this type of joint responsibility in a shared role space (Gronn & Hamilton, 2004).

AD relationship

When board members felt comfortable and stimulated about the mission and the ADs leadership, they adopted an advocacy relationship on behalf of the AD and mobilized their networks to acquire resources to promote and support the artistic vision. This dynamic is described in

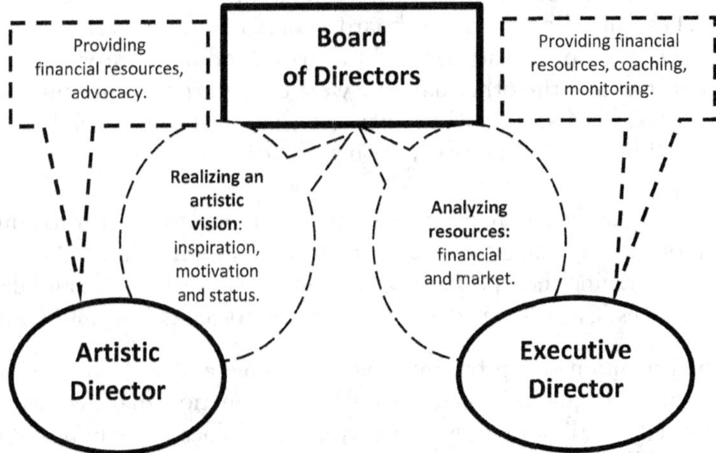

Figure 8.1 Pattern 1: Unique board and co-leadership relationships.

the board role on the left side of Figure 8.1. The incoming chair in one case reflected:

> We have a responsibility – towards the artists and towards the company as board members. What we are trying to do currently is to find financing in new places, in a new way that can help to stabilize the company. It is a major preoccupation – in financial terms.

A board member in another case expressed the need to expand the financial horizon in order to support the growing needs of the artistic vision:

> The more we can raise, the further we can advance AD's vision and artistic aspirations. My motivation is to facilitate and to provide the necessary resources for AD to take the company where it is necessary, and I think AD is being restricted by the dollar.

Being close to and supportive of the AD without being judgmental appeared to enhance the board members' sense of identity, purpose, and importance. This benefit is identified for board members on the left side of Figure 8.1. In one case, board members expressed interest in understanding the artistic process and how a season was constructed. The AD was keen to participate, and neither the board nor the AD perceived this as a monitoring initiative. Rather, the board chair explained how the connection with the AD and the insights "behind the scenes" excited and motivated board members to donate or to encourage others to donate:

> AD has to feel that the board is supportive, that AD has connections to them, they get to know AD as well as the ED. And so, we have organized over the course of the last year, numerous social opportunities, lunches, and dinners where board people can get together and listen to AD. ... And we had AD and the artistic administrator come to the board meeting the other day. We were enraptured about how they got the guest artists, and when they got this person, they had to cancel other things because it wasn't going to work.

Atypically, two board chairs in other cases attempted to elevate this familiarization process to a strategic evaluation of artistic programs. Their ADs reacted strongly, leveraging their professional and informational power, and discouraging the investigation – an effective gesture to protect artistic autonomy.

> I had mentioned a programming committee and AD reacted: 'If you do that, I'll quit ...' that's a pretty core function that AD does, and we need to talk about what that committee does ... helping the Board check off all the governance requirements.
>
> If we're going to pursue excellence in all we do, what does that mean? How do you define it? And AD gets all upset and imagines all these

> people who know nothing about the artistic product sitting around the board table ...

Similar to researchers in other Anglo-Saxon countries (Bieber, 2003; Kushner & Poole, 1996; Ostrower, 2002), we found that these boards and their artistic leader eventually succeeded in side-stepping debate about mission fulfilment as a formal governance practice at the board level. The concerns about managerial hegemony presented by Cornforth (2003a; 2003b) arise here as the board either chose or was forced to "blindly" trust the ADs artistic judgement and decisions. This choice demonstrates the power of the artistic ideal and professional autonomy linked to the professions order. Competing logics between governance norms and artistic autonomy present significant dilemmas. These concerns lead to pattern two where governance responsibilities are delegated to the ED, explored in Figure 8.2. But before we look at this pattern, we focus next on the board's relationship with the ED.

ED relationship

Although many admired the AD and the art, board members expressed their lack of competence to debate the merits of art and artistic decisions and their preference to work directly with the ED. One ED commented:

> So, AD doesn't have a relationship with very many board members because they're afraid. They don't understand. They don't mind talking to me, they understand business, they're all over it...

Board members expressed their separate relationship with the ED where they felt comfortable applying business logics to monitor, to assess, and to offer guidance. "Now the board's jurisdiction is mainly with the ED, not the AD" (Board chair). Board members' comments in two different cases reflect their distance from artistic decisions and their proximity to the ED and to the managerial point of view.

> The board has only marginal involvement in the artistic direction – a place I would say "no comment" – but otherwise we have a very significant involvement through the operations, the finances and that's what occupies us at our board meeting.
>
> Board chair

> The ED provides all the tools - building, seats, money, payroll, all that sort of thing. And that's the board's concern.
>
> Fundraising chair

Co-leadership researchers suggest that co-leaders are jointly responsible for the overall well-being of the organization (Gronn, 2002; Gronn & Hamilton, 2004). Instead, we found that board members focused a monitoring role almost exclusively on the ED, seeing this person as responsible for the organization. In that relationship, they are seemingly inspired by an agency theory logic. They approved budgets and grant applications and expected detailed treasury, fundraising, and marketing reports and break-even financial results. This dynamic is illustrated in the right side of Figure 8.1.

In numerous cases, a collegial stewardship approach with the ED was also reported. For instance, a board chair explained how a key board member engaged in mentoring when promoting a less experienced candidate from within the organization into the ED position.

> The [previous] chair had run a big company - a corporate type. This chair recognized talent, energy and said: 'This is the right choice. We've got to give this person a chance, they're up to the ED job'.

In a context of organizational stability and balanced budgets, board members appeared to trust the ED and senior management. They engaged in long-range planning and human resource issues. The past chair of the board of an institution expressed the board's relationship in partnership and stewardship terms:

> I guess my job was to lead the board in assisting the ED and staff to fulfil the strategic vision of the organization. How we can do that best is ... through our own reaction to the ideas and assisting in making them happen.

Consistent with their monitoring and mentoring relationship with their EDs, boards undertook performance evaluations. On the other hand, board evaluation of AD performance seemed rare, which perhaps further demonstrates a response to claims for artistic autonomy as well as information asymmetry. When there was an AD evaluation, it was very different from that of the ED. In Figure 8.1, monitoring is included in the ED-board relationship but not in the AD-board relationship. A board member in one case observed:

> Now performance evaluation has been driven the last couple of years by one of the MBA types - very hardnosed about ED and what ED's doing and not doing. But if AD doesn't do one of those things, the reaction is very forgiving - doesn't have the same sort of negative response to it ... doesn't feel as able to stand in judgment of AD as that of the ED. Being from a business management background, that's where ED is supposed to be.

The ED of the same organization compared an ED performance evaluation to that of the AD:

> When we started to do performance reviews of me...that was different than with AD. With AD, it was - let's go for lunch and see how things

are going. With me it was OK, what are your benchmarks and what are your goals for the year, and did you achieve them?

I stopped that ... [The ED explained that the process was subsequently re-calibrated to make the evaluations similar.]

However, if the ED reported less than stellar financial results, board members would adopt a classic agency stance: Change the executive, reflecting their perception that co-leadership involves separate roles. A board member commented:

> The MBAs on the board tend to have the attitude that a board stands back, hands off, you just set goals and objectives for your management and then...if they don't meet them, you replace the management. And we've had some deficits the last few years and that's been hard to deal with. Their solution is: change the management [or the ED].

An ED remarked:

> As your employer, the only role they play is either a cheerleader or a disciplinarian. They are there in an oversight role, not ...as a resource or a sounding board, which I think is unfortunate...

Commentary

Boards feel both comfort and discomfort with co-leaders in arts organizations. To solve the tensions in their relationship with each co-leader, board members divide the normally shared role space and make use of different logics to guide their separate relationship with these leaders. Board members are familiar with the business and market logics that orient the EDs domain and so, interact comfortably through an agency or stewardship perspective (Cornforth, 2003b). But boards generally distance themselves from the discomfort of monitoring the ADs performance that results from their lack of artistic expertise (information asymmetry), the societal power of artistic logics, and the ADs expectation of artistic autonomy. Instead, board members mobilize their role as promotional ambassadors and fundraisers to resolve this distance and which may lead them to negotiate with funding stakeholders as a response to resource dependence logics. This dynamic may also suggest potential for managerial hegemony by ADs (Cornforth, 2003b).

From our analysis, many boards seem to lack an understanding of the joint co-leadership responsibilities situated in the shared role space (Gronn & Hamilton, 2004). Some board members were concerned with how the two leaders worked together. However, to guide their relationship with the co-leaders, they focused their governance relationship at the level of the individual leader's organizational role, mobilizing the specific logics affiliated with that role, rather than the joint leadership role. This separation may contribute to an explanation of why, in Chapter 5, most relationships appeared to have high role differentiation (Hodgson et al., 1965), implying a limited overlap between the roles. In contrast to this practice in our data, we have found a more recent practice in Québec arts organizations where the titles and job descriptions of the co-leaders recognize both separate and joint roles (Lavoie, 2021).

Pattern 2: Delegation of a governance relationship with the AD

Given board members' need to distance themselves from evaluating ADs and the fulfilment of the artistic mission, the board directed their governance oversight and monitoring of the AD through the ED. This is demonstrated in Figure 8.2.

Board members perceived power and knowledge differences between themselves and the AD due to the ADs public profile and professional expertise related to the artistic ideal (Chapter 2) (Lindqvist, 2017). In Figure 8.2, the ADs "professional expertise" is key to the AD-board relationship. Qualitative assessment of art is subjective, contributing to the ambiguity of leading and managing these organizations (Lampel et al., 2000). As we understand from Pattern 1, most board members expressed anxiety about monitoring the artistic side of the organization, despite their passion for the mission and art (Rentschler, 2015). They felt unqualified to evaluate artistic decisions, processes, and performance, hence they avoided an assessment of the AD. The board's reaction is summarized at the left

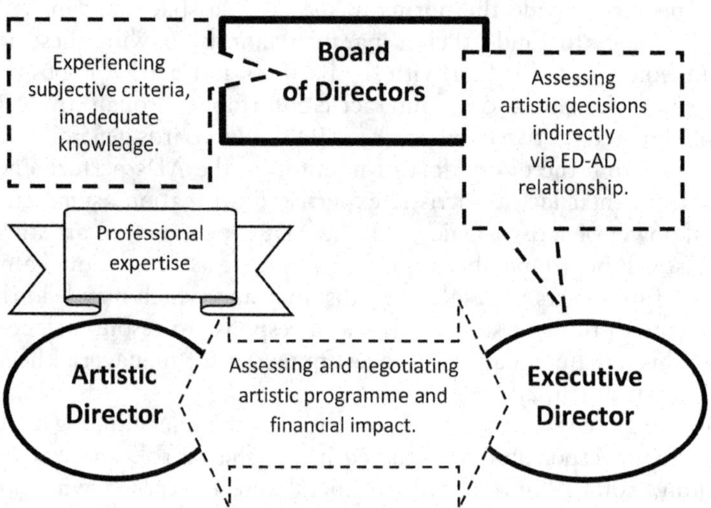

Figure 8.2 Pattern 2: Delegation of governance responsibilities to the ED-AD relationship.

in Figure 8.2. ADs also contributed to the underlying distance by insisting on the maintenance of artistic autonomy. A board chair explained the dilemma:

> It's very hard for a board to manage an artistic person with a huge ego. It's very difficult.... because they (board members) lead busy lives and they have other things to worry about and then all of a sudden, you've got this person who you can't argue the art form with unless you're most unusual. You're never going to have half a sense of it, and if you don't rein them in, it's a question of getting rid of them. And nobody likes to face situations where they fire somebody. ... And when that person has an enormous artistic reputation, and may well be beloved in the community, it's a tough thing to do.

Instead, boards preferred that the ED negotiate artistic and associated financial risks directly with the AD, deploying the ED as their proxy for overseeing the ADs decisions. As one board member explained: "the ED is there to control the egotistical budgetary excesses of the AD".

While boards related to the co-leaders separately, they formally mandated joint responsibilities and parity between the ED and AD in order to enable this delegated governance function to occur within the shared role space. As a result, functional differentiation is maintained between the two leaders as boards assessed the impact of co-leadership executive decisions through financial and marketing reports. The co-leadership structure serves the board as a monitoring and governance mechanism at the executive level, shielding the board from perceptions of direct intrusion into the artistic domain. This unconscious governance dynamic is illustrated in Figure 8.2 through the descriptions of relationships between the ED and board, and between the AD and ED.

In some cases, this delegated approach was, in fact, articulated as an institutionalized policy. A past chair in one case expressed this perspective:

> I don't think a board meddles with artistic matters. In other words, we don't say "you should be doing this work." There's no way a board should be involved in that sort of process.

This approach contrasts with the two cases identified earlier in our discussion, where the board chairs viewed direct assessment of artistic mission performance as a strategic governance responsibility. Later in the chapter, we reintroduce this dilemma in light of #MeToo! and increasingly vocal concerns raised during the recent pandemic about AD abuse of power.

Some board members expressed an appreciation for the relationship and the day-to-day exchange between the ED and the AD, symbolized by the two-directional arrow in this relationship in Figure 8.2. In five cases,

EDs were perceived as capably understanding the artistic objectives and how they might be achieved, and as a result, were able to negotiate acceptable trade-offs and provide suggestions for artistic programming within the AD-ED relationship. These cases reinforce the interest in hiring EDs with arts training or related knowledge (Chapter 7). ED familiarity with art appears to be as much a governance concern for boards as a trust issue for ADs. One of the board chairs expressed the AD-ED relationship in terms of risk management, part of the assessment function of governance:

> ...the two of them can have good, frank, open discussions on a daily basis about the artistic productions, and vice versa, the financial ramifications of those [artistic productions].

A member of a different board observed how the two executives worked:

> And the constructive tension has allowed one person to focus on one element like the managerial aspect, and another one on the artistic leadership aspect, and one is like the gas pedal and the other one is like the brake, and you need both to drive a car.

The ED in the same organization interpreted the role as: "You come to accept that there's a watchdog aspect". The treasurer on a board with a more conflicted AD-ED relationship perceived his own role as trying "to assess with the ED the risks of what is going on" regarding relationship health and financial problems.

The co-leadership relationship varied across the cases. In four of the cases, the co-leaders contained the tension resulting from the board members' delegation into the shared role space. Some board members indicated admiration for the complementary talents of the co-leaders. The chair of the board of the largest organization reflected on each co-leader's ability to balance the integration of their own and the other's logic:

> You've got ED who could weigh in and have an understanding and a deep appreciation of the artistic side and the business side, and AD who could do the same. You've got four possibilities. I guess it's possible that, out of four, you could get zero. ... But I think in this situation you've probably got a three or a three and a half out of four, which is pretty good.

A fundraising chair also indicated:

> I would like to see the AD accept more credit for being a very good leader when it comes to the artistic element of the company; he's pretty modest on that front ... And ED is a very good facilitator, very good - good at execution, good at trying to bring the various parties together.

Commentary

These organizations function with multiple objectives and attempt to balance the artistic ideal with business, market, and community logics. Ambiguity around priorities and goals results from the pluralism of these logics. Boards are often uncomfortable within the nexus of these logics, especially when box-office revenue is a significant portion of the budget, as occurred in our data. Sustaining this balancing act among logics requires professional knowledge to judge the implications of prioritizing decisions. For boards of directors, co-leadership has become a delegated response to this governance dilemma regarding information asymmetry and the necessity for a delicate balance respecting artistic autonomy and organizational stability.

Many co-leaders appear to accept the additional assignment of a monitoring role that demands further political and relational skills within the role space. Hence, the problem of the board's information asymmetry in the arts appears to be solved by a co-leadership configuration in these organizations. However, combining monitoring responsibility delegated to the ED by the board and the EDs subsequent accountability to the board may produce more pressure than the co-leadership relationship can bear. This pressure may produce negative conflict as the co-leaders navigate their own relationship with artistic autonomy (Røyseng, 2008). The delicate negotiation necessary to render this governance solution successful may become untenable. In the next pattern, we observe how boards are compelled to intervene directly when a balance of logics within a co-leadership relationship breaks down.

Pattern 3: Board intervention in problematic co-leadership relationships

Our data yielded examples of relationships which had evolved to either very negative or very positive co-leadership relationships – toxic conflict or perceived "collusion" – which instigated board intervention. These alternative patterns are illustrated in Figure 8.3 (a and b).

Pattern 3 (a): AD-ED negatively conflicted relationship

In one case, the artistic administrator related several instances from the past when a previous AD had gone directly to the board to pre-empt and manage conflict with an ED. The AD prevailed.

> ...board chairs are very intimidated by artistic leaders. ... That's usually one of the final stages, where the AD asks for a private meeting with the executive of the board. That's usually where you know you've got trouble.

Another very negative case provides an illustration of a board intervention requested by the ED to resolve a financial crisis and significant conflict within the co-leadership relationship. The AD refused to control accelerating production costs in a deficit situation, and the board increased its monitoring pressure on the ED to control these same costs. The co-leadership relationship deteriorated quickly, and the ED sensed that cost-control efforts were failing. The ED explained how the board needed to manage the AD directly:

> I realized that I was living an insular life of trying to solve the problems without getting any sense of partnership from AD… I decided I'd put it out on the table in a more public venue…The board finance committee began to see that there was this blatant disregard for financial responsibility … people were grappling with the notion of trying to bring AD back under control.

The open conflict drew the board into the operations of the organization, typically as a result of an appeal for allegiance by one or the other executive co-leaders, as depicted in Figure 8.3 (a) (Chapter 6). This required the board to manage budgeting processes closely, to act as a direct check and balance with the AD, and to solve the daily managerial questions that the two executives could not. The delegation of negotiating and monitoring functions to the ED had ceased to function. This dynamic is further illustrated in Figure 8.3 (a) by the lightning bolt between the AD and ED and the intervening arrow descending from the board. Agency theory logic required the direct intervention in a crisis (Reid & Karambayya, 2009; Reid & Turbide, 2012). Board members' anxiety increased through direct engagement with the AD. The board treasurer expressed discomfort in his mediating role because the ED and AD were not a functional partnership:

> But the spending side, clearly that has got to be controlled by somebody - I think it should be the ED with an oversight by the treasurer. I found that I got pegged with it probably more than I would have liked. And more than I think is necessary. … I don't know what model you could have to break the deadlock. It's ultimately the board that can do that. … you really have to mediate between the AD and the ED any time there is a disagreement.

In this case, the new board chair's leadership energy was taken up mediating the conflict, expressing despair about how to manage the organization's problems at the executive level.

> We as a board had to play a significant role in managing the relationship between them … You're putting out fires everywhere. Maybe halfway into the year that I'd been there, I started to see that, if you clear the smoke away, you might get a glimpse that there are some problems here. You can hear that there's a problem, but you can't fix it because there's nothing you can do.

After the crisis was resolved through board intervention and the departure of the ED, the AD insisted that the board withdraw from close engagement with the rest of staff. The artistic administrator explained:

> AD has been protective, like the board getting involved with the staff … but AD overwhelmingly wants [the new ED] to be the

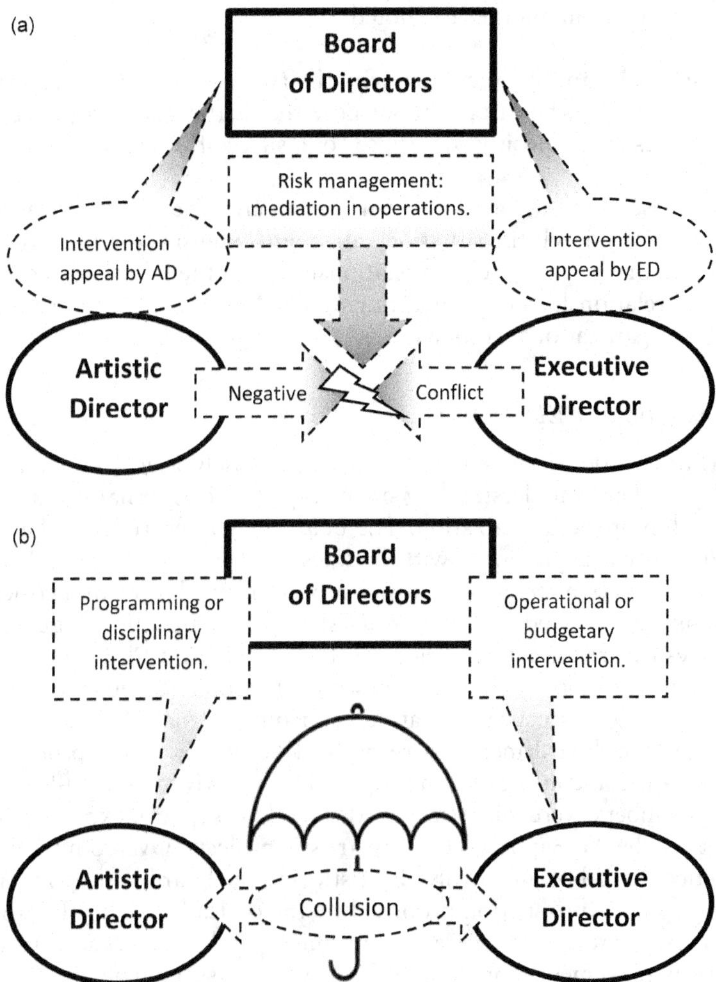

Figure 8.3 Pattern 3(a): Board intervention in AD-ED negatively conflicted relationship Pattern 3(b): Board intervention AD-ED "collusive" relationship.

> contact ... with the board, and not have the board really involved in the lives of the staff.

Board intervention has political implications for the relationship and consequently, for the organization. The co-leaders abdicated their joint responsibility within the shared role space and the board crossed the governance line to adopt a managerial role, entering the role space to ensure all responsibilities were fulfilled. This situation highlights how the board's intervention dissolves the parity that was intended by the board at the beginning of the relationship.

As confirmation, another ED noted:

> The checks and balances are why the two positions were created [by the board] ...when I talk about how the dual roles work, checks and balances isn't a positive descriptor of a successful relationship.

These cases demonstrated that without an effective ED-AD relationship at the executive level, the situation can create extensive discomfort for the board, requiring a much closer relationship with the AD than the board's preferred relationships described in patterns 1 and 2. There were implications for organizational stability.

Pattern 3 (b): AD-ED "collusive" relationship

In certain relationships, co-leaders became closely allied, either through a collegial shared understanding or in response to external threats to the relationship or the organization. The board may interpret the relationship as collusive when presented with budgets that predict a deficit. The ADs ambitions do not appear to be sufficiently counterbalanced and co-leaders' decisions are perceived to constitute a risk to the organization. Figure 8.3 (b) illustrates this relational challenge for boards and AD-EDs. The umbrella in this figure symbolizes how the trusting effort undertaken by the AD and ED attempts to protect their relationship from external intervention.

In one case, board members responded negatively to the program and budget for the upcoming season proposed by a newly minted co-leadership. Board members were surprised by the level of support expressed in the budget for the ADs apparently risky artistic projects. Overcoming the normal reticence to become involved artistically, the board voted to eliminate a contemporary production proposed by the co-leaders. They felt that the EDs revenue projections were too optimistic and so intervened to regain the risk management that they believed was necessary. The board crossed a line into artistic programming where most boards would not have ventured. Unfortunately, their intervention had consequences. The AD chose to leave the organization at that point and the ED left a year later.

In another case, the board expressed great concern about and criticism of the founder AD and ED for undertaking an additional artistic project in the season's creative program. This project was outside of the budget and activity approved for the year but was in response to an external invitation accompanied by funding. The ED had collaborated with the AD in logistics planning for this new project because it was very prestigious. For them, the project was funded outside of the organization's budget and so they felt they could proceed. The board stayed within its normal governance limits but exerted high agency control to restrain the AD's entrepreneurial initiative regarding the artistic programming. The co-leaders were reprimanded but are still with the organization. Two board members left.

Commentary

Earlier, we observed that boards work with each co-leader independently and often do not understand the jointly conceived responsibilities within the shared role space. However, we also observed that in the context of a perceived crisis, boards are ultimately forced to consider the consequences of an inappropriate dynamic in the relationship itself.

Conflict is often anticipated in co-leadership. Toxic conflict ruptures the shared executive role space and the organization's well-being is threatened. The tension of the co-leadership relationship becomes intolerable, and boards are vulnerable to appeals for allegiance from one or the other co-leader (Chapter 6). Collegiality and perceived collusion may also undermine the board's confidence in the co-leadership configuration as a solution to their problem of information asymmetry and artistic autonomy. In both situations, a direct intervention by the board results, and the board is drawn into the day-to-day management of the organization and the co-leadership shared role space. Boards are rarely experienced in this role and they appear to find it threatening. They may be criticized for their disrespect for artistic autonomy and their intervention disturbs the joint responsibilities that are normally fulfilled by the co-leaders.

Discussion and conclusion

From this research, we have learned how co-leadership is the board's hedge against managerial hegemony. Despite the rewards and the passions of their implication in the arts, boards face a number of challenges in their efforts to achieve a governance balance in these organizations. At the field level, several competing logics inform governance (Cornforth, 2003a, 2003b) resulting in accountability relationships that can be unclear and ambiguous (Cohen & March, 1974; Denis et al., 1996). At the organization and individual levels, ADs can project the authority of celebrity based on their artistic achievement and quality accomplishments. Their personal vision is often recognized as leadership by their professional peers (Lindqvist, 2017), reflecting how evaluation criteria in the arts are rooted in personal taste (Lampel et al., 2000). As community volunteers or government representatives, it is difficult for boards to assess artistic accomplishment and ADs often resist a board's efforts to that end (Bieber, 2003; Kushner & Poole, 1996; Ostrower, 2002).

In this chapter, we reported on our investigation of two research questions. The first asks how the relationship between boards and co-leaders works in the arts. The second explores how co-leadership provides solutions in board-staff relations in the non-profit arts as well as investigating the implications for the role space shared by the co-leaders. We identified four patterns of practice in the board-co-leadership relationship that were intended as solutions to perceived challenges of governing in a pluralistic arts context. These patterns are portrayed in Figures 8.1–8.3.

Two governance concerns were uncovered in our research: Information asymmetry between the board and the AD (agency theory) and the role tension between advocate and critic of the AD (stakeholder theory). These concerns generated changes in the traditional dynamics of accountability in a board-staff agency relationship (Fama & Jensen, 1983). With co-leadership, boards hire an ED as an equal peer to the AD to compensate for their reluctance to directly assess the AD and the ADs demand for artistic autonomy. They delegate to the ED the responsibility to analyse and negotiate with the AD the risks of the artistic program and to interpret this negotiation to the board as part of risk assessment. This delegation injects governance responsibilities into the shared executive role space (Gronn & Hamilton, 2004) influencing its power dynamics, logics, and tensions. It solves the general organizational discomfort around board assessments of artistic performance and the artistic vision, and it isolates the board from direct monitoring responsibilities. As a result, board members feel comfortable embracing their role as advocates of the AD, following their passion for the art and the ADs vision.

The delegation pattern relies heavily on the complementarity of the co-leadership relationship (Hodgson et al., 1965). However, over-enthusiastic agency-inspired demands by the board on the ED in relation to the AD may increase tensions in the relationship, instigating difficulties in the shared role space in response to the board's delegation. Boards should probably become mindful of the implications of these tensions, suggesting the value of a stewardship approach. However, the delegation may rebound to the board, requiring their direct intervention in the co-leadership dynamic, undermining the balance of logics within that relationship and the potential of this solution for a board's governance responsibilities.

On the other hand, the ADs and EDs may align on a certain strategy involving some risk in a budget. As a result of this united front, the board may perceive that the co-leadership relationship lacks the necessary debate to ensure balanced and well-informed decision-making (Gibeau et al., 2020). Board interventions into the co-leadership role space risk negative reactions regarding the need for artistic autonomy, a point of high sensitivity in the arts (Røyseng et al., 2020) (Chapter 2). Some executives may leave in response to board interventions, reflecting the potential fragility of co-leadership (Denis et al., 2012) (Chapter 3).

Despite a board effort to solve governance issues in the arts with co-leadership, a newly urgent and uncomfortable imperative has emerged regarding ethics and power in the arts (Lederman, 2018). Since 2017, intense media coverage of social justice movements like #MeToo! has sensitized internal and external stakeholders about the need for leadership accountability regarding abuse of power and the strategic need to change social norms within these organizations. This criticism has particularly focused on artistic leaders and may clash with the prioritization of the artistic imperative (Lindgren, 2009; Quigg, 2007), augmenting the pressure on EDs who function in a delegated governance role. For boards, working with charismatic ADs has traditionally been an effective leadership strategy to attract funding and collaborators (Nisbett & Walmsley, 2016; Ostrower, 2002) and to enhance stakeholder relations. This strategy allied with delegated governance of the AD through co-leadership has allowed boards to side-step this ethical imperative until recently. New solutions for boards may be necessary to address these issues more directly. While not reflected specifically in our data, we raise it in Chapter 10 as a compelling and necessary concern to research in the future.

Recently, scholars in non-profit governance have addressed power issues through the lens of a dominant coalition where informal alliances arise to solve issues in the organization (Andersson & Renz, 2021). These alliances can be temporary or permanent. They often cross and change the formal accountability relationships traditionally in place in the organization. We wonder about how our description of co-leadership and boards may reveal other forms of dominant coalitions. Deploying this lens for explaining board-staff relations with co-leaders may extend our theorizing of co-leadership further.

In summary, passionate board members in the arts are confronted with ambiguous goals and competing logics in their governance role, thus complicating their responsibilities as a board. Their decision to engage a co-leadership enables them to solve information asymmetry and demands for artistic autonomy, and hence, manage risks more effectively in arts organizations. However, this solution is limited due to the fragile and dynamic nature of the co-leadership relationship, the constraints of ambiguity within and around the organization as well as recently emerging representation and inclusion logics, like diversity and equity issues, that challenge norms that were accepted in the past. We wonder if there are further solutions to the board's information asymmetry that might restore the parity between AD and ED, which would recognize and enhance their ability to lead the organization jointly.

References

Abbott, A. D. (1988). *The System of Professions: An Essay on the Division of Expert Labour.* University of Chicago Press.

Abzug, R., & Simonoff, J. S. (2004). *Nonprofit Trusteeship in Different Contexts.* Ashgate.

Alvarez, J. L., & Svejenova, S. (2005). *Sharing Executive Power: Roles and Relationships at the Top.* Cambridge University Press.

Andersson, F., & Renz, D. (2021). Who really governs? Nonprofit governance, stakeholder theory and the dominant coalition perspective. In G. Donnelly-Cox, M. Meyer, & F., Wijkström (Eds.), *Research Handbook on Nonprofit Governance* (pp. 196–219). Edward Elgar Publishing.

Ansell, C., & Gash, A. (2007). Collaborative governance in theory and practice. *Journal of Public Administration Research and Theory*, *18*, 543–571. https://doi.org/10.1093/jopart/mum032

Bieber, M. (2003). Governing Independent Museums: How Trustees and Directors Exercise Their Powers. In C. Cornforth (Ed.), *The Governance of Public and Non-profit Organisations: What Do Boards Do?* (pp. 164–184). Routledge.

Brown, W. A., Hillman, A. J., & Okun, M. A. (2012). Factors that influence monitoring and resource provision among nonprofit board members. *Nonprofit and Voluntary Sector Quarterly*, *41*(1), 145–156. https://doi.org/10.1177/0899764011402510

Chait, R. P., Ryan, W. P., & Taylor, B. E. (2005). *Governance as Leadership: Reframing the Work of Nonprofit Boards*. John Wiley & Sons, Inc.

Cohen, M. D., & March, J. G. (1974). *Leadership and Ambiguity: The American College President* (2nd ed.). Harvard Business School Press.

Cornforth, C. (2003a). Conclusion: Contextualising and Managing the Paradoxes of Governance. In C. Cornforth (Ed.), *The Governance of Public and Non-profit Organisations: What Do Boards Do?* (pp. 237–253). Routledge.

Cornforth, C. (2003b). Introduction to the Changing Context of Governance - Emerging Issues and Paradoxes. In C. Cornforth (Ed.), *The Governance of Public and Non-profit Organisations: What Do Boards Do?* (pp. 1–19). Routledge.

Cornforth, C. (2004). The governance of cooperatives and mutual associations: A paradox perspective. *Annals of Public and Cooperative Economics*, *75*(1), 11–32. https://doi.org/10.1111/j.1467-8292.2004.00241.x

Cornforth, C. (2012). Nonprofit governance research: Limitations of the focus on boards and suggestions for new directions. *Nonprofit and Voluntary Sector Quarterly*, *41*(6), 1116–1135. https://doi.org/10.1177/0899764011427959

Coule, T. M. (2015). Nonprofit governance and accountability: Broadening the theoretical perspective. *Nonprofit and Voluntary Sector Quarterly*, *44*(1), 75–97. https://doi.org/10.1177/0899764013503906

Denis, J.-L., Langley, A., & Cazale, L. (1996). Leadership and strategic change under ambiguity. *Organization Studies*, *17*(4), 673–699.

Denis, J.-L., Langley, A., & Rouleau, L. (2010). The practice of leadership in the messy world of organizations. *Leadership*, *6*(1), 67–88. https://doi.org/10.1177/1742715009354233

Denis, J.-L., Langley, A., & Sergi, V. (2012). Leadership in the plural. *The Academy of Management Annals*, *5*(1), 211–283. https://doi.org/10.1080/19416520.2012.667612

Döös, M., & Wilhelmson, L. (2021). Fifty-five years of managerial shared leadership research: A review of an empirical field. *Leadership*, *17*(6), 715–746. https://doi.org/10.1177/17427150211037809

Döös, M., Wilhelmson, L., Madestam, J., & Örnberg, Å (2019). Shared principalship: The perspective of close subordinate colleagues. *Leadership and Policy in Schools*, *18*(1), 154–170. https://doi.org/10.1080/15700763.2017.1384503

Fama, E. R., & Jensen, M. C. (1983). Separation of ownership and control. *Journal of Law and Economics*, *26*(June), 301–325.

Fanelli, S., Donelli, C. C., Zangrandi, A., & Mozzoni, I. (2019). Balancing artistic and financial performance: Is collaborative governance the answer? *International Journal of Public Sector Management*, *33*(1), 78–93. https://doi.org/10.1108/IJPSM-05-2019-0138

Fjellvær, H. (2019). An unpublished study of boards in Scandinavian non-profit arts organisations. Norwegian University of Science and Technology.

Freeman, R. E. (1994). The politics of stakeholder theory: Some future directions. *Business Ethics Quarterly*, *4*(4), 409–421.

Gibeau, É, Langley, A., Denis, J.-L., & van Schendel, N. (2020). Bridging competing demands through co-leadership? Potential and limitations. *Human Relations*, *73*(4), 464–489. https://doi.org/10.1177/0018726719888145

Gronn, P. (2002). Distributed leadership as a unit of analysis. *The Leadership Quarterly*, *13*(4), 423–451. https://doi.org/10.1016/S1048-9843(02)00120-0

Gronn, P., & Hamilton, A. (2004). 'A bit more life in the leadership': Co-principalship as distributed leadership practice. *Leadership and Policy in Schools*, *3*(1), 3–35. https://doi.org/10.1076/lpos.3.1.3.27842

Hambrick, D. C., & Mason, P. (1984). Upper echelons: The organization as a reflection of its top managers. *Academy of Management Review*, *9*(2), 193–206.

Hernandez, M. (2012). Toward an understanding of the psychology of stewardship. *Academy of Management Review*, *37*(2), 172–193. https://doi.org/10.5465/amr.2010.0363

Heskia, T. (2021). Public boards; Questions of representation in supervisory boards of German, Austrian and Swiss theatres. *International Journal of Arts Management*, *24*(1), 32–47.

Hodgson, R. C., Levinson, D. J., & Zaleznik, A. (1965). *The Executive Role Constellation: An Analysis of Personality and Role Relations in Management*. Harvard University: Division of Research, Graduate School of Business Administration.

Hood, C. (1991). A public management for all seasons? *Public Administration*, *69*(1), 3–19. https://doi-org.proxy2.hec.ca/10.1111/j.1467-9299.1991.tb00779.x

Hwang, H., & Powell, W. W. (2009). The rationalization of charity: The influences of professionalism in the nonprofit sector. *Administrative Science Quarterly*, *54*(2), 268–298.

Jegers, M. (2009). 'Corporate' governance in nonprofit organizations. *Nonprofit Management & Leadership*, *20*(2), 143–164. https://doi.org/10.1002/nml.246

Jensen, M., & Meckling, W. (1976). Theory of the firm - managerial behavior, agency costs and ownership structure. *Journal of Financial Economics*, *3*(4), 305–360.

Jocelyn, M. (2021). International theatre and opera director, former AD and ED Toronto, Canada: Canadian Stage. Interview.

King, I., & Schramme, A. (Eds.). (2019). *Cultural Governance in a Global Context: An International Perspective on Arts Organizations*. Palgrave MacMillan.

Kushner, R. J., & Poole, P. P. (1996). Exploring structure-effectiveness relationships in nonprofit arts organizations. *Nonprofit Management and Leadership*, *7*(2), 119–136. https://doi.org/10.1002/nml.4130070203

Lampel, J., Lant, T., & Shamsie, J. (2000). Balancing act: Learning from organizing practices in cultural industries. *Organization Science*, *11*(3), 263–269. https://doi.org/10.1287/orsc.11.3.263.12503

Laughlin, S. (2019). USA. In I. King, & A. Schramme (Eds.), *Cultural Governance in a Global Context: An International Perspective on Art Organizations* (pp. 267–300). Palgrave MacMillan.

Lavoie, D. (2021). Administrative director and director general Montréal, Canada: Festival TransAmériques (FTA). Interview.

Lederman, M. (2018). When the #MeToo reckoning came for Canadian arts. *The Globe and Mail*.

Lindgren, A. C. (2009). The National Ballet of Canada and the Kimberly Glasco legal arbitration case. *The Journal of Arts Management, Law, and Society*, *39*(2), 101–116. https://doi.org/10.3200/JAML.39.2.101-116

Lindqvist, K. (2007). Public governance of arts organizations in Sweden: Strategic implications. *International Journal of Arts Management*, *13*(3), 303–317.

Lindqvist, K. (2017). Leadership in Art and Business. In E. Raviola & P. Zackariasson (Eds.), *Arts and Business: Building a Common Ground for Understanding Society* (pp. 404–422). Routledge.

Lorsch, J. W., & MacIver, E. (1989). *Pawns or Potentates: The Reality of America's Corporate Boards*. Harvard Business School.

Nisbett, M., & Walmsley, B. (2016). The romanticization of charismatic leadership in the arts. *The Journal of Arts Management, Law, and Society*, *46*(1), 2–12. https://doi.org/10.1080/10632921.2015.1131218

Ostrower, F. (2002). *Trustees of Culture: Power, Wealth, and Status on Elite Arts Boards*. University of Chicago Press.

Pfeffer, J., & Salancik, G. (1978). *The External Control of Organizations: A Resource Dependence Perspective*. Harper & Row.

Quigg, A.-M. (2007). Bullying in theatres and arts centres in the United Kingdom. *International Journal of Arts Management*, *10*(1), 52–64.

Reid, W., & Karambayya, R. (2009). Impact of dual executive leadership dynamics in creative organizations. *Human Relations*, *62*(7), 1073–1112. https://doi.org/10.1177/0018726709335539

Reid, W., & Turbide, J. (2012). Board/staff relationships in growth crisis: Implications for nonprofit governance. *Nonprofit and Voluntary Sector Quarterly*, *41*(1), 82–99. https://doi.org/10.1177/0899764011398296

Reid, W., & Turbide, J. (2013). Dilemmas in the Board-staff Dynamics of Nonprofit Governance. In C. Cornforth & W. A. Brown (Eds.), *Nonprofit Governance: Innovative Perspectives and Approaches* (pp. 163–182). Routledge.

Rentschler, R. (2015). *Arts Governance: People, Passion, Performance* (1st ed.). Routledge.

Røyseng, S. (2008). Arts management and the autonomy of art. *International Journal of Cultural Policy*, *14*(1), 37–48. https://doi.org/10.1080/10286630701856484

Røyseng, S., Di Paolo, D., & Wennes, G. (2020). As you like it! How performance measurement affects professional autonomy in the Norwegian public theater sector. *Journal of Arts Management, Law and Society*, *50*(1), 52–66. https://doi.org/10.1080/10632921.2019.1693458

Stewart, R. (1991). Role Sharing at the Top: A Neglected Aspect of Studies of Managerial Behaviour. In S. Carlson, H. Mintzberg, & R. Stewart (Eds.), *Executive Behaviour* (pp. 120–136). Studia Oeconomiae Negotiorum.

Sundaramurthy, C., & Lewis, M. (2003). Control and collaboration: Paradoxes of governance. *Academy of Management Review*, *28*(3), 397–415.

Thornton, P. H., Ocasio, W., & Lounsbury, M. (2012). *The Institutional Logics Perspective: A New Approach to Culture, Structure, and Process*. Oxford University Press.

Tschmuck, P. (2006). The budgetary effects of 'Privatizing' major cultural institutions in Austria. *The Journal of Arts Management, Law, and Society*, *35*(4), 293–304. https://doi.org/10.3200/JAML.35.4.293-304

Zan, L., Bonini Baraldi, S., Ferri, P., Lusiani, M., & Mariani, M. M. (2012). Behind the scenes of public funding for performing arts in Italy: Hidden phenomena beyond the rhetoric of legislation. *International Journal of Cultural Policy*, *18*(1), 76–92. https://doi.org/10.1080/10286632.2011.573849

9 Following and influencing co-leaders

> If you have the right people in the right leadership positions among the department heads, then your company will do well.
>
> Development director

Introduction

Followers of co-leadership are rarely studied (Döös & Wilhelmson, 2021), but as observed by one senior manager in our cases, they can make a difference for the well-being of the organization. In arts organizations, each co-leader heads up their expert team of professional or management specialists. They also jointly lead the whole organization. In contrast to single leadership, a co-leadership constellation is dynamic because the shared role space is subject to pluralistic logics (Chapters 2, 3, and 5). As a result, followers may discover variations of leadership and communication styles, strategic orientations, and the possibility of executive conflict that can emerge unless some degree of logic integration is accomplished. Understanding the culture of followership that occurs in co-leadership contexts would be useful to extend research about co-leaders and their followers. Several arts management scholars have been attracted by the benefits of sharing or distributing leadership beyond the shared role space of co-leadership (Hewison et al., 2013; Schrauwen et al., 2016). Other scholars have found that immediate followers may attempt to solve issues in co-leaders' relationships and influence the dynamics in the co-leaders' role space through expanding and crafting roles (Ebbers & Wijnberg, 2017). Initiating organizational leadership among co-leaders' followers in the arts may be unconscious or deliberate, passive or active.

Traditionally, research about co-leadership has been focused on achieving the ideal relationship dynamics in order to lead as one (Alvarez & Svejenova, 2005; Gibeau et al., 2020) (Chapter 3). Some consideration has been given to strategic decision-making in co-leadership in the arts, but the impact is framed at the organizational level without followers in mind (Bhansing et al., 2016; Voss et al., 2006). The research undertaken by Reid

DOI: 10.4324/9780429504259-12

and Karambayya (2009) is an exception where co-leadership conflict was found to interfere with followers' ability to accomplish their responsibilities. However, followers' aspiration to leadership was not directly considered. In order to develop our investigation into the relationship between co-leaders and their followers, we link perspectives from follower-centred leadership theories (Shamir et al., 2007), plural leadership (Denis et al., 2012), and role theory (Ebbers & Wijnberg, 2017; Gronn & Hamilton, 2004).

Follower-centred leadership

How leaders and followers interact is passionately debated across a continuum of perspectives in the follower-centred leadership literature. At one end of the continuum, followers may respond passively to inspiring leaders (Bass, 1990), while at the other end, they may actively and directly participate in shared or distributed leadership (Shamir, 2007). Through the continuum, followers gain agency and increasingly become "active co-producers" of leadership. Plural leadership theorists of collective, shared, and distributed leadership suggest that everyone in the organization or group is potentially a leader (Denis et al., 2012; Gronn & Hamilton, 2004). However, co-leadership, situated earlier in the continuum, is a separate form of plural leadership. It involves "pooling to direct others from the top" as an executive configuration (Denis et al., 2012). Followers do not necessarily participate in leadership roles.

The "romance" of leadership is found mid-point in the continuum. It describes how followers construct the illusion of strong leadership and direction (Meindl et al., 1985). The professional celebrity of artistic directors (ADs) is often linked with charismatic leaders who attract support for the organization, including many types of followers (Nisbett & Walmsley, 2016). Inspiration – called "covert" leadership (Mintzberg, 1998) – can be key to motivating high performance from the professional artists of the organization. This inspirational role may produce an elevated status for the AD through attribution (DeRue & Ashford, 2010), contributing to power differences and relationship issues within co-leader configurations (Chapter 6). Celebrity in co-leadership is a factor unique to the arts.

In later theorizing along the continuum of perspectives, leader-member exchange (LMX) explores vertical relationships between single leaders and followers, as well as collaborative follower influence on that leadership (Shamir, 2007). Co-leadership has only recently been explored using an LMX theoretical lens. Two sets of scholars have investigated situations focussing on communication and leadership effectiveness in relationships between co-leaders and followers (Barkela, 2019; Vidyarthi et al., 2014). One study looks at major German theatre companies where ADs and executive directors (EDs) relate to different types of professionals and staff, and the other study involves two leaders in separate but closely related organizations as supplier and client. In the LMX dynamic in arts co-leadership, the vertical relationship with employees is compounded by followers' need to relate to separate expert and differentiated leaders, and the horizontal and equal relationship of the joint co-leadership. It is compelling to understand who initiates the collaboration when senior managers are motivated to engage in leadership.

Plural leadership

In their literature-structuring analysis of plural leadership, Denis et al. (2012) question how co-leadership might be different from a top management team (TMT), which is a group of senior executives surrounding a single CEO (Hambrick & Mason, 1984). In addressing this definitional concern, Gronn and Hamilton (2004) consider the possibility of co-principals sharing leadership with a group of senior managers. They observe the implications of a malleable leadership role space that accommodates other organizational members on a periodic basis. In fact, co-leaders in larger arts organizations are often surrounded by a senior management group that provides the expertise necessary to lead the organization's various domains (Hewison et al., 2013). While each team member might report more consistently to one of the co-leaders, they also report collectively to the co-leaders in their jointly mandated role responsibilities. Their implication in the co-leaders' shared role space has yet to be considered.

Scholars of plural leadership find that single leaders can generate a shared leadership culture within groups of managers who report to them (Pearce, 2004). Several arts management scholars have expressed an affinity for the relevance of shared and distributed leadership. They describe co-leadership as part of a team with other senior managers who participate in leading (Hewison & Holden, 2011). Other preliminary research indicates increased effectiveness when leadership is distributed beyond co-leaders (Schrauwen et al., 2016). This potential effectiveness suggests the value of investigating co-leadership within a culture of shared or distributed leadership and its influence on the co-leaders' shared role space.

Role theory

Job or role crafting, found in role theory, is a process that may influence the relationship between co-leaders and their followers (Biddle, 1986; Wrzesniewski & Dutton, 2001). A role is defined in response to the expectations of other members in the role set, those who surround the role of interest. Role conflict and ambiguity arise from pluralistic expectations by the role set. Arts co-leaders face further challenges in defining their role because of the two roles they perform – their individual functional role and the joint role. As a result, they respond to multiple role sets. For co-leaders in permanently established organizations, trust and collaboration mechanisms are often deployed within the shared role space to assist in resolving conflict and ambiguity, and to integrate logics (Chapters 5, 6, and 7). Their close managerial associates in the organization may also contribute to the resolution of co-leaders' role challenges. Their involvement suggests distributed leadership if these associates are invited to enhance their organizational role. This context may also offer an opportunity for independently initiated role crafting by these managerial associates (Wrzesniewski & Dutton, 2001). Role crafting can occur when co-leader relationships are not functional (Ebbers & Wijnberg, 2017).

The study of short-term film production projects provides a significant empirical demonstration of independently initiated role crafting in the context of arts co-leadership. If there is room in the space between the film's director and producer, the first assistant director (1st AD) becomes implicated in the process of decision-making and may complete the co-leadership role space. In these projects, the 1st AD can implicate themselves by expanding and crafting their role to solve production problems and make creative decisions (Ebbers & Wijnberg, 2017; Ebbers et al., 2014). However, if co-leaders are tightly engaged in their relationship because of close collaboration and complementarity, the 1st ADs intermediary role may not grow to the same degree. In a more distanced co-leader relationship, often caused by tension or conflict, there may be openness to increased input and enhanced roles for senior managers (Ebbers & Wijnberg, 2017). Ironically, a contradiction emerges between the collaborative harmony idealized in shared and distributed leadership and the opportunity for such wider participation in leadership as the result of conflict within the leadership configuration (Bolden, 2011).

We have observed similar dynamics and stories from the permanently established organizations in our data where senior functional managers have also been observed to participate in the leadership role space. Of course, we have already analysed how members of boards of directors are drawn into the shared role space due to co-leaders' destructive conflict or lack of debate (Chapter 8). Our research extends and enriches both the role crafting findings from research on temporary film production projects and distributed leadership by answering the following questions:

> How do co-leadership dynamics create opportunities for leadership participation by senior organizational followers?
>
> How do followers influence co-leadership dynamics?

Studying senior management followers of co-leadership

Our data is fortunately rich, allowing us to explore the relationships between co-leaders and members of their senior management teams. The type of co-leader relationship is key to understanding the realization of different practices that senior managers deploy to engage in co-leaders' shared role space and the relationship dynamics. In our research, access to the space may be in response to a deliberate invitation from one or both co-leaders. The modest expansion of roles occurring in response to co-leader invitation suggests delegation and, as a result, distributed leadership (Gronn & Hamilton, 2004).

On the other hand, when co-leadership communication is weak and distanced, when particular responsibilities are overlooked by neglect or abstention, or when co-leadership conflict appears, the senior manager may initiate their own involvement in the shared role space. These circumstances provided opportunities for senior managers to expand their roles or may be seen by followers as a dire organizational need to be solved. This reinforces insights reported from the study of role-crafting in film production (Ebbers & Wijnberg, 2017).

We identify senior management engagement practices according to three types of co-leadership relationships that reflect high to low logic integration and complementarity: (1) Collaborative, (2) tolerant "negative peace" (Chapter 5), and (3) toxic conflict. We found 11 examples of engagement practices with executive leadership by members of the senior management team in eight organizations. We identified five engagement practice types from these 11 examples reflecting passive to active followership: Providing expertise, debating strategy, reinforcing, mediating, and compensating. These practice types appeared across the different relationship types. Table 9.1 charts the practice types in relation to the three co-leader relationship types.

Co-leaders in positive or tolerant relationships deliberately invite senior managers to provide their expertise that ultimately enriches co-leadership complementarity and effectiveness through expanded information sharing. Occasionally, these managers participate in decision-making for the organization which provides opportunity for expanding job responsibilities.

On the other hand, in tolerant or poorly functioning co-leadership relationships, a senior manager often feels compelled to act independently and without invitation to stabilize the organization or to accomplish specialized tasks. In some examples, the senior manager engages directly with the co-leaders and their relationship, facilitating decision-making by functioning as a mediating go-between. In other examples, the senior manager expands their specialist role directly with external stakeholders without the executive leaders' participation. In both types of practices, role crafting and expansion is involved, fulfilling a gap in the executive role space that is created by co-leadership distance, conflict, or being silent (Chapter 6).

Providing expertise

In this first practice type, the co-leaders in two organizations enjoyed a positive relationship with extensive communication. In one organization, the AD travelled, but was regularly connected with the ED through many

Table 9.1 Senior management engagement in the co-leadership shared role space

	Co-leader relationship types		
Engagement practices	*Positive co-leadership relationship*	*"Negative peace" or tolerant co-leadership relationship (Chapter 5)*	*Toxic co-leadership relationship*
Providing expertise	Senior managers share expertise to support strategic decisions by ED and AD (alliance seeking).		
Debating strategy		Senior managers invited to engage with ED and AD in round-table debates (influence, job crafting).	
Reinforcing		Co-AD spouse adjusts artistic program at home (alliance seeking, no job crafting). Senior manager listens with empathy to ED (alliance seeking and job crafting).	
Mediating		Production director hired to shape AD logistics and share with ED (facilitating decision-making, limited job crafting). Senior manager debates ED strategies with AD (alliance seeking and job crafting).	Artistic administrator intervenes between ED and AD (facilitating decision-making, extensive job crafting).
Compensating		AD travels externally and artistic administrator developed strategies with AD to ensure ADs presence with board of directors (advocating, job crafting).	Development director advances sponsorship program without artistic program (entrepreneurship, extensive job crafting).

modes of communication. In another organization, co-leaders' frequent and daily conversations enabled active debates and abundant information sharing. Each set of co-leaders exhibited a balanced perspective to logics. In one of the organizations, the co-leaders developed an over-arching logic that enabled exceptional collaboration and regular debate, effectively covering the shared role space (Chapter 5). However, in the other organization, the board objected to the co-leaders' overly coherent programming vision that projected a deficit budget. The board intervened to force a change (Chapter 8).

In both organizations, senior managers representing marketing, business, artistic, and production domains were deliberately invited to provide their functional expertise as the co-leaders made decisions. They were deliberately invited by one or the other co-leader to whom they individually reported. This kind of involvement was satisfying for the participants, since their competence was being recognized. However, in general, this practice did not involve extensive job expansion for these senior managers. They remained within their functional role definition, drawing on their area of expertise, to advise the pertinent co-leader. Despite the requests for suggestions for solutions, the invitation did not engage them directly in decision-making. Their input expanded expert information sharing at the co-leadership level, but it neither disturbed nor enhanced the balanced perspective shared by the co-leaders. The impact of the senior manager was through the individual leader's ability to participate in the co-leadership dynamics.

> I generally would feed information back to ED – I've kind of got my finger on the organization a little bit, just because of who I'm meeting with and talking to... when you come to ED with things, you have to have at least started to formulate what a solution might look like.
>
> Administrative director

> The budget is developed with ADs main collaborators – production director and artistic administrator – who do some shopping around in the field for décor and costumes to see what it's going to cost and if it seems to make common sense. They will look for artists who are available. Then AD will come to the board of directors and say: For the year X-Y, I propose these shows, and of the five, one is not yet certain. That last production might be a choice between this one or that one.
>
> Board treasurer

In the first organization in this practice type, the organization was stable and its artistic fare remained at a high quality, but increasingly, critics commented on the need for more innovation and development in the artistic vision. The artistic administrator attempted to reinforce an exclusively artistic perspective in the shared role space. However, this manager's influence was limited because of the frequent daily communication and complementarity between AD and ED.

In these examples, little co-leadership role space was left unfulfilled. As a result, opportunities for role crafting were limiting, but a form of distributed leadership was attempted. The co-leaders developed an over-arching logic that focused on balancing the organization's regional and artistic communities' needs. Therefore, the interests of an integrated but respectful co-leadership were served, but any further development of senior management roles was limited.

Debating strategy

In another organization, the AD and ED were actively developing a new relationship. Their adjoining offices facilitated communication and the ED was dependent on the AD for learning a new art discipline while inhabiting the executive leadership role space. This new relationship contrasted with the previous toxic co-leadership relationship in the organization.

The AD enjoyed debates, whereas the ED preferred to avoid tensions and differences. They decided to expand the opportunity for debate by inviting their directors of marketing and finance to participate in regular round-table discussions. As a result, they were able to influence executive perspectives and decision-making. They felt that including these senior managers in an expanded, unstructured, and ongoing conversation with both of them together would enable practical sharing of information and reflexivity without pressure. An agenda was rarely prepared, but pertinent and timely organizational topics were considered by consensus. Different perspectives were debated without needing to make immediate decisions, but the debate process enabled a collective change in points of view.

> I instituted a kind of weekly meeting, call it brainstorming, with ED, the director of finance and director of marketing in which we just kind of blue-sky ideas. Because I felt I wasn't getting the opportunity to sit around and just talk. I wanted to start to question some of our assumptions. ... We decided there'd be no agenda... it's very freeform. And nobody takes minutes.
>
> AD

This format suited both co-leaders by delegating task conflict to others in a "neutral" forum. When important strategies were subsequently under consideration, solutions had already been discussed and debated, a decision-making process that included others with specific and pertinent expertise.

For these senior managers, some initiative on their part was needed to navigate the conversation with their well-informed and engaged AD and their conflict-avoiding ED to maximize their opportunity to influence. As well, the opportunity to debate depended on co-leaders who initiated the invitation to participate in the round-table debates. While follower expertise and strategies were respected, executive decision-making was not delegated to them.

> AD loves to spar ... was on the university debating team. I think AD and the marketing director are really good at it, and AD and the finance director mostly do well with it. ...I mean that we're all equals. And we're just there to spin ideas around and see what grabs hold and,

> here's a topic, let's talk about this one. AD might approach it that way, I don't know about the marketing director, but I know the finance director told me that "as round as that table may or may not be, you people are still the boss. So, it isn't absolutely round. My opinion isn't as equal as your opinion really".
>
> ED

Despite the co-leaders' invitation and expression of confidence in the senior managers' input, they were also focused on developing their new and positive relationship. This emphasis may have constrained their openness to involve those senior managers in a more distributed leadership mode. Because of the concern about the co-leadership relationship and the social hierarchy that remained in the group, role crafting appeared as an opportunity to expand influence. The two senior managers expanded their roles by navigating the debates, influencing decisions, despite their reservations.

Reinforcing

In other organizations, we found two examples of reinforcing practices. AD-ED co-leader relationships were tolerant but somewhat distanced, as found in the middle column in Table 9.1. In each case, the AD had a co-AD, who was a spouse. While this co-AD spouse was an artistic contributor, the AD was the public voice of the duo and the EDs day-to-day primary contact. We have chosen to consider these co-AD spouses as followers because they were not actively involved in the co-leadership, despite their title.

> ED is trying to give AD a greater understanding of how the larger picture works… I think you can get places with AD but where we have issues is that co-AD is not involved in that process. So, you can bring AD to a certain point, but then co-AD gets involved at home, and AD comes in with the little notes and you take four steps backwards again.
>
> Marketing director

The ED needed to anticipate the "off-stage" reinforcement of the AD role in the shared role space after home consultations occurred, and the possibility that decisions might be adjusted. While this process rarely created significant conflict or serious difficulties, it produced some tension with a two-against-one co-leadership dynamic, slowed the process of decision-making, and reinforced artistic autonomy. This version of leadership distribution demanded flexibility on the part of the ED and the staff. However, it diminished the complementarity of the primary AD-ED relationship in the co-leadership.

Another reinforcing practice was observed in one of the organizations considered earlier. The AD and ED shared a carefully managed trusting relationship. The AD was the founder and a very dynamic artistic leader at the centre of all their productions. The senior manager, a marketing director, demonstrated a different form of a reinforcement practice. In this small organization, the ED needed a sounding board to share concerns about balancing finances and managing cash flow. At times, this senior manager adopted a therapy mode in an effort to encourage an appreciated superior. This conversational approach supported the ED and reflections on the company's strategic concerns. This provided protection from other influences, like the board, that would rebound on the co-leader relationship. It also allowed the development of distance and solutions that reduced the tension in the co-leadership relationship. This was clearly role crafting since it was not by invitation or within the job description of the marketing director. The dynamics could also be considered distributed leadership, given the influence on strategic organizational thinking by this senior manager.

> When EDs got a problem, the only person that is comfortable to confide in is me. There's something wrong with that, don't you think? I don't mind that I'm a sounding board for the quivery voice at the other end of the phone call saying I'm really scared I don't have any cash flow right now. I don't mind that. I'm happy to do that.
>
> Marketing director

Mediating

Examples from two organizations illustrate mediating. In the organization founded by the AD, there had been terrible conflict between the first board-appointed ED and the AD. The new co-leadership relationship was under construction. Both co-leaders disliked conflict, creating some distance and leaving some space for others in the organization to solve issues that they perceived in the shared role space.

> We certainly don't do conflict well together. We avoid it. So, if there is an issue, I would tend to raise it orally. If there is an issue, AD tends to wait it out. Or [leaves] a phone message. AD doesn't like direct one-on-one conflict. I prefer not to have it, but it's the nature of my job, I have to have it all the time.
>
> ED

In this new relationship, the ED wanted to ensure some judicious and arm's length control of production costs without having to confront the AD directly. As a result, the ED hired a production manager to coordinate artistic logistics and to ensure that budgets and union procedures were followed by the ambitious and entrepreneurial AD. The ED asked the production manager to use expertise to anticipate and manage the production process and the ADs expectations. This had previously been undertaken by the ED alone.

> I found the production manager and brought that person on board.
>
> ED

> I have a great relationship with AD so it's really easy to keep those avenues open ... I feel like I can walk in that room and be honest no problem... I can say no, I can say yes, I don't feel afraid by the authority... I'm trying to take a lot away from ED in terms of union contracts and individual contracts with the people we hire ... the designers, the wardrobe, lighting directors and that sort of thing.
>
> Production manager

The production manager's involvement in the executive role space focused on ensuring conformity to established production constraints. Communicating judgement about the implications of the process to the ED was a modest expansion of the production role. As a result, the ED was never surprised by concerns expressed by production stakeholders, eliminating confrontation with the AD. This mediating role allowed the ED to delegate any direct conflict with the AD, enabling stability and some complementarity in a tolerant "negative peace" relationship (Chapter 5). Distributed leadership was at play.

In another example in the same organization, if criticism of the ED arose, the reinforcing senior manager defended the ED in conversations with the AD by insisting on his competence and good faith.

> AD made a comment, "I am the one left holding the bag around here all the time". And I looked and I said, "excuse me, that is completely inappropriate, and you know I do not want to hear you talking that way about ED."
>
> Marketing director

This manager had played a similar mediating role in the ADs very toxic relationship with the prior ED. Distributed conflict is identified as a common practice in arts organizations (Reid & Karambayya, 2009). This senior manager's role did not require direct involvement in the co-leaders' decisions, but the individual recognized that a mediating role was useful to stabilize the relationship for the organization's sake. As a result, some role crafting was undertaken by the marketing director since the role did not involve relationship mediation with the charismatic AD.

In another organization, the co-leaders were experiencing increasingly toxic conflict. Communication between the two leaders had become minimal and decisional processes were confrontational. Almost no complementarity existed within the relationship. Each leader increased their focus on a dominant logic and limited integration occurred (Chapter 5). The role space was poorly occupied, leaving a lot of room for others.

The artistic administrator filled the only role working on both sides of the organization, attending separate meetings led by each of the co-leaders that grouped specialists on each side of the organization.

> There's an artistic meeting and then an administration meeting… I'm sitting in both of those meetings and having to pull out all the information that needs to go to each of those other meetings, because I'm the only one that's sitting in the two of them.
>
> Artistic administrator

As a result of the toxic and limited co-leadership relationship, this senior manager was forced to expand the artistic administration role to accomplish significant mediation and overcome communication deficits between the two co-leaders in a dire situation.

> I would talk to AD about [an issue]. We would have a great discussion about it, but it might not go anywhere, and the reality was for me to get my point across I'd have to take it through to ED. Whereas I would have thought the better way would be me [to communicate] to AD [and then AD] to ED, around that way, instead of me to AD [and] ED [independently]…
>
> Artistic administrator

The artistic administrator unconsciously expanded the role as a result. This significant increase in responsibilities was somewhat stressful. Role crafting became a challenging process.

> So, it's that challenge to keep that communication open, and to keep that involvement there, and to keep that artistic side in the administrative world… I don't know, it's a real sort of conundrum…
>
> Artistic administrator

As the one balancing agent present in the role space, this senior manager was required to find a creative approach to share difficult information across uncomfortably opposing logics to stimulate decision-making.

Compensating

This practice occurred in two organizations where the AD was either absent or they abstained from or neglected their larger organizational responsibilities. The relationship was tense although there was no open conflict. There was limited complementarity and much role space needed to be filled in order to avoid fundamental organizational problems.

As a result, individual senior management specialists on either the artistic or the marketing sides of the organization expanded their specific roles. They were motivated to compensate when certain responsibilities in the leadership role space were not fulfilled, and the well-being of the organization was threatened.

In one organization, the AD was often away from the organization travelling for other artistic responsibilities. While ADs in other organizations also travelled, the ED in this situation viewed the AD role as less strategic, suggesting that it was unnecessary for AD to attend board meetings. There was physical and psychological distance among AD, ED, and the board.

The artistic administrator felt strongly that the AD role should be recognized and consulted as an equal in the organization. The artistic imperative needed to be present in some or all board meetings. This senior manager felt responsible for promoting the ADs vision as well as keeping the AD informed. The individual took the initiative to make presentations at board meetings and travel to meet with the AD to engage in planning.

These activities actively expanded this role, reflecting significant role crafting. These compensating efforts at integrating the AD into the organization's strategic decision-making process produced an AD-ED relationship that functioned symbolically but without much complementarity. However, because of the efforts of the artistic administrator, financial and artistic logics were relatively well-integrated.

In another organization and example of compensating, the AD and ED were not fulfilling their responsibilities in the role space, and not meeting the role set of senior managers' expectations as executive co-leaders. They were very distant, resulting in limited joint decision-making. As a result, there were many responsibilities in the role space unfulfilled, resulting in limited complementarity in the shared executive role space.

The company's development and sponsorship director needed information about artistic plans to negotiate with sponsors. The previous AD had been a public figure at the heart of the fundraising program, but the new, more reticent AD was unprepared to commit to programming decisions on an appropriate schedule for fundraising needs. The senior manager was caught between the timing of market decision-making and artistic planning. So, in their role responsibility for philanthropy and sponsorship, this senior manager initiated a creative strategy with the staff to acquire market commitments from new sponsors using less specific program information.

> So, based on the little bit I have been able to glean from AD, I've had to go out and sell and build a case for [sponsorship].
>
> Development director

> ...absence of leadership ... An absence of vision, and so that has created a real sense of autonomy within my own department.
>
> Development director

The ED was aware of the frustration experienced by the senior managers, also finding it difficult to draw out the AD. ED commented on how the co-leadership relationship affected others' ability to function effectively.

> And I think there is a bit of frustration in that … not that one person is failing, or one person is succeeding. I think they're accepting that there are probably two interests not quite connected, and that they're caught in it…
>
> ED

Nonetheless, the development director and staff achieved significant and independent job crafting for the department. As a result of compensating, conflict was avoided for the organization, and a marketing logic was realized despite minimal integration with the artistic logic.

Insights regarding co-leadership, role crafting, and distributed leadership

In this chapter, we have explored mutual influences between co-leaders and their senior managers by analysing the boundary dynamics of the co-leadership shared role space. This investigation suggests how co-leadership and other forms of plural leadership may intersect. We found that the quality of an arts co-leadership relationship and the joint completion of the role space contributes to the potential for distributed leadership.

There are two perspectives in this discussion about the occupation of the shared role space: Those of the co-leaders and those of the surrounding senior managers. These senior managers may be deliberately invited to participate in co-leadership or may independently initiate engagement in the unconsciously created gaps in the shared role space. As they respond to invitations, senior managers may be in a responsive mode but on the other hand, when role space gaps occur, they are pre-emptive and actively engage in leadership in the role space by either mediating or compensating.

Previous research in film production projects suggests that when co-leaders leave room in the role space, their 1st AD engages in role crafting (Ebbers & Wijnberg, 2017). Filling available space is stimulating for senior managers and expands the resources of expertise and talent in the co-leadership shared role space. This initiative produces a culture of leadership distribution and sharing in these short-term projects.

In our research, we extend the understanding of both role crafting and distributed leadership. It reveals responsive and proactive practices by senior managers to engage in the shared leadership role space. These practices contribute either to increased information sharing or compensate for overlooked responsibilities in the space. When co-leaders deliberately involve senior managers for their expertise, we suggest that distributed leadership is being practiced (Gronn & Hamilton, 2004). However, when senior managers themselves initiate engagement in the role space, role crafting occurs (Wrzesniewski & Dutton, 2001). We suggest that this role crafting is a form of unconscious distributed leadership undertaken by the co-leaders. As a result, we contribute this dynamic to the understanding of distributed leadership, which is another form of plural leadership, but linked to co-leadership.

Role crafting practices can provide opportunities for expanded roles at the senior management level. This can be stimulating for senior managers (Ebbers & Wijnberg, 2017). However, we discovered a darker side to these opportunities for the longer-term relationships that exist in permanently established organizations. Role-crafting practices can create tension in the co-leadership relationship and although expanded opportunities occur, they may also be demanding and risky for the senior managers. They can also involve the board and generate governance implications (Chapter 8).

This dynamic contrasts with the relatively benign short-term initiatives in film production projects (Ebbers & Wijnberg, 2017). These projects last only weeks and are very focused on the intense logistics and aesthetic decision-making under pressure on the film set – a constrained circumstance. The senior manager is able to step in to take over specific tasks that are normally part of the co-leaders' roles. They involve routines and swift trust (Ebbers & Wijnberg, 2017; Meyerson et al., 1996). It is a quick fix but appears ultimately to be a satisfying one for all. The expansion of senior managers' roles in permanent organizations is more free-form than the expansion investigated in the film production project management context (Ebbers & Wijnberg, 2017).

Permanently established organizations require co-leaders to engage with a wide range of stakeholders: Artists and technical personnel, public and private funders, community relationships, and a variety of audiences. Co-leaders make decisions that have longer-term implications like season programs, artistic creation projects, and budget planning. In these situations, artistic reputation and organizational stability are concerns that generate tension across the co-leadership role space. In these ongoing organizations, co-leaders find themselves on a complex playing field that requires them to manage multiple strategic perspectives. We highlight these relationships in the triangle discussed in Chapter 1. Accountability and political dynamics are continuous and demanding, and complicated by the plurality of perspectives and values around the leadership (Chapter 2), limiting the co-leaders' motivation to include others in the executive role space. They also require political skills for followers who are role crafting.

Gronn & Hamilton (2004) observed that as co-principals exchanged with their management team in regularly scheduled meetings, sharing information and expertise was appreciated. Arts management scholars are attracted to these inclusive concepts of distributed and shared leadership, but few recognize the difference between these plural leadership forms and co-leadership where social hierarchy exists between the co-leaders and followers (Hewison & Holden, 2011; Schrauwen et al., 2016). Extending leadership participation from the executive and shared role space to include the senior management team is one means for co-leadership to participate in other plural leadership forms. But ironically, unconscious distributed leadership occurs only when the co-leader relationship is poor and organizational stability is threatened. We found that the highest degree of job crafting occurred in organizations with co-leaders who found it difficult to lead as one.

In one of our organizations, the round-table conversations with key senior managers appeared to be an effective distributed leadership mechanism that anticipated and redirected conflict in the co-leadership – perhaps similar to co-principals. It enabled fuller exploration of risks for the organization without confrontation and became a deflecting mechanism to avoid conflict within the co-leadership. Despite the benefits for the co-leadership that included an increase in complementarity and a balance of logics, there was only some opportunity for role crafting by the senior managers. Of course, decision-making for these non-profit organizations is ultimately negotiated with boards of directors who expect their mandated co-leaders to bear the responsibilities assigned to them. To include other senior managers may be helpful in the process of decision-making but it does not reflect the accountability expected by the board, suggesting potential limits to the co-leaders' ability to delegate and distribute leadership, consciously or unconsciously.

Managing the co-leadership relationship is an important aspect of leading as one. If co-leaders are unable to accomplish this coherently, in certain extreme conflict situations, others may perceive the circumstance as dire and intervene in recognition of its importance for the organization. They initiate communication work when co-leaders abstain, enabling decisions to occur. They provide leadership to their staff when there is lack of executive leadership and initiate external relations on behalf of the organization. These practices provide more immediate and appropriate operational intervention than that of the board when serious conflict occurs (Chapter 8). Mediating the relationship or compensating in the shared executive role space over an extended period and in a difficult set of circumstances are potent examples of management of co-leadership by others. This engagement by senior managers is an even more political process than role crafting to complete a film production project.

Our insights are new for the study of co-leadership. They consider the boundaries of the shared role space, and extend the understanding of co-leadership further into the organization. Scholars sometimes idealize distributed or shared leadership as a means to engage others in the leadership and strategy of the organization. Delegating appears more inspiring than abstention or conflict, whereas these latter unconsciously create room for senior managers in the joint role space. More insights are needed to challenge and nuance our findings.

References

Alvarez, J. L., & Svejenova, S. (2005). *Sharing Executive Power: Roles and Relationships at the Top*. Cambridge University Press.

Barkela, B. (2019). Theatre leadership from a communication perspective. *Zeitschrift für Kulturmanagement*, *5*(2), 135–164.

Bass, B. M. (1990). *Handbook of Leadership* (3rd ed.). Free Press.

Bhansing, P., Leenders, M., & Wijnberg, N. (2016). Selection system orientations as an explanation for the differences between dual leaders of the same organization in their perception of organizational performance. *Journal of Management & Governance*, *20*(4), 907–933. https://doi.org/10.1007/s10997-015-9330-4

Biddle, R. J. (1986). Recent developments in role theory. *Annual Review of Sociology*, *12*, 67–92.

Bolden, R. (2011). Distributed leadership in organizations: A review of theory and research. *International Journal of Management Reviews*, *13*(3), 251–269. https://doi.org/10.1111/j.1468-2370.2011.00306.x

Denis, J.-L., Langley, A., & Sergi, V. (2012). Leadership in the plural. *The Academy of Management Annals*, *5*(1), 211–283. https://doi.org/10.1080/19416520.2012.667612

DeRue, D. S., & Ashford, S. J. (2010). Who will lead and who will follow? A social process of leadership identity construction in organizations. *Academy of Management Review*, *35*(4), 627–647. https://doi.org/10.5465/amr.35.4.zok627

Döös, M., & Wilhelmson, L. (2021). Fifty-five years of managerial shared leadership research: A review of an empirical field. *Leadership*, *17*(6), 715–746. https://doi.org/10.1177/17427150211037809

Ebbers, J., & Wijnberg, N. (2017). Betwixt and between: Role conflict, role ambiguity and role definition in project-based dual-leadership structures. *Human Relations*, *70*(11), 1342–1365. https://doi.org/10.1177/0018726717692852

Ebbers, J., Wijnberg, N., & Bhansing, P. (2014). The Producer-Director Dyad: Managing the Fault-line between Art and Commerce. In J. C. Kaufman, & D. K. Simonton (Eds.), *The Social Science of Cinema* (pp. 157–184). Oxford University Press.

Gibeau, É, Langley, A., Denis, J.-L., & van Schendel, N. (2020). Bridging competing demands through co-leadership? Potential and limitations. *Human Relations*, *73*(4), 464–489. https://doi.org/10.1177/0018726719888145

Gronn, P., & Hamilton, A. (2004). 'A bit more life in the leadership': Co-principalship as distributed leadership practice. *Leadership and Policy in Schools*, *3*(1), 3–35. https://doi.org/10.1076/lpos.3.1.3.27842

Hambrick, D. C., & Mason, P. (1984). Upper echelons: The organization as a reflection of its top managers. *Academy of Management Review*, *9*(2), 193–206.

Hewison, R., & Holden, J. (2011). *Cultural Leadership Handbook: How to Run a Creative Organization*. Ashgate Publishing Group.

Hewison, R., Holden, J., & Jones, S. (2013). Leadership and Transformation at the Royal Shakespeare Company. In J. Caust (Ed.), *Arts Leadership: International Case Studies* (1st ed., pp. 145–160). Tilde University Press.

Meindl, J., Ehrlich, S. B., & Dukerich, J. M. (1985). The romance of leadership. *Administrative Science Quarterly*, *30*(1), 78–102.

Meyerson, D., Weick, K., & Kramer, R. M. (1996). Swift Trust and Temporary Groups. In R. M. Kramer & T. R. Tyler (Eds.), *Trust in Organizations: Frontiers of Theory and Research* (pp. 166–195). Sage Publications.

Mintzberg, H. (1998). Covert leadership: Notes on managing professionals. *Harvard Business Review*, November–December.

Nisbett, M., & Walmsley, B. (2016). The romanticization of charismatic leadership in the arts. *The Journal of Arts Management, Law, and Society*, *46*(1), 2–12. https://doi.org/10.1080/10632921.2015.1131218

Pearce, C. L. (2004). The future of leadership: Combining vertical and shared leadership to transform knowledge work. *Academy of Management Executive*, *18*(1), 47–57. https://doi.org/10.5465/ame.2004.12690298

Reid, W., & Karambayya, R. (2009). Impact of dual executive leadership dynamics in creative organizations. *Human Relations*, *62*(7), 1073–1112. https://doi.org/10.1177/0018726709335539

Schrauwen, J., Schramme, A., & Segers, J. (2016). Do Managers Run Cultural Institutions? The Practice of Shared Leadership in the Arts Sector. In K. Dalborg, & M. Löfgren (Eds.), *The FIKA Project: Perspectives on Cultural Leadership* (pp. 103–116). Nätverkstan Kultur.

Shamir, B. (2007). From Passive Recipients to Active Co-producers: Followers' Role in the Leadership Process. In B. Shamir, R. Pillai, M. Bligh, & M. Uhl-Bien (Eds.), *Follower-centered Perspectives on Leadership: A Tribute to the Memory of James R. Meindl* (pp. ix–xxxix). Information Age Publishing.

Shamir, B., Pillai, R., Bligh, M., & Uhl-Bien, M. (Eds.). (2007). *Follower-centered Perspectives on Leadership: A Tribute to the Memory of James R. Meindl*. Information Age Publishing.

Vidyarthi, P. R., Erdogan, B., Anand, S., Liden, R., & Chaudhry, A. (2014). One member, two leaders: Extending leader–member exchange theory to a dual leadership context. *Journal of Applied Psychology*, *99*(3), 468–483. https://doi:org/10.1037/a0035466

Voss, Z. G., Cable, D. M., & Voss, G. B. (2006). Organizational identity and firm performance: What happens when leaders disagree about 'Who we are?'. *Organization Science*, *17*(6), 741–755. https://doi.org/10.1287/orsc.1060.0218

Wrzesniewski, A., & Dutton, J. (2001). Crafting a job: Revisioning employees as active crafters of their work. *Academy of Management Review*, *26*(2), 179–201.

Section IV

Structuring co-leadership research and practice

10 Charting insights and a future research course

What and who, how, where, and why?

Introduction

This final chapter provides an opportunity to look back on the learning in this book and to look forward to future research possibilities about co-leadership. To accomplish this task, we synthesize our insights for future research through an open-ended interrogation: What and who, how, where, and why? We end the chapter with an analysis and discussion on research methods on the topic – a different kind of how.

We begin with "what and who" because these questions return to the initial working definitions of co-leadership. They open the discussion into other possibilities. "How" responds to the counter-intuitive nature of co-leadership. Its critics insist that it is improbable and they challenge the feasibility of its integrative role, and therefore, its ability to lead as one leader does (Chapter 3). As a result, how the relationship works is crucial. With competing logics and the concern for artistic autonomy, collaborative relationships among co-leaders may not be easy to realize (Chapter 2). Issues of social hierarchy, conflict, and trust are all dimensions that contribute to the dynamics of how (Chapters 6 and 7). On the other hand, partnering co-leadership with other types of plural leadership may also enable practices that share responsibilities further into the organization, and so may contribute to theory and new practices (Chapter 9).

"Where" has been a major finding in our research. Co-leadership is not a universal arrangement geographically, suggesting numerous opportunities for comparative research. "Where" links closely to the question of "why" does co-leadership exist? As we mentioned, the phenomenon is counter-intuitive for successful leadership and the contextual environment may not provide support for sharing leadership at the top. In many contexts, we discovered governance reasons for its mandated nature (Chapters 4 and 8).

Finally, we developed an analysis of research methodology for co-leadership. Qualitative research has dominated study in the arts field, although three sets of scholars have engaged in quantitative investigations with interesting results (Chapter 3). We explore what has happened and make suggestions of approaches that might enrich future insights.

DOI: 10.4324/9780429504259-14

Structuring this chapter through the use of elemental questions rather than reviewing chapter topics provides an alternative understanding of the book, focusing on the language of research questions. We hope to encourage colleagues to undertake further research on co-leadership. We look forward to reading the results of your work. One caution: Our insights in this chapter may interact and overlap. Separating them was challenging.

What and who?

Co-leadership is a plural leadership constellation that leads by pooling at the top (Denis et al., 2012; Hodgson et al., 1965). Founding scholars of co-leadership focus on the presence of two to five individuals who join together with the intention to lead an organization or an organizational unit (Chapter 3). They may be mandated or they initiate the leadership group themselves. In certain contexts, similar professionals occupy one leadership role, like co-principals in the education field. In the same manner, co-leaders in the private sector who are similarly qualified occupy the one leadership role dividing the labour among constellation members. Health care co-leaders are distinct professionals who typically share one role responsible for a clinic or a department in the institution. In professional service firms, there is an elected lead partner and an appointed administrative leader. Authority for both is ambiguous because of the horizontal partnership arrangement which they lead. Co-leadership in the arts stretches the definition of co-leadership beyond that developed in these key professional sectors of the literature.

In this discussion of what and who for co-leadership in the arts, we consider two topics. The first involves different structures of arts co-leadership and the challenges of social hierarchy. The second concerns the different possibilities for participation by others in the shared leadership role space.

Arts co-leaders have separate but equally valued responsibilities in the organization – an artistic role (artistic director (AD)) and a management role (executive director (ED)). Each co-leader leads a particular side of the organization (Reid & Karambayya, 2009) and their responsibilities are guided individually by the logics affiliated with their expertise. However, each leader occupies another role which is the co-leadership role. In this second role, they are responsible for integrating the competing logics that guided the leaders individually (Chapters 2 and 5) (Thornton et al., 2012). Investigating the structure and dynamics of both separate and joint co-leadership roles in the arts amplifies and extends structuring theories about co-leadership (Döös & Wilhelmson, 2021). We feel that arts co-leadership requires a more complex definition than in other sectors, reinforcing the suggestion that context nuances the general case (Denis et al., 2010) and contributing to plural leadership theorizing. Exploring the practices of co-leadership in different sectors in more detail will enhance the definition and understanding further.

To achieve organizational strategic effectiveness, leadership scholars argue for unity of command because they find mandated equality in co-leadership confounding (Fayol, 1949; Krause et al., 2015). This argument for social hierarchy provokes reflection about formal parity in co-leadership. Despite the intention of equality in the co-leadership shared role space, it may be subverted by informal differences in status and power that emerge. On the other hand, co-leaders may be formally mandated with unequal authority but can affect operational equality through sophisticated and informal influence (Schmidt, 2020). Both formal and informally structured relationships that are truly equal and functional may be rare. This would be convincing to scholars of unitary leadership. In fact, research in the for-profit sector demonstrates that slight differences in status appear to make a difference in co-leadership effectiveness (Krause et al., 2015). Similar research in the non-profit sector might help extend this finding, especially in such passionately charged environments as in the arts. But many have noted that the co-leadership relationship needs ongoing work by its members for success, leading us to the how section that is next in our discussion (Alvarez & Svejenova, 2005).

In most research on co-leadership, social hierarchy functions at a relational level (Magee & Galinsky, 2008). However, we also see status influenced by societal-level logics. Co-leadership members' views of themselves are shaped by powerful logics like the value of art in society. These logics are filtered through hiring and mandating authorities and found in institutionalized structuring practices across disciplines and regions (Katz & Kahn, 1966) (Chapter 4). Contextual circumstances influence the initial structuring of the constellation, the evolution of the relationship (Denis et al., 2001), and organizational fluidity (Alvehus, 2019; Reid & Karambayya, 2016). More finely grained study of contextual differences and their logics will help create specific insights about these differences in executive arts leadership.

Calls for new ways of producing art and relating to the public are increasing and this may require a review of co-leadership membership. Opening up to audience engagement in programming and in performance, as well as orienting towards social innovation may lead to new and different organizing practices (Glow, 2013; Janamohanan et al., 2021; Rånlund et al., 2016). Much of this organizing in the arts literature has been studied in case analyses and Chapter 4 provides a tentative explanation for these variations through societal values and arts funding practices. For both scholars and practitioners alike, it may be time to theorize the nature of co-leadership across cases and regions in response to the evolving landscape. Consequently, the field will remain up-to-date and gain sophistication about changing requirements of leadership.

Gronn and Hamilton (2004) acknowledge that there may be other executives who lead sub-units in the organization who can temporarily participate in the shared role space. In both Chapters 8 and 9, we examined how either members of a board of directors or key actors in the senior management might temporarily participate in the shared role space and become engaged in leadership. Plural governance logics, concerns about assessment capabilities, and co-leaders' ability to debate issues effectively encouraged board members to participate in the role space, sometimes temporarily and at other times on a more on-going and strategic level (Chapter 8). In cases where conflict and lack of communication in the co-leadership occurred, other senior actors in the organization have enabled the co-leadership to debate and connect (Chapter 9). A study about board chairs' involvement with EDs in the National Health Service in Britain inspired the conceptualization of shared role space (Stewart, 1991). Further developing the value of the role space and who functions with others in close or distant proximity would stretch strategic insights on co-leadership (Döös & Wilhelmson, 2021).

Denis et al. (2012) comment on the distinction between top management teams and co-leadership, asking where one ends and the other starts. Other plural leadership theorizing has influenced arts leadership analysis. "Distributed" leadership has been a lens for viewing arts leadership in Britain (Hewison et al., 2013), suggesting that executive leadership should include other senior management executives beyond the co-leaders. As well, "shared" leadership has been mobilized to consider organizational effectiveness in Belgian and Dutch arts organizations (Schrauwen et al., 2016). The ideas about sharing leadership are attractive for many who are concerned about the directive and sometimes abusive leadership that has been justified by a Romantic notion of artistic leadership and the artistic imperative (Lindgren, 2009; Quigg, 2007). Investigations would be welcome from both arts management and plural leadership scholars to discover new leadership practice and theorizing that examines the interaction of different plural leadership types and the resulting impact on organizational dynamics. To date, much of this investigation has been normative, favouring a distributed practice without theorizing and perhaps critical insights about the co-leadership partnership or the shared role space dynamics within that practice (Hewison et al., 2013).

Our research has investigated co-leadership as a standard duo or trio with an ED and one or more ADs. But there are also arts constellations that are extended collectives, as found in Spain in a long-standing theatre collective (Padrissa, 2017) or intimate family partnerships like Christo and Jeanne-Claude who wrapped buildings as art projects (Svejenova et al., 2010). We also found that the collective was a common organizational structure in South East Asia (Janamohanan et al., 2021) and was part of the history of arts management in Latin America (Ruiz-Gutiérrez et al., 2016). The separate co-leadership roles (AD and ED) as well as their joint decision-making role may be realized differently in collectives and special relationships. How these arrangements vary across cultural contexts may also reveal more insights. They provide alternatives to single leadership other than co-leadership. The impact of their structure and roles on organizing in the arts merits more attention. Many dimensions of relational processes like trust and conflict could be investigated and much more theorizing on how co-leadership functions is possible. We explore those possibilities in the next section on how.

How?

Arts organizations are challenging to lead. They are fragile; successful realization of art is uncertain; and audience response is difficult to predict (Lampel et al., 2000). The perspectives of multiple stakeholders like artists, audiences, funders, recipients of social impact activities, and boards of directors converge around the co-leadership shared role space, producing a demanding, pluralistic context in which to lead. The art-management collaboration can be expressive and enabling for art and for organizations (Røyseng, 2008) or it can limit artistic autonomy (Alexander, 2018; Chiapello, 2004). The literature on arts co-leadership relationships considers logics, identity, or strategic orientations as guides to how co-leaders integrate and make decisions (Bhansing et al., 2016; Voss et al., 2006).

However, understanding how the co-leader relationship works is key to understanding successful leadership in the arts and has been the focus of several empirical chapters in this book. Effectively debating and negotiating decisions need a balanced perspective on the logics involved (Chapter 5). Collaborative communication skills enable debate to gain that balance to integrate but discomfort with the ambiguity of equal status may lead to different forms of conflict (Chapter 6). However, knowledgably prioritizing the organizational mission may focus a process of trust development (Chapter 7).

The following themes and sub-themes serve as a base for new questions about how co-leadership functions.

First, the co-leaders' relationship in the shared role space is a leading perspective for understanding how they may lead as one.

- Parity and social hierarchy,
- Collaboration and conflict,
- Trust.

The second theme considers influences from and integration of competing logics where we consider the legitimizing guidance of the environment for co-leadership.

- Institutional logics' influence on leader attention,
- Integrating and reconciling logics.

Finally, leadership and governance interact strategically. For this theme, we study processual connections between co-leadership and their organizations.

- Co-leadership and organizational effectiveness,
- Governance and board-staff relations.

The co-leaders' relationship in the shared role space

How co-leaders inter-relate can be analysed in structural terms or through their joint behaviour. Social hierarchy or parity play an important role in supporting or undermining co-leadership effectiveness. Sources of ED power can include tenure and expertise, counterbalancing the dominance of the artistic profession logic – the artistic imperative. Succession and engaging co-ADs may alter power differences in the relationship. Collaboration or competition can also solve or increase these differences. Trust is necessary to pre-empt negative behaviours, but it is fragile. In the following discussion, we synthesize our findings and suggest research questions within these topics.

Parity and social hierarchy

Single leadership calls on the need for social hierarchy to achieve efficiency, accountability, clarity, and organizational confidence (Fayol, 1949; O'Toole et al., 2002). Scholars argue that having more than one executive leader, especially on an equal basis, would undermine these goals. This concern about parity in co-leadership has been tested in the private sector in the US, finding that some difference of power between co-CEOs generates organizational effectiveness (Krause et al., 2015).

Despite concerns about how co-leadership can function effectively, it has been found in numerous professional contexts like the arts. Other than the American for-profit research cited above and a study of leadership structures in Australian arts organizations (MacNeill & Tonks, 2013), social hierarchy within co-leadership has rarely been investigated. Despite the formal parity among co-leadership arrangements in the arts, the artistic imperative is a powerful profession logic that gives the AD an advantage (Chapter 6). This has proven true in our data despite ADs sense that they lack power. Scholars and managers have questioned the strategic value of formal parity with the ED. However, since the 1970s in North America, management training has demystified the ED role (Peterson, 1986), suggesting a growing acceptance of equality between artists and managers in co-leadership in this context. But variations of formal parity in co-leadership exist in Britain and Europe according to company websites and press reports (Chapters 4 and 6). To investigate the factors that influence social hierarchy, qualitative interviews with all of an organization's co-leaders and their colleagues are needed to analyse a further and nuanced internal perspective on parity dynamics in organizational decision-making.

Collaboration and conflict

Formally mandated parity in a co-leadership can render individual authority ambiguous within the relationship and generate anxiety about status. In response to this anxiety, status conflict challenges this formal parity and changes co-leadership power differences. In Chapter 6, we report on subtle practices of status conflict within the co-leadership that confirm artistic superiority but avoid a negative impact on decisional efficiency. In contrast, mobilizing powerful allies was found to break trust and diminish power on both sides, undermining the relationship's functionality and its legitimacy with the board of directors. Status conflict can build on other conflict types or generate toxic relationships that cause relationship and values conflict. Downward spirals result, influencing relational and leadership effectiveness. A further exploration of strategies that counter status conflict and generate collaboration with organizational implications would be valuable for executive co-leaders and arts leadership scholars.

Because of pluralism, ambiguity about priorities for goals and objectives overlays the organizational context (Chapter 2). As a result, co-leaders may mobilize ambiguous messaging as they navigate these contexts (Denis et al., 2010). Research about such messaging in status conflict would provide insights on how the relationship manages power differences (Abdallah & Langley, 2014; Sillince et al., 2012).

Another aspect of the relationship concerns power sources that generate informal differences of status within the shared role space. These include dimensions such as celebrity and proximity to the mission, formal training, relative tenure, professional peer evaluation, attributions of leadership by key senior actors in the organization, and links to environmental actors like board members, private donors, and government funders (Chapter 6).

Celebrity ADs stereotypically enjoy an authority that translates into an informal power difference inside the shared role space. A successful relationship with a very accomplished AD appears to require an ED with highly developed interpersonal skills to respectfully navigate the power difference within the relationship. Celebrity that personifies the organization's mission is specific and typical within artsleadership. Arts co-leaders offer extreme examples to investigate the development and application of these interpersonal skills. Further research on the circumstances that promote the mythological profile of difficult celebrity ADs might generate theory and insights on solutions to its problems. Beneficial implications may also exist (Nisbett & Walmsley, 2016).

Longer tenure of one of the co-leaders suggests another source of power (Chapter 6). With time, ambitions for both artistic and management careers evolve and new organizational projects arise. New partners arrive and predecessor history either casts its shadow on current co-leadership or is forgotten (Reid & Karambayya, 2016). A new partner's training and skills may introduce different interpretations of institutional logics and disrupt the standard operating procedures and routines of past relationships. With different status dynamics, trust development begins anew (Chapters 6 and 7). The negotiated balance changes and incumbents confront possible challenges to their power and status. Succession within co-leadership in the arts has enjoyed little attention (Reid & Karambayya, 2016) and investigation is necessary to extend an understanding of the organization's stability. How incumbents and new partners relate to each other, shape the shared role space, and strategize has organizational impact. The expertise and orientation of AD or ED as incumbent may cause different processes and outcomes of succession, calling for insights on practices in those circumstances that either undermine or enrich the process.

Since the power of an AD in the West has been questioned recently (Chapter 6), co-ADs have begun to be appointed. Often, they share programming on a time basis or by expertise. This arrangement is not completely new, but the objective to counterbalance concentrated AD power is new. A plurality of equal ADs with an ED may re-shape the separate leadership roles that AD and ED play outside the shared role space. This would potentially influence the ED's power and relationship with the board, a new dynamic to consider for co-leadership research (Chapter 8). In our data, we observed a case with three co-ADs where the EDs continuous presence brought greater influence to bear on the organization's strategies. On the other hand, three co-leaders can result in complicated decision-making and a two against one power dynamic (Alvarez & Svejenova, 2005). As well, this structure may significantly influence how the senior management team relates and interacts with the co-leaders (Chapter 9). Investigation is needed to understand how the multiplication of AD roles influences the operation of the shared role space and impacts the organizational dynamics and decision-making.

Dynamics at the relational level of co-leadership are vital to the constellation's ability to lead jointly and as one (Gibeau et al., 2016; Gronn & Hamilton, 2004). Despite the apparent separation of functions within the co-leadership constellation in the arts, the strategic triangle in Chapter 1 (Figure 1.1) and our study of integration of logics suggest overlap and interdependence within the shared role space (Gronn & Hamilton, 2004) (Chapters 2 and 5). Like other professional organizations, arts organizations are complex and pluralistic (Kraatz & Block, 2008, 2017). Co-leaders' mutual recognition of leadership parity and interdependence and respect for the other appear to be essential dimensions of co-leadership stability and decisional efficiency (Fleming & Spicer, 2014). Scholars emphasize how collaboration solves difficult conflict and supports co-leadership success (Reynolds et al., 2017). Its role in the interplay of debate and task conflict in co-leadership should be an ongoing topic of investigation. As well, co-leadership theorizing will benefit from an investigation of the drivers, characteristics, and impact of competitive and collaborative practices.

Trust

In the shared role space, trust is another behavioural dimension that preoccupies scholars of co-leadership. Overcoming the vulnerability of interdependence is fundamental to launching trust (Rousseau et al., 1998).

Artists recognize vulnerability in their art practice because a willing suspension of disbelief is often necessary for a performance to succeed (Goffman, 1959). For an artist as a co-leader, making leaps of faith may be familiar, such as swift trust that occurs among technical professionals on a film set. But relying on assumptions of swift trust can lead to disappointments. For sustained trust beyond individual moments of suspending doubt, various mechanisms are necessary for ongoing development in the relationship (Möllering, 2006). In our research, we offered trust-positive and trust-negative experiences to explore the mechanisms for developing trust. Extending our study of positive and negative situations of trust will provide greater clarity regarding this important dimension of the relationship.

The ongoing routine of defining an artistic mission to frame decision-making was an important trust-enhancing mechanism for our co-leaders (Chapter 7). This mechanism relies on the power of the artistic imperative that is embedded in the profession logic. Making time for and openness for co-leaders to permit information-sharing and reflexivity is another trust-development mechanism. Further research could analyse how mutual trust supports co-leaders as they balance logics, debate differences, and fulfil the joint responsibilities in the shared role space. As a result, this research would extend understanding about complementarity. Our research also uncovered assumptions that partnering with hybrid professionals produced trust benefits. Further research could provide insights confirming the possibilities of these assumed benefits.

Competing logics – Their influence and integration

In the previous section, we explored relational-level social psychology dynamics in co-leadership to understand how the shared role space may provide a fertile setting to craft a joint leadership vision (Alvarez & Svejenova, 2005). In the following section, we suggest research opportunities as we examine two aspects of the interaction between socially constructed institutional logics and the co-leadership: How logics influence the relationship and how co-leaders integrate the logics.

Institutional logics' influence on leader attention

Each co-leader has links with and pays attention to stakeholders who manifest a variety of institutional logics. Co-leaders' individual and collective priorities are guided by the legitimizing influences exerted through these logics and stakeholders, which shape daily routines of joint decision-making. The ADs choices are shaped by profession logics, which are manifested in the peer evaluations of how the work aligns with the artistic ideal and professional autonomy. These assessments are most often provided in response to grant requests made to public funders. The ED's and board's organizational orientation to audiences as well as public and private funders is embedded in market and business logics. These logics are manifested in marketing and strategic plans as well as ticket sales and fundraising campaigns that typically adopt a relationship orientation based on compelling artistic experiences to prioritize the artistic ideal over a purely market logic (Boorsma, 2006). Community logics may also provide the foundation for social impact objectives motivated by criteria from all types of funders (Kawashima, 2006). How these influences are introduced, negotiated, and experienced by co-leaders in the shared role space is worthy of further analysis. How social hierarchy defined by a variety of factors plays a role in the valuation, balancing or integration of these logics would also contribute to our understanding.

A community animation role for the arts has gained increasing interest and influence. This turn to social impact activities appears linked to the logic of the artistic imperative as Romantic ideal – art perceived as a source of inspiration, education, mental health, and social change (Kawashima, 2006; Löfgren, 2016). Inclusion and artistic development for community cohesion and well-being are new for co-leaders who might be revising and innovating organizational missions and allocating resources to these new projects. Further exploration is needed about how co-leaders break free from a former duality of balanced logics (business and art) to include this social imperative in their mission.

Scholars have expressed concern whether adding social impact to an artistic mission has been adopted to justify public funding, questioning to what extent funders have influenced this orientation (Belfiore & Bennett, 2007). Little research on this potential shift to a more instrumental motive has been conducted outside of Britain and rarely has it been examined at the executive leadership level where logic integration is very important. Tracking co-leaders' decisional patterns might reveal how the interaction of community logics with artistic and managerial logics is manifested at organizational and relational levels. Investigating whether and how funders influence the decision-making process could also shed contextual light.

Integrating and reconciling logics

Lucid and meaningful arts co-leadership is dependent on the ability to integrate and balance managerial and market logics with the artistic imperative (Chapter 2). In Chapter 5, we found that co-leaders in our data largely demonstrated a balanced view and were able to integrate logics, compared to those reported in the health sector (Gibeau et al., 2020). The contrast may be related to the significant presence of the audience in the life of performing arts organizations. Artists do want their art to be seen, heard, and experienced. This orientation to market and the associated business logic may promote an easier coherence and integration with the profession logic. An investigation of this orientation could begin with the nature of the marketing function, where it resides organizationally with each of the co-leaders, and how the relationship responds to institutionalized practice. Comparing co-leadership practices in different cultural policy and funding contexts may produce insight on factors that influence these patterns of practice. Our analysis was based on North American data where revenues from the box office are proportionately more significant than in other contexts with larger amounts of government funding.

Integration of competing logics is a principal rationale for adopting co-leadership and we will explore the possibilities in the upcoming section on why. Empirically, we analysed each individual's cognitive orientation towards managing conflicting logic imperatives within the shared role space (Chapter 5). If each co-leader adopts a balancing approach, they might reach an overarching logic to guide their organizational mission more clearly. We suggested however that "negative peace" may be sufficient in many contexts because of its minimal conflict approach, despite imbalanced relationships. However, we need to understand how fluidity and change over time at the organizational and relational levels can have an impact on co-leaders' relationships. Change can inhibit co-leaders' ability to resolve conflict and clarify ambiguous goals for stakeholders. Studying patterns of logic manifestation in an organization's co-leadership constellation over time would provide insights about these macro influences and micro responses.

The functionality of the relationship has strategic implications for the organization. We have observed that the pressure to achieve the coherence and harmony of a "positive peace" may be more than is necessary and is rarely achieved in these relationships. Given the differentiation inherent in arts co-leadership and the need for artistic autonomy, a "negative peace" approach allows logics to be well-debated and integrated across the functional differences with respect and without acrimony in the role space.

Leadership and governance

To broaden our horizon of inquiry beyond the relational aspect to the organizational level, we pursue an executive leadership and governance path: Co-leaders relate to both internal followers and environmental stakeholders, including governance actors. As a result of these connections outside the shared role space, co-leaders assume their strategic leadership role in the larger ecosystem of organizational members and boards of directors. The following discussion examines each approach.

Co-leadership and organizational effectiveness

Co-leadership is described as "pooling leadership at the top to direct others", thus recognizing the existence of followers in this type of plural leadership (Denis et al., 2012). We observe that in the arts, each co-leader heads a separate, but interdependent, functional side of the organization.

They are often individually mandated by boards of directors or government to take on these separate roles. Together, they then perform a joint co-leadership role for the whole organization and its community.

Research has focused either on the dynamics within the joint relationship and its shared role space or the logic integration necessary for strategic decision-making (Bhansing et al., 2016; Voss et al., 2006). While decision-making is part of the general study of leadership, the organizational effectiveness of co-leadership with its members has attracted sparse consideration. We lack insights on how stakeholders like artists and employees interact with and are led by these individuals in their separate and joint roles (Döös & Wilhelmson, 2021). Analysis of leader-member exchange (LMX) with co-leadership has appeared in the private sector (Wang, 2017) but has only recently emerged in the non-profit arts in Europe (Barkela, 2019).

Role crafting has been recognized as a means to expand an individual's role and responsibilities. This expansion in proximity to a co-leader's shared role space may be developed consciously by the co-leaders or unconsciously in a conflicted and distant co-leader relationship. Our research (Chapter 9) demonstrated how a negative relationship provided opportunity for followers to expand and possibly grow as leaders. Despite this, the trajectory can be a bit perilous. More insight is needed from other contexts and other relationships.

Our identification of the combination of individual and joint roles undertaken by the same people has not previously been recognized in the plural and co-leadership research. This combination is challenging because of the ambiguity it presents to the leaders as they respond to the institutional logics that guide their own individual roles and as they also attempt to balance and integrate these logics with other logics embedded in the joint role. The interaction of these separate and joint roles and how they shape the organization's leadership would benefit from further study. This study could deconstruct the ambiguity experienced between the two roles through identifying patterns of leadership behaviour and manifestations of how the two roles are realized by each leader.

The profession logic of artistic imperative often involves the engagement of a celebrity artist as AD. These people galvanize the organization (Nisbett & Walmsley, 2016) and their recognition within the arts and society is based on their reputation for artistic innovation or virtuosic performance (Lindqvist, 2017). Stakeholders, funders and donors, and board members are attracted to the organization in response to this leadership (Ostrower, 2002). The link between freedom of expression – an important societal value – and artistic autonomy confers legitimacy on the leadership vision of a well-recognized and inspirational AD. How celebrity reinforces the legitimacy of the co-leaders' ideas and thus the leadership of the organization in the arts needs further study.

The wider literature on co-leadership suggests that humility and lack of pretention on the part of the co-leaders is essential for the success of these relationships and co-leadership (Gronn, 1999; Heenan & Bennis, 1999). In the case of the arts, the intensity of the public and organizational spotlight on the realization of the artistic mission requires the AD to be convinced about the validity of their personal aesthetic taste and judgement to realize their leadership. Faced with potential business and market logics debates, ADs ambitions for their artistic ideas may require more personal commitment to the profession logic than required of professionals in other sectors. It may be more difficult for a celebrity AD with power derived from status in the organization and in the community to be self-effacing in the shared role space. The substantial literature on leadership and followers (Shamir, 2007) may be enhanced through research using the lens of co-leaders paired with celebrity in the arts and the romance of leadership (Meindl et al., 1985).

Our data included some very charismatic and creative ADs with a community and media following. These ADs provided some insight about the effect of artistic conviction and celebrity on interpersonal dimensions like social hierarchy, conflict, and trust in the relationships with EDs (Chapters 6 and 7). However, not all the ADs fit this charismatic profile, approaching logic integration with a balancing perspective (Chapter 5). How co-leadership constellations lead in conjunction with the power of artistic celebrity would benefit from further investigation. Considering the social justice logics inherent in contemporary movements like #MeToo! and Black Lives Matter, the relationship between an ED and a celebrity AD entangled in accusations of abuse of power needs observation and theorizing for relational and governance practices. We return to this concern in the next discussion on governance.

Governance and board-staff relations

Co-leadership constellations in the arts are often mandated by either a board of directors or a government ministry. Co-leadership also emerges when artists found their own non-profit or civil-society organization, and typically in the West, they function with a board of directors (Chapter 4). Since the AD and ED are executive leaders in the arts, they are ultimately accountable for the organization. The governance dynamics with a high-profile professional and their managerial partner are in contrast with a single executive leadership, and except for this book, have not been explored (Chapter 8). The societal importance of the artistic ideal grounded in the profession logic establishes a unique status for the AD role and raises issues of artistic autonomy, especially with a board of directors. Our data in North America revealed board member hesitancy to directly monitor artistic programming. Efforts to evaluate the ADs artistic work and fulfillment of the mission were blocked by expression of concerns about preserving artistic autonomy. Other research about artistic leadership and governance exposes similar responses (Bieber, 2003; Ostrower, 2002). In our research, the ED became a balancing intermediary between the board and the AD, responding to a governance need for stability and enabling the integration of business, market, and artistic logics. Exploring patterns and practices of relationships between co-leaders and boards may provide more insights into trustees' relationships with profession logics in different funding and governance contexts.

Relationships between co-leaders and boards provide insight into power and status differences. An emerging theoretical frame in non-profit governance observes that a dominant coalition can shape governance dynamics in non-profits. Informal groups of stakeholders can maneuver with organization members and board members to acquire decision-making power temporarily or over the long-term (Andersson & Renz, 2021). Consequently, board and executive leaders' formal influence may be diminished. Applying the lens of dominant coalition to co-leadership in the arts may explain the EDs engagement in governance that we observed. Through informal patterns of control, a coalition may counterbalance an ADs efforts to determine an artistic program or long term vision for the organization. A coalition may also challenge formal equality in the shared role space. These dynamics reveal a dark side of delegating board governance responsibilities to the ED. They may influence the strategic effectiveness of the co-leadership relationship and question artistic autonomy.

Although trust between AD and ED has been declared important for successful co-leadership (Alvarez & Svejenova, 2005), it may also appear to subvert the EDs ability to perform the role of monitoring and managing the AD as delegated by the board. If the board perceives that co-leaders are making decisions without sufficient debate, they may assume that collusion has overtaken the relationship. Thus, trust can be viewed as both positive and negative for the relationship. An investigation of how collaboration between ADs and EDs could balance both trust and debate might advance the study of trust and governance.

Boards infrequently undertake performance evaluation of ADs because of a societal concern for artistic autonomy. Recently, boards have been confronted by media coverage of abusive AD leadership. In the past, concerns about ethical leadership have rarely been a focus in board-AD relationships. Normally, the ED has an internal responsibility for organizational and administrative HR issues, but until recently, similar evaluation principles have not been considered relevant to the ADs leadership of artists (Lindgren, 2009) despite union regulations in certain regions. ED and AD relationships have focused mainly on integrating profession and market-business logics. Similar to the research suggestion mentioned earlier, further investigation is warranted to understand how the governance of individual leadership within co-leadership may responsibly take these ethical concerns into consideration to preserve artistic and organizational integrity.

Our research focused on boards and their relationship with the co-leaders. In other parts of the world, boards are less important or may not exist.

Other governance instances are found with different relational dynamics. The practice of co-leadership is also not universal, and this was an important discovery in this book. Our study of this variation in practice is in its initial stages and more research is warranted. The following section explores the possibilities for this research. We follow this section with why, since through our study of where we were inevitably led to the question of why or why not instigate co-leadership practice.

Where?

Arts co-leadership is common in the Anglo-Saxon tradition as well as Northern Europe but less in the Global South. While it appears scarce elsewhere in the world, efforts to document leadership globally have revealed interesting but isolated cases in Asia, Africa, and India (Carneiro, 2019; Caust, 2015; Rånlund et al., 2016). As mentioned in Chapter 4, other leadership arrangements exist resulting from variations in cultural policy and funding environments, and how arts management is understood in the sector. As well, co-leadership is not standard in certain arts disciplines like museums and in North American opera companies. These other structures may be vertical co-leadership, a single leader, or a CEO with a team of functional specialists reporting to them, like top management teams (Chapter 4). Our research demonstrates that hybrid constellations of leadership have developed around the world. Nonetheless, pluralistic contextual influences and competing logics remain present, including the artistic ideal as a key part of the mix. As a result, artists are typically key executive leaders in arts organizations globally.

In this discussion about where co-leadership is found, we consider three topics. The first is a consideration of practices according to a variety of social values in different contexts. The second is related to disciplines, and the third is the practice as it is found in other sectors. Each contextual discussion provides perspectives that have not been considered in the literature on co-leadership.

Arts management scholars have situated their theorizing work on co-leadership within the regions where it is most found (Chapter 3) usually responding to the practices of their own region. Our categorizing contribution in Chapter 4 regarding leadership practice globally expands these perspectives but is exploratory and the nascent ideas there need further investigation. More research is needed to detail, expand, and consolidate the current understanding of leadership practices in different cultural contexts in the arts around the world. The sector offers a research terrain broad enough to expand our understanding of co-leadership beyond anti-management and post-heroic leadership polemics. It is a rich territory for nuanced investigations of all variations of leadership structures, their benefits, and issues in a wide range of contexts. It could lead to useful comparative theorizing about the phenomenon. Arts management and plural leadership scholars will benefit from the theoretical impact that this kind of diversification of contexts provides.

Co-leadership practice also straddles a continuum of funding contexts from significant public funding in Europe to mainly private funding in the US (Laughlin, 2019). Societal values and logics influence funding practices, but the dynamics of competing logics may evolve these practices (Chapters 2 and 4). In the US, consideration of the market value of programming dominates AD-ED conversations and negotiations. Programming plays an important role in maintaining financial sustainability as well as fulfilling artistic objectives. On the other hand, in significant publicly funded environments, revenues have been more stable, especially in institutions. Nonetheless scholars in Europe and Britain have expressed concern about pressure coming from public funders of the arts to increase ticket revenue (Alexander, 2018), potentially changing the focus and issues to be negotiated within the co-leadership. Indeed, co-leaders in each context have different decisions to make regarding art and the organization. Where box-office revenues are significant, the tastes of artistic leaders and audiences are interdependent, influencing the co-leaders' ability to integrate logics (Chapter 5). With substantial public funding, EDs adopt an administrative role, ensuring cost control measures. If the government funds operating deficits, past imbalances have little consequence. The comparative impact of regionally different revenue composition on co-leadership existence and behaviour has not been researched.

We have noted that, in particular arts disciplines, certain types of major institutions feature single leaders, not co-leadership: Museums and opera institutions. The reasons for these structural traditions are intriguing and not yet well-understood. These single leadership situations appear similar to top management teams in the private sector where a collection of functional executive leaders report to a CEO; team-member inclusion in decision-making can be variable (Denis et al., 2012; Roberto, 2003). Despite the prevailing top management team (TMT) single leadership practice in museums and opera institutions, some museums and several smaller opera companies have moved to co-leadership (Chapter 4). A comparison between TMT and co-leadership across these institutional settings may provide new insight into structural and process dynamics and organizational impact for these two leadership arrangements.

In contrast, symphony orchestras are major institutions that adopted the co-leadership constellation from early days, particularly in North America (Hart, 1973). Since the 1960s with the advent of air travel, music directors started travelling as guest conductors. As a result, the ED is present throughout the year playing an important and leading role in the strategic positioning of the organization within its community of stakeholders (Chapter 1). In contrast, the artistic celebrity of the music director (AD) is a year-round hallmark of the organization's image in the community. Rehearsing and conducting the musicians in the moments of residence in the organization involve symbolic and "covert" leadership accomplished through inspiration (Mintzberg, 1998, p. 140). But symphony orchestra ADs appear less implicated in organizational leadership than the ED. This specific contrast of the co-leadership roles in symphony orchestras is worth investigating for insights about social hierarchy and celebrity, organizational influence, and the dynamics of the shared role space. The off-stage reality behind public celebrity may contest the metaphoric importance of symphony orchestra conductors in the traditional management literature.

Ironically, there has been very limited research on arts co-leadership in the US, where it was first practiced. There are two exceptions (Beard, 2012; Voss et al., 2006). Sustainability in US arts organizations is dependent on a high level of philanthropic support (Laughlin, 2019). The EDs leadership role in developing this revenue stream may be a significant reason for the prominence of co-leadership in this region. Certain scholars of American cultural policy argue that accountability is the reason for the need of the constellation, but historical research demonstrates its presence earlier than the National Endowment for the Arts (London, 2013; Peterson, 1986). The US revenue model involves both private funding and commercial ticket income, whereas direct funding models in Europe and Asia depend on proportionally little box-office revenue. Comparing co-leaders' focus of attention across different arts revenue models could inform logic integration practices within the co-leadership. We provide one such comparison in Chapter 5. These integration practices have relational, organizational, and governance impacts. A consideration of both public and non-profit governance perspectives could enrich this comparative co-leadership research. We introduced these possibilities in Chapters 4 and 8 and encouraged further exploration.

As we have mentioned, co-leadership has been found in the for-profit cultural sector. Film directors and their executive producers share leadership of both their production house and related film projects. Closely aligned producers have been found to facilitate the distinctive vision and taste of their partnering directors by protecting idiosyncrasy while balancing with audience appeal (Alvarez et al., 2005). Artistic autonomy is a relevant issue, especially in a for-profit enterprise where financial concerns may prevail. Major fashion designers in the early years of haute couture often allied closely with financially expert co-owner executives to establish and run their design firms (Alvarez & Svejenova, 2005). An example of this co-leadership is Yves Saint-Laurent and Pierre Bergé (Müller & Farid, 2010). The current business conglomerates in fashion have begun engaging and integrating high profile designers as artistic or creative directors at the executive management level to both innovate and to ensure ongoing design and brand legitimacy (Parmentier & Fischer, 2018). Comparing the cultures of for-profit and non-profit cultural co-leadership may discover newly emerged or reinforced dimensions of the shared role space because of the financial implications for the enterprise in contrast with artistic autonomy. For instance, celebrity impact on revenue and profitability may be crucial in both fashion and film projects.

Finally, leading one-time artistic projects like producing commercial theatre or film also requires functional differentiation and artistic autonomy at the top. Hence co-leadership is frequently found in these projects: A producer financier and the artistic creative leader who acts as the director. Institutionalized routines manifest in the technical production side and in the organizational support activities for the project (Chapter 7). These routinized manifestations reflect the logics that guide these projects. However, there is also creative judgment involved in developing the artistic product. Managing the fluidity and efficiency of that co-leadership arrangement generates tension in these projects (Schreyögg & Sydow, 2010). Such projects are often nested into the framework of an ongoing project management company that may influence the co-leaders. This structural arrangement might be similar to non-profit organizations, although these support organizations are typically smaller compared to their much larger one-time projects. Comparing the impact of context on co-leadership in for-profit and non-profit organizations merits exploration to expand our findings in this book. As well, studying co-leadership in larger ongoing organizations and leadership in one-time projects in either sector may also produce intriguing insights about why.

Why?

We found that the separate executive roles in arts co-leadership exist for eight different reasons distributed across four topics. First is the influence of mission:

- Confirming the artistic mission by an ADs presence as a senior executive,
- Maintaining artistic autonomy and protecting the craft.

Second considers the balancing of pluralism:

- Developing artistic excellence at the same time as organizational and financial well-being,
- Adding managerial expertise and capacity to lead at the top,
- Balancing the artistic, market, and managerial logics.

The third topic highlights the challenges of ambiguity:

- Managing and negotiating the ambiguity that results from pluralistic objectives.

Finally, the fourth considers governance dynamics:

- Governing and managing risk,
- Accounting to external stakeholders.

Justifying arts co-leadership is a significant concern for many around the world. It appears improbable and perhaps expensive.

Influence of mission

The artistic imperative is the distinctive logic in this field, calling for artistic autonomy to innovate and achieve excellence (Chiapello, 2004; Røyseng, 2008; Shiner, 2001). Artists are key for confirming the existence of this imperative within the profession logic, one of the primary logics for organizations led by co-leaders. Situating an AD within the executive leadership of the organization embodies this artistic authority for internal, audience, and public stakeholders, thus legitimizing the artistic mission.

In a for-profit sector outside the arts, protection of the professional craft is suggested as an important reason for co-leadership (Fjellvær, 2010). As we have already mentioned, this protective aspect underscores concerns about artistic autonomy. As an example, in the field of journalism, commercial interests can be seen to influence journalistic integrity, justifying the presence of co-leadership as a means to safeguard this craft (Fjellvær, 2010). The arts are also perceived as threatened by commercial needs (Alexander, 2018). However, dependence on ticket sale revenue varies within a budget from one cultural policy context to another and co-leaders appear to adapt accordingly. Exploring how this influence varies across regions and sectors may enrich our understanding of co-leadership responsibilities and logic integration in the shared role space. Scholars are divided on how well-protected the artistic craft may be and how respected the artistic autonomy might be. Comparisons between the US and Europe would be pertinent as extreme examples of competing logics. In the US, co-leaders function with almost no government funding and often 50% or more of their revenue from ticket sales. In many major arts institutions in Europe, revenue may be funded up to 85% from government.

Balancing pluralism

Balancing art, business, and market is a key orientation arising from the discussion of the role of art in co-leadership (Lampel et al., 2000). Despite the resistance to managerial partners in some regions, integrating an ED with an AD increases organizational understanding of management (Peterson, 1986) and legitimizes the business and market logics to support the organization's functions. Around the world, programs in arts management are increasing. In the US, training in the arts discipline as well as in arts management or business training are quite prominent in ED bios on organizational websites. Ironically, management training is also mentioned in biographies for intendants (AD) in numerous German operatic institution websites. We have suggested that the presence of arts management training is a contributing factor to the practice of co-leadership practice in a region. But the type of training and co-leadership structures varies, suggesting different needs in different cultural contexts. Research on training effectiveness exists in Europe and in the US, and our overview in Chapter 4 links these perspectives with research elsewhere such as in India and in South-East Asia. However, exploring these differences through the lens of funding or business logics might generate greater insight into this connection between arts management training and the existence of co-leadership globally.

We have observed that artists were often founders of organizations in regions where entrepreneurship dominates in the arts, like non-profits in North America and civil society organizations in Europe. Through a co-leadership, EDs in the executive role space contribute additional skills and capabilities to the organization's leadership, albeit informally at the beginning (Chapter 4). This addition may generate market-related and commercial opportunities (Lampel et al., 2000); broaden public access to artistic achievements; and stabilize finances for the organization. The ED may also lead significant fundraising initiatives to support new capital projects that can enlarge the artistic program for the organization (Frumkin & Kolendo, 2014).

Contextual pluralism and ambiguity

Pluralistic contexts generate goal ambiguity. This ambiguity can generate confusion and conflict. Furthermore, scholars are concerned about the potential managerial constraint of artistic autonomy and therefore creative innovation of art. How to research this potential constraint is a passionate question and may require comparisons across funding contexts where audiences and funders have a different impact on the financial balance of the organization. Once analysed, it may help clarify and nuance the dynamics of the competing logics that have generated unease in the scientific literature, opening-up the need to study the goal ambiguity faced by co-leaders in the arts.

Scholars in other sectors with co-leadership argue that this form of plural leadership appears in professional organizations as a means to manage pluralism and ambiguity, reflecting the competing logics in these pluralistic contexts (Denis et al., 2012). In the arts, we have observed that additional imperatives such as social impact missions supplement the artistic imperative. These social impact objectives enrich the organization's relationship with its community, but they also extend the landscape of competing logics beyond the art-business dichotomy. The relative importance of the artistic imperative and the profession logic may require further reflection when these community-based logics are embraced. As well, there has been some recognition of the role that technical and production employees play in both performing organizations (Barkela, 2021). Adding objectives and logics to the portrait may reconfigure the co-leadership constellation by inviting other professionals into the role space and by influencing how the responsibilities in the role space are structured and fulfilled (Chapter 9). Exploring what that means particularly for co-leadership of major institutions may evolve mainstream arts co-leadership and provide insights into the flexibility of co-leadership as the landscape changes.

The multiplicity of objectives in these organizations generates ambiguity about goal priorities. Decision-making becomes challenging and sometimes confusing. Co-leadership is intended as a solution to these challenges. Debate across the specialized expertise of co-leaders may clarify goal ambiguity. More exploration of debate as a manifestation of logic integration will further enlighten the dilemmas of ambiguity in pluralistic environments.

Governance dynamics

Co-leadership may be mandated and seen by boards and by funders as a governance mechanism to balance artistic priorities and generate stability for the organization (Peterson, 1986; Radaelli, 2012). One expert referred to it as providing "four eyes" for ensuring accuracy and eliminating bias (Abfalter, 2019). Board intentions regarding the mandating of co-leadership are sometimes criticized within the arts field. Co-leadership is seen as too controlling and constraining to the artistic efforts and mission of the organization (Beirne & Knight, 2002; Macdonnell & Bereson, 2019). Our research in Chapter 8 confirmed that boards rely on co-leadership because of information asymmetry that restricts their ability to monitor the artistic process. We found that boards were reluctant to intervene in artistic programming and creation. When they did attempt to monitor artistic quality, they were confronted with refusals by their ADs, which we interpreted as insistence on artistic autonomy. Our research observed that the ED served as an interpretive intermediary between the board and the AD, as a result. Therefore, this delegation provides for artistic autonomy. These perspectives might differ in publicly funded or in largely philanthropic contexts. Studies on arts governance and co-leadership would be useful with regional differences in mind to explore the role of the ED in governance and the importance of an AD on organizational image and legitimacy.

The charisma of artistic leaders appears important to the symbolic and financial well-being of arts organizations (Nisbett & Walmsley, 2016; Ostrower, 2002). However, concern about AD power has grown and boards have been confronted by cases where complaints of abuse have become public and significant. Monitoring leadership competence in an organization requires that boards consider two facets of AD leadership – artistic expertise as well as managerial leadership. Researching these combined governance and leadership issues within a co-leadership arrangement may be beneficial in the current context.

Related to governance, co-leadership may provide boards of directors with continuity when succession occurs. Evidence has shown waves of change on alternating sides of the co-leadership. We explored succession with ADs as incumbents to understand trust in Chapter 7. Experts have explained that in major institutions in Europe, continuity is maintained through the ED or commercial director, rather than the publicly recognized intendant (AD). Canadian symphony orchestras have recently appointed a wave of new music directors and the role that EDs play in the selection of ADs merits research. This research could provide insights in how co-leadership relationship evolves through this other kind of change.

Traditional leadership theorists criticize co-leadership as unable to produce a motivating and clear vision for the organization because of the number of actors involved (Locke, 2003) and blurred accountability (Fayol, 1949). Arts scholars criticize it for imposing instrumental and managerial constraints on artistic autonomy (Beirne & Knight, 2002). These criticisms ignore co-leadership's objective of integrating competing logics that are embedded in the co-leadership relationship and shared role space. These logics have the potential for conflict and goal ambiguity, suggesting the strategic necessity of effective relationships.

In the next section, we reflect on the rather extensive research that has occurred regarding co-leadership in the arts. We suggest other means that might evolve and enrich this literature.

Research methodology issues

In this section, the suggested research questions in this chapter are further developed through an understanding of related issues about research methodology. The following discussion is consolidated under three themes and reflects on methods embedded in past research and future possibilities.

The first theme considers how comparative research on co-leadership is conducted across different contexts, theoretical frames, and levels of analysis. By making these differences explicit across arts co-leadership research, a more coherent and comprehensive literature about the phenomenon may be constructed. The second theme of stakeholder relationships considers how to investigate the views of actors being led by co-leaders, extending beyond the traditional focus on co-leaders and their role space. Finally, ontological and epistemological intentions influence the choice of qualitative and quantitative research approaches. Arts co-leadership research includes both approaches. By explicitly justifying a research philosophy, scholars can create an awareness of how different approaches contribute to an understanding of the phenomenon, developing the literature on arts co-leadership. A greater understanding of these methodological considerations may expand interest in study of co-leadership beyond the traditional community of scholars.

Comparative research

Different contexts

While results from research focused within a particular context can reveal lessons for application elsewhere, recognizing this specificity and its limitations enables more effective learning. To date, research on co-leadership appears to assume a homogeneous environment, ignoring cultural and funding differences as explanations for variation in practice. Multi-region research partnerships may invigorate comparative insight about cultural context and its impact on organizational and leadership practice.

Theoretical frames

The tradition of co-leadership research has been anchored in a socially constructed orientation, evolving through role theory (Alvarez & Svejenova, 2005; Gronn & Hamilton, 2004) and logics and practice theory. In the field of arts co-leadership, relational social-psychology theories (Reid & Karambayya, 2009, 2016; Reynolds et al., 2017) and approaches to strategic decision-making (Bhansing et al., 2016; Voss et al., 2006) have further enabled insights on how co-leaders integrate the logics of the arts context. Scholars have rarely recognized how this theoretical variety contributes to the collective development of an arts co-leadership literature. Traditionally, scholars have oriented their contributions to the specific theoretical frame. Recognizing the theoretical variety within the research may provide more coherence for future arts co-leadership research.

Levels of analysis

Analysis of levels of activity functions as an important structuring mechanism. Co-leadership environments are replete with potentially conflicting forces that can result in dilemmas manifested at different levels. To understand these dilemmas and the potential theorizing for leadership, there needs to be clarity about where these forces and logics originate and how they interact. Analysis by level enables researchers and managers to define and resolve differences in cultural meanings. Previous research crosses levels of analysis, but explicit mention of this analytical structure is sparse; definitional clarity and discussion about the implications of crossing levels are lacking. Recognizing this structure will improve the rigour and quality of research about co-leadership. A call in the general leadership literature to declare perspectives by level (Yammarino et al., 2005) reinforces our suggestion about research methodology.

Stakeholder engagement in co-leadership

A balanced research perspective would include data from all members of the co-leadership, not just one member of the constellation, triangulating and enriching insights from within the relationship. In addition, research about how co-leadership coherence influences others' ability to do their work requires data collection from subordinate and superordinate actors

(Döös & Wilhelmson, 2021). Rarely have these organizational perspectives been considered in co-leadership research. Some leaders may be reluctant to give access to internal perspectives on their performance, despite reassurances of confidentiality. However, interviewing close observers of the co-leadership can reveal the full spectrum of organizational dynamics, enriching the analysis and theorizing if this is a desired objective for the research. This approach requires an intensive investment in trustworthy participant-researcher relationships.

Research methodology and theorizing

Process research

In both quantitative and qualitative research, data collection over time is useful to observe how fragility and change occur within the constellation. As well, in qualitative research, data over time provides opportunities to consider co-leaders' interactivity with the organizational context. Observation of meetings and interactions also provide rich insights beyond interviews and documents about co-leaders' relationship with the organization. The benefit of process research reveals the co-leadership relationship in direct action and comparative possibilities for insights are elevated. Lessons for scholars and managers are richer by engaging in research over time, as a result.

Qualitative and quantitative research

Our research in this book is both qualitative and analytical. However, the concepts and models that we have proposed here could benefit from further exploration and testing in quantitative studies to push and confirm the theorizing of the field. More quantitative research would provide a useful contrast in the literature of arts co-leadership that has been dominated by qualitative research. Recognition of the contribution to the methodological contrast will further develop the breadth of the literature and deepen insights about the phenomenon.

Conclusion

There is still much to investigate in the realm of co-leadership. This may surprise some scholars who consider co-leadership a nuisance and not strategic. However, we have found co-leadership to be a rich research terrain. Its internal dynamics are fundamental to understanding the ability to lead as one. It has symbolic value in a contextual dynamic of pluralistic logics and powerful stakeholders. The artistic imperative is no doubt its most important driver, justifying its presence in the field. Our suggested future research questions create a kaleidescope of topics around the phenomenon. We are excited to see the future structured in such a manner and are keen to see the upcoming responses to these questions.

References

Abdallah, C., & Langley, A. (2014). The double edge of ambiguity in strategic planning. *Journal of Management Studies*, *51*(2), 235–264. https://doi.org/10.1111/joms.12002

Abfalter, D. (2019). Associate Professor. Vienna, Austria: Universität für Musik und darstellende Kunst. Interview.

Alexander, V. D. (2018). Heteronomy in the arts field: State funding and British arts organizations. *British Journal of Sociology*, *69*(1), 23–43. https://doi.org/10.1111/1468-4446.12283

Alvarez, J. L., Mazza, C., Pederson, J. S., & Svejenova, S. (2005). Shielding idiosyncrasy from isomorphic pressures: Towards optimal distinctiveness in European filmmaking. *Organization*, *12*(6), 863–888. https://doi.org/10.1177/1350508405057474

Alvarez, J. L., & Svejenova, S. (2005). *Sharing Executive Power: Roles and Relationships at the Top*. Cambridge University Press.

Alvehus, J. (2019). Emergent, distributed, and orchestrated: Understanding leadership through frame analysis. *Leadership*, *15*(5), 535–554. https://doi.org/10.1177/1742715018773832

Andersson, F. O., & Renz, D. O. (2021). Who really governs? Nonprofit governance, stakeholder theory and the dominant coalition perspective. In G. Donnelly-Cox, M. Meyer & F. Wijkström (Eds.), *Research Handbook on Nonprofit Governance* (pp. 196–219). Edward Elgar Publishing.

Barkela, B. (2019). Theatre leadership from a communication perspective. *Zeitschrift für Kulturmanagement*, *5*(2), 135–164.

Barkela, B. (2021). Leadership communication and knowledge integration across the artistic, technical and administration area in theaters. *Journal of Arts Management, Law and Society*. https://doi.org/10.1080/10632921.2021.1974628

Beard, A. (2012). *'No money, no mission' - Financial performance, leadership structure and budgeting in nonprofit and performing arts organizations*. Doctoral dissertation, New York University, New York.

Beirne, M., & Knight, S. (2002). Principles and consistent management in the arts: Lessons from British theatre. *International Journal of Cultural Policy*, *8*(1), 75–89. https://doi.org/10.1080/10286630290032459

Belfiore, E., & Bennett, O. (2007). Rethinking the social impact of the arts. *International Journal of Cultural Policy*, *13*(2), 135–151.

Bhansing, P., Leenders, M., & Wijnberg, N. (2016). Selection system orientations as an explanation for the differences between dual leaders of the same organization in their perception of organizational performance. *Journal of Management & Governance*, *20*(4), 907–933. https://doi.org/10.1007/s10997-015-9330-4

Bieber, M. (2003). Governing Independent Museums: How Trustees and Directors Exercise Their Powers. In C. Cornforth (Ed.), *The Governance of Public and Non-profit Organizations: What Do Boards Do?* (pp. 164–184). Routledge.

Boorsma, M. (2006). A strategic logic for arts marketing: Integrating customer value and artistic objectives. *International Journal of Cultural Policy*, *12*(3), 73–92. https://doi.org/10.1080/10286630600613333

Carneiro, M. (2019). *How do dual executive leadership practices of theatre production companies around the world make decisions for their artistic and organizational wellbeing*? Master's thesis, HEC Montréal, Montréal.

Caust, J. (Ed.). (2015). *Arts and Cultural Leadership in Asia*. Routledge.

Chiapello, È. (2004). Evolution and co-optation: The 'artist critique' of management and capitalism. *Third Text*, *18*(6), 585–594. https://doi.org/10.1080/0952882042000284998

Denis, J.-L., Lamothe, L., & Langley, A. (2001). The dynamics of collective leadership and strategic change in pluralistic organizations. *The Academy of Management Journal*, *44*(4), 809–837. https://doi.org/doi.org/10.2307/3069417.

Denis, J.-L., Langley, A., & Rouleau, L. (2010). The practice of leadership in the messy world of organizations. *Leadership*, *6*(1), 67–88. https://doi.org/10.1177/1742715009354233

Denis, J.-L., Langley, A., & Sergi, V. (2012). Leadership in the plural. *The Academy of Management Annals*, *5*(1), 211–283. https://doi.org/10.1080/19416520.2012.667612

Döös, M., & Wilhelmson, L. (2021). Fifty-five years of managerial shared leadership research: A review of an empirical field. *Leadership*, *17*(6), 715–746. https://doi.org/10.1177/17427150211037809

Fayol, H. (1949). *General and Industrial Management*. Isaac Pitman.

Fjellvær, H. (2010). *Dual and unitary leadership: managing ambiguity in pluralistic organizations* (Publication Number 2010/10). Doctoral dissertation, Norwegian School of Economics and Business Administration, Bergen. https://openaccess.nhh.no/nhh-xmlui/bitstream/handle/11250/164362/fjellver%20avh%202010.PDF?sequence=1

Fleming, P., & Spicer, A. (2014). Power in management and organization studies. *Academy of Management Annals*, *8*(1), 237–298. https://doi.org/10.1080/19416520.2014.875671

Frumkin, P., & Kolendo, A. (2014). *Building for the Arts: The Strategic Design of Cultural Facilities*. University of Chicago Press.

Gibeau, É., Langley, A., Denis, J.-L., & van Schendel, N. (2020). Bridging competing demands through co-leadership? Potential and limitations. *Human Relations*, *73*(4), 464–489. https://doi.org/10.1177/0018726719888145

Gibeau, É., Reid, W., & Langley, A. (2016). Co-leadership: Contexts, Configurations and Conditions. In J. Storey, J. Hartley, J.-L. Denis, P. 't Hart, & D. Ulrich (Eds.), *Routledge Companion to Leadership* (pp. 225–240). Routledge.

Glow, H. (2013). Cultural Leadership and Audience Engagement: A Case Study of the Theatre Royal Stratford East. In J. Caust (Ed.), *Arts Leadership: International Case Studies* (1st ed., pp. 132–144). Tilde University Press.

Goffman, E. (1959). *The Presentation of Self in Everyday Life*. Doubleday.

Gronn, P. (1999). Substituting for leadership: The neglected role of the leadership couple. *The Leadership Quarterly*, *10*(1), 41–62. https://doi.org/10.1016/S1048-9843(99)80008-3

Gronn, P., & Hamilton, A. (2004). 'A bit more life in the leadership': Co-principalship as distributed leadership practice. *Leadership and Policy in Schools*, *3*(1), 3–35. https://doi.org/10.1076/lpos.3.1.3.27842

Hart, P. (1973). *Orpheus in the New World: The Symphony Orchestra as an American Cultural Institution*. W. W. Norten.

Heenan, D. A., & Bennis, W. G. (1999). *Co-leaders: The Power of Great Partnerships*. John Wiley & Sons.

Hewison, R., Holden, J., & Jones, S. (2013). Leadership and Transformation at the Royal Shakespeare Company. In J. Caust (Ed.), *Arts Leadership: International Case Studies (1st ed., pp.* 145–160). Tilde University Press.

Hodgson, R. C., Levinson, D. J., & Zaleznik, A. (1965). *The Executive Role Constellation: An Analysis of Personality and Role Relations in Management*. Harvard University: Division of Research, Graduate School of Business Administration.

Janamohanan, S., Sasaki, S., & Wong Wai Yen, A. (2021). *Managing Creativity and the Arts in South-East Asia*. UNESCO, Paris and Bangkok.

Katz, D., & Kahn, R. L. (1966). *The Social Psychology of Organizations*. Wiley.

Kawashima, N. (2006). Audience development and social inclusion in Britain: Tensions, contradictions and paradoxes in policy and their implications for cultural management. *International Journal of Cultural Policy*, *12*(1), 55–72. https://doi.org/10.1080/10286630600613309

Kraatz, M. S., & Block, E. (2008). Organizational Implications of Institutional Pluralism. In R. Greenwood, C. Oliver, K. Sahlin-Andersson, & R. Suddaby (Eds.), *The SAGE Handbook of Organizational Institutionalism* (pp. 243–275). SAGE Publications Limited.

Kraatz, M. S., & Block, E. (2017). Institutional Pluralism Revisited. In R. Greenwood, C. Oliver, T. Lawrence, & R. E. Meyer (Eds.), *The SAGE Handbook of Organizational Institutionalism* (2nd ed., pp. 532–557). SAGE Publications.

Krause, R., Priem, R., & Love, L. (2015). Who's in charge here? Co-CEOs, power gaps, and firm performance. *Strategic Management Journal*, *36*(13), 2099–2110. https://doi.org/10.1002/smj.2325

Lampel, J., Lant, T., & Shamsie, J. (2000). Balancing act: Learning from organizing practices in cultural industries. *Organization Science*, *11*(3), 263–269. https://doi.org/10.1287/orsc.11.3.263.12503

Laughlin, S. (2019). USA. In I. King, & A. Schramme (Eds.), *Cultural Governance in a Global Context: An International Perspective on Art Organizations* (pp. 267–300). Palgrave MacMillan.

Lindgren, A. C. (2009). The National Ballet of Canada and the Kimberly Glasco legal arbitration case. *The Journal of Arts Management, Law, and Society*, *39*(2), 101–116. https://doi.org/10.3200/JAML.39.2.101-116

Lindqvist, K. (2017). Leadership in Art and Business. In E. Raviola & P. Zackariasson (Eds.), *Arts and Business: Building a Common Ground for Understanding Society (pp.* 135–147). Routledge.

Locke, E. A. (2003). Leadership: Starting at the Top. In C. L. Pearce, & J. A. Conger (Eds.), *Shared Leadership: Reframing the Hows and Whys of Leadership* (pp. 271–284). Sage.

Löfgren, M. (2016). On the Public Value of Arts and Culture. In K. Dalborg, & M. Löfgren (Eds.), *The FIKA Project: Perspectives on Cultural Leadership* (pp. 75–99). Nätwerkstan Kultur.

London, T. (Ed.). (2013). *An Ideal Theater: Founding Visions for a New American Art*. Theatre Communications Group.

Macdonnell, J., & Bereson, R. (2019). Arts Management and Its Discontents. In W. J. Byrnes, & A. Brkić (Eds.), *The Routledge Companion to Arts Management* (1st ed., pp. 1–12). Routledge.

MacNeill, K., & Tonks, A. (2013). Leadership in Australian Arts Companies: One Size Does Not Fit All. In J. Caust (Ed.), *Arts Leadership: International Case Studies* (1st ed., pp. 69–82). Tilde University Press.

Magee, J. C., & Galinsky, A. D. (2008). Social hierarchy: The self-reinforcing nature of power and status. *Academy of Management Annals*, 2(1), 351–398. https://doi.org/10.1080/19416520802211628

Meindl, J., Ehrlich, S. B., & Dukerich, J. M. (1985). The romance of leadership. *Administrative Science Quarterly*, *30*(1), 78–102.

Mintzberg, H. (1998). Covert leadership: Notes on managing professionals. *Harvard Business Review*, November–December, 140–147.

Möllering, G. (2006). *Trust: Reason, Routine, Reflexivity*. Elsevier.

Müller, F., & Farid, C. (2010). *Yves Saint Laurent*. Abrams.

Nisbett, M., & Walmsley, B. (2016). The romanticization of charismatic leadership in the arts. *The Journal of Arts Management, Law, and Society*, *46*(1), 2–12. https://doi.org/10.1080/10632921.2015.1131218

O'Toole, J., Galbraith, J., & Lawler, E. E. (2002). When two (or more) heads are better than one: The promise and pitfalls of shared leadership. *California Management Review*, *44*(4), 65–83. https://doi.org/10.2307/41166143

Ostrower, F. (2002). *Trustees of Culture: Power, Wealth, and Status on Elite Arts Boards*. University of Chicago Press.

Padrissa, C. (2017). How the artists's collective La Fura dels Baus developed from Catalan street theater into a global cultural benchmark. *The Focus*, *XV*(1).

Parmentier, M.-A., & Fischer, E. (2018). What's New? Institutional Work in Updating Taste. In Z. Arsel, & J. Bean (Eds.), *Taste, Consumption and Markets* (pp. 65–82). Routledge.

Peterson, R. (1986). From Impresario to Arts Administrator: Formal Accountability in Nonprofit Cultural Organizations. In P. DiMaggio (Ed.), *Nonprofit Enterprise in the Arts: Studies in Mission and Constraint (pp.* 161–183). Oxford University Press.

Quigg, A.-M. (2007). Bullying in theatres and arts centres in the United Kingdom. *International Journal of Arts Management*, *10*(1), 52–64.

Radaelli, E. (2012). American Cultural Policy and the Rise of Arts Management Programs: The Creation of a New Professional Identity. In J. Paquette (Ed.), *Cultural Policy, Work and Identity: The Creation, Renewal and Negotiation of Professional Subjectivities (pp.* 145–159). Ashgate.

Rånlund, S., Dalborg, K., & Löfgren, M. (Eds.). (2016). *The FIKA Project: Narratives by Cultural Change Makers*. Nätverkstan Culture.

Reid, W., & Karambayya, R. (2009). Impact of dual executive leadership dynamics in creative organizations. *Human Relations*, *62*(7), 1073–1112. https://doi.org/10.1177/0018726709335539

Reid, W., & Karambayya, R. (2016). The shadow of history: Situated dynamics of trust in dual executive leadership. *Leadership*, *12*(5), 609–631. https://doi.org/10.1177/1742715015579931

Reynolds, S., Tonks, A., & MacNeill, K. (2017). Collaborative leadership in the arts as a unique form of dual leadership. *The Journal of Arts Management, Law, and Society*, *47*(2), 89–104. https://doi.org/10.1080/10632921.2016.1241968.

Roberto, M. A. (2003). The stable core and dynamic periphery in top management teams. *Management Decision*, *41*(2), 120–131. https://doi.org/10.1108/00251740310457560

Rousseau, D. M., Sitkin, S. B., & Burt, R. S. (1998). Not so different after all: A cross-discipline view of trust. *Academy of Management Review*, *23*(3), 393–404. https://doi.org/10.5465/amr.1998.926617.

Røyseng, S. (2008). Arts management and the autonomy of art. *International Journal of Cultural Policy*, *14*(1), 37–48. https://doi.org/10.1080/10286630701856484

Ruiz-Gutiérrez, J., Grant, P., & Colbert, F. (2016). Arts management in developing countries: A Latin American perspective. *International Journal of Arts Management*, *18*(Special Edition Latin America Spring 2016), 6–31.

Schmidt, U. (2020). *Former Managing director.* Germany: Hamburg Ballett. Interview.

Schrauwen, J., Schramme, A., & Segers, J. (2016). Do Managers Run Cultural Institutions? The Practice of Shared Leadership in the Arts Sector. In K. Dalborg, & M. Löfgren (Eds.), *The FIKA Project: Perspectives on Cultural Leadership* (pp. 103–116). Nätverkstan Kultur.

Schreyögg, G., & Sydow, J. (2010). CROSSROADS—Organizing for fluidity? Dilemmas of new organizational forms. *Organization Science*, *21*(6), 1251–1262. https://doi.org/10.1287/orsc.1100.0561

Shamir, B. (2007). From Passive Recipients to Active Co-producers: Followers' Role in the Leadership Process. In B. Shamir, R. Pillai, M. Bligh, & M. Uhl-Bien (Eds.), *Follower-centered Perspectives on Leadership: A Tribute to the Memory of James R. Meindl* (pp. ix–xxxix). Information Age Publishing.

Shiner, L. (2001). *The Invention of Art: A Cultural History.* University of Chicago Press.

Sillince, J. A., Jarzabkowski, P., & Shaw, D. (2012). Shaping strategic action through the rhetorical construction and exploitation of ambiguity. *Organization Science*, *23*(3), 630–650. https://doi.org/10.1287/orsc.1110.0670

Stewart, R. (1991). Role Sharing at the Top: A Neglected Aspect of Studies of Managerial Behaviour. In S. Carlson, H. Mintzberg, & R. Stewart (Eds.), *Executive Behaviour* (pp. 120–136). Studia Oeconomiae Negotiorum.

Svejenova, S., Vives, L., & Alvarez, J. L. (2010). At the crossroads of agency and communion: Defining the shared career. *Journal of Organizational Behavior*, *31*(5), 707–725. https://doi.org/10.1002/job.702.

Thornton, P. H., Ocasio, W., & Lounsbury, M. (2012). *The Institutional Logics Perspective: A New Approach to Culture, Structure, and Process.* Oxford University Press.

Voss, Z. G., Cable, D. M., & Voss, G. B. (2006). Organizational identity and firm performance: What happens when leaders disagree about 'Who we are?'. *Organization Science*, *17*(6), 741–755. https://doi.org/10.1287/orsc.1060.0218

Wang, Y. (2017). Shared leadership and team effectiveness: The examination of LMX differentiation and servant leadership on the emergence and consequences of shared leadership. *Human Performance*, *34*(4), 155–168.

Yammarino, F., Dionne, S., Chun, J. U., & Dansereau, F. (2005). Leadership and levels of analysis: A state-of-the-science review. *The Leadership Quarterly*, *16*(6), 879–919. https://doi.org/10.1016/j.leaqua.2005.09.002

Index

Note: **Bold** page numbers refer to tables and *italic* page numbers refer to figures.

inted in the United States
aker & Taylor Publisher Services

Printed in the United States
by Baker & Taylor Publisher Services